WINGS OF FIRE

THE HISTORY OF THE DETROIT RED WINGS

I

WINGS OF FIRE

THE HISTORY OF THE DETROIT RED WINGS

FOREWORD BY
SID ABEL

EPILOGUE BY
BILL GADSBY

PAUL R. GREENLAND

PHOTOGRAPHS FROM THE COLLECTIONS OF
JAMES D. McCARTHY,
RICHARD A. MARGITTAY
AND
THE HOCKEY HALL OF FAME

TURNING LEAF PUBLICATIONS
ROCKFORD, ILLINOIS

ISBN 0-9659128-0-9
Library of Congress Catalog Card Number: 97-090768

Graphic Design and Layout: Jeff Hultgren
Cover Design: Jim Jacoby
Cover Art: Vincent S. Chiaramonte
Illustrations: Michael S. Cascio
Editorial Services: Scott M. Fisher and Donna Bacidore

The photographs in this book, unless otherwise credited, are from
the collection of James D. McCarthy, Richard A. Margittay or the Hockey Hall of Fame.
Every effort has been made to trace the ownership of copyrighted photographs. If we have
failed to give adequate credit, we will gladly make changes in future printings.

The quotations cited throughout the book from
the *Detroit News* are used with permission.

DEDICATION

Dedicated to the men who have donned the winged wheel with pride;

to my parents for their endless love, support and encouragement;

and to Tracey, my best friend.

ACKNOWLEDGEMENTS

Sid Abel
Donna Bacidore
Mike Bacidore
Doug Barkley
George H. Bathje, III
Gary Bergman
Wally Crossman
Jeff Davis
The Detroit News
Scott M. Fisher
Bill Gadsby
Edna Gadsby
Danny Gare
Tom Gaston
Robert Giles
Barbara Greenland
David R. Greenland

Rollin Greenland
Glenn Hall
Dennis Hextall
Hockey Hall of Fame
Dale Hornickel
Jeff Hultgren
Greg Innis
Jim Jacoby
Brian Kendall
Joan Lane
Matthew R. Lane
Tracey L. Lane
Nick Libett
Nicklas Lidstrom
Douglas H. Liedberg
Carl Liscombe

Harry Lumley
Budd Lynch
Richard A. Margittay
Lois Morgan
John Ogrodnick
Marty Pavelich
Pierre Pilote
Bill Quackenbush
Leo Reise
Paul Stewart
Mark E. Thate
Elliott Trumbull
Norm Ullman
Harry Watson
Johnny Wilson
Ross "Lefty" Wilson
Pat Zaccharias

FOREWORD

Dear Red Wings fan,

I have many fond memories of being associated with the Detroit Red Wings as player, coach, manager, and Bruce Martyn's sidekick in the broadcast booth. I had the good fortune of being on three Stanley Cup teams and centering "The Production Line" with Ted Lindsay and Gordie Howe. The Norris family, Jack Adams, teammates and players I coached all contributed greatly to the rich heritage of the Red Wings. And accolades to Mike and Marion Ilitch, who brought the Stanley Cup back to Detroit! They truly made the city "Hockeytown." I am proud to have been a part of the history of the Detroit Red Wings.

Paul Greenland has conducted a great deal of research in order to bring you this book on the Red Wings' colorful history. So please, sit back and enjoy yourself as you leaf through the pages. I hope that you enjoy reading about Detroit's hockey past as much as I enjoyed being a part of it.

Best Wishes,

Sid Abel
Hockey Hall of Fame, 1969

INTRODUCTION

It was January 1993. A cold winter's day. I sat waiting for the hands of the clock to reach high noon. The morning sun burned brightly and the wind blew hard outside, sending a cool draft through the window. It was definitely hockey season. Soon, I would make a phone call—the first of many since that day—to a former National Hockey League defenseman whom I now consider my friend. At the time, I was hard at work on a book covering the history of the Chicago Blackhawks. I could hardly wait to talk with Bill Gadsby, whose NHL career had begun with Chicago in 1946. It was he who inspired me to write about the rich history of the Detroit Red Wings.

The sport of hockey is perhaps the greatest on earth. It has speed, action, skill, aggression and, most of all, stories. The game hockey fans know and love today—that characterized by 26 teams—has rich and colorful roots. It was not long ago that a mere six teams comprised the National Hockey League, and only 120 men had the honor of playing in it. During that time, most fans knew almost every player in the league by name. The going was tough and the rivalries intense.

It was the romanticism of that "golden age" and the conversations I've had with former players that inspired me to pen my first book on the Chicago Blackhawks. Once I finished the first project, I did not want to stop. Several years after our first conversation, Bill Gadsby hinted at the storied history of the Detroit Red Wings. The hint made me decide to embark upon another journey through hockey history, one that ended happily with a Stanley Cup victory.

During my journey, I met many gentlemen who wore the famous winged wheel during their NHL careers. I got to know them through our personal conversations and through written accounts of their endeavors. Figuratively speaking, I also met a few ghosts along the way. It was intriguing to gaze at photographs of the earliest players, long dead, and read interviews they had done with sportswriters. They were men who played for little more than the simple love of the game. It was also moving to meet, through my research, men like Terry Sawchuk, Syd Howe, Herbie Lewis and Mud Bruneteau.

It is my hope that, as a Detroit Red Wings' fan, you will take the time to think about the times in which the players of each era lived and the sacrifices many of them made to play the game we enjoy today. As you will discover in the pages ahead, there was a time during the Great Depression when Jack Adams actually paid some of his players out of his pocket.

I have done my best to be as comprehensive as possible in my coverage of the team's history. Sometimes, it was difficult to find the information I was after. For remedying that, I must thank former players and employees at the Hockey Hall of Fame for their help. Gregg Innis was also an invaluable resource. There are many areas of the book that I would have loved to take into further detail, many smaller treasures that I would have loved to unearth. However, given the constraints of space and time, there is only so much one man can do!

I am sure that this book will bring you, the reader, a considerable amount of enjoyment—especially if you are a die-hard Detroit Red Wings' fan. So find a comfortable place to sit down and leaf through the book. Be prepared to meet figures from the past, some legendary and some not, that have carried Detroit's hockey torch since the team's inception in 1926. Relive the excitement of Gordie Howe rushing down the ice to score a goal, or Terry Sawchuk diving to make an incredible save. The journey is yours to enjoy!

Paul R. Greenland

CONTENTS

CHAPTER ONE

THE BUILDERS

JAMES D. NORRIS

Born: December 10, 1879, St. Catharines, Ontario
Died: December 4, 1952, Chicago, Illinois
Awards & Honors
- Hockey Hall of Fame (builder), 1958
- Lester Patrick Trophy (outstanding service to hockey in the U.S.), 1967
- Red Wings Hall of Fame, 1959
- Hockey Hall of Fame, 1958

BIOGRAPHY

James D. Norris truly loved the sport of hockey. He moved to Montreal at a very young age and played the game on the city's corner lots. The son of a grain dealer, Norris played hockey for the Montreal Victorias and received his prep education at the Tucker School. In Montreal, he attended both McGill University and the Montreal Collegiate Institute. He was known for his ability in both hockey and lacrosse at the latter school.

Known among business associates as "Big Jim,"

Norris came to Chicago in 1907 and became a wealthy grain broker and international businessman after starting the Norris Grain Company. He later held business interests in a variety of different enterprises, including hotels, the Rock Island and Pacific Railroad Companies, the First National Bank of Chicago, the Upper Lakes and St. Lawrence Transit Companies, Toronto Elevators, Ltd., and the West Indies Sugar Corporation. In addition, he had interests in arenas like Chicago Stadium, Madison Square Garden, St. Louis Arena Corporation, Indianapolis Coliseum Corporation, and Detroit's Olympia Arena. Norris was also a trustee of the Atlantic Mutual Insurance Company. Once he was established in the grain business, he invested portions of his fortune in sports, especially hockey teams.

At one time, Norris attempted to place a second NHL franchise in Chicago, but the owner of the Chicago Blackhawks, Major Frederick McLaughlin, wouldn't allow it. Norris subsequently formed the Chicago Shamrocks of the American Hockey

1

Association and later became owner of the Detroit Red Wings. He relished it whenever the Red Wings beat the Blackhawks because of his rivalry with the Major.

The Detroit Red Wings were Norris' passion, and the team's success was always his concern. His association with the club began in May of 1932, when he acquired both the Detroit Olympia and the Detroit Falcons, then in financial trouble. On October 5, 1932, he renamed the team the Red Wings, after the Winged Wheelers, a team for which he played in the upscale Montreal Amateur Athletic Association.

"He was a great man for hockey, a sincere lover of the game, with a tremendously constructive mind," said former NHL President Clarence Campbell, in an article by Elmer Ferguson. "I don't believe the National Hockey League could have continued without him. As it is, thanks to his tremendous constructive ability, the National League today is in its best shape in years."

Norris was also well-respected by many players. A *Detroit Program* article said that he was both a modest and gracious team owner. It recalled an incident which showed these qualities when, in 1938, he sold Turk Broda to the Toronto Maple Leafs for only $8,000. Said Norris at the time of the sale: "It isn't the money which I'm concerned about. I'm interested in the future of this young man who deserves the chance to play major league hockey. We have a great goalie in Normie Smith and Broda would have little opportunity to play here. I'm not going to stand in the boy's way of enjoying the greatness for which he has worked."

Writer Elmer Ferguson gave a good description of Norris shortly after his death. He said: "Norris was everything a Hollywood director would select as a typical tycoon of Big Business. He was a square-built man, with a solid chin, a gruff voice, strong rugged face, a man of determined ideas, and with the personality and wherewithal, to enforce these. ... He was a fine person. And, a very charming person, outside business. Perhaps a charming man in business, too, so long as he had his own way, which was generally the right way, about it. We know he was very fond of Jack Adams, the Red Wing maestro, a personality not unlike James Norris himself, because

he was eminently successful in directing the policies of the Red Wings, built teams, scrapped them at the crucial points and built up new machines, always keeping the Red Wings in the forefront of the hockey race."

Norris lived in Lake Forest, Illinois. He built a hockey rink behind his mansion so his family and servants could play hockey. He was well-known for flying from his estate to watch the Red Wings play. On Sunday afternoons, he would often fly to Detroit, have dinner, attend the game, and fly home to Chicago. In later years, his physicians recommended against his attendance at the games, as the excitement was simply too much for him. He then insisted upon regular telephone reports of games.

At the age of seventy-three, Norris died of a heart attack in Chicago's Passavant Hospital. Shortly before his death, he withdrew controlling interest in the Chicago Stadium; and a syndicate composed of his sons, James Jr., and Bruce Norris, as well as Chicago Blackhawks' owner Arthur Wirtz, took over. At the time of his death, his son, James D. Norris, Jr., was co-owner and vice president of the Blackhawks.

JAMES D. NORRIS, JR.

Born: November 6, 1906
Died: February 25, 1966
Awards & Honors
- Red Wings Hall of Fame, 1968
- Hockey Hall of Fame, 1962
- Lester Patrick Trophy, 1972

BIOGRAPHY

Known to friends as "Young Jim," James Norris was affiliated with the Detroit Red Wings while his father ran the club. After his father passed away, siblings Marguerite and Bruce Norris took over the Red Wings, and the younger Norris purchased all of the stock in the Chicago Blackhawks from the estate of the late Major Frederick McLaughlin. Along with partner Arthur Wirtz, he became owner of both Chicago Stadium and the Blackhawks.

Opposite: James Norris, Jr., Jack Adams and James Norris, Sr. were instrumental in the success of the Detroit Red Wings. Detroit News Photo

MARGUERITE NORRIS

Born: 1927
Died: Waterbury, Connecticut, 1994
Awards & Honors
  • Red Wings Hall of Fame, 1977

BIOGRAPHY

On December 13, 1952, nine days after the death of her father, James Norris, Sr., Marguerite Norris became President of the Detroit Red Wings. At the time of her appointment, she had never seen the Red Wings play a home game in the city of Detroit.

When she took control of the team, Marguerite became the NHL's very first female executive. The world of sports had other female executives in 1952, but not many. Mrs. Grace Comiskey held controlling interest in the Chicago White Sox and served as the team's president. Margie Lindeheimer was an executive with the Los Angeles football team of the former All-American Conference and was also an official at both Arlington and Washington Park race tracks. The youngest of four children, Norris was the first woman to have her name engraved on the Stanley Cup.

In the December 15, 1952 issue of the *Toronto Daily Star*, she commented on her new role. "[I am] very thrilled by it all, and very humble. ... I hope to be so close to the picture I won't have to get my information by telephone," she said, referring to her father's reception of game reports by phone. "Will I attend practices? Yes, I think I will see them, too. The only part of the program I am pondering now is the pre-game dressing-room pep talks. Maybe I'll have to pass them up. That's a shame, because they were a specialty with Father."

In the December 16, 1952 issue of the *New York Journal-American*, she elaborated further on the locker

room dilemma, commenting: "I know I can't go in the dressing room after hockey games. Maybe I'll install a microphone and loud speaker system so I can offer the team my congratulations after a big victory. I have no favorite players. I have a favorite hockey team—the Red Wings. There's never been another hockey team."

Marguerite Norris grew up in Lake Forest, Illinois, and graduated from Smith College. She learned about hockey on the outdoor rink at her father's Lake Forest estate.

"She understood hockey and was very kind to us, too kind," said Jimmy Skinner in the May 14, 1994 issue of the *Toronto Sun*. "Every time she came on a trip, she bought all the players gifts. They would be on the seats of the train when the team boarded."

Before her involvement with the Detroit Red Wings, Norris worked in Chicago for West Farm Management, part of her father's grain empire in Chicago, and in New York doing market research for Dunn and Bradstreet.

BRUCE A. NORRIS

Born: February 19, 1924, Chicago, Illinois
Died: January 1, 1986
Awards & Honors
- Hockey Hall of Fame, 1969
- Red Wings Hall of Fame, 1968
- Lester Patrick Trophy, 1975

BIOGRAPHY

Bruce Norris became associated with hockey at a young age. As a child, he skated on the outdoor rink on his family's Lake Forest estate. He played defense for Yale University until an injured knee forced him to quit. When he was Detroit's president, Norris was known to lace up the skates and scrimmage with players.

Before he took over the Wings, Norris' father James, Sr., owned and operated the club. His brother, James, Jr., was both Detroit's vice president and a co-owner of the Chicago Blackhawks. It was in 1955-56 that Bruce took over the team's operations from his sister, Marguerite Norris-Riker. Besides serving as the president of the Norris Grain Company, which he inherited from his father, Norris maintained his position as president of the Red Wings until 1982.

He was the last member of the Norris family to own the Red Wings before current owner Mike Ilitch purchased the club.

"Bruce had a lot of money, and his dad was a dedicated hockey man," says former Red Wings trainer Lefty Wilson. "Jim was dedicated and Bruce, he listened to everybody else but the right people. His dad left him $400 million. In the end he didn't have a dime. He was a very shy man. He would get in to the tomato juice when he came into town. He'd get into the tomato juice, I call it tomato juice. But I got along with him alright until I got fired, and then he didn't know my name."

"[The image of Bruce Norris presented was] very overstated in that damn Net Worth [television] show," says former Red Wings PR man Elliott Trumbull. "They showed Bruce drinking out a flask at the NHL meetings. Come on, he never did that. Bruce was a millionaire, billionaire playboy and pretty high liver and all that, but when he had business to do, he ran his business. Both the Norris Grain Company and the Detroit hockey club."

Besides business and hockey, Norris was an avid cattle rancher and raised purebred Herefords on his 500-acre Daybreak Farm in Libertyville, Illinois, his permanent residence. One positive thing Norris did during his tenure as president was a 2.5 million dollar renovation of the Detroit Olympia, which saw all of the seats padded. Norris was particularly proud of the move.

MIKE ILITCH

Awards & Honors
- Lester Patrick Trophy, 1991

BIOGRAPHY

The Detroit Red Wings are presently owned by Detroit native Mike Ilitch. An All-City baseball player at Detroit Cooley High School, Ilitch turned down an offer from the Detroit Tigers in 1947, when he opted to join the Marine Corps. Ilitch continued playing baseball in the Marine Corps and, upon his discharge, signed with the Tigers. He never made it to the big club but did play in their minor league system for three years until an injury ended his career.

Besides owning the Red Wings, Ilitch also owns

the Detroit Tigers and is a successful businessman. He started the very first Little Caesars Pizza store in 1959. Since that time, Little Caesars has blossomed into an international franchise, with many stores in the United States and Canada.

Ilitch purchased the Red Wings for ten million dollars in June of 1982. He acquired the team when it was in the basement of the NHL, having literally crumbled under former owner Bruce Norris. "The franchise would never have been up for sale if everything was rosy," said Ilitch in the March 29, 1983 issue of the *Toronto Sun*. "They [the Norris family] would have kept it for another 50 years if that had been the case. What we bought were a lot of problems caused by many years of bad housekeeping."

It was somewhat difficult for Ilitch getting used to being the driving force behind a LOSING team. "It's funny how your perspective changes," commented Ilitch in the same article. "For 20 years, I've been sponsoring amateur teams, spending thousands of dollars, sometimes hundreds of thousands, and if we finished second or third in a national championship, it was a disappointment. Now, here I've spent many, many millions on the Red Wings and the rink for the privilege of fighting for last place in the National Hockey League. A little strange, isn't it?"

Since Ilitch took the helm, things have improved greatly and, because of his continued support, the team is now among the league's elite clubs and a Stanley Cup winner. Besides his efforts to support the team itself, Ilitch has also improved the Joe Louis Arena, spending over two million dollars in renovations.

Intent on keeping the Red Wings in Detroit, Ilitch also acquired the assets of Olympia Corporation for an undisclosed price in December of 1982. The purchase included the leases for Joe Louis Arena and Cobo Arena, marking the end of the Norris family's long-time involvement in Detroit hockey. The lease required the Red Wings to play at Joe Louis Arena for at least 30 years.

"He went out and got some good players and he spent a lot of money," says former Red Wings defenseman Bill Gadsby. "He has had some pretty good draft choices, they made some good trades, and they got a hell of a coach in Scotty Bowman. He's got

a great record. You put all of those things together and you've got something going for you."

"I think he changed some personalities," says former Red Wings center Dennis Hextall. "He wasn't afraid to sit pat. He made some changes with management, he made changes with players, and you know he was very aggressive. [He] fixed up the Joe Louis Arena [and] made it pleasant for people to come down. [He was] very, very involved. I think Bruce Norris, in his later years, was sort of an absentee owner, and it was run by people in Detroit that were more concerned about themselves, I think, than the team. He is very involved [in the community]. He moved his offices down there to the Fox Theater. He refurbed that. I think Mike Ilitch is doing tremendous things for the City of Detroit. At the present time he's trying to get a new ball stadium, and I think he's offered to put up $150 million of his own money. A lot of people don't do that. Most of the other cities build the stadium for the owners."

Ilitch is well-known for being a very supportive member of the Detroit business community and often sponsors a myriad of different youth athletic teams in different sports. According to the October 20, 1995 issue of the *Detroit Free Press*, his Little Caesars National Love Kitchen, a mobile pizza kitchen which travels around the United States, stopping at different soup kitchens to feed the nations hungry, recently had its tenth anniversary and fed its 1,000,000th person.

Ilitch's family is very involved in the operation of the Detroit Red Wings. He and his wife have seven children: Denise, Ron, Mike, Jr., Lisa, Atanas, Christopher, and Carole. Atanas and Christopher Ilitch serve as team vice-presidents.

JOSEPH FRANCIS (BUDD) LYNCH

Born: August 7, 1917, Windsor, Ontario
Awards & Honors
- Hockey Hall of Fame, 1985
- Michigan Sports Hall of Fame, 1992
- The Beaver Award, 1945
- Foster Hewitt Memorial Award, 1985

BIOGRAPHY

Budd Lynch was known for years as the "Voice of the Red Wings," doing play-by-play radio and television broadcasts for them from 1950 to 1975. He was also a member of the Red Wings' public relations department and today is the team's game announcer. Besides hockey, Lynch has also done broadcasts of Michigan State football, University of Detroit football and worked with broadcasters covering the Detroit Lions and other NFL teams in the early 1950s. During the 1960s, he served as the public relations director for the Detroit Race Course.

Lynch attended Cathedral High School in Hamilton, Ontario, and secured his first job in radio at the age of 20 in 1937, doing play-by-play of senior hockey games on CHML radio. Later that year, Lynch moved to CKOC in Hamilton to do play-by-play of Canadian football and baseball games. In 1939, he moved to CKLW in Windsor to work as both a sportscaster and newscaster.

Lynch enlisted in the Canadian Army in 1940 and served with the Essex-Scottish Regiment of Windsor during World War II. He was commissioned with the rank of lieutenant after attending officer's training school in Brockville, Ontario. Overseas by 1941, Lynch was in combat in France and Belgium and attained the rank of major. While with the Combat Infantry Division, he was wounded but returned to serve as a Major Liaison Officer at the Canadian Infantry Bridge Headquarters. However, he then sustained another, more serious injury, losing his right arm and shoulder on August 28, 1944, near the village of Caen, France.

One month after losing his limb, Lynch was back working, this time for the BBC's Armed Forces Expeditionary Forces Program, co-producing a show called "Combat Diary" in London. Working with American, Canadian and British radio personnel, Lynch was awarded a citation by Prime Minister Winston Churchill and SHAEF headquarters, which was operated by American General Dwight D. Eisenhower. In February of 1945, Lynch returned to Canada to work for the Canadian Broadcasting Company in Montreal but soon went home to Windsor to work for CKLW. There, he was director of sports, special events and public relations, handling all of the Mutual Broadcasting System's assignments in the Detroit area. In 1945, he received The Beaver Award, which is Canada's equivalent of an Oscar, for Distinguished Service to Canadian Radio

during World War II. Lynch became the voice of University of Michigan football in 1948 and did play-by-play broadcasts of Windsor Spitfire games, then Detroit's top junior club, in 1947-48 and 1948-49.

It was during his association with the Spitfires that he met Jack Adams, who recommended Lynch for the job when the Red Wings decided to televise the last 1-1/2 periods of 12 games during the 1949-50 season. He thus became the "voice" of the team and would remain so for 26 seasons. He did radio play-by-play with Al Nagler on WXYZ radio. Lynch stepped down in 1974-75 and was named director of public relations by then-general manager Alex Delvecchio. In 1982, he became the team's director of community relations.

In a May 6, 1985 *Detroit Red Wings News Release*, he remembered a few of the most memorable moments of his career. "The greatest moment was Tony Leswick's overtime goal which won the seventh game of the Stanley Cup finals against the Montreal Canadiens in 1954 ... I also remember what a kick it was to meet Foster Hewitt when I was a young broadcaster in the 1930s, then having the privilege to work with him in later years. He was the idol of all hockey broadcasters."

THOMAS NATHANIEL IVAN

Born: January 31, 1911, Toronto, Ontario
Awards & Honors
- Hockey Hall of Fame, 1974
- Red Wings Hall of Fame, 1977
- Lester Patrick Trophy, 1975

BIOGRAPHY

Tommy Ivan grew up in the Perth Square area of West Toronto and was first involved with the game as a player. However, while playing junior hockey, he was injured and turned to coaching and officiating in Brantford, Ontario. It was in Brantford that Ivan got Jack Adams' attention. Ivan learned many of his hockey skills under Adams' wing. "I played Junior with Tommy," recalled former Detroit Red Wing Leo

Opposite: As Detroit's general manager, Tommy Ivan led the team to six straight league championships and three Stanley Cups in three years.

Tommy Ivan

DETROIT

Reise. "Tommy coached the Brantford Lions Club when I played Junior B there. He was a good coach and guy. Quiet. He had a system he tried to get you to work. He was very good. He was a very personable man."

During World War II, Ivan served in the capacity of gunnery instructor in the Canadian Military. However, he maintained his association with the game he knew and loved. Soon, Adams had Ivan scouting for Detroit and eventually coaching their top farm clubs in Omaha and Indianapolis, before he took over the big club in 1947-48. After coaching in the United States Hockey League and the American Hockey League, Tommy Ivan became a successful coach and general manager of the Detroit Red Wings. As Detroit's general manager, he led the team to six straight league championships and three Stanley Cups in three years.

"The biggest thrill I got, as far as coaching is concerned, was when I was coaching Detroit," says Ivan. "I think it was '52, you'd have to go through the record books. At that time, there were only six teams. In the first round of the four of seven series, we won four straight. In the finals, a four of seven series, we won four straight. It was pretty incredible."

Ivan was eventually sent to the Chicago Blackhawks by the younger Jim Norris, who called upon him to rebuild the then-crumbling hockey club. "The biggest obstacle," commented Ivan, when asked about his role in rebuilding that team, "was just getting a contender. ... When I came over to Chicago and eventually got a contender, it was a big thing, at least to me it was."

An example of Ivan's no-nonsense approach to the game can be seen by looking at a game during the 1958 season. While serving as Chicago's G.M., he fined every man on the team $100 for "indifferent play" when they lost to the Canadiens 9-1, with five of the Montreal goals coming in the third period.

Ivan was quoted in the October 25, 1958 *New York Times* the day after the game: "It [the game] was a lousy effort from a bunch of players who call themselves major leaguers. Any time a team can score

nine goals against you in one game, it's obvious that the players aren't putting out. That third period, when Montreal scored five goals against us, was a disgrace. I know Montreal always is tough on home ice but we were never in the game at any time. We have tried everything without getting any results. Maybe this will do some good—hitting them in their pocketbooks." Ivan was reportedly the first G.M. in the history of the NHL to fine an entire team.

In Chicago, through numerous deals, Ivan also acquired many key players, including the likes of Ed Litzenberger, Eric Nesterenko and Pierre Pilote. These men would make important contributions to the team for years to come. After spending enormous amounts of the owner's money, Ivan finally established a farm system made up of 11 teams and over 300 hundred players.

"He built the system [in Chicago]," says former Red Wings trainer Lefty Wilson. "He was a good coach. He was a good coach with us [in Detroit], and he was a good a coach in the minor leagues. He understood the guys and he wasn't that tough on us, you know. He said, 'Just play your game and things will come around.' I believe he won it in Omaha. He didn't win it in Indianapolis, he was only there one year. Then he won it up here in the big time. He was a very understanding man and a great guy. I really like Tommy. Nice man. Very, very nice, and he hasn't changed a bit since he was on the top."

JAMES DONALD (JIMMY) SKINNER

Born: January 12, 1917, Selkirk, Manitoba
Awards & Honors
• Red Wings Hall of Fame, 1977

BIOGRAPHY

Jimmy Skinner played junior hockey for the Winnipeg Rangers and senior hockey in Flin Flon, Manitoba. A defenseman, he was discovered by Detroit scout Fred Pinkney, who signed him in 1944. Skinner played a season in Indianapolis and two in Omaha, where he was the team captain and an unofficial aid to coach and former Red Wings great Mud Bruneteau.

Playing professional hockey was not in the cards for Skinner, but coaching certainly was. Jack Adams

---

Opposite: Jimmy Skinner coached the Red Wings to the Stanley Cup as a first-year coach in 1955.

convinced him of this and soon had him behind the bench of Detroit's best junior club, the Windsor Spitfires. He also coached junior hockey for Detroit in Hamilton, Ontario when the club moved there. In Windsor, Skinner's teams made the playoffs five times and won the OHA season schedule championship twice during the six seasons he was there. Skinner coached many of the men who developed into prominent Red Wing regulars and sent a total of 27 players into the NHL. Men like Marcel Pronovost, Terry Sawchuk, Johnny Wilson, Glen Skov and Dutch Reibel were a few who went on to play for Detroit.

Skinner didn't have to say goodbye to the high caliber athletes he honed to perfection in the junior ranks. When Tommy Ivan departed to rebuild the Chicago Blackhawks, Skinner stepped up as head coach of the Detroit Red Wings. The pressure was on, but he did well, becoming the very first rookie coach to win both the Prince of Wales Trophy (1st place) and the Stanley Cup.

Skinner considers his appointment to lead the Red Wings the highlight of his career.

"The pinnacle of my career, my biggest thrill, was when I was first appointed the coach of the Detroit Red Wings, because they had a pretty good record at that time. Tommy Ivan won quite a few championships—I think seven straight National League titles. Then he won four Stanley Cups, I think it was. When Tommy moved to Chicago and I was appointed, I was just out of junior hockey. I was kind of surprised, but I was quite thrilled to be appointed the coach of the champion Red Wings at that time. That was my biggest thrill. My second thrill was winning the Cup. A lot of people were amazed that I said that my biggest thrill was being appointed the coach. We had quite an exciting year that year (1954-55)."

In the NHL, Skinner was more reserved than he was during his junior hockey days. At the same time, he had the respect of his players and knew how to accomplish his objectives. A Hockey Hall of Fame write-up on Skinner provides a good description of him as a coach: "He appears to be the type of coach who inspires respect without developing the baldness and ulcers which are seemingly physical manifestations of so many of his fellow men. ... Basically, Skinner has achieved the philosophic mirth of humanity and leadership, which have enabled him to be a stern disciplinarian and still to retain his players' touch."

"Just to have the players respect me [was important]," he says today. "If they came to me with a problem...you know they were scared to go to Jack [Adams]. Jack was a competitor and he believed in discipline. A lot of players wouldn't go to him. They'd come to me and I always [smoothed things out with Adams]. I did it for them, and they respected me for it. I think the big thing in coaching is respect. If the players don't have any respect for you and they don't have any confidence in you, you're not going to be a successful coach. I had a few players on that club that played for me in junior hockey. They grew up with me, I had their respect, and I had a feeling all the time that they put out for me. ... Those players stuck by you. They backed you 100%. We fought together and I fought the referees."

Skinner coached the Red Wings from 1954 to 1958, posting a 123-78-46 record in 247 games. He gave up coaching during his fourth season because of the pressure, which was causing him to experience migraine headaches. Skinner remained with the organization for a long time, 39 years in all. Altogether, he served as head scout, director of farm club operations, director of hockey operations, and both assistant and head general manager. He returned in 1982 after the Norris family sold the club. During his career, Skinner made his permanent home in the Winnipeg suburb of Lockport, Manitoba. There, he operated several drive-in restaurants with his family. After retiring to Windsor, Ontario, Skinner continued following junior hockey, which he felt was the most exciting form of the game.

CHAPTER TWO

THE CLUB THAT JACK BUILT
- JACK ADAMS -

JOHN JAMES (JACK) ADAMS

Born: June 14, 1895, Fort William, Ontario
Died: May 1, 1968
Junior
  • Fort William, 1911-1914
Senior
  • Fort William (NMHL), 1914-15
  • Peterborough (OHL), 1915-16
  • Sarnia (OHA), 1916-1918
Professional
  • Toronto Arenas (NHL), 1918-19
  • Vancouver Millionaires (PCHA), 1919-1922
  • Toronto St. Pats (NHL), 1922-26
  • Ottawa Senators (NHL), 1926-27
Career - Administrative
  • Detroit Red Wings Coach, 1927-1947
  • Detroit Red Wings General Manager, 1947-63
  • President, Central Hockey League, 1963-68

Career Awards & Honors
  • Red Wings Hall of Fame, 1945
  • Hockey Hall of Fame, 1959
  • Lester Patrick Trophy, 1965-66
  • First All-Star Team (RW, PCHA), 1920-21, 1921-22
  • First Team All-Star Coach, 1937, 1943
  • Second Team All-Star Coach, 1945
  • All-Star Game Coach, 1937
  • Michigan Sports Hall of Fame
  • Fort William, Ontario Hall of Fame
Career Milestones
  • PCHA scoring leader, 1922
  • As Red Wings GM, led team to 12 regular-season championships, seven consecutively.

BIOGRAPHY

Jack Adams brought an awareness and an appreciation of the sport of hockey to both the city of Detroit and the United States. Known as "Jolly Jack" and "Genial Jawn," among other nicknames, Adams built the Red Wings into true champions. During the 35 years that he served as Detroit's general manager, his team won the Stanley Cup seven times and won 12 regular-season championships, seven of them consecutively. Loved, hated, honored and respected, many different opinions exist regarding Jolly Jack, and they are explored in the following pages. A symbol of both competitiveness and Detroit Red Wings hockey, one thing that cannot be disputed is that Adams was tremendously successful in getting the results he demanded.

The son of a passenger train railroad engineer, Adams' childhood ambition was to be a surgeon. He made a commitment to himself at a young age to abstain from smoke and drink. To buy his first pair of skates, Adams sold newspapers in saloons. To get ice time, he worked scraping the ice at a local rink, and, at the age of 15, went to work in a grain elevator so that he could save money for school. He moved to Calumet, Michigan for a time and while working there met George Gipp, a future Notre Dame football star. Adams played for the Northern Michigan Senior Hockey League where, as he said in the January 9, 1954 issue of *The Saturday Evening Post*, "If you could play hockey and fight, you were in."

Thus, Adams' association with the sport of hockey began as a player. He learned to play on his neighbor's backyard rink. He played for the local Fort William YMCA team and later for the amateur Fort William Maple Leafs. Adams also played junior and senior hockey in Fort William (now Thunder Bay), Ontario, and continued playing senior hockey in the Ontario Hockey Association, first for Peterborough in 1915-16, and then for Sarnia the following two seasons.

Adams eventually turned professional, playing both center and right wing. World War I took him away from hockey for a short time, and he served in the Canadian Army. His professional career began with the Toronto Arenas in 1917-18. He remained with the Arenas until 1919-20, when he went to the Vancouver Millionaires of the Pacific Coast Hockey League with his brother Bill and NHL star Alf Skinner.

Adams found a great deal of success in the PCHA. In 1921-22, he led the league in scoring with 25 goals in 24 games, adding six more in the post-season final match up against Toronto, which the Millionaires

ended up losing. That season, he recorded four hat tricks and one four-goal game! He was named to the PCHL first All-Star team at right wing. Adams returned to Toronto to play for the St. Patricks in 1922-23, when he was traded there for Harry Cameron on October 30, 1922. He remained with the St. Pats until 1926-27 and spent his last professional season with the Ottawa Senators.

As a player, Jack was a nuisance to opposing teams and was very crafty in the way he wove through their defenses. He was tough and got into fights on a regular basis. Once, he ended up in the hospital after taking a bad beating. Bandaged and mangled, it required 14 stitches to close a wound he had sustained. His sister happened to be a nurse at the hospital and did not recognize her brother in this condition. When Adams identified himself, his sister fainted and later told Jack that if he did not quit hockey, it would kill him. She added that hockey was changing his personality for sure.

Adams joined the Detroit Red Wings, then known as the Detroit Cougars, in 1927-28. While Ottawa was in Boston for a playoff game against the Bruins, he received word that Detroit was in need of a coach. Detroit's current coach, Art Duncan, was stepping down to resume a playing career with the Toronto Maple Leafs. The coaching job was appealing to Jack, and he made a request to then-NHL president Frank Calder to give him the job. Calder obliged and thus cemented the fate of the Detroit Red Wings for years to come.

The tender, young years of the team were not easy ones. When Adams came to town, Detroit residents had very little knowledge of the game. It was commonplace for knowledgeable Canadian fans from nearby Windsor, Ontario, to fill the Olympia and boo the Red Wings. These fans opted to root for the more familiar Canadian teams that visited Detroit. In an effort to educate Detroit fans about the game, Adams wrote a column for the *Detroit Times* entitled "Following the Puck."

The Great Depression added to the difficulty of operating a young hockey club. During the team's first year, it lost $84,000 at the gate. In 1928-29, the team made a small gain when it took in $175,000, but the Depression quickly took care of that. The syndicate that owned the Cougars soon went broke,

Jack Adams exits the train station with Sid Abel, Marty Pavelich and Alex Delvecchio.

and Adams found himself working for the bankers who took over.

Things were not good. As stated in Phil Loranger's book *If They Played Hockey In Heaven–The Jack Adams Story* in 1931-32, Adams commented that he had to chip in some of his own money to pay players. He said: "Things are so bad around here that I'm having to put up my own money sometimes to meet payroll. We've been riding day coaches all season on the road and eating cold sandwiches, candy bars, and oranges when we can't afford to buy them from hawkers. I just hope we don't break any more of our sticks, because we're at a point where we just can't afford to buy any new ones. Last week, a gang of kids over near the stadium stole some of our sticks and if the police hadn't recovered them, we'd be kicking the puck with our skates."

In 1933, the team was spared from dissolution by

millionaire Jim Norris, who loved the sport of hockey. A native of Canada, he had played the game and knew it well. A tough, hard-nosed businessman, he met with the stockbrokers in a downtown Detroit bank office. Present were his son Jim, Jr., Arthur Wirtz and Adams, whom he had met for the very first time. He acquired both the Olympia and the Falcons, which he renamed the Red Wings, and put Adams on probation for one year. It was sink-or-swim for Jack, and he certainly did not sink. Adams did a good job for Norris, handling scouting, promotion and publicity, in addition to his job as the team's coach. It was not long before the Wings won two consecutive Stanley Cups.

Adams continued to do well for "Big Jim" and during his long association with the Red Wings never required a contract. He and Norris, whom he affectionately referred to as "Pops," hit it off right from the start. Even when things didn't go so well, the two men got along. In a January 22, 1952 *Detroit News* article, he said: "I don't think there's any job I have that is tougher than explaining to Pops why we lost a game. He hates defeat ... can't understand it. In my whole life, I've never been criticized by him about a deal. If it goes sour—and a lot of them do—he just shrugs it off and observes that we all agreed on it, so what."

In 1934, Adams started to put together a farm system for the Red Wings. The team had minor league affiliations but not a good system that would keep supplying the parent club with a consistent supply of young, fresh legs. Adams sought players who were very young, ones that he could develop the Red Wings' way. Even when playing junior hockey, players would be put through drills that Adams instructed their coaches to run. They were evaluated in many different areas (temperament, ability, etc.). Eventually, men like Terry Sawchuk, Ted Lindsay, Red Kelly and Gordie Howe came up through the system's ranks.

It wasn't long before Detroit's system had produced a surplus of talent. However, the Wings were not greedy. In the January 9, 1954 issue of *The Saturday Evening Post*, Adams said: "If a boy is a big league hockey player, we'll see that he gets a chance to play in the big league—even if it isn't with the Red Wings."

With the Red Wings, Adams proved to be a master trader and pulled off many successful deals. He worked on the theory that the ideal time to insist on quality as well as quantity was when a top notch player was put on the block and was known for unloading "star" players when they were in their prime.

Sometimes his deals were successful, and sometimes they were not. Two that backfired on him involved Red Kelly and Bill Quackenbush. In the first trade, he sent Kelly to Toronto in exchange for Marc Reaume. The other trade, in 1949, involved his unloading of All-Star Quackenbush, who had just become the first defenseman to win the Lady Byng Trophy, and Pete Horeck for Lloyd Durham, Jimmy Peters, Clare Martin and Pete Babando. That season, the Red Wings won the Stanley Cup, with Pete Babando scoring the winning goal. Despite the

goal, Adams got rid of him less than three months later.

Two other deals that Adams made were especially shocking to many hockey fans. In 1955, he traded Terry Sawchuk, Vic Stasiuk, Marcel Bonin and Lorne Davis to the Boston Bruins for Warren Godfrey, Ed Sanford, Real Chevrefils, Norm Corcoran and Gilles Boisvert. Then, prior to the beginning of the 1957-58 season, he sent Ted Lindsay and Glenn Hall to the Chicago Blackhawks in exchange for Bill Preston, Hank Bassen, Forbes Kennedy and Johnny Wilson. Lindsay was just coming off of a career-high, 85-point season and was an established Detroit star. Lindsay claimed his dismissal was because of his involvement in the formation of the NHL player's association. Adams said that he needed fresh players and that Lindsay was getting older.

When asked about the trades that Adams made around that time, in the May 7, 1995 issue of the *Detroit News*, former Red Wing Johnny Wilson said: "There's no question that we could have won another four or five Cups. We had the talent, and the other teams weren't getting any better. Those Stanley Cups were so important. Then, all of a sudden to just get rid of nine guys, it kind of breaks your heart."

One of the most unpopular trades that Adams made was the 1957 trade of Johnny Bucyk, with cash, to the Boston Bruins to reacquire Terry Sawchuk. Although Sawchuk was an established goaltender, Bucyk developed into an excellent player in Boston and would have been a tremendous asset to the Red Wings had he remained in Detroit.

Besides successfully piloting the Red Wings, Adams left his impression on the league as well. Along with Dick Irvin and the Patrick brothers, Lester and Frank, he pushed for the penalty shot's introduction into the NHL rule book. The shot had already been in use in the Western League for some time. Detroit's Ralph "Scotty" Bowman was the first player in NHL history to score a goal on a penalty shot when he put the puck past Alex Connell of the Montreal Maroons, 36 feet out from the net.

The Red Wing career of Jack Adams came to an end in 1962 when Norris decided that the time had come. Although he had anticipated the end was near, he felt that he had been fired, according to Loranger's book. However, at an April 26, 1962 press conference, he said: "It was pretty much my own decision. My doctor has been after me to quit. He is a good friend of mine and he was worried I'd keep wanting to keep continuing for one more year and then one more year. The fact that we finished out of the playoffs had nothing to do with this. I never quit under fire and I'm not doing it now."

In 1965-66, Jack Adams was the first recipient of the Lester Patrick Trophy. He was presented with the award on February 7, 1966, in Toots Shor's restaurant in New York.

After leaving the Red Wings, he was appointed president of the Central Hockey League by the NHL Board of Governors. He retained the position until his death in 1968. At the time, the CHL was the NHL's farm league and during its inaugural season had six hockey teams: St. Louis, Indianapolis, Omaha, Tulsa, St. Paul, and Minneapolis. In 1962, a trophy was named after him and was awarded to the league's playoff champions. The Omaha Knights were the first recipients, and Adams personally presented them with the trophy.

Today, a National Hockey League Trophy bears his name and is given to the NHL coach judged to have contributed the most to his team's success. When the first trophy was given his name, Adams was presented with lifetime passes to the Detroit Lions, Tigers, Red Wings and Olympia for his continued interest in and contributions to the world of sports. In 1962, then-NHL president Clarence Campbell also presented him with a gold pass to all NHL arenas.

The hospital incident in which Adams' sister told him to quit hockey because it was changing his personality had some truth to it. Supposedly, a seasoned hockey writer once gave the following advice to a rookie journalist, as told in a *Detroit News* article: "Don't pay any attention to what you hear from Adams now. It's hockey season. During the season, he simply cannot be understood. He hates his best friend. He just lives to win. But wait until summer comes. There won't be a finer, more thoughtful gentleman in Detroit. He can't do enough for anybody then."

Even in the off-season, Adams was still very concerned about the Red Wings. He rarely vacationed but often was seen in attendance at baseball games,

which he enjoyed a great deal. In the same *Detroit News* Paul Chandler article, he explained: "I can't enjoy myself. I keep thinking that there is something I should be doing with the club. I've seen too many guys get in trouble vacationing while the pot was boiling back home."

WHAT IS YOUR OPINION OF JACK ADAMS?

Jack Adams was a multi-faceted individual. Those who had dealings with him offer a variety of descriptions, ranging from the most bitter portraits to the most positive, endearing caricatures.

William Barry Furlong, in the January 9, 1954 issue of *The Saturday Evening Post*, gave the following description of Adams at the age of 58: "To his players, Jack Adams is a kindly, sweet tempered, if sometimes strong-willed overseer. To his rivals, Adams is a sharp-tongued, irascible tyrant. He is a man of emotional extremes. He may deliver a scorching denunciation of an opponent's rough tactics; then rush from the rink and break into tears in a hospital corridor while one of his players undergoes an emergency operation. In the heat of a game, he has blisteringly reviewed the shortcomings of the league's referees and linesman, but he has also gone before the league's board to advocate higher pay and a pension system for the officials."

In Philip Loranger's book *If They Played Hockey In Heaven—The Jack Adams Story*, Loranger said:

Jack never cheated his fans. He brought the city champions and trophy winners because he brought in the finest players available. Most of his players were gate-pleasers and just about all of them could make the big plays when they were called upon. There were few rumdums in the Adams' organization and Jack kept reaching into the barrel and pulling out talented players whenever it looked like one of his regulars was beginning to limp along on past glories. Adams helped his players in every way he could because he knew that fellows in good health and without worries would perform better than those who couldn't concentrate on the game. Even the Detroit equipment was the finest. Jack's players had some gear that other teams only saw in Detroit or their dreams. Jack had long ago posted a sign above the door of Wings' dressing room which simply stated: 'We supply everything but the guts.' It was the truth.

Adams was a fiery, competitive man for sure, and there are numerous stories of him "skinning his players alive" for poor performances, throwing orange wedges at them in the dressing room or walking around with one-way tickets to Indianapolis visibly protruding from his pocket. "There's more freedom now," says Red Wings' locker room attendant Wally Crossman. "Before, when Adams had the team, you couldn't even talk back to him. He did all of the talking, he did all of the bawling out of the players. If you talked back to him, it was too bad. I used to pass oranges around at that time between periods. I would cut up the oranges in quarters and pass them around on a tray. Adams would come into room and he'd take a piece of orange off of there and throw it at the player and bawl him out for something he did on the ice before. If he did that now-a-days, he'd be sued. One guy talked back to him once and the next day he was sent out to the farm club."

Once, in a game against the Montreal Canadiens, Adams broke NHL rules and burst into the official's room in disagreement over a call. "He [Adams] raised the devil with referee Red Storey," said Habs coach Dick Irvin in the January 20, 1953 issue of the *Toronto Globe and Mail*. "He went into the room at the end of the second period and, at that time, Detroit had four penalties to our three. That Adams! I think the new authority he possesses (following death of James Norris, Sr., club owner) has gone to his head."

Adams was also known for having had different personality "quirks" during his career. As stated in a *Montreal Gazette* article: "At one stage in the early 1930s Jack was obsessed by the idea that the only promising hockey prospects had to come from the Ottawa Valley, which he loved so dearly. This was probably his most distressing period in hockey; that is until the fatal day when Norris interests decided to retire him."

The following reflections on Jack Adams by those who knew him reveal that he was both loved and hated, both respected and despised. It is to those opinions that we must turn to get a real feel for Jack Adams.

REMEMBERING A FRIEND

Elliott Trumbull, former director of public relations for the Detroit Red Wings, remembers Jack Adams in a very positive light.

[Adams was] my confidant...I was very close to him. Towards the end, he was losing all of his friends and he didn't have too many confidants. On road trips that I didn't go on and he didn't go on, we'd meet back at Olympia to watch the ticker to see how the games came in. We just shared a lot of time together. He got a bum rap, a bad deal. Because at the end, I think that it did pass him by. But my God, he was a hell of hockey guy. He built that franchise. He brought those players in to make the Red Wings the Stanley Cup winners they were in the late 1940s and 1950s. Yes, he really was a great judge of talent.

He was gruff, but he had a heart of gold. He [had] a gruff exterior, but he was a smiling Irishman underneath it. I think he had to be gruff because of the type of background he came from. Hockey, when he played it, was damn rough, the whole thing was rough. When the NHL was getting started in the 1920s and early 1930s, it was rough, and he had to be tough dealing with everybody. So he got that reputation. But on the other hand, one of his nick names was Jolly Jack. So he was sort of a contradiction of himself. I didn't find him that gruff. He was a good guy to work with. He was tough when we lost, of course, but deservedly so. He kept those guys going because he had the fear of God in them, those young players. They knew if they didn't do their job, they were gone. Well that's the way it should be.

They showed [him throwing the orange wedges at players] in [the television movie] Net Worth. He came in, they were on the table and he just took his arm and swept them off. Oh, the movie was terrible. Anybody that didn't know any background and they saw that, they'd say, 'My God! Who the hell was this guy? Was he a raving maniac? What were his credentials?' It wasn't fair. It didn't show the side of him as a hockey man, that he built this franchise and that he brought those players in.

I remember we used to train up in the Soo [at the Pullar Ice Rink] when I first joined the team. Jack would sit up there, it was colder than hell, and he'd

As general manager, Jack Adams piloted the Red Wings to 12 regular season championships, seven of them consecutively.

sit up there and, Jesus, he'd watch the practice without saying a word. And he just knew, this guy can go here, this guy can go there, he's not going to make it, let's put him with so and so. Hell of a judge of talent. I think that's his legacy, he judged that talent. He brought the guys in.

Johnny Wilson tells the story that at Olympia, the guys would be on the ice—this was when Jack wasn't coaching, he was general manager and Sid [Abel] was coaching—and Sid would have the guys just skating around to start off with. It would be a light mood and everything, a fairly light mood, depending on how the game went the night before. There was one place in the Olympia where they could see through the glass out into the parking lot. And when the 'Old Man,'—that's [what] Johnny and the guys called him—when the 'Old Man's' car arrived, they knew, 'Whoop, we better get skating here.'

But that's the way he was. I liken him to baseball's Branch Rickey. He was hockey's Branch Rickey. Look at the wonderful reputation Branch Rickey has for baseball. He [Adams] built that franchise, the league, he made a hell of a lot of players, but towards the end, people will always just remember what happened at the end and it was pretty bad. Bruce let him go. That was the worse thing I had to do, I had to write the release when Jack got let go in 1962, I think it was. Oh, it was terrible. It was the end of an era.

REMEMBERING JACK - DIFFERENT OPINIONS OF ADAMS -

"He was an inspiration to me as a player. I played against him when he was at Toronto, with him on a Stanley Cup championship team at Ottawa, and against him when he managed at Detroit. As a player and later as a coach, he fought every second. That's why I admire him and think he is the greatest hockey man Detroit will ever have. If he didn't beat you he'd say, 'I'll get you next time.'"
-Frank "King" Clancy, October 9, 1962
Detroit News

"Jack Adams was the greatest juggler of talent in the history of hockey, who made more winning teams out of average talent than any other manager in

the game."
-Former Detroit Times sportswriter Lew Walter, Phil Loranger's If They Played Hockey In Heaven–The Jack Adams Story

"We had a great manager in Jack Adams. He was a competitive manager. He was a tough competitor and he was tough to play for, but he was a very fair man. He was very fair to the players. He looked after them, he did everything for them, but he wanted discipline and that's what we had in our club. We didn't have any foolhardy players or stuff like that. It was a great hockey club and we had a great owner. He was very good to the players and I think that has a lot to do with it."
-Former Detroit coach Jimmy Skinner

"Jack Adams is a vitally important part of this community and the hockey-playing youth of Detroit shall be forever thankful there was a Jack Adams."
- Former Detroit Mayor Jerome P. Cavanagh, Phil Loranger's book If They Played Hockey In Heaven–The Jack Adams Story

"Jack's a tough loser. But win or lose, he's with you. He imbues you with a spirit not to be satisfied with average play. He wants you to give your best all the time. If you don't, you're not his type of player and you're not going to be around long. At the same time he is considerate. He says everybody is due for a certain number of bad nights. You'll have a bad night and he won't criticize you. He's making allowances, balancing up your performances. Over the years he has had some great competitors, some fine leaders in the Red Wings' lineup."
-Former Detroit Red Wing Marty Pavelich, March 10, 1956 Detroit News

"He had quite a bit of success in Detroit. You can't knock success, can you? He sure did [do a lot for Detroit]. He was quite fiery."
-Former Detroit Red Wing Harry Lumley

"Jack Adams was the greatest personality I knew. I was always grateful to him for giving me my start as Red Wings broadcaster. He was the dominant person during the glory years, and the best general manager

and coach I ever saw."
   -Budd Lynch, May 6, 1985 *Detroit Red Wings News Release*

"[He was] very competitive, a good, down-to-earth man, with a heart of gold, but he could be as tough as anybody in the business. You had deep respect for the man. He was the greatest person I ever had anything to do with. He had great foresight and did things that you respected."
   -Jimmy Skinner in the November 26, 1976 *Detroit News*

"I never had any trouble with Jack. The problems that people bring up when they [mention] that network show [*Net Worth*] was that 'Jack was a bully' type of thing, but I never found him that way. It was never a part of my experience with him. He was just a gentle manager and I have no criticism for him at all."
   -Former Detroit Red Wing Leo Reise

"He treated us right. You had to know where you stood with him. If he liked you [you were alright]. As I said, trades were made on personality. I got along with Jack Adams good and he did me right. Of course, he never paid us too much. That remains to be seen. The big guys didn't get paid too much, but that was the wages those days. I was even sorry when he got cut. But they probably figured he was getting too old or something. He was a dedicated man and he lived hockey and he did a lot for the game. Like Connie Smythe, Frank Selke and Dick Irvin and the Patricks, they kept the league going, you know. They were dedicated men in the business. They were the big guys. They were the roots."
   -Former Detroit Red Wings trainer Lefty Wilson

"Jack was with the club, of course, when I came there—he was already the coach. He was the coach in the 1930s. He was still the coach in the 1940s. Then he handed it over to Tommy Ivan. Adams was a very stern disciplinarian, and he was very tough on the players. He was really gruff. Ivan was just the opposite. He was really a nice acting coach. He got along very well with the players. They really played for him, too. Of course, they had to play for Adams or they were gone."
   -Long-time Locker Room Attendant Wally Crossman

"[If we were playing poorly], he'd start chewing on an orange and his face would start turning red. We'd sit there, almost cowering in our cubicles, never taking our eye off him for a minute. You knew he was going to throw that orange and you wanted to be ready if it was coming at you.
   He had a great trick he used on us in practice. He'd let us play for a while and then all of a sudden he'd blow his whistle. You had to stop in your tracks . . . and lord help anyone who wasn't where he was supposed to be on the ice. We'd try to edge over when he blew the whistle but he'd scream at you, 'Abel, where are you going! Stay right there!' He would tell us he wanted us to go up and down our wings like we were riding a trolley car–18 feet from the boards, up and down, up and down. He'd say, 'The puck will come to you enough without chasing it all over the place.'
   I'll tell you what kind of a man he was. He got me my first coaching job in Chicago—he arranged the whole thing for me—and then when I came back to town with the Black Hawks he wouldn't even talk to me. I was one of the enemy and he'd have nothing to do with me.
   I LOVED that man."
   -Sid Abel, April 14, 1985 *Detroit News*

CASCIO

"He just wanted us to be better, that's all. I wasn't afraid of him. In fact, you had to laugh at the way it worked. Adams was the general manager, and he would come into the room and yell at us between periods. He'd be as red as a beet and throw orange slices at us. When he was done screaming, he'd go back into the first-aid room and our coach, Tommy Ivan, would come around and talk to the guys one by one, telling us not to worry, saying everything was going to be fine."
-Ted Lindsay, November 8, 1991 *Detroit News*

"My first ten years in the league I could kick Jack in the rear end and he'd hug and kiss me. When Marty Pavelich and I went into business in the off-season, he became a different person. And of course it got worse when we tried to get the Player's Association up and running. Why? Because he was losing control of us. It's that simple. He didn't realize that we had brains and could think for ourselves."
-Ted Lindsay, February 1996 *Inside Line*

"It was rough [playing for Adams]. He was a dictator. Yeah, he didn't give a damn for you or anyone else. He said his job was to put people in the building and you had to win hockey games. I was really not too happy with Jack when I was traded to Toronto because a couple of weeks before he told me

that I should move my family down to Detroit because I would be there for a long time, and two weeks later I was traded to Toronto for Billy Taylor."
-Former Detroit Red Wing Harry Watson

"I'll just put it this way, the man never spoke to me for nine straight years. If we passed in the corridor, he'd turn his head. The only time he spoke to me was to give me hell getting on and off the ice. In fact, he fined me $25 in practice one day. He said I made a bad pass. Now that's how bad he was. Let's not get on him. I really, highly disliked the man. Of course, you won't get anybody to say a good word about him anyway. I wasn't the only one. That's why we never had any problem, we never had any cliques on the team, we never had anything because we were all basically covering up for one another around Jack. He tried to get rid of me every year. For year after year, he'd try to waive me out of the league. But everybody else would pick me up. He could put you on the waiver list, and then pull you off. ... Did you see the Jack Adams movie [referring to the television movie *Net Worth*]? Well, that man that played Jack Adams [Al Waxman] was a dead, spittin' image of the way Jack Adams handled his players. Oh, did he ever [look like him]! He had the same expression in his eyes too. He was a good actor."
-Former Detroit Red Wing Carl Liscombe

CHAPTER THREE

THE OLYMPIA, THE JOE, THE FANS!!!

The author wishes to acknowledge that the factual information given in this chapter regarding the actual Detroit Olympia building was taken almost entirely from a report written on June 30, 1986, by Charles K. Hyde, who, at the time, was an Associate Professor at Wayne State University. Mr. Hyde's report was written for the City of Detroit in accordance with an agreement between the City of Detroit, the State Historic Preservation Office, and the National Park Service as a mitigative measure prior to building demolition.

THE DETROIT OLYMPIA

The Detroit Red Wings played their very first hockey at the Border City Arena in Windsor, Ontario. However, after their inaugural season, they moved into a dark brownish-red structure called the Olympia, a name that for many years was synonymous with Detroit Red Wings hockey.

OLYMPIA DESCRIPTION

When the Olympia opened its doors in 1927, it was the largest rink in the United States. A polygonal, six-sided structure built of dark, reddish-brown brick with terra cotta trimmings, the arena was composed of five main levels (ground level,

mezzanine, main-seating section, balcony and a fifth section which contained the roof supports). At the time of the Olympia's construction, it had a floor space of 77,393 square feet, an ice surface of 110 x 242, and it took up 7.3 million cubic feet. The original interior colors were buff, red and green. A three-sided marquise sat above the building's entrance on Grand Avenue to announce upcoming events and information.

The Olympia's ice surface was kept cool by an elaborate pipe system. As stated in a report by Charles K. Hyde: "Underneath the oval ice-skating rink ... was a labyrinth of 74,880 feet of 1 1/4 inch pipe, placed four inches apart, center-to-center, which carried the brine coolant to create the ice surface. A layer of concrete covered the pipes. The center of the basement housed brine coolers and pumps to move the brine throughout the piping system."

Hyde's report reveals that, before the Olympia was constructed on its home site, the land was undeveloped until the mid-1880s. In 1890, a large farmhouse was erected on the site. It was occupied by James Scovel, a partner in the Scovel Brothers seed growing company, who operated a seed farm there. Residential construction soon flourished in the area, and on February 3, 1927, a building permit was issued to the Detroit Hockey Club and A.A. Scovel to erect the Detroit Olympia, valued at $1,259,300.

The Olympia was designed by internationally - known theater architect C. Howard Crane. Born in Hartford, Connecticut, in 1885, Crane began an illustrious architectural career as a draftsman with the firm of Bayley & Goodrich. He later moved to Detroit, where the design of movie theaters became his specialty. By the end of his career, Crane had completed 250 theaters, over 50 of which were in Detroit. Among those in the Motor City were the Capital Theater (1922), the State Theater (1925), the United Artists Theater (1928) and the Fox Theater (1928), which is now owned by Mike Ilitch. Crane also built Orchestra Hall (1919), which until 1955 was home to the Detroit Symphony.

THE MEMORIES

Over the years, hundreds of Detroit Red Wings called the Olympia home. Following are words from a few players and team associates who fondly recalled their thoughts on one of the greatest sports arenas of all time.

"It was absolutely [beautiful]. It was built for hockey. The first balcony that they had, it was in line with about the second row of seats from the ice. The people were only up in the air 40 or 50 feet maybe. You know, they were like sitting on your bench. They could lean over the boards and yell at us. I know I had a lot of good hockey fans up there over the years. It was real nice to get on the ice and hear them yell, "Hi, Carl, Hi, Carl" before the game. Because after the game started, of course, you never heard anything. It's just yelling and shouting and that is just background noise."
-Carl Liscombe (Left wing, 1937-38 to 1945-46)

"The Detroit Olympia goes down [as one of the greats]. Everybody that I've ever talked to, even fans, just say they sure miss the Olympia. It was built for hockey, and mostly hockey was played in there. It was one of the best buildings in the circuit for hockey, and we hated to see it go. It could only seat 12,000 people and we had 15,000 to 16,000 in there standing. They finally had to move because the expenses were getting higher, player's salaries were getting higher, equipment was getting higher, so they had to move out of there."
-Former Detroit Coach Jimmy Skinner

"The Olympia, when I first started to play, was known as having the fastest ice. Also, they had the liveliest boards. They were the first ones to have it.

OLYMPIA FACTS

Location: 5920 Grand River Avenue (Grand Avenue at McGraw Avenue) Detroit, Michigan

Construction Date: 1927

Additions: 1965 - A four-story, rectangular steel & concrete addition to the rear (northeast) side of the building was made to add 1,800 seats. The addition cost about $2,000,000. At the same time, 13,000 new seats, new boards, and new time clocks were also installed.
1967 - New piping system installed beneath the playing surface.
Early 1970s - Box seats installed.

Olympia opened: October, 1927

Olympia closed: December, 1979

Events: Besides being the home for the Detroit Red Wings, the Olympia was host to a myriad of different events. Among them were basketball games, ice shows, circuses, rodeos, rock concerts, track meets, boxing matches, bicycle races, political & social conventions.

First Red Wings Game: November 22, 1927. Loss to the Ottawa Senators

Last Red Wings Game: December 15, 1979. 4-4 tie with the Quebec Nordiques

Formal Opening: October 17, 1927. Boy Scout Day

First Event: October 22, 1927. "The March of the Flags," a US Navy Band concert & the International Cowboy Rodeo Championships

Last Event: February 22, 1980. Old-timers hockey game

When the Detroit Olympia opened its doors in 1927, it was the largest rink in the United States.

At the bottom of the boards there was about an eight-inch piece that was so lively, they [the Red Wings] could use it to their advantage. They'd practice on how to shoot the puck in and it would bounce a certain way out. It was very lively. If you didn't know how to work that board, you could get caught very, very seriously. I don't know if they started making the ice differently, at one time they just used ordinary water, and then after that they started using water that was cleaner. It would make the ice surface a lot faster. They were the first ones to use that kind of system. They had the best ice that I remember, as compared to the other teams."
  -Pierre Pilote (Defense-Chicago Blackhawks, 1955-56 to 1967-68)

"The Olympia was super. They had the best ice in the league. It was a nice building and the ice maker there really did a super job. And it was a big rink, it was bigger than most of the other ones. That's what I liked about it."
  -Harry Watson (Left-wing, 1942 43 and 1945-46)

"It was great. One of the old, great buildings.

You know, it was tough to play in, coming into [it as] another player because it was sort of egg-shaped, and any time you shot and missed the net, the puck seemed to go back to the blue line. If you knew how to play those boards, it was a definite advantage. Delvecchio was a master at it. He knew every board there. He used to have a spot where he could shoot and that puck would come out at the top of circle for the guy coming in. I mean, he had it perfected"
  -Dennis Hextall (Center, 1975-76 to 1978-79)

"I think the thing with the fans and the building, the fans were right on top of you. That was number one. I mean, they were really close to you. And number two, we had the best ice of anybody in the league. Everybody came to our rink, they'd just fly on that ice and God, it was just terrific ice and everybody loved it. Howe and Lindsay would stay out there and practice shooting pucks in the corner and seeing how the puck would come out and so forth, and those guys had that down pat. Gordie would just be going down there as fast as he could go and Lindsay would shoot it in. The defensemen would be playing Lindsay, but the puck would be shot in the corner,

An aerial view of the Detroit Olympia. The addition to the rear (northeast) side of the building was completed in 1965.

Fans wait in line to buy Red Wings tickets at the Detroit Olympia.

and by the time he'd turn around, Gordie would know exactly where it was coming from."

-Marty Pavelich, (Left wing, 1947-48 to 1956-57)

"[The Olympia] was fantastic. It was just rockin' and rollin'. [If] you've been in Chicago Stadium, [it's the] same thing, just those old buildings. That's why they were so special, because of the proximity of the people to the sport, with the balconies hanging out over the top. All those old buildings were [great] for center court sports: boxing, basketball, hockey, that type of thing. I always felt that probably some of the best seats in the house were the first row in the balcony in those places. In fact, when there were only six teams, when I first came, we played a lot of home-and-home on weekends. When you'd come home, traditionally, Sunday night in Detroit was the big night. Like a lot of times Sunday night in Chicago is a big night. You'd play a home-and-home with Toronto or Montreal or something like that, and you'd come home Sunday night and that place was literally vibrating, literally shaking. It'd get the juices running, I'll tell you that."

-Gary Bergman (Defense, 1964-65 to 1974-75)

"It was one of the classics, just like the Stadium in Chicago. For the time they used it, it was great. Obviously you couldn't play in it now, because it was too small [with] no private suites. It was a good, old stadium that had a good, long life, but its time was up."

-Nick Libett (Left wing, 1967-68 to 1978-79)

REFEREE'S PERSPECTIVE

I played in the Olympia during the Great Lakes Tournament. It was interesting because...the funny thing I remember about the Olympia was that the top of the dashers weren't level, they were beveled. They sloped in toward the rink, so if the puck hit on top, it would angle down to the ice. And during one of the games [against] the University of Pennsylvania, a guy shot the puck around the dasher and it hit and came off the front and they scored and beat us.

I'll always remember that. It was funny because, not just on the top of the dasher, but along the sideboards, they had funny little bounces, and it reminded me of the Boston Arena where BU used to play before they built their own rink. They knew that rink so well that they used to punch the puck off the boards and it would come out in front of the net and guys would be standing there banging them in. That's why they had such a successful power play. But in Detroit, of course, everything was shaped like an egg and [that] sort of ovaled everything in toward the net, similar to Boston Garden or the old Boston Arena.

The one other thing I remember about the

The destruction of the Detroit Olympia marked the end of an era. Photo by John Jacobs.

Olympia is that in order to take a shower, we had to go out of the dressing room and across the hall and go over to shower across the hall. Rather than get up and walk across the hall to take a leak in between periods, the guys would just pee into the...there was a hole in the wall. It was pretty grungy. But overall, you know, we were just a college team coming in from the east, we didn't get any of the, I suppose, 'nicer' accouterments that the other people got?

-National Hockey League referee Paul Stewart

THE OLYMPIA FAMILY

Elliott Trumbull once served as the Director of Public Relations for the Detroit Red Wings and worked for the Olympia Corporation before that time. During his long association with the building, he knew many of the individuals that also called the arena home. Mr. Trumbull thoughtfully recalled the Detroit Olympia below not as a brownish-red, brick structure standing on Grand River and McGraw, but as a home that contained people he considered family.

It was wonderful. That was my home. I mean, I really loved it because the year I joined the whole deal, I didn't work for the hockey club. In 1957-58, I worked for the Olympia. I did PR for the Olympia, for the ice shows, for wrestling and boxing, the Globetrotters, and it was the best thing I ever did because I really got a hand into everything. I had written a few things for the program, so I had my hand in a little bit of hockey. I worked on the junior programs.

The building was great. We had some good people working there, the maintenance crew, the concession people, it was like a family. [There are a lot] of great memories and we had fans that had been with us since the 1930s, and back even into the 1920s—fans that had supported that team [for many years]. They would talk about Larry Aurie and Marty Barry and Mud Bruneteau, like they would talk about Gordie Howe and Sid Abel. The legacy of support was wonderful, and I think the building helped that. It was the continuity of always being in the same building. That wonderful building with great sidelines and not a bad seat in the house. The balcony. The first couple rows in the balcony were probably the best seats in the house, because it was built in such a way that it was an overhang, like in Chicago, like the old Chicago Stadium. It was wonderful.

I think our fans are very knowledgeable. I think the older fans, the ones that supported us for all those years at the Olympia, they knew their hockey and they really appreciated beautiful hockey, the way the game was played when there were only the six teams. It was just wonderful.

The Olympia was just wonderful. I started a players' children's Christmas party. We covered up the ice and went in and put tables down and chairs. We had balloons and the concessions. The other end of the ice we'd leave free and the little kids would come and skate. Gordie would bring Mark and Marty to this Christmas party. All of the concession people would be there. All of the maintenance people. It was a real family.

There's an armory built on the site of the old Olympia. Fortunately, the commander in chief of the National Guard Armory is a hockey fan, so I contacted him and I told him we wanted to memorialize the site or commemorate the site, and we got a plaque. We put up a beautiful bronze plaque [that Alex] Delvecchio's company made. There's a picture of the Olympia and the Red Wing Crest and it says, to paraphrase it, "Be it known to future generations that this site was the location of the Olympia Stadium, home of the Detroit Red Wings of the National Hockey League.

In the October 1995 issue of *Inside Line*, Joe Louis Arena concessions worker Bernie Opalewski, who is one of the few remaining employees that also worked at the Olympia, confirmed Trumbull's story. He said: "It was like an oversized home. Everyone knew everyone else at Olympia. An usher at Olympia was assigned a section and he kept that section throughout the season. By doing that, the usher got to know all of the season-ticket holders in his section. It was like one big, happy hockey family every night at Olympia."

JOE LOUIS ARENA

In 1979, the Detroit Red Wings moved into their current home, the Joe Louis Arena, named after the legendary Hall-of-Fame, World Champion Heavyweight boxer. Owned by the City of Detroit, the building is leased by Mike and Marian Ilitch's Olympia Arenas, Inc. Since 1982, the Ilitch's have invested over ten million dollars into the Joe Louis Arena to improve the facility Red Wings fans know and love.

PERSPECTIVES

"I think it's a great arena. I never, *per se*, played in it. It holds nearly 20,000 people and there is not a bad seat in the house. But the trouble with the new buildings, I think, is when you get up in the top few rows, you're so far from the ice. All of the old arenas had that ... upper level coming out. The new ones don't."

-Dennis Hextall (Center, 1975-76 to 1978-79)

Fans cheer as Al Sobotka removes a giant octopus from the ice during the 1995 Stanley Cup finals. Rich Margittay Photo.

JOE LOUIS ARENA FACT SHEET

*Building Construction
Started, 1977
Finished, 1979
Total Construction Cost: $26,500,000
*Demographics
Total Number of Seats: 19,275
Rink Size: 200 x 85 feet
Five Levels
33 Food & Beverage Counters
5 Novelty Counters
88 Executive Suites
Total Annual Attendance: Over 2 Million
*Event Information
First Event: December 12, 1979, College Basketball.
University of Michigan vs. University of Detroit

First Detroit Red Wings Game: December 27, 1979
Red Wings lost 3-2 to the St. Louis Blues
Notable Events: 1980 NHL All-Star Game
1981 Republican National Convention
Concerts: Frank Sinatra, Neil Diamond, Diana Ross,
Whitney Houston
College Hockey: Great Lakes Invitational & Central
Collegiate Hockey Association Playoffs
Other: Detroit Turbos Lacrosse
World Figure Skating Tours
Ringling Brothers & Barnum and Bailey Circus

***Factual information provided by Sharon Arend,
Little Caesar Enterprises, Inc.**

"Although it was a necessary move for the team, due to the deterioration of both the arena and the surrounding area, you just don't have the same feel in some of the newer buildings that was present in the older arenas. But the Wings got a heck of a deal on a great building, so it was definitely a move worth making."

-Hall of Fame broadcaster Bruce Martyn, October 1995 *Inside Line*

"Well, the guy who built the Detroit Joe Louis Arena is the same person that built the Met Center in Minneapolis, and the same person that built Cincinnati's Riverfront Coliseum that I played in for a couple of years. So, I find that in the first level, you can see up about the first 15 to 20 rows and then after that the rink slopes away from you, so you don't have the same type of feeling as you did in Boston, Buffalo,

Chicago or maybe even the Philadelphia Spectrum, the hanging over bit.

"For the most part, I think it's pretty hard not to be up for the game in Detroit because you've got a pretty good crowd, you can feel the pulse in the building, the atmosphere, electricity is running, people are busy going about all their business underneath the stands, and it's really like a mini production, almost like a small city.

"All the different things that are happening between the restaurants and next to our dressing room—[that] is where they have the beer cooler, so there's a lot of activity there—and the Zamboni and the ice crew, the police officers and all the waiters and vendors and all of the other different people coming in and out. There is a lot of activity. It can't help but charge you up. Plus, the rink is bright. It's very bright. A lot of times, these new buildings might be new and

Loyal fans enter the Joe Louis Arena, home of the Detroit Red Wings since 1979. Rich Margittay Photo.

A member of the Little Caesar's AAA midget team removes octopi from the ice during the 1995 Stanley Cup finals. Rich Margittay Photo.

A giant artificial octopus hangs from the rafters of Joe Louis Arena. Rich Margittay Photo.

they might be clean, but they are not bright. They are not really so illuminated. [Detroit is so bright] that it's just instantly charging you up!"

-National Hockey League referee Paul Stewart

AL SOBOTKA - A JOE LOUIS ARENA "LINK TO YESTERYEAR"

Years ago, when the Detroit Red Wings were still playing in the Olympia, their present day building manager was just getting started with the team, sweeping and mopping floors after games. As time passed, Sobotka worked his way up the Olympia ladder and today has become somewhat of a legend in Detroit, driving the Zamboni, tending to unfortunate octopi that land on the ice, and preparing the arena for game time.

In the January 1996 issue of *Inside Line*, Sobotka commented on his job, saying: "Everyone thinks it's such a laid-back job–I mean, how tough can it be to drive a Zamboni and twirl an occasional octopus? But they don't realize the all-nighters we have to put

in to get the place ready to go. During the hockey season, we can be here seven days a week, 15 hours a day, easily–depending on what events we have." Red Wings fans can be glad that a man like Sobotka is on the job, making sure that the Joe Louis is in top condition for their team.

THE FANS

Detroit Red Wings fans have been around ever since the team came to the Motor City. They come in all shapes, sizes, demeanors and temperaments. They are often described as wild. However, they have not always been *loyal*. Since the team is located just across the border from Canada, many of the earliest "fans" were loyal to Canadian teams like the Toronto Maple Leafs and Montreal Canadiens. They would fill the Olympia not to cheer the Red Wings on to victory, but to boo them like crazy and root for the opposing Canadian clubs. In a 1936 article that appeared in the *Detroit News*, Jack Adams said: "[Detroit] was the first place I ever saw that the home team wasn't popular. The crowds used to come out to see us lose. We were a new team in this part of the country and we weren't popular. The crowd in Detroit was mostly Canadian and the Canadians had their favorites. They had always followed the fortunes of the established teams and they wanted to see them win. It wasn't strange for us to get a good jeering for knocking off one of the well-known teams."

Although conditions improved, such behavior did not necessarily dissipate in later years, to which former Detroit defenseman Bill Gadsby can attest. Said Gadsby: "I remember the first night I came here and I think we played against Toronto or Montreal. Especially against Montreal, we would have 2,000 or 3,000 French Canadians living in Windsor who were real Montreal Canadiens fans, and they would come over here and have a few beers or whatever before the game. They were very robust and very vocal. I remember the first night I played here, Montreal scored a goal. Hell, I thought I was in Montreal. I thought I was in the Montreal Forum instead of the Olympia. I heard this big cheer go up and I thought, 'Boy that's strange, here I'm in Detroit with the Red Wings and all of a sudden they score a goal and half the crowd is cheering for them.' I remember going up to Gordie [Howe] and saying, 'Are we in the right building?' He said, 'Oh, you get that every night that we play Toronto and Montreal.' And it was like that every night we played them."

Today, the Red Wings have gained a home town following and have established themselves as the greatest, most storied American National Hockey League franchise. What exactly are the fans like? In the January 11, 1991 issue of the *Detroit News*, Red Wings fan Larry Fox, then a season ticket holder for both the Detroit Red Wings and Pistons living in Southfield, Michigan, said: "Red Wings crowds are more workman, blue-collar people. I have more fun at Joe Louis. The Palace is a circus, a showplace. There are girls in shorts and ladies all dressed up in furs. Everyone is more concerned with who they can say hello to and what kind of jewelry they're wearing."

Sportswriter Joe Falls, in the February 12, 1987 issue of the *Detroit News*, made a statement about Detroit fans at a time in the team's history when it had been struggling. Said Falls: "You see, we are a crazy town. Not many understand us. We draw

A die-hard fan proudly displays the image of an octopus on his head. Rich Margittay Photo.

crowds of 20,000 for a hockey team that sometimes can't clear the puck from in front of its net. Who but Detroit would buy such an inferior product for such a long time? Who else would line up through the night and stand in the cold outside of the stadium to buy tickets to stand up inside the stadium? Who else would go to the fish market and buy an octopus and toss it onto the ice at the first moment of exultation? ... The Red Wings have gotten far more from their fans than they've given them in these last 30 years."

The following segments attempt to describe the personalities and characteristics of a few of the more wild Red Wings fans through actual newspaper accounts of their behavior.

HOLY OCTOPI!!!

"Every Tom Dick and Harry has a bag full of octopuses up their sleeve."
-Police Officer Carl Dolechek, April 7, 1984
Detroit News

Fans share their excitement during Game 2 of the 1995 Stanley Cup finals. Rich Margittay Photo.

Perhaps the "trademark" of a Red Wings fan is the octopus, which has gained a great deal of recognition in recent years as the team has become more successful. A giant artificial octopus hangs from the rafters of Joe Louis Arena, a tangible statement of this trademark. Despite the fact that a Detroit city ordinance forbids throwing anything onto the playing surface, the ritual of tossing the eight-limbed creatures out onto the ice has been a long-time Detroit tradition. It died out in the 1960s, but by the late 1970s, the octopi were back again.

Its roots can be traced all the way back to 1952, when only eight games were required to win the cherished Stanley Cup. That season, the Red Wings had beat the Maple Leafs in four, first-round games. They won the next three final-series games against the Canadiens, requiring only one more to win the Cup. Supposedly, two Detroit brothers, Pete and Jerry Cusimano, took an octopus from their family's fish market and brought it with them for the final game. They believed that the eight tentacles symbolized

good luck for the Red Wings, and they must have been right, as Detroit won the prize.

"I thought it was great years ago when they'd throw one in the playoffs," said Sid Abel in the April 7, 1984 *Detroit News*. "We looked forward to it coming each year. It seemed to grow on us. The octopus was a real part of our playoff tradition. But it's been carried too far. Now, they're coming from all over the place and for no reason whatsoever—even during the regular season."

Has octopus-tossing gotten out of hand? The unofficial record for octopi thrown was set during the 1994-95 Stanley Cup finals, when 54 of the creatures were thrown to the ice. One of the octopi, a 25-pounder, had a rubber ball sewn into its head. Another had a red bandana tied around its neck! In order to keep up with the volume of creatures that were obstructing the ice, five high school-aged members of the Little Caesar's AAA Midget team were on hand to zip around the rink and dispose of them. In the June 19, 1995 issue of the *Detroit Free*

Press, building manager Al Sobotka said: "There's no way we're going to stop the tradition, but we have to keep it under control. I imagined hundreds of octopi on the ice, and I was so worried. But we were able to manage. Fifty-four is still too many, but it could have been a lot worse."

Due to the volume of octopi being thrown to the ice, Red Wings captain Steve Yzerman pleaded with fans to restrain themselves. Animal rights activists voiced their anger in the papers as well. In the June 27, 1995 issue of the *Detroit Free Press*, several made their feelings public. Mary M. Grab said: "Throwing an animal onto the ice is abhorrent. As a diver, I know these cephalopods to be graceful, intelligent, and beautiful. It's rewarding to see an octopus dance and change color on a night dive. To have these animals taken merely to be flung and not as food is deplorable."

Diane E. Claiborne said: "Why have genuine Red Wing fans continued to tolerate the barbaric tradition of tossing octopuses onto the ice? This has nothing to do with real sportsmanship or the honorable values of athletic competition. I suppose an octopus has few friends, but this is—or was—a living creature, just as sacred in God's eye as Lassie, Man O' War, or even a hockey fan. Nothing deserves the indignity and lack of respect demonstrated by the octopus-throwers."

A new NHL policy prohibits fans from throwing anything onto the ice. Doing so can result in the home team being penalized for two minutes. Because of this, today fewer octopi make their way to the ice at Joe Louis Arena.

Octopi are not the only creatures that Red Wing fans have thrown into the rink. In the 1961 Stanley Cup playoffs against the Chicago Blackhawks, a variety of things sailed out from the Olympia crowd. Aside from programs, bits of paper and coins, ink bottles, firecrackers, a steak, and both live and dead animals (among them a guinea pig) were also among the various projectiles employed by the crowd.

They also threw eggs. One egg just barely missed referee Frank Udvari, who was officiating the game. A fan was quoted in the April 14, 1961 issue of the *Detroit News* as he waited for the mess to be cleaned up: "I wouldn't mind waiting if he'd hit him," said the fan. "Wouldn't that have been great with the egg running down his face? I'm not complaining. Maybe

he'll get him next time."

After that game, Gordie Howe appealed to the fans in the *Detroit News*, asking them to refrain from throwing things on the ice, as they had the potential to injure the players (Red Wing Vic Stasiuk once required 24 stitches to his head after skating on a heated penny).

BANNED FOR LIFE

Red Wings fan E. Steiner gained notoriety many years ago for an incident which caused him to be banned for life from the Detroit Olympia. After a game against the New York Rangers, Olympia fans threw various objects (as well as insults) at the boys from the Big Apple. A few of the Rangers charged the crowd, and headed towards Steiner's seat. New York's Camille Henry slipped while charging toward Steiner, dropping his stick in the process. Steiner picked up the stick and clobbered Henry, opening a big gash in his face. In the end, Steiner lost out big. Aside from being banned from the Arena, Henry chased him (on skates), caught him 50 yards outside of the Olympia on Hooker Street and had his revenge!

COME HERE, CHICKEN!

Some of the antics displayed by Detroit fans have been down right clever. In February of 1974, St. Louis Blues' defenseman Ted Harris got his from an Olympian. According to a newspaper article shortly after the incident, during the week, a fan had somehow made his way into the arena and up to the central catwalk near the Olympia's roof. It was there that he did his dirty work for the upcoming game against the Blues. Somehow, the fan rolled up a sign that read "Chicken Harris." Using an elaborate system of strings, the fan managed to "roll out" the sign after Detroit's Red Berenson scored the Wings' third goal of the game during the second period. As an added feature, a rubber chicken and a massive quantity of sawdust emerged from the sign as it unrolled!

WHOPPER, ANYONE?

In the April 7, 1996 issue of *The Blueline*, an underground publication devoted mainly to Chicago Blackhawks hockey, a short excerpt read: "People in

Detroit love the Wings so much, they're risking jail for them. At least 75 Red Wing hockey puck promotional displays have been stolen from local Detroit-area Burger Kings in the last few weeks. The fast food chain is running a hugely successful promotion in which fans can buy pucks with the pictures of their favorite Wings for $3.49. Each outlet receives between 300-500 pucks each Monday, and many locations have run out by the end of the day. The stolen displays and pucks have begun to appear at Michigan memorabilia shows. The displays are being sold for hundreds of dollars and the pucks are selling for $10 each." The Red Wings player pucks continued to be hot items in 1996-97.

CHAPTER FOUR
THE EARLY YEARS
1926 - 1930

Hockey was a different sport when Detroit's first NHL team took to the ice. "Hockey, in my day as a player, may have been dirtier—but it was not tougher to play," said the legendary hockey pioneer Dick Irvin, in a February 13, 1956 *Sports Illustrated* article by Whitney Tower. "By dirtier, I mean plain brutal. The butt end of a stick could break off in a man's ribs and the referee would never call it. Today the refereeing is better and the hockey is better too. A man does more skating now than he used to in a whole game. It was the total legalizing of the forward pass in 1929 that opened up hockey. In my [day they had] board-checking, but the game was so slow that if you tried it today, you'd put 15,000 people to sleep—or else they'd walk out on you."

The men who played were tough. In a press advance, a Canadian sportswriter of years past once said that they were "prime targets of fans who hurled empty spirit bottles, pieces of boards and even chairs in their direction. On outdoor rinks, where tobacco-chewing spectators perched on adjoining snow banks,

goalies had to contend with another hazard: A squirt in the eye at the most crucial moments."

The world of sports in general was a different place when the city of Detroit received its very first professional hockey team. It was often referred to as the Golden Age of Sports. Athletes like Babe Ruth, Jack Dempsey, and Red Grange entertained American Sports fans. Salaries were not even a fraction of what today's professional athletes make. It was possible to run an entire hockey club on a payroll smaller than the average salary of today's NHL player.

Many of the very first men who donned the Detroit uniform did not spend the majority of their careers playing in the National Hockey League. Most were born before the turn of the century and played in various different leagues, professional and otherwise, some of which were forerunners of the NHL. Among these leagues were the National Hockey Association, the Western Canadian Hockey League and the Pacific Coast Hockey League. It is interesting to hear the tales of the men who are the

The Detroit Cougars - Detroit's Hockey Pioneers.

pioneers of the game we know and enjoy today. These men wore the different Detroit crests of Cougar, Falcon and Red Wing while playing for the first professional hockey club in the Motor City.

On September 25, 1926, a group of businessmen purchased an NHL franchise, and Detroit joined the NHL along with the New York Rangers and Chicago Blackhawks. They were called the Cougars, taking the name with them from Victoria of the Western Hockey League. Having no home arena during their first season in Detroit, the Cougars played all of their home games in Windsor, Ontario, at Border Cities Arena. Their first game, a 2-0 loss to the Boston Bruins, was played on November 18, 1926.

Prior to Detroit's inaugural season, the league consisted of a mere seven teams, all of which were located in the eastern half of Canada and the United States (Ottawa, Montreal [Maroons], Pittsburgh, Boston, New York [Americans], Toronto and Montreal [Canadiens]). With the addition of the

newcomers, the NHL was comprised of ten teams altogether, divided into the American and Canadian Divisions. The league would retain this format until Ottawa and Philadelphia left in 1931-32, leaving only eight teams.

THE MEN

CLARENCE E. (DOLLY) DOLSON

Born: May 23, 1897, Hespler, Ontario
Position: Goaltender
Junior: Galt Juniors (Northern Ontario League), 1914-15
Senior: Galt Seniors (Northern Ontario League), 1919-23
Stratford Seniors (OHA), 1923-26
Minor Pro: Stratford (CPHL), 1926-28
London (IHL), 1929-30
Detroit: 1928-29 to 1930-31
Best NHL Season: 1928-29: 2,750 min., 1.43 GAA
Career Milestones
  • Recorded ten shutouts in 44 games, 1928-29
  • Recorded six shutouts in 44 games, 1930-31

BIOGRAPHY

Jack Adams discovered Dolly Dolson while he was playing in a game for Stratford of the former Canadian Professional League. That game against Kitchener was a playoff match, and the Olympia had been selected as a neutral site for the game. Dolson did so well that he left the arena as a Detroit Cougar. He remained in Detroit for the remainder of his NHL career. During the two full seasons in which he was goaltender for Detroit, he didn't miss a single game, playing the entire 44-game schedule.

Unlike many of his contemporaries, Dolson was one of professional hockey's first "acrobatic" goalies. Compared to Hap Holmes, the goalie whom he replaced, Dolson was more of a showman. As an article in the January 26, 1928 issue of the *Detroit News* said: "Dolson ... is the kind of goalie that keeps the crowd convinced that he is just the pepperiest gent on two skates. He can do all of the tricks that any of them can do, including some of the best ground and lofty tumbling ever seen outside of a circus."

Dolson's strong point as a goalie was his ability to clear the puck from Detroit's end of the ice after making a save. Very few shots were scored on him on the rebound. He was an excellent judge of distance and had a knack for judging when to leave the goal to chase down a loose puck. Besides being very skilled, Dolson had a real love for his position. As a youth, goaltending was the position he chose, never expressing a real interest in any other role. He instilled a similar interest in his son, Jack, who played goal for the Auto Club of the International Amateur League during the 1940s.

HAROLD (HAP, HARRY) HOLMES

Born: April 15, 1889, Aurora, Ontario
Position: Goaltender
Died: 1940
Professional
- Toronto Blueshirts (NHA), 1913-15
- Seattle Metropolitans (PCHA), 1916, 1917, 1919-24
- Victoria Cougars (WCHL & WHL), 1925-26

Detroit: 1926-27 to 1927-28
Best NHL Season: 1927-28: 1.8 GAA in 44 games
Career Awards & Honors
- Hap Holmes Memorial Trophy now given to AHL top goalie each season (since 1961)
- Hockey Hall of Fame, 1972

Career Milestones
- Played in five professional hockey leagues during his 16-season career.
- First goalie to win the Stanley Cup with four different teams.
- Played on seven championship teams.

BIOGRAPHY

Although he had a lengthy professional hockey career, Hap Holmes spent only four seasons in the NHL, two with Detroit, recording 17 shutouts. Twice during his professional career, he registered goals-against averages below 2 (1.8 in 1926 with Victoria and 1.8 in 1928 with Detroit) and was referred to by sportswriters as being "nerveless." If there had been a trophy for leading goaltender during the time that Holmes played, he would have won the award on eight occasions.

Holmes turned professional in 1912-13 with the Toronto Blueshirts of the NHA. Three seasons later, he moved to Seattle with Toronto teammates Frank Foyston and Jack Walker to play for the Metropolitans, where he helped them become the

CASCIO

first U.S. team to bring Lord Stanley's Cup to an American city. After returning to Toronto for a year, he went back to the PCHA for eight more seasons. Holmes had a great deal of success playing hockey out west and was the league's leading netminder on six occasions. In 1918-19, he nearly won a second Stanley Cup with Seattle, but a Spanish flu epidemic there caused the cancellation of the series against Montreal. Holmes retired from professional play in 1928 at the age of 39.

CARSON E. (SHOVEL SHOT) COOPER

Born: Cornwall, Ontario
Position: Forward
Died: Hamilton, Ontario, April, 1955
Senior: Hamilton Tigers
Detroit: 1927-28 to 1931-32
Best NHL Season: 1929-30: 18 goals, 36 points
Career Awards & Honors
- Team Captain, 1931-32
- Red Wings Hall of Fame, 1949

Career Milestones
- 1928-29 - Led Red Wings in goals (18), assists (9), points (27), and penalties (68)

BIOGRAPHY

Carson Cooper was a true hockey pioneer in both Boston and Detroit. Before his debut with the very first Boston Bruins team in the fall of 1924, Cooper learned the game in his native town of Cornwall, Ontario. After that, he moved to the city of Hamilton, where he played for the Hamilton Tigers Senior team, helping them win the World's Amateur Championship in 1918 and 1919. He broke into the National Hockey League with Boston in 1924-25, but was traded to Montreal for a half-season in 1926-27. After that, Cooper was a Red Wing until his career ended in 1931-32.

During his NHL career, Cooper gained a reputation for possessing one of the game's most accurate shots. In his very first professional game with the Bruins, Cooper scored three goals on the legendary Georges Vezina, which he rated as the greatest thrill of his career. In the February 8, 1934 issue of the *Detroit News,* Albert Landy described Cooper's shot. He said: "As a member of the Detroit

Falcons, he unsettled rival goaltenders with his unique method of shooting the puck with a sweeping motion of the stick, rather than with the wrists. Sports writers called it the 'shovel shot.' It was particularly hard to stop because it was aimed to go under the goaler's right arm and Cooper's aim in his heyday was seldom bad."

Cooper was not only a member of the very first Boston Bruins team but was also on right wing for the first Detroit team to skate at Olympia. "After three seasons with Boston, I came to Detroit," he said in the February 8, 1934 issue of the *Detroit News,* in an article by Albert Landy. "I got here in time for the first hockey game ever played on Olympia ice. That was in the fall of 1927. Detroit had been in the league the year before, but had played its home games in Windsor. On the first night in Olympia we met Ottawa, which had won the Stanley Cup in the previous season. They had Alex Connell in goal and King Clancy on defense. They had Frank Neighbor, one of the all-time greats, at center. Hec Kilrea was on the left wing. They beat us 2 to 1 on a third-period goal by Frank Finnegan."

After playing five years with the Red Wings, Cooper coached the Detroit Olympics for a short time and then became the Red Wings' head scout. Along with fellow scout Fred Pinkney, Cooper spent many years scouring the frozen Canadian countryside for talent to place in Detroit's farm system. He was compared to Detroit Tigers scout A.J. (Wish) Egan in his value to the club. Among the players he found for the Wings were goalies Harry Lumley and Johnny Mowers, forward Ted Lindsay, and defensemen Bill Quackenbush and Red Kelly.

FRANK CORBETT FOYSTON

Born: February 2, 1891, Minesing, Ontario
Position: Center
Died: 1966
Junior: Barrie Dyment Colts (OHA)
Senior: Eaton's senior company team (OHA)
Professional
- Toronto Blueshirts (NHA), 1912-16
- Seattle Metropolitans (PCHA), 1916-24
- Victoria Cougars (WCHL)

Detroit: 1926-27 to 1927-28
Career Awards & Honors
- Hockey Hall of Fame, 1958

BIOGRAPHY

Frank Foyston spent his entire two-year tenure in the NHL with Detroit, playing there in 1926-27 and 1927-28. Like many of the players of his era, he played hockey in several leagues, five altogether. With the Toronto Blueshirts, Foyston centered a line with Jack Walker and Alan Davidson, taking home the Stanley Cup in 1914. A 1928 *Olympia Official Program* states that in Toronto "his play from the very first was of the highest type, and his headwork was responsible for many brilliant attacks and sallies on the opponent's goal, resulting with great frequency in scores for his team."

In 1914-15, like many of his contemporaries, Foyston traveled west to play for the Seattle Metropolitans of the PCHA, where he stayed for nine seasons. In 1916-17, Foyston won an award for being the league's best all-around player. That season, he scored four goals in seven games against Montreal to help Seattle become the first American club to win the Stanley Cup. In 1919, with future Detroit teammate Hap Holmes, he played in the famous Stanley Cup match between Seattle and Montreal that was canceled due to an outbreak of the Spanish flu. Foyston played on several PCHA all-star teams while with the Mets and led the league in scoring on two occasions (1920 & 1921).

Foyston later played for the Victoria Cougars of the WCHL, helping his team win the coveted Stanley Cup in 1925, the last time a non-NHL club won the prize. Altogether, he played in a total of six Stanley Cup finals. Foyston became a Detroit Cougar when Victoria was sold in 1926. He came to Detroit along with Jack Adams and was made the playing-manager

of the new club after it moved. A 1928 *Olympia Official Program* says: "In order to put the new team on the map, a man of outstanding ability in the great winter pastime had to be secured, and Frank Foyston was the ultimate choice for the responsible position."

Foyston was fearless and aggressive on the ice and a true and personable gentleman off it. He was bold and clever around the net and possessed a choppy style of skating that gave him the illusion of being faster than he actually was. "You missed one of the all-time greats if you never saw Frank Foyston perform with a hockey stick," revealed a 1966 article in the *Seattle Post Intelligencer*. "He wielded it like Fritz Kreisler his bow, Willie Mays his bat and Arnold Palmer his two iron." Foyston lived in Seattle, Washington, after retiring from professional hockey.

FRANK (FREDDIE) FREDERICKSON

Born: June 11, 1895, Winnipeg, Manitoba
Position: Center
Died: May 28, 1979
Amateur
- Winnipeg Falcons (MIHL), 1913-16 & 1919-20

Professional
- Victoria Aristos (PCHL), 1920-22
- Victoria Cougars (PCHL & WCHL), 1922-26

Detroit: 1926-27 to 1930-31
Best NHL Season: 1926-27: 18 goals, 31 points
Career Awards & Honors
- Hockey Hall of Fame, 1958

Career Milestones
- Manitoba Senior Hockey League scoring title: 1916-17 & 1919-20
- Pacific Coast Hockey League scoring title: 1920-21 & 1922-23

BIOGRAPHY

Frank Frederickson played hockey for Detroit on two occasions, first in 1926-27 as a Cougar and again in 1930-31 as a Falcon. He also played for Boston and Pittsburgh during the five NHL seasons of his 20-year, professional career. Although he did not play with Detroit for a lengthy period of time, he is one of the city's hockey pioneers. Frederickson was a colorful and dynamic individual. Different articles written about him reveal that he was a scholar, hockey star, coach, Olympian, aviator, musician and heartful promoter of the game.

The son of John and Gudlaug Frederickson,

Frank had to learn how to speak English, as he was fluent in only the Icelandic language of his immigrant parents.

He dropped out of school at the age of 15 to be an office boy at a law firm. While working at the law firm, he played his first organized hockey for the firm's commercial league team. "We won the first game I played something like 9-1 and I got all but one goal," he once recalled in an unidentifiable source. "I became something of an overnight hero around the office and the people there took an interest in me and prodded me into returning to school." Frederickson later attended the University of Manitoba, where he was the captain of their varsity hockey team and graduated from Winnipeg's Kelvin Technical School. For a time, he also pursued a law education but gave it up for hockey.

Frederickson was a passionate musician. He married a member of the Toronto Conservatory, and played violin in a dance band. During World War I, he joined the Royal Flying Corps and served a tour of duty in Egypt, winning his wings. Returning to England from the Land of the Pyramids, his ship, the Leassowe Castle, was torpedoed by a German submarine. Frederickson spent 12 hours adrift on a life raft, clutching his violin before being rescued by a Japanese destroyer.

After the war, Frederickson returned to Winnipeg to play for the Falcons in 1919-20 and helped them win the Allan Cup (presented to the Senior A champion of Canada and the US). In 1920, he played in the Antwerp Olympic Games, where Canada won the gold medal. "After winning the Manitoba title, we beat University of Toronto to win the Allan Cup and the right to represent Canada," he recalled in a May 24, 1972 *Ottawa Journal* article. "At Antwerp we won all our games but encountered a strong United States team in the final. We didn't know it, but one of the Americans was sure they'd beat us and offered a good size bet. Our treasurer never told us, but he took him up on that wager. Afterwards, he presented each of us with a new suit of clothes, and I went for a visit to Iceland. It was later that we heard that P. J. Mulqueen, then the head man in the Canadian Olympic circles, found out about us getting those suits. He wanted to have us deprived of our title and medals for having accepted these gifts, but nothing happened." Sadly, the members of that squad were disinherited when the Olympic committee decided to honor only those games that were played after 1924.

After having much hockey success in Winnipeg and the Olympics, Lester Patrick lured Frederickson to the Pacific Coast Hockey League, where he played for the Victoria Aristos and Victoria Cougars, winning the Stanley Cup in 1924-25.

Frederickson came to Detroit in 1926-27, when the Cougars were purchased by Detroit interests. His move to Detroit is an interesting story. When the Patricks sold their WCHL interests, he was supposed to become property of the Boston Bruins at the price of $2,000. However, he signed a $6,000 deal with Detroit instead, infuriating Boston general manager Art Ross. R. Phillips of the British Columbia Sports Hall of Fame, who compiled a biographical outline on Frederickson in 1983, said "the ill feeling between the two lasted for many years and ultimately hastened Frederickson's departure from the league." Phillips also pointed out that "ironically, Frederickson went sour with Detroit. His linemates were so mad when they heard about the deal that they wouldn't pass the puck to him. Mid-way through the season he was sold to Boston, then in the NHL cellar. He was in 27th place in scoring when the sale was made. He immediately regained his form and paced the Bruins to the Stanley Cup finals against Ottawa. The Senators took the series."

While playing for the Boston Bruins, Frederickson won another Stanley Cup in 1928-29. He later played for Pittsburgh of the NHL and then returned to Detroit and finished his career with the Falcons in 1930-31.

After retiring as a player, Frederickson turned to coaching and promoting hockey and selling insurance. He coached in Winnipeg from 1931-32 to 1932-33 and then for several years at Princeton University. He spent many hours of volunteer service promoting the game of hockey during his lifetime.

GORDON BLANCHARD (DUKE) KEATS

Born: March 1, 1895, Montreal, Quebec
Position: Center
Amateur: 228th Sportsman's Battalion (Military)
Professional
- Toronto Blueshirts (NHA), 1914
- Edmonton (WCHL), 1919-1926

Minor Pro: Tulsa (AHL)
Detroit: 1926-27 to 1927-28
Best NHL Season: 1926-27: 16 goals, 24 points
Career Awards & Honors
- Hockey Hall of Fame, 1958
- Edmonton Sports Hall of Fame, 1964

Trades
- 1926-27: Traded from Boston to Detroit with Archie Briden for Frank Frederickson and Harry Meeking.
- 1927-28: Traded to Chicago for Gord Fraser.

BIOGRAPHY

One of hockey's legendary figures, Duke Keats grew up in North Bay, Ontario. At the age of six, he was given the nickname "Duke" by his peers, who named him after a warship. At the age of 14, he was playing for the O'Brien Mines team in the rough and tumble Cobalt Mining League of Northern Ontario at the salary of $75.00 per month. He also played for Haileybury of the Temiskaming League and later with Peterborough.

In 1914, Keats signed his first professional contract with the Toronto Blueshirts of the National Hockey Association for $600. His coach was Eddie Livingstone, who had a great deal of influence on Keats and shaped the raw talent he saw into a polished player. It took hours of extra practice on the ice when the rest of the players were through, but Keats soon made it to the professional ranks and became one of the most gifted stickhandlers of his day.

The great Lester Patrick once said: "Keats may not be a fast skater, but he is a stick-handling wonder; he never wastes energy when he knows there is no opening. He waits and calculates carefully, always chancing the break, when it comes, and then puts everything into it, leading a powerful attack. He may be a little slow on his feet, but makes up for that with his brilliant stick work and ... maneuvering. He has the wicked shot in the league and his accuracy at finding the goal is amazing. Besides that, Keats is most unselfish, not refusing to make a pass when there is the slightest chance of a break."

While in the Canadian Army, Keats played for the 228th Sportsman's Battalion before going overseas. Once overseas, he was spotted playing baseball by scout Deacon White. White told Keats that while he was no great baseball player, he possessed a wealth of natural athletic ability. White persuaded him to come to Edmonton after the war and play hockey for the Edmonton Eskimos of the old Big Four in 1919-20. The following season, Keats was named team captain. He became a 50-50 partner of the team in 1920 with Kenny McKenzie when Edmonton joined the Western Canada Hockey League. In 1922, he led the Western League in scoring with 31 goals and 24 assists.

Throughout his career, Keats was well-known for getting ejected from hockey rinks for his actions. In Saskatoon, he would get showered with hunks of coal from angry fans. He once joked that either a lump of coal came with every ticket purchased or the Saskatoon rink in which they played was built atop a coal mine.

When the Patricks sold the Western League, Keats went to Boston for the salary of $8,500 in 1926-27. That same season, he went to Detroit in a trade for Frank Frederickson. In 1927-28, Keats was traded to Chicago, where he had problems with the eccentric owner, Major Frederick McLaughlin. As the story goes, one night in Chicago Stadium, Keats lost his temper and swung his stick at a fan. The problem was that he nearly hit the Major's famous wife, Irene Castle. NHL president Frank Calder fined him $100 and handed him an indefinite suspension for the incident.

Fed up after the Chicago incident, Keats bought his release from the Blackhawks and moved to Tulsa of the American Hockey Association in 1928, where he was the scoring champion. He later focused on rebuilding hockey in Western Canada. In 1931-32, Keats served in four different capacities with the Edmonton Eskimos (player, coach, manager and owner). That season, the Eskimos won the championship. In 1934, he sold the Eskimos to Henry J. Roche and turned to coaching in Saskatoon. He eventually ended up back in Chicago with the Blackhawks for a short time as assistant coach to Clem Loughlin.

REGINALD (REG) NOBLE

Born: June 23, 1895, Collingwood, Ontario
Position: Left-wing
Died: January 19, 1962, Alliston, Ontario
Junior: Collingwood Juniors (OHA)
Senior: Toronto Riversides (OHA)
Minor Pro: Cleveland (IHL)
Detroit: 1927-28 to 1932-33
Best NHL Season:
  • 1919-20 (Toronto): 24 goals, 31 points
Career Awards & Honors
  • Red Wings Hall of Fame, 1944
  • Hockey Hall of Fame, 1962
  • Team Captain, 1927-30

BIOGRAPHY

One of the National Hockey League's pioneers, Noble broke into organized hockey with Collingwood Business College in Ontario. He then played junior hockey for Collingwood of the OHA, who won the championship in 1914-15. The following season, he helped the Toronto Riversides win the OHA senior championship.

Noble turned professional in 1916 with the Toronto Blueshirts of the NHA and ended up with the Montreal Canadiens when the Blueshirts dissolved that season. In 1917-18, the NHA itself dissolved and Noble returned to Toronto to play for the Stanley Cup champion Toronto Arenas of the newly formed NHL. Noble was the team's leading scorer, with 28 goals in 22 games, playing with men like Jack Adams and Corbett Denneny.

The Arenas changed their name to the Saint Patricks the following year and, with scoring ace Cecil "Babe" Dye and Noble, took home the Stanley Cup once more in 1921-22, beating Vancouver.

Noble made a three-year stop in Montreal to play with the Maroons. While there, he was on yet another Stanley Cup winner in 1925-26. Noble then came to Detroit where for, five seasons, he played center, left wing and defense. *Toronto Telegram* sportswriter Ted Reeve rated Noble as one of the best left-wingers of all time. An excellent positional hockey player, he was a good skater and also quite a stickhandler and poke-checker.

A January 26, 1962 *Toronto Telegram* article revealed that: "As a defense player with Detroit he

[Noble] often scored more goals than some of the regular forwards, and in the last game of his career he had a goal and two assists. Jolly Jack [Adams] figured he could have used Noble as insurance on defense for several more years but Reg knew that his sturdy legs were going and he eased off."

After Detroit, Noble went back to Montreal to finish out his NHL career. He stopped playing altogether with Cleveland of the International League. After playing, Noble served as an NHL official for several seasons. He came out of retirement briefly during World War I to help entertain crowds with the Married Men of Alliston, who had put together a hockey team.

The Detroit Falcons—Forerunners of the Red Wings

CHAPTER FIVE
IN WITH A BANG
• THE 1930s •

In 1930-31, the Great Depression was taking its toll on the city of Detroit, just as it was everywhere else. Citizens had little money to spend on recreational activities like attending hockey games. In 1930, the Detroit Cougars changed their name to the Falcons in an attempt to spice up falling interest in their team. On a league-wide basis, the NHL instituted the All-Star team during this season. Although the outlook appeared bleak, the 1930s proved to be successful times for Detroit, as they won the Stanley Cup twice consecutively.

Hockey was a very different game during the 1930s. In a February 7, 1962 *Detroit News* article, former Detroit Red Wing Ebbie Goodfellow reflected on how the game was during the 1930s and how it had changed since he played. "Hockey is faster, the pace is terrific and the players are better conditioned," he said. "In my time you could pace yourself. You're yanked if you coast now. We checked more and harder. That Bucko [McDonald] would put them up

in the rafters when he was having a good night."

Even though the players checked hard and played hard, they did not, as a rule, play dirty. Carl Liscombe, who played for Detroit during the 1930s, recalls the fact that sticks seldom went above the waist. "That was an unwritten rule," he says. "Nobody high sticked back then and if you did high stick, you didn't touch the puck the rest of the night because you had five guys chasing you all night long. That's just a figure of speech, of course. But you kept your head up. Of course with the helmets and the plexiglass shields today, the kids are pretty safe."

Detroit's Stanley Cup success started with a bang, as the team became the first American NHL team to win the coveted trophy in two consecutive seasons (1935-36 & 1936-37). Their first taste of victory might have come earlier had it not been for a defeat by the Chicago Blackhawks, who, coached by Tommy Gorman, won their first Cup in 1933-34.

1933-34 STANLEY CUP FINALS

FIRST GAME: (April 3, at Detroit)
Black Hawks 2, Red Wings 1
First Period
Chicago - Conacher 17:50
Second Period
No scoring
Third Period
Detroit - Lewis (Aurie, Graham) 4:45
First Overtime
No scoring
Second Overtime
Chicago - Thompson 1:10

SECOND GAME: (April 5, at Detroit)
Black Hawks 4, Red Wings 1
First Period
Chicago - Couture 17:52
Second Period
Detroit - Lewis (Weiland) 9:58
Third Period
Chicago - Romnes (Thompson) 1:28
Chicago - Coulter (Gottselig) 5:34
Chicago - Gottselig 18:02

THIRD GAME: (April 8, at Chicago)
Red Wings 5, Black Hawks 2
First Period
Chicago - Thompson (March, Romnes) 0:28
Detroit - Pettinger (Starr, Carson) 6:07
Detroit - Aurie (Buswell) 8:40
Second Period
Chicago - Gottselig (McFayden, Couture) ..18:07
Third Period
Detroit - Young 13:50
Detroit - Weiland (Aurie, Lewis) 18:20
Detroit - Aurie 19:53

FOURTH GAME: (April 10, at Chicago)
Black Hawks 1, Red Wings 0
First Period
No Scoring
Second Period
No Scoring
Third Period
No Scoring
First Overtime
No scoring
Second Overtime
Chicago - March (Romnes) 10:05

The defeat Detroit suffered at the hands of the Chicago Blackhawks in 1934 brought the Stanley Cup to the Windy City for the first time in its team's history. Detroit was first place in the American Division. Chicago had just finished off the Montreal Maroons in the semifinals. Prior to that, they hadn't won a game in the Motor City for over four years! In a best of five series, the Blackhawks beat the Red Wings 3-1.

The Blackhawks took the first two games. However during the third game, held in Chicago, the tables turned. Chicago's goaltender, Charles Gardiner, played poorly due to an illness that caused his death soon after the series, and Detroit skated away with a win. They managed to defeat the Blackhawks 5-2, especially dominating the third period with three unanswered goals.

THE FINAL GAME - APRIL 10, 1934

On April 10 in Chicago, the Blackhawks won the fourth and final game, and their first Stanley Cup. Chicago's goalie was still very ill but played anyway. Opening at a fast pace, the Blackhawks dominated the first period with the line of March, Thompson and Romnes. Detroit's Gus Marker and Chicago's Rosie Couture both served two minutes in the penalty box for tripping before the period ended. Chicago's Doc Romnes came close to putting a shot past Detroit goalie Wilf Cude, but it hit the post. After Marker was sent to the penalty box for charging Chicago's Johnny Gottselig into the boards, the Blackhawks began playing more offensively.

Early in the first period, Detroit's Herbie Lewis nearly scored on Gardiner with a high shot, and had a second chance on the rebound. However, the puck was swept away by Chicago defenseman Roger Jenkins. After that, the Red Wings went at full steam in an attempt to score, only gaining an advantage for a short while. Unfortunately, their efforts were fruitless and the game's first period ended with no score.

During the second period, Chicago's Harold "Mush" March completely escaped the Detroit defense on a mad rush for Cude, and his shot barely missed the net. The third period was played defensively, with most of the action occurring at mid-ice. The tension began to build as the game remained scoreless. Detroit's Hap Emms gave Gardiner his toughest moment of the entire game with a high, hard shot which caused the ill goalie to fall and take a time-out to catch his breath.

After the third period ended with no score, the teams progressed through two periods of overtime play. Several near fights developed as the tension built, but no penalties were called. Then, at 10:05 of the second overtime period, March finally scored, ending the series.

In that final game, Detroit's Cude stopped 53 shots while Gardiner had to stop only 40. It was a strange twist of fate that Gardiner and Cude played goal on the opposing teams. As boys, they were friends back in Winnipeg, and even walked back and forth to school together.

The 1934-35 Detroit Red Wings.

1935-36 STANLEY CUP VICTORY

FIRST GAME: (April 5, at Detroit)
Red Wings 3, Maple Leafs 1
First Period
Detroit - McDonald 4:53
Detroit - Howe (Young) 5:37
Detroit - W. Kilrea (Bruneteau) 12:05
Toronto - Boll (Thoms) 12:15
Second Period
No scoring
Third Period
No scoring

SECOND GAME: (April 7, at Detroit)
Red Wings 9, Maple Leafs 4
First Period
Detroit - W. Kilrea (Sorrell) 1:30
Detroit - Barry (Bowman) 4:25
Detroit - Lewis (Sorrell, Barry) 10:05
Toronto - Boll (Thoms) 12:35
Detroit - McDonald (H. Kilrea) 16:55
Second Period
Detroit - Sorrell (Barry, Howe) 7:15
Detroit - Pettinger (Howe, Young) 9:10
Toronto - Primeau (Shill) 14:00
Third Period
Detroit - Sorrell (W. Kilrea, Bruneteau) 7:30
Toronto - Thoms (Boll, Horner) 9:40
Detroit - Pettinger (H. Kilrea) 12:05

Toronto - Davidson (Finnigan, H. Jackson) ..16:10
Detroit - McDonald 17:15

THIRD GAME: (April 9, at Toronto)
Maple Leafs 4, Red Wings 3
First Period
Detroit - Bowman (Pettinger) 9:25
Second Period
Detroit - Bruneteau 1:06
Third Period
Detroit - Howe (Pettinger, H. Kilrea) 11:15
Toronto - Primeau (Davidson, Horner) 13:10
Toronto - Kelly (Finnigan) 15:21
Toronto - Kelly (Primeau) 19:18
Overtime
Toronto - Boll (Horner, Kelly) 0:31

FOURTH GAME: (April 11, at Toronto)
Red Wings 3, Maple Leafs 2
First Period
Toronto - Primeau 18:11
Second Period
Detroit - Goodfellow (Sorrell) 9:55
Detroit - Barry (Lewis) 10:39
Third Period
Detroit - Kelly (Lewis) 9:45
Toronto - Thoms 10:57

In the Spring of 1936, the Detroit Red Wings skated away with their very first Stanley Cup. Taking home the Prince of Wales Trophy (their second in three years) with a first-place, American Division

finish, Detroit faced off against the defending Stanley Cup champion Montreal Maroons in the semifinals.

This particular series proved to be one of the most historical of all time. It was, in many respects, a record-setting series. It began with a telegram to the team from then-Detroit Mayor Couzens. As quoted in a Sam Greene article in the March 25, 1936 issue of the *Detroit News*, Jack Adams read the telegram aloud to his players: "Permit me to join with the many ardent fans in expressing to you [Jack Adams] and every member of the Red Wings my sincere good wishes and confidence that you will come through the play-off series with flying colors. Best of Luck."

The game which followed that telegram on March 24-25, 1936, would turn out to be the longest in Stanley Cup history. Detroit eventually won it in the sixth period of overtime when Mud Bruneteau scored at 2:25 a.m., ending 176 minutes and 30 seconds of hockey, 5 hours and 51 minutes after the game started! The game broke the previous record of 2:44:46 set by Toronto on April 3, 1933. Ten thousand fans, the largest crowd to assemble in Montreal that winter, witnessed most of the game (many actually left early from fatigue).

An excerpt from the same *Detroit News* article reveals: "The regulation 60 minutes finished and the overtime started. It became monotonous to the spectators as the rival forces sallied up and down the ice in a vain effort to break the tie. Some of the crowd started to leave. Others ordered coffee and drank it in their seats. Wives explained facetiously that they had to go home to prepare breakfast. A wit suggested that the teams flip a coin to settle the issue. Another countered with the idea that they decide the ownership of the Stanley Cup in the same fashion. It was even less fun for the men on the ice. They were tiring under the grind. Adams ordered hot tea for the Wings, and it was served during the 10-minute intermissions." Adams not only gave his men hot tea, but also sugar soaked in brandy in an effort to keep them on their toes.

Bruneteau was the youngest member of the team, but turned out to be the most valuable player during that game. It was only a few weeks before that he had been skating for the Detroit Olympics, the Red Wings' farm team. His famous game-winning goal came when he took a pass from teammate Hec Kilrea. Then, to the left side of Lorne Chabot, 12 feet out from the Montreal net, Bruneteau fired a shot, not towards the half of the net that was wide open, but to the other side. The puck sailed past Chabot and

Detroit could finally breathe a sigh of relief! Mud was mauled by his teammates on the way to the dressing room. Once there, reporters asked him how he had done it. In the same *Detroit News* article, he said: "I don't know. All I know is I hope my old man was listening to the radio. I showed 'em they didn't bring me up for nothing this time."

During that long game, both goalies played superbly. Detroit's Norm Smith stopped 91 shots. Montreal's Chabot turned aside 66. Critics had placed Smith at a disadvantage because they felt he lacked poise and experience. They thought he would certainly crack under the pressure, but he did not. That night, Smith made one miraculous save after another, amazing the crowds.

Although Detroit's powerful line of Larry Aurie, Herbie Lewis and Marty Barry did not score any goals that night, they would prove a force to be reckoned with as the Wings went on to win the series 3-0. The Wings' defensive corps of Bucko McDonald, Doug Young, and Ebbie Goodfellow would also be a large factor in the team's continued success during the series. Characteristically, McDonald played a very tough game that night. A newcomer to post-season hockey, he flattened the opposition with his patented, bone-jarring body checks time and time again.

STANLEY CUP FINALS

In the finals, the Red Wings faced off against the Toronto Maple Leafs, who finished second in the Canadian Division. The tired Maple Leafs beat the New York Americans 2-1 and, for the fourth time in five years, advanced to the finals where a rested Detroit team was waiting to beat them. The second game of the finals, played in Detroit on April 7, 1936, was especially embarrassing for Toronto, as Detroit set what, at the time, was a league Stanley Cup record by spanking them 9-4! Just as in the first game, Detroit scored three unanswered goals before Frank "Buzz" Bohl, assisted by Bill Thoms, was able to put one in the net for the Leafs.

THE FINAL GAME - APRIL 11, 1936

The Detroit Red Wings finished off Toronto in four straight games. The final game, which brought Detroit its first Stanley Cup, started out well for

Toronto, raising the hopes of 14,728 Maple Leafs fans at the Gardens, the largest crowd of the season, and at the time, the second-largest in the history of the building. To the delight of the crowd, Toronto's Joe Primeau scored the game's first goal in what was the last game of his NHL career. Detroit was not able to answer back with a goal in the opening period, but got two past George Hainsworth in the second, and another goal during the third period from Pete Kelly. Toronto's Bill Thoms also scored in the third period, but it was not enough to keep Toronto's series alive. Detroit had won its very first Stanley Cup!

When the victory siren sounded, all of the Maple Leafs threw their sticks to the ice and skated over to congratulate the victors. Marty Barry and Herbie Lewis shook hands with Charlie Conacher, who because of their efforts, had been held scoreless the entire series. The Stanley Cup was not presented to the Wings on Toronto ice. Instead, amidst the continuous clicking of cameras, then-NHL President Frank Calder gave it to team owner James Norris, Sr., at Toronto's Royal York Hotel.

The Red Wings boarded the train home at 8:30 Sunday morning, and arrived in Detroit at 2:40 that afternoon. When they arrived in Detroit, they were met by mobs of happy fans from a city that had earned a reputation for being a real sports town. Carl Liscombe, then playing for the Detroit Olympics, remembered: "We won our championship [in] the IHL, the Red Wings won the Stanley Cup, the Detroit Tigers won the baseball championship [World Series] and the Detroit Lions won the [NFL] football championship. Joe Louis won the boxing championship of the world that year. They called us at that time, the City of Champions!"

The 1938-39 Detroit Red Wings (L to R): Jack Adams (manager), Carl Liscombe, Syd Howe, Herb Lewis, Cecil Thompson, Doug Young, Hec Kilrea, Eddie Wares, Bucko McDonald, Pete Kelly, Mud Bruneteau, Ralph "Scotty" Bowman, Sid Abel, Marty Barry, Maurice Gerts, Ebbie Goodfellow, Alex Motter.

1936-37 STANLEY CUP VICTORY

FIRST GAME: (April 6, at New York)
Rangers 5, Red Wings 1
First Period
New York - Keeling (Murdoch, Cooper) 5:23
New York - Patrick (Boucher, Coulter) 9:40
New York - Cooper (Keeling, Dillon) 18:44
Second Period
New York - Boucher (Johnson) 18:55
Third Period
Detroit - Howe (Pettinger, Goodfellow) 17:12
New York - Patrick (Boucher) 18:22

SECOND GAME: (April 8, at Detroit)
Red Wings 4, Rangers 2
First Period
Detroit - Sorrell 9:22
Detroit - Bruneteau (Howe) 12:07
Detroit - Gallagher (W. Kilrea, Sherf) 13:31
Second Period
Detroit - Lewis (Howe, Goodfellow) 11:02
New York - Pratt (N. Colville, M. Colville) . . .15:08
New York - Keeling (Coulter) 18:18
Third Period
No scoring

THIRD GAME: (April 11, at Detroit)
Rangers 1, Red Wings 0
First Period
No scoring
Second Period
New York - N. Colville (Pratt, Cooper) 0:23
Third Period
No scoring

FOURTH GAME: (April 13, at Detroit)
Red Wings 1, Rangers 0
First Period
No scoring
Second Period
No scoring
Third Period
Detroit - Barry (Howe, Sorrell) 12:43

FIFTH GAME: (April 15, at Detroit)
Red Wings 3, Rangers 0
First Period
Detroit - Barry (Howe) .19:22
Second Period
Detroit - Sorrell (Barry, H. Kilrea) 9:36
Third Period
Detroit - Barry (Sorrell) 2:33

STANLEY CUP FINALS

The defending Stanley Cup champion Detroit Red Wings completed the regular season with a first-place, American Division finish in 1936-37. Norm Smith won the Vezina Trophy as the goalie allowing the fewest goals during the regular season. Marty Barry and Larry Aurie, who ended up breaking his leg and missing the playoffs, finished third and fourth, respectively, in league scoring. Early in the playoffs, Detroit eliminated the Montreal Canadiens in five games, the fifth of which went into a third overtime period. In the finals, they faced off against the New York Rangers, who had erased the Montreal Maroons.

Norm Smith, who had sparkled between the pipes the previous post-season, was injured in the series against Montreal when he fell during a pileup and somebody sat on his elbow, causing it to hyperextend. Many thought that with the Red Wings depending upon rookie goalie Earl Robertson, they could not win. Robertson had been called up from the Pittsburgh Hornets, and Jack Adams felt that he was adequate for the job.

The Stanley Cup finals series went to five games.

The Rangers had many new faces on their roster, including Lester Patrick's son Lynn, Art Coulter, and Babe Pratt. They gave Detroit a beating in the first game, winning 5-1. However, they found themselves at a disadvantage when they lost their home ice to a circus that came to New York and were able to win again only once. In the end, the Red Wings won the series and their second consecutive Stanley Cup.

THE FINAL GAME - APRIL 15, 1937

The fifth and final game, played in Detroit, was the proving ground for the hungry Red Wings. They were able to shut out the Rangers, tapping in one goal each period.

During the first period, with the Rangers' Joe Cooper in the penalty box for holding Herbie Lewis, Detroit sent five forwards to the New York net and scored a goal. As it happened, Ranger defenseman Ott Heller attempted to clear the puck, but instead passed it to Detroit's Syd Howe just inside the Rangers' blue line. Howe passed to Marty Barry, who, positioned to the left of the goal, scored with a low shot.

The second period brought a second goal for the Wings. With the assistance of Marty Barry, Johnny Sorrell outsmarted New York goalie Dave Kerr, who dove to the ice to block his shot. Sorrell retrieved the puck, and with Kerr flat on the ice, scored on the rebound.

Ahead by two goals, Detroit entered the third period and scored again, bringing their goal total to three. The final goal was scored by Marty Barry, with an assist from Sorrell. After receiving a pass from Sorrell, Barry went in on Kerr alone, with New York's Joe Cooper chasing after him. Barry fired a shot from 10 feet out, and the puck sailed into the far corner of New York's net, just out of Kerr's reach. Detroit had won the Stanley Cup!

THE MEN

ALEX (THE OTTAWA FIREMAN) CONNELL

Born: February 8, 1902, Ottawa, Ontario
Position: Goaltender
Died: 1958
Amateur: Ottawa Cliffsides, 1919
Detroit Red Wings: 1931-32
Best NHL Season
• 1925-26 (Ottawa): 2,231 MIN, 1.17 GAA, 15 SO
Career Awards & Honors
• Hockey Hall of Fame, 1958

BIOGRAPHY

Alex Connell was a fireman when not playing goal. Because of his other occupation, Connell was appropriately dubbed "The Ottawa Fireman." Besides playing goal for the Senators and Red Wings in the NHL, Connell also played for the Montreal Maroons. With Ottawa and Montreal, he played on two Stanley-Cup-winning teams under manager Tommy Gorman, in 1926-27 and 1934-35 respectively.

Connell was the very first goaltender in NHL history to have two seasons with 15 shutouts. While playing for Ottawa in 1927-28, he set an NHL record after shutting out the opposition six consecutive times, for a total of 416 minutes, 29 seconds.

In an obituary issued by the Canadian Press, Gorman reflected upon Connell's net-minding skills in the series against the Maple Leafs: "I remember Connell as putting on the greatest goalkeeping performance in the history of hockey in Toronto in 1935," he said. "It was in the Stanley Cup playoffs when the Maroons were two men short. For three minutes Connell put on an astounding effort against the Leafs and the Maroons went on to win the Cup."

Connell was quite a prankster during his time. In a 1949-50 *Toronto Maple Leaf Program, Montreal Star* Sports Editor Baz O'Meara recalled a humorous event in which Alex was the perpetrator. He explained:

Connell is the chap who once sent the Maroon directors a wire from Winnipeg telling them that they were lighter by $10,000 because he had just bought Joe Selkirk from an American Association club. He described him as an Indian, six foot two, weighing two forty and a great snow shoe runner. He signed Tommy Gorman's name to the wire. Gorman, who is smart at that sort of thing, was mystified when he got an answering wire telling him they couldn't get a line on the new player in any of the newspaper offices. In the wire it wasn't specified who the new player was, so Tommy had to get on the long distance wire to find out what was what. It was about three days afterward when Connell blandly inquired of Gorman if he would like to look over a promising new rookie named Selkirk that he knew. Then he knew he had been "had."

Besides his 29-year career with the Ottawa Fire Department, and his net-minding endeavors, Connell was also quite a baseball player. In the 1920s, he helped Ottawa win two Eastern Canadian League championships while catching in the Interprovincial League. He also had a short stint as coach of the Quebec Hockey League's Ottawa Senators, but resigned the post in 1949 because of failing health.

JOHN ROSS ROACH

Born: June 23, 1900, Fort Perry, Ontario
Position: Goaltender
Died: July, 1973
Amateur: Toronto Granites
Minor Pro: Syracuse Stars (IHL), 1933-34
Detroit Red Wings: 1932-33 to 1934-35
Best NHL Season
• 1928-29 (Rangers): 2,760 MIN, 1.48GAA, 13 SO
Career Awards & Honors
• NHL All-Star Team: 1932-33

BIOGRAPHY

Before his debut with Detroit, John Ross Roach began a professional career at the age of 20 with the Toronto St. Patricks. The legendary Frank "King" Clancy signed with the Ottawa Senators at the same time, but spent much of his first season sitting on the bench, while Roach was a regular contributor from the start. After Toronto, Roach spent several seasons with the New York Rangers before being acquired by Detroit late in his professional career for $11,000.

As an athlete, Roach had a reputation for being a fearless net-minder, despite his small size. He stood at 5 feet, 5 inches, and at one stage of his career, weighed only 130 pounds. Former New York Ranger Bill Cook, one of the exceptional shot-makers of his day, rated Roach and Chicago's legendary Chuck Gardiner as the two toughest goalies he had ever faced. He also considered Roach the hardest net-minder to feint out of position, as he would wait to the absolute last minute to commit himself when facing an opposing attacker.

"He was one of the real good ones," said former Red Wing Ebbie Goodfellow in the July 11, 1973 issue of the *Detroit News*. "He was on the small side, but he was all there. He was awfully good. He had some really good years."

Roach was the first Detroit player to make the NHL All-Star Team, and at one time, was the oldest player in the NHL. He had two especially proud moments in Detroit. First, on January 17, 1933, he shutout the New York Rangers, 2-0. Far from an ordinary shut-out, the feat snapped what, at the time, was the longest consecutive scoring streak in NHL history. The Rangers had scored one or more goals in 77 consecutive games before that particular contest. Then, on January 15, 1935, Roach shutout the Montreal Maroons, 1-0, ending their scoring streak of 55 consecutive games.

A humorous story exists about Roach. While playing for Detroit, a young boy by the name of John Downey used to occupy a seat directly behind Roach, on the Grand River side of the Olympia. Detroit's goal was on that side of the ice for two of the game's three periods. Before the start of each game, Downey would toss a pack of chewing gum onto the ice in front of Roach, who was a big gum-chewer. As the

Larry Aurie, Ebbie Goodfellow and John Ross Roach were key players for Detroit during the 1930s.

season wore on, Roach came to expect the small gift before each game, and would often catch the package with his glove. One night, other fans joined in with Downey, and showered Roach with 28 packages of 5-stick chewing gum!

NORMAN SMITH

Born: March 18, 1908, Toronto, Ontario
Position: Goaltender
Senior
- Toronto (Senior Commercial League), 1928-29
- Toronto (Mercantile Senior League), 1929-30
- Montreal Royals
Minor Pro:
- Windsor Bulldogs (IHL)
- St. Louis Eagles
Detroit Red Wings
- 1934-35; 1938-39; 1943-44 to 1944-45
Best NHL Season
- 1936-37: 2,980 MIN, 2.13 GAA, 6 SO
Career Awards & Honors
- Vezina Trophy: 1936-37
- First All-Star Team: 1937
- All-Star Game: 1937 (Howie Morenz benefit game)
- Red Wings Hall of Fame, 1963 (second goalie elected)
Career Milestones
- NHL-leading six shut-outs: 1935-36, 1936-37
- Played in longest game in Stanley Cup playoff history.
Trades
- Traded to the Detroit Red Wings from the St. Louis Eagles in 1934 for Burr Williams

Opposite: Norm Smith tended goal for Detroit in the longest game in Stanley Cup playoff history.

BIOGRAPHY

Alert and aggressive, Norm Smith was an excellent goaltender and a major factor in the Red Wings' first two consecutive Stanley Cup victories. After playing minor league hockey for the Detroit Olympics, Smith succeeded John Ross Roach in goal for the Red Wings. He would sometimes play wearing a cap to avoid the glare he claimed existed in some minor league rinks.

Carl Liscombe, Smith's former teammate, remembered: "Normie was a good goaltender. All goaltenders back in those days were stand-up goaltenders. They never went down. But it was a different game all together. We didn't have the pile-ups in front of the net like they do now. You see, they didn't have any masks on either. If they were going down, they were going to get hit in the face."

With the Red Wings, Smith became part of hockey history when he played in the longest playoff game of all time. In a January 24, 1987 article by Paul Patton, Smith remembered that game. "Somebody at Guinness figured out that I set a world record with 92 saves in the longest shutout in history," he said. "The ice was soft because they didn't have the Zambonis then and had to flood by hand, and my pads got heavy from the water, and my underwear from the sweat. They started giving us a little brandy, just a sprinkle, between periods to give us energy to keep going." In the next game, Smith again shut out the Maroons. Montreal's Gus Marker finally ended the shut-out streak when he scored in the third game, 248 minutes, 32 seconds later. The feat still stands in the record books.

Norm Smith was the very first Detroit Red Wing to be suspended (with pay) and fined by Jack Adams. As it happened, Smith once missed the train ride from New York to Montreal, and Adams caught him. Smith had been visiting friends on Staten Island the evening before the team's departure, and they failed to get him to the train on time the following morning.

In the November 16, 1938 issue of the *Detroit News*, an infuriated Adams said: "I'm absolutely fed up. I've protected some of these guys long enough. That's all over now. I can't say definitely that he broke training because I don't know. However, I do know that he wasn't in his hotel room, and that he isn't on the train. I put his roommate, Syd Howe, on the spot today when I asked him whether Normie was in his room last night. Like anyone would, Syd tried to cover up for him, but he finally admitted Normie wasn't there." A week later, Adams ordered Smith to report to the team's minor league affiliate in Pittsburgh, or be suspended without pay. Smith refused to report and temporarily quit the team.

Norm Smith became an American Citizen in 1935, and retired from playing after four years and part of a fifth to work for Ford Motor Company in 1939. With Ford, he worked as an assistant to Harry Bennett, former personnel director. At the Red Wings' request, he returned to help out when needed during the Second World War. After working at Ford, Smith went to work for Hewitt Metals, where he served as the company's vice president.

Norm Smith proudly displays the Vezina Trophy he won in 1937.

WILFRED KENNEDY (BUCKO) McDONALD

Born: October 31, 1911, Fergus, Ontario
Position: Defense
Died: July, 1991
Minor Pro
- Buffalo (IHL)
- Detroit Olympics (IHL), 1934-35

Detroit Red Wings
- 1934-35 to 1938-39

Best NHL Season
- 1941-42 (Toronto): 2 goals, 21 points

Career Awards & Honors
- Red Wings Hall of Fame, 1961
- Canadian Lacrosse Hall of Fame, 1972
- Second All-Star Team, 1942

Trades
- Traded to the Detroit Olympics midway through the 1934-35 season with Desse and Earl Roche in a deal for Buffalo's George Patterson and Llyod Gross.
- Traded to the Toronto Maple Leafs for Bill Thomson and $10,000 in 1938.

BIOGRAPHY

Before playing hockey, Bucko McDonald was one of Canada's best lacrosse players. He played for the Brampton Excelsiors, who were the Minto Cup champions in 1931. It was Bucko's desire to turn professional in the sport of lacrosse, and he did in 1932. The league in which he played folded, however, and fate put him in skates for Detroit. "When the league folded I had to stay out of amateur sports for three years and in those days employment was hard to come by," he said in a *Herald* article by Dan Ralph. "Well, every job I had was related to sports so I decided to give hockey a try."

Bucko could hardly stand up on skates at first, but improved with time and many extra hours of hard practice. After being signed by Toronto, who farmed him to Buffalo, he played for the Detroit Olympics, and eventually made it to the big team. During his NHL career, McDonald won the Stanley Cup three times. His first two victories came successively with the Red Wings in 1935-36 and 1936-37, and his third with Toronto in 1941-42.

During the opening game of the 1935-36 series, which was the longest match in NHL history, McDonald set an unofficial record when, according to an article by Jim Proudfoot of the *Toronto Star*, he

Before playing hockey, Bucko McDonald was one of Canada's top lacrosse players. Hockey Hall of Fame archives.

knocked no fewer than 37 opposing players to the ice!

McDonald was a fierce competitor during his professional hockey career, and he was also tough, earning the nickname "Socko" for his thundering, bone-jarring body checks. "Bucko was one of the best body checkers the NHL ever saw," said Jack Adams in the January 1, 1961 issue of the *Detroit News*, in an article by John Walter. "He had a knack of hitting opposing players standing straight up. I think it was the carry-over from his lacrosse playing days. He was one of Canada's top lacrosse players before he took up hockey professionally."

Although he was tough, McDonald was not one who relished mixing it up with the opposition on a regular basis. "He never had a fight," recalled Adams in the same article. "He hit them so hard and clean

they didn't have any fight left. I'll never forget seeing Mervyn (Red) Dutton, then the New York Americans' playing coach, getting a lesson from Bucko. 'That's nonsense,' Red said after he saw several of his players flattened by Bucko. 'I'll show you,' he said, hopping over the fence. Down the ice he came with the puck. He zigged when he should have zagged. Bucko knocked him unconscious. That was one of the last times Red played." Humorously, long-time Red Wings locker room attendant Wally Crossman shed some light on one of the possible motivating factors behind Bucko's hits when he said: "I remember Bucko McDonald. We had a florist that sat behind the bench and he'd offer Bucko McDonald $10 every time he'd knock a player down."

The nickname "Bucko" came differently than the nickname "Socko." In a *Herald* article by Dan Ralph, McDonald recalled the nomenclature, explaining: "As a boy growing up in Sundridge I remember a general store owned by Andy Steele. Next to it was a drug store and there was a road running through the two buildings. One day I got into a wrestling match with two buddies and had them piled up one on top of the other. I turned around and looked right into the eyes of Mr. Steele who said, 'My, my, you'll be a bucko someday.' I guess it means some kind of character, but as soon as I let my friends up they said 'Bucko let's go.' It has been one of my greatest fortunes to have such a nickname." McDonald was also referred to as "Two Steak" McDonald because of his huge appetite!

Besides Detroit and Toronto, McDonald also played for the New York Rangers during his NHL career, which spanned 10 seasons. After the NHL, he continued playing hockey with Hull of the Quebec Senior League, and also served as playing coach for the Sundridge [Ontario] Beavers Intermediate "B" team in 1948-49. A humorous incident occurred while he played there. As it happened, Sundridge was playing against the Georgetown Raiders in the Ontario Provincial Championship that year. While sitting in the penalty box, a fan pulled a lady's corset over Bucko's head. Instead of throwing it aside,

McDonald put it on and skated around the rink so that everyone could see!

After playing, McDonald turned to coaching professionally with the Rochester Americans of the AHL in 1958, and with the Sault Ste. Marie Greyhounds as well. He then coached junior hockey in Parry Sound, Ontario, where a young man named Bobby Orr was but one future NHL player under his tutelage. "I used to have some lively arguments with Doug Orr, Bobby's father, said McDonald in the July 21, 1991 issue of the *Toronto Star*. "He wondered why I had Bobby on defense. He thought his son should be a forward. I told him Bobby was the greatest defense prospect I'd ever seen. And he was. He was the greatest defenseman there ever was."

In 1945, McDonald was elected to the Canadian Parliament as a Liberal. He was reelected to Parliament in 1949 and 1957. A January 14, 1976 *Toronto Star* article by George Gamester said that "despite carping from opponents who complained he spoke only a few dozen words during three terms, he was a jovial, easy-going guy who preferred to leave the speech-making to the party bigwigs while he worked behind the scenes to get new post offices, bridges and docks for his constituents."

In 1968, McDonald coached the Montreal Canadiens of the National Lacrosse Association. He lived in retirement in Sunridge, Ontario, until his death from a long illness in July, 1991.

JAMES V. ORLANDO

Born: February 27, 1916, Montreal, Quebec
Position: Defense
Died: October 24, 1992
Amateur
- Montreal Vic (seniors and juniors)
- Montreal Royals
- Sons of Italy (Montreal)

Minor Pro
- Rochester Cardinals (IHL), 1935
- Pittsburgh Hornets (AHL), 1936
- Springfield Indians (AHL), 1937
- Valleyfield Braves (OSHL)

Detroit Red Wings
- 1936-37 to 1937-38; 1939-40 to 1942-43

Career Awards & Honors
- AHL All-Star Team, 1937
- Red Wings Hall of Fame, 1962

Opposite: Known as "The Bad Man On Ice" Jimmy Orlando was fiery and exciting to watch. Hockey Hall of Fame archives.

BIOGRAPHY

Jimmy Orlando spent his entire six-year, NHL career with the Detroit Red Wings. Orlando played some of his earliest hockey with the Belmont School on Montreal's Guy Street. Ultimately, after playing minor league hockey, he won a regular job with the big club. He had an unimpressive tryout with the Red Wings in 1937, and was sold to the Springfield Indians of the American Hockey League. Luckily, Springfield failed to come up with the money for his purchase and Orlando ended up back in Detroit.

Known as the "Bad Man on Ice," Orlando was fiery, exciting to watch, and as tough as they came. He not only mixed it up with many an opponent, but with fans as well. Easy-going off of the ice, he was considered by many players to be the game's hardest hitting defenseman.

In Detroit, Jimmy Orlando was often the defensive pair of Black Jack Stewart. The two made up one of the most fearsome defensive duos in the league. Guaranteed punishment awaited unsuspecting opponents who crossed the pair's blue line with their head down. "That's for darn sure," recalled former Red Wing Carl Liscombe. "Because they both could hit you. Jack Stewart was a hard hitter, [and] so was Jimmy Orlando. I will honestly say, if they would have left those two together—they only played part of a year together, but Jack split them up because they were so good together—that nobody would come over our blue line."

Orlando had many memorable battles during his career, the most famous of which was with Gaye Stewart of the Toronto Maple Leafs. On November 7, 1942, in Maple Leaf Gardens, Orlando started to poke fun at Stewart, then a rookie. Stewart retaliated, and the two went at it. Orlando recalled the incident in an article by Paul Patton. Said Orlando: "We're in the corner scuffling, and he gets a 2-minute penalty. The play goes down the other end, and all of a sudden he comes out of the penalty box and I know he's not there to give me a kiss, so I throw a punch and hit him. But King Clancy, who is refereeing, doesn't see anything, so I don't even get a penalty and he gets an extra 2 minutes for coming out too soon. Five minutes later he's going down the left wing, and I'm checking him when he raises his stick and hits

me, and I end up with 20 stitches."

Joe Carveth and Clancy helped Orlando get off the ice, blood dripping from his face. A picture of Orlando in this state is supposedly the very first hockey picture to make the cover of *Life* magazine. Each player was suspended for the next three games between their respective teams, and was ordered to pay $100 to his country's Red Cross organization for the war effort. In the same article, Orlando said: "It didn't seem right, me giving money to the Red Cross since I was the one who had lost all the blood."

Because of his tough style of play, Orlando was a marked man. In an article by Andy O'Brien, he once explained: "Yeah, I must be a ba-a-a-ad boy. Mr. Calder is never wrong. If he says I'm bad, I must be REALLY bad. But I'll say this . . . I got two strikes on me before I go on any ice in the National Hockey League circuit. ... But I never hit a guy with my stick—the dukes are good enough for me, especially that left hook. I never looked for a fight in my life, but I've never dodged one. It brings me lots of trouble. Two years ago in Chicago I got into a scrap with a spectator. He was a millionaire, and the last I heard of it he was intending to sue me for a few hundred grand—wow!"

Well-dressed, and often seen with a big cigar in his mouth, Orlando was of Italian heritage. His teammates called him "Little Caesar," "Mussolini, Jr.," and "Kid Capone." These names didn't bother the tough blue-liner. His heritage sometimes drew ruder comments from fans at Maple Leaf Gardens. "I don't mind," he recalled in the same article, reflecting upon the rude comments hurled at him. "I suppose the cash customers pay for the privilege, but I'm just as good a Canadian as any of them. It strikes me, though, as being a bit below the belt."

Orlando took home the Stanley Cup on two occasions with the Red Wings. The first silver chalice came in 1936-37, and the second in 1942-43. When his playing days with the Red Wings ended, Orlando continued playing hockey with the Valleyfield Braves of the OSHL until he hung up the professional skates for good in 1951. He played with the Quebec Old-timers after that time, where he helped to raise money for charity. After hockey, Orlando ran a Montreal nightclub called Champ Showbar, and even served as a wrestling referee. He passed away at the age of 77.

DOUGLAS GORLEY YOUNG

Born: October 1, 1908, Medicine Hat, Alberta
Position: Defense
Died: May, 1990, Tamarac, Florida
Junior
- Calgary Canadian Juniors, 1926-27

Minor Pro
- Kitchener (CPHL), 1927-28
- Toronto Millionaires (CPHL), 1928-29
- Cleveland Indians (IHL), 1929-31

Detroit Red Wings
- 1931-32 to 1938-39

Best NHL Season
- 1935-36: 5 goals, 17 points

Career Awards & Honors
- Red Wings Hall of Fame, 1951
- Team Captain, 1935-38
- NHL All-Star Game: 1939 (Montreal)

Trades
- Traded to the Detroit Red Wings in 1931 from the Cleveland Indians (IHL) in the inter-league draft.

BIOGRAPHY

Doug Young grew up in the snowy town of Gleichen, Alberta, where his father raised show horses. He spent the majority of his NHL career with Detroit. As a hockey player, Young was well-known for his deceptive shift on the ice. In the January 26, 1932 issue of the *Detroit News*, a reporter told of Young's "shift," and his assets as a player, saying, "Doug's shift has caused much comment around the League. To a football player a shift would mean hip motion. He has unusual ability in carrying his body one way and apparently maneuvering the puck the other. He is a strong skater and one of the hardest Red Wings to knock off his feet. When he is knocked down, Doug gets up as fast as any of them and is ready for more. He's not hurt easily and is an expert hook checker. He has the right kind of hockey temperament. For such a good defenseman and body checker he spends comparatively little time in the penalty box. He trains conscientiously, is good natured and an easy player to manage."

While with the Red Wings, Young served as team captain and helped them win their first two Stanley Cups in 1935-36 and 1936-37. Humorously, he was once sued for $25,000 by a Doris Geldhart. As it happened, Young swung his stick and missed the puck in a February 24, 1935 game against the Toronto Maple Leafs at the Olympia. His stick struck Mrs. Geldhart in the forehead, breaking her nose and giving her two black eyes!

HARRY LAWRENCE (LARRY) AURIE

Born: February 8, 1905, Sudbury, Ontario
Position: Right wing
Died: December 11, 1952
Junior
- Sudbury Juniors

Senior
- Galt Seniors (OHA), 1925-26

Minor Pro
- London Tecumsehs (CPHL), 1927

Detroit Red Wings
- 1927-28 to 1938-39

Best NHL Season
- 1934-35: 17 goals, 46 points

Career Awards & Honors
- NHL All-Star Game, 1934

BIOGRAPHY

In the summer of 1927, when Jack Adams was named Detroit's coach, his first move was to draft a small, flashy, right wing from Sudbury, Ontario, named Larry Aurie. Aurie was a member of the team that skated in the very first hockey game at the Detroit Olympia on November 22, 1927. He electrified Olympia fans during many more games in the future, as the team's name changed from the Cougars to the Falcons, and finally to the Red Wings.

On both the 1936 and 1937 Stanley Cup-winning teams in Detroit, Aurie played with Marty Barry and Herbie Lewis on what many claim to be one of the most successful lines of all time. He was an excellent penalty killer, known for his skill at ragging (keeping the puck away from the opposition when short-handed) the puck, earning him the nickname "The Little Rag Man." Although he played an aggressive game, he was selective in his approach, and was not known for losing his head when things got hot.

As a player, Aurie was as tough as they came. In an era when tough players like Ching Johnson, Nelson Stewart, Dit Clapper and Eddie Shore were associated with the game, Aurie knew how to take punishment and send it back at the opposition, despite his small size. Never one to use his stick in entanglements, Aurie preferred a good, clean fight.

In the December 27, 1952 issue of *The Hockey News*, in an article by Marshall Dann, an incident revealed his toughness After being put in the hospital by Eddie Shore, Aurie told reporters: "It wasn't Shore's fault. He got me with a legal check." Two weeks after his hospital stay, Aurie was back playing hockey.

Jack Adams proclaimed that Aurie was one of the greatest competitors he had ever seen. "Pound for pound," said Adams in the February 28, 1936 issue of the *Detroit News*, "he has more courage than any player hockey has ever known. The only time I have ever gone on the ice in street clothes in my life was the night in New York four years ago when Larry was knocked unconscious. I thought he was dead. I couldn't restrain myself and before I knew what was happening I was out there with him in my arms. I took one look at the kid and just knew he was either dead or dying. That's a night I never can forget. And do you know the little rascal accused me the next day of giving him something to make his head ache so I would have an excuse for not letting him play the next game. Aw, I tell you he's a grand fellow—one of the very greatest."

Many, including Adams, considered Aurie the best two-way player in the league. "He has developed offense and defense to such a degree of perfection that we use him both when we are one man short and when the other team is one man short," recalled Adams in the February 28, 1936 issue of the *Detroit News*.

After playing for the Red Wings, Aurie went on to coach hockey in Pittsburgh of the International-American League. One day he received an emergency order to send help to the Red Wings who had been shorthanded. Rather than send help, he notified Jack Adams that he was coming to personally help the club. On January 10, 1939, he returned and helped the Red Wings beat their opponents 3-0, scoring the game's first goal, and the last of his professional career. He later returned to coaching with the Pittsburgh Hornets until the club folded. He then found work in Detroit as a probation officer for the juvenile court, and later as a worker in a wartime plant.

Hockey was still in Aurie's blood, and he eventually became a coach and part-time scout for Detroit, and later the New York Rangers. He then coached the Oshawa Generals of the OHL, where he

Marty Barry centered a highly successful line with Herb Lewis (lw) and Larry Aurie (rw) in Detroit. Hockey Hall of Fame archives.

was an influence on players like Alex Delvecchio. "I learned a lot from Aurie," recalled Delvecchio in the December 13, 1962 issue of the *Detroit News*. "He was my coach at Ottawa (Ont.) in my last year in junior hockey. I learned a lot about stickwork and playmaking from him." After coaching, his last working days were spent as an automobile insurance salesman.

On December 11, 1952, at the age of 47, Aurie died after a stroke. The incident occurred as he was driving home that night. The stroke caused him to collapse over the steering wheel and collide with another car in a minor collision. He never regained consciousness and was pronounced dead several hours after the stroke. At his funeral, Herbie Lewis, Ebbie Goodfellow, Jack Adams, Ted Lindsay and

Gordie Howe served as pall bearers. He was buried at Detroit's Holy Sepulcher Cemetery.

In 1938-39, Aurie's number 6 was ordered retired by James Norris. His jersey was enshrined in a case which was displayed in the hallway of the Detroit Olympia. However, one will notice that his sweater does not hang from the rafters of Joe Louis Arena, nor did it at the Olympia. If it had been officially "retired" it would have been the team's first retired number. According to an article in the February 4, 1995 issue of the *Detroit News*, the Red Wings say the number is not retired, but simply out of circulation. In 1955-56, and from 1957 to 1959, Aurie's nephew, Cummy Burton, became the only other Red Wing to wear the number.

MARTIN A. (MARTY) BARRY

Born: December 8, 1904, Valcartier, Quebec
Position: Center
Died: August 20, 1969
Amateur
- Gurney Foundry (MRIL): 1922-23
- St. Michael's (MRIL): 1923-24
- St. Anthony's (MRIL): 1924-25, 1925-26
- Bell Telephone Team (Montreal)

Minor Pro
- Philadelphia Arrows (Can-Am League): 1927-28
- New Haven Eagles (Can-Am League): 1928-29

Detroit Red Wings
- 1935-36 to 1938-39

Best NHL Season
- 1936-37: 17 goals, 44 points

Career Awards & Honors
- Hockey Hall of Fame, 1965
- Red Wings Hall of Fame, 1944
- All-Star Games: 1937 (Howie Morenz benefit game)
- Lady Byng Trophy, 1936-37 (first Red Wing recipient)
- First All-Star Team: 1937

Trades
- Traded to Detroit from Boston in 1935-36 with Art Giroux for Cooney Weiland and Walter Buswell.

BIOGRAPHY

An amazing athlete, Marty Barry was a durable, hard-skating centerman (and occasionally left-wing) for Detroit. Totally bypassing junior hockey, he played amateur hockey in the Montreal area in the Montreal Intermediate League at the former Mount Royal Arena. He was the league's leading scorer there, and was given the nickname "Goal-a-Game"

Barry by local sportswriters. At the same time, Barry also played for the Bell Telephone team, which won a championship under coach Jack Laviolette and manager Harry Bowen.

After that, he made it to the NHL with the New York Americans in the spring of 1927, but lasted for only one game. Stints with the Philadelphia Arrows and the New Haven Eagles of the Can-Am League were to follow. With the Eagles, Barry won the scoring title and became a member of the Boston Bruins in 1929-30. He remained there until he was traded to Detroit in 1935-36. According to former Detroit sportswriter Sam Greene, when Boston general manager Art Ross executed the trade, it was considered one of the most mutually satisfactory deals ever made in hockey. Jack Adams said that Barry was the best stickhandler in the league, a great playmaker, and that he'd gladly make such a trade every season.

During his professional career, Barry scored 20-or-more goals for six consecutive seasons, which was more than respectable at the time. Six times during his career, he finished in the top 10 in scoring, and twice ended up in second place (1935-36 and 1936-37). Barry found a great deal of success in Detroit, centering one of the league's most successful lines with left wing Herb Lewis and right wing Larry Aurie. He played on Stanley-Cup-winning teams in both 1935-36 and 1936-37. The latter season, Barry helped his teammates win the Cup, received first All-Star team honors as well, and won the Lady Byng trophy for gentlemanly play.

Besides having a productive career, Barry was also an iron man, missing only one game in 11 seasons of play. He played through some painful injuries. The year after he made his debut with the Red Wings, he played with a hurt hip. While playing in a game with the Boston in 1932, he took six stitches to close a throat wound inflicted by the stick of a Chicago player. Three days later, he returned to the ice for a game against the Red Wings in Detroit.

The legendary Charlie Conacher commented on Barry's amazing games-played streak in the November 23, 1933 issue of the *Detroit News*: "I've never gone through a season without being out of at least a few games," he said. "I can appreciate better than anyone else what a really great accomplishment that is."

As a person, Barry was a fine family man. In the

Mud Bruneteau was an excellent checker and stickhandler and had a reputation for his dashing style of play.

February 25, 1936 issue of the *Detroit News*, reporter Bob Murphy said the following of Barry: "As in hockey, so it is in life with Marty Barry. He moves along the even tenor of his way. He looks for the good in people and strives quickly to forget the bad. Truly, here is a man in this warring cycle of sports who seems definitely at peace with the world."

After playing for Detroit, Barry finished his NHL career with the Montreal Canadiens in 1939-40. He later served as playing coach in Minneapolis. After his playing days ended, Barry turned to coaching and later managed a grocery store called Shannon Park Canteen, at Tuft's Cove, near Halifax, Nova Scotia.

MODERE (MUD) BRUNETEAU

Born: November 28, 1914, St. Boniface, Manitoba
Position: Right wing
Died: April, 1982
Amateur
• Winnipeg Commercial League
Minor Pro
• Detroit Olympics (IHL)
Detroit Red Wings
• 1935-36 to 1945-46
Best NHL Season
• 1943-44: 35 goals, 53 points
Career Awards & Honors
• Red Wings Hall of Fame, 1944

BIOGRAPHY

Mud Bruneteau spent his first night in the Motor City in a bath tub. An article in the March 9, 1943 issue of the *Detroit News*, explains that "Mud, along with Eddie Singbush and Walter Broda, ... received letters from Jack Adams requesting them to report to the Olympia for tryouts. The threesome arrived in Detroit, bewildered, tired and frightened at 10 p.m. one fall evening. They made their way to the stadium, where after depositing their luggage in front of the Grand River entrance, they were informed that the building was closed for the night. Their combined resources at the Fisher Y.M.C.A. netted them a small room with a single bed and an adjoining bath. They flipped their remaining coin to see who slept in the bath, and Modere lost."

Bruneteau was one of the better players the Red Wings had during the '30s. Before the NHL, he played for the Detroit Olympics, whom he helped to

win their first International League championship in 1934-35. Bruneteau was an excellent checker and stickhandler, earning a reputation for his dashing style of play. He played frequently when the team was short handed, and was utilized as a defensive forward.

As a person, it was said that Bruneteau had few enemies on or off of the ice, and was very popular with his teammates. He was also a good family man. During the off-season, Bruneteau worked for James Norris, Sr., as a clerk in Winnipeg, and also for the Ford Motor Company's service department.

Bruneteau is best remembered for ending the longest Stanley Cup playoff game in history against the Montreal Maroons. As stated previously, the game was the first in a best-of-five series that Detroit eventually won 3-0. In February 1946, after playing more than a decade in Detroit, Bruneteau and teammate Syd Howe were sent to Indianapolis of the American League. The decision was in part to make room for Jimmy Conacher from Indianapolis, and Sid Abel, who had been serving with the Royal Canadian Air Force.

In August 1946, Bruneteau was named as the coach of Detroit's farm club in Omaha. His brother Eddie, also a right-winger, played for the Detroit Red Wings in 1941-42, and from 1943-44 to 1948-49.

EBENEZER RALSTON (EBBIE) GOODFELLOW

Born: April 9, 1907, Ottawa, Ontario
Position: Center
Amateur
• Ottawa Montaguards
Minor Pro
• Detroit Olympics (IAL)
Detroit Red Wings
• 1929-30 to 1942-43
Best NHL Season
• 1930-31: 25 goals, 48 points
Career Awards & Honors
• First All-Star Team: 1936-37, 1939-40
• Second All-Star Team: 1935-36
• Hart Memorial Trophy: 1940 (first Red Wing recipient)
• All Star Games: 1937 (Howie Morenz benefit game), 1939 (Earl Seibert benefit game)
• Hockey Hall of Fame, 1963
• Red Wings Hall of Fame, 1944

BIOGRAPHY

Ebbie Goodfellow played his earliest hockey in his

home town of Ottawa with the Montaguards. Later, while playing for the Detroit Olympics, his team had a big rivalry going with the Windsor Bulldogs, and Goodfellow led the Olympics in scoring with 26 goals and 34 points.

Jack Adams brought Ebbie to the Olympia in 1929-30, and he responded by leading the club in scoring. Once with the Red Wings, he was one of the main attractions of his time, much like Gordie Howe would become in later years. In 1930-31, he was only three points behind the legendary Howie Morenz in league scoring, with 48 points to Morenz's 51.

While in Detroit, Goodfellow was the original center for Larry Aurie and Herbie Lewis. However, he was replaced in the middle by Marty Barry when Jack Adams moved Ebbie to right defense when he thought he was losing speed. The move gave Goodfellow a new life, and as a high-scoring, rushing defenseman, he became even more of an asset to the team. He often gave Dit Clapper of the Bruins a run for his money in the goal-scoring race for defensemen.

An unselfish playmaker, Goodfellow was a large contributing factor to Detroit's first two consecutive Stanley Cup victories. He held many of the team records until Sid Abel, Gordie Howe and Red Kelly found their way to the Motor City.

As an athlete, Goodfellow possessed a hard, dangerous shot. In a February 7, 1962 *Detroit News* article, sportswriter George E. Van provided a good description of Goodfellow, explaining that he was "a strong man of honest expression ... [who] played like a high class businessman on the ice where his deportment seemed almost serene. He was never a fierce fellow spoiling for a battle but when he had a scrap he worried that he might have to share it with one of his teammates. He was big and fast for 185 pounds, and could punch with both hands. Rivals respected him and stayed clear. But he was always the workman rather than the showboat. He has been likened to Charlie Gehringer in baseball ... efficient without being ostentatious."

In 1940-41, during post-season play against the New York Rangers, Goodfellow suffered a knee injury that eventually ended his career. Despite seeing specialists, he was never able to regain all of his strength. He served as playing coach of the Red Wings for a while, staying in excellent playing condition and filling in when needed. The late years of World War II took him temporarily away from the game. However, he returned and managed the St. Louis Flyers in 1947, and the Chicago Blackhawks in the early 1950s.

Besides playing hockey, Goodfellow partook in golf and softball, and was the best golfer on Detroit's roster during his career. At one time, he was the caddie master at Oakland Hills golf course. After playing, Goodfellow remained active with hockey by serving as the president of the Detroit Red Wing Alumni Association, and went to work for International Tool Company.

HERBERT A. (HERBIE) LEWIS

Born: April 17, 1907, Calgary, Alberta
Position: Left wing
Died: 1991
Junior
- Calgary Junior Canadians, 1923-24

Minor Pro
- Duluth Hornets (CHL & AHL), 1924-25 to 1927-28
- Detroit Cougars (CPHL), 1928-29

Detroit Red Wings
- 1928-29 to 1938-39

Best NHL Season
- 1934-35: 16 goals, 43 points

Career Awards & Honors
- Hockey Hall of Fame, 1989
- Red Wings Hall of Fame, 1944
- Team Captain: 1933-34
- NHL All-Star Game, 1934

Career Milestones
- On February 9, 1931, Lewis scored four goals in a game against the Pittsburgh Pirates.
- On February 14, 1934, Lewis played in the first-ever All-Star game, a benefit for Ace Bailey. After the game, Toronto architect Conn Smythe said Lewis and teammate Larry Aurie were undoubtedly the best All-Stars in the game.
- Played in the longest game in Stanley Cup playoff history.

BIOGRAPHY

Herbie Lewis spent his entire 11-season, NHL career at left wing with Detroit, wearing the crest of the cougar, falcon, and winged wheel. He was one of the most popular hockey players to skate at the Olympia.

In 1923-24, Lewis played for the Calgary Junior Canadians. With Calgary, he led his team to the Alberta Junior Hockey Championship, the Western Canada Junior Championship (winning the Abbot Memorial Cup), and the finals of the Canadian Junior Championship for the Dominion Cup. That particular team was dubbed by many to be one of the best junior amateur teams ever developed. On it, Lewis played with men like Vic Ripley (Boston Bruins) and Ronnie Martin (New York Americans).

In 1924-25, Lewis began playing for the Duluth Hornets of the Central Hockey League, which later turned into the American Hockey League. The following season, he was named captain of the team, and led the Central League in scoring. Again team

captain in 1926-27, Lewis continued playing in Duluth until he was drafted by the Detroit Cougars in 1928-29.

While playing for the Duluth Hornets, Lewis was dubbed "The Duke of Duluth" for his memorable four-season tenure with the Hornets. A Hockey Hall of Fame write-up on Lewis points out that "he was the undisputed chief drawing card in the American Hockey League ... [and was also the] most sought after man in the loop." Lewis came to be known as the "$20,000 Man." In 1927-28, he attempted to join the NHL Montreal Maroons, and Duluth had to obtain a court injunction to bring him back during a heated dispute that developed between the two leagues. The same season, he led his team to the AHL championship.

When Jack Adams brought Lewis to the Motor City in 1928, he made a move that few could argue against. An early Detroit Program labeled him: "Ace of the Wings," and pointed out to everyone the facts. That he was: "A Junior Star at 17, A Professional at 18, [and] A Veteran Star at 26."

Lewis was a gifted athlete. In addition to hockey, he excelled at rugby, football, track and basketball. However, it was hockey in which he made a name for himself. Over the course of his career, Lewis was among the NHL's leading scorers on a regular basis and was considered to be one of the best defensive forwards in the NHL. He was a fast skater, accurate playmaker, and great sportsman.

In a January 23,

1991 *Detroit Free Press* article by Bernie Czarniecki, former Red Wing teammate Pete Kelly said the following of Lewis shortly after his death: "He was a real steady-eddie type and harmonized very well with [linemates] Barry and Aurie. He was a good defensive wingman ... a very fast skater with short, choppy strides. He would pick up speed behind the net and skate through entire teams occasionally." In the same article, former teammate Bucko McDonald said of him: "Herbie was a hell of a player, good offensively and defensively. A defenseman like me could always count on him to be where he was supposed to be."

"He combines everything a manager wants in a player," said Jack Adams in an article by Leo MacDonnel. "Besides being a brilliant puck carrier and an expert shot, Herbie is one of the best back-

Herbie Lewis skated on Detroit's "Kid Line" with Ebbie Goodfellow and Larry Aurie. Hockey Hall of Fame archives.

checkers in hockey. Aurie and Lewis form the best back-checking combination to be found on any club. On top of all that, Lewis is always in shape, popular and an inspiration to other members of the club— being especially helpful to the younger men."

While with the Red Wings, Lewis skated on the famed Kid Line with Ebbie Goodfellow and Larry Aurie. He also played on a line with Aurie and Marty Barry. The line was instrumental in Detroit's two consecutive Stanley Cup victories in 1936 and 1937. During the latter victory, Lewis scored four goals and had three assists.

Besides his success at athletics, Lewis was also a very mature man who assumed a great level of responsibility at an early age. He was but 18 years old when he got married to a girl he met in high school and was a father by age 20. As the years went by, Lewis became skilled at business, and by the age of 26, was in charge of 26 gas stations in Duluth, Minnesota and Superior, Wisconsin. By age 30, he was sales manager of Duluth's Harbour City Oil Company, and owned a very nice summer home in Bergen Lake, Minnesota.

In a *Spring 1938 Detroit Program* article by Elmer W. Ferguson, Jack Adams said: "There's a hockey player, and a smart boy. He's an example of an athlete who knows how to take care of himself. ... A lot of our boys were sitting on top of the Empire State Building, looking down. In the summer, they had let themselves go, didn't train, or look after themselves. Not Herbie Lewis. He's saved his money, and will have an annuity of $42,000 when he's forty-five. Has his own oil business, and is still a great hockey player. Has a couple more years left. No, I couldn't back-check with Lewis."

Lewis was both organizer and participant in the first professional hockey game ever played in Indianapolis, Indiana. In November 1939, in a game to which more than 10,000 fans attended, Lewis was player-manager of the Indianapolis Capitols, a team that had been recently established by James Norris and Arthur Wirtz. He remained with the Capitols until 1943, when he retired as their manager. While there, he managed the club to the American League Championship in 1941-42, and won both the Calder and Ted Oke Cups.

The Red Wings celebrate a 3-1 playoff victory over Toronto on March 30, 1939.

HARRY CARLYLE (CARL) LISCOMBE

Born: May 17, 1915, Perth, Ontario
Position: Left wing
Junior
- Hamilton Tigers
- Galt Juniors

Minor Pro
- Detroit Olympics (IHL)
- Pittsburgh Hornets (AHL)

Detroit Red Wings
- 1937-38 to 1945-46

Career Awards & Honors
- Detroit Red Wings Hall of Fame, 1964

Career Milestones
- Former record holder for the fastest three goals in NHL history.
- Seven-point game in November of 1942 against the New York Rangers.
- 73-point season, 1943-44

BIOGRAPHY

Carl Liscombe played senior hockey for the Hamilton Tigers with his brother Frank, where he was a linemate of the legendary Toe Blake. He spent his entire nine-season, NHL career, which began in 1937-38, playing for the Detroit Red Wings. While playing for Hamilton, the Tigers won the Allan Cup and Liscombe led the league in scoring. Before making it to the Wings, he broke into the professional ranks with the championship Detroit Olympics in 1935-36. He also played for the Pittsburgh Hornets, the Red Wings' other farm club, before being called up for service on November 23, 1937.

Liscombe was a man on a mission. His eyes were set on the National Hockey League, and on leaving an impression once he got there. In the October 17,

1933 issue of the *Detroit News*, Liscombe said: "I never have thought about playing baseball in the big leagues. I like baseball, but I like hockey better. I'd like to be a big league star."

Upon recommendation from Larry Aurie, who had been following Liscombe since his junior days, Jack Adams brought him up from the minors when he anticipated the retirement of Herbie Lewis. Once with the big club, Liscombe made quite an impression. In the March 20, 1938 issue of the *Detroit News*, teammate Hec Kilrea said: "[He is] one of the best first year men I've ever seen. ... He's fast, packs a hard shot and burrows in after the puck like a terrier digging for a bone. He's going to be one of the greats some day."

A short and stocky left-winger, Liscombe turned out to be one of the NHL's least-penalized players during his career, and played like one of the "greats" right from the start. His first season in Detroit, he was a strong candidate for Rookie of the Year, but was beaten by Cully Dahlstrom of the Chicago Blackhawks. He possessed a fast shot, was an excellent playmaker, and was both smart and skilled at the art of stickhandling.

Liscombe was quite a record setter during his NHL career. He recently reflected upon the records he set. Commenting on the seven-point game, he recalled: "That [game] was against the New York Rangers. We beat them, I think the score was 12 to 0, I know it was because that was the biggest shut out that they have ever had. You never see it, but it really was. They didn't get a goal that night. I got three goals and four assists. That was a record that stood with the Red Wings for quite a few years. Then, I don't know who the devil broke it. Somebody got more than that, but I can't remember who it was.

"I know in 1939 I scored three goals in 1 minute and 52 seconds in Chicago," he continued. "It was a funny damn thing [about the crowd]. They never realized it until after the game was over. Yeah, one of the reporters came up to me and said, 'Carl, do you know that you broke a record tonight?'"

Liscombe also had a 73-point season in 1943-44 (36 goals and 37 assists), which at the time was the highest season total in Detroit Red Wings history. However, there were also other marks set during his career. On January 23, 1944, on Olympia ice, Liscombe scored two goals in what at the time was the most one-sided game in NHL history. The Red Wings ended up spanking the Rangers 15-0 that night. "We were hotter than a pistol," he said in the January 23, 1982 *Toronto Globe and Mail*, in an article by Paul Patton, "and it was unbelievable in front of the net. We were just walking in from the blue-line like there was nobody there." The Rangers had beaten the Maple Leafs 5-1 the night before.

After playing for the Red Wings, Liscombe played for Providence of the American Hockey League. In the American League, he continued to be a record-setter. In 1947-48 he had a 50-goal season, a prelude to the 55 goals he scored in 68 games the following season. The 55 goals tied an AHL record set by Sid Smith of Pittsburgh, and lasted 34 years. In Providence, Liscombe led the AHL in points his first season with 118, and the mark stood for six seasons. He was named the AHL's most valuable player on two occasions. According to the same *Toronto Globe and Mail* article, Liscombe didn't mind the demotion to Providence, explaining that he made more money in Providence than in Detroit, and that he was able to get away from the fiery Jack Adams!

After retiring from hockey, Liscombe owned a carpet business and worked in the insurance field. He currently resides in the Detroit area, and still follows the Red Wings.

CHAPTER SIX

CLOSE CALLS
▪ THE 1940s ▪

The 1940s were a different era in professional sports in many ways. Leo Reise, who played for Detroit during the 1940s and 1950s, described what it was like to play during this decade: "You were making $10,000 to $15,000, depending on when it was and how it was. Some more when you got to the bonuses for the playoffs. Whether or not you were winning, you made a little bit more. People came there to play hockey, they did their job and that's what it was. There were no clubhouse lawyers. ... You either wanted to play or you didn't. You were there to do a job and that's what it was thought of. It was a job that you did."

Describing the travel conditions of this era, former Detroit Red Wing Harry Watson commented: "Well, we never traveled by air, we were on the trains all the time. So if we had one trip from Chicago to Boston, we were on the train all day and we got five dollars a day for meal money. The cheapest meal on the train was over five dollars. So you would be on the train all day and have to try to live on five dollars a day."

"They fooled around a lot on the train," added long-time Red Wings locker room attendant Wally Crossman. "They played jokes on each other and they put things in their bed. It was different. Now, of course, it's all flying and there is no time at all until you are at your destination again. Yes, there was a lot more fun traveling by train. It was tedious because the train rides were so long, especially to Montreal."

It was a different time. A time when players didn't have huge homes, but lived in boarding houses and apartments during the hockey season. One of those boarding houses was owned by Ma Shaw. During the '40s, she boarded Bill Quackenbush, Harry Lumley, and Blackjack Stewart. In later years, she would board the likes of Ted Lindsay and Gordie Howe.

"When I was with Detroit, we stayed in homes and private houses," says Harry Watson. "[People would board players]. [Gordie Howe and some of the other players] were with Ma Shaw. I was with another lady, and not too far from where they were. [The

The 1941 Detroit Red Wings

1940-41 STANLEY CUP PLAYOFFS

FIRST GAME (April 6, at Boston)
Bruins 3, Red Wings 2
First Period
Boston - Wiseman (Smith, Conacher) 13:26
Second Period
Boston - Schmidt (Dumart, Crawford) 14:45
Third Period
Boston - McCreavy (Schmidt, Crawford) 9:16
Detroit - Liscombe (Jennings, Brown) 10:55
Detroit - Howe (Brown) 17:45

SECOND GAME (April 8, at Boston)
Bruins 2, Red Wings 1
First Period
No scoring
Second Period
No scoring
Third Period
Detroit - Bruneteau (Howe, Orlando) 2:41
Boston - Reardon (Cain, Smith) 13:35
Boston - Conacher (Schmidt) 17:45

THIRD GAME (April 10, at Detroit)
Bruins 4, Red Wings 2
First Period
Detroit - Jennings (Grosso, Abel) 3:15
Boston - Wiseman (Conacher, Hollett) 3:57
Detroit - Abel (Stewart) 7:45
Boston - Schmidt (Dumart, Bauer) 14:07
Second Period
Boston - Schmidt (Dumart, Clapper) 0:59
Third Period
Boston - Jackson (Reardon, Clapper) 17:20

FOURTH GAME (April 12, at Detroit)
Bruins 3, Red Wings 1
First Period
Detroit - Liscombe (Howe, Giesebrecht) 10:14
Second Period
Boston - Hollett (Schmidt) 7:42
Boston - Bauer (Schmidt) 8:43
Boston - Wiseman (Conacher, McCreavy) . .19:32
Third Period
No scoring

1941-42 STANLEY CUP PLAYOFFS

FIRST GAME (April 4, at Toronto)

Red Wings 3, Maple Leafs 2

First Period

Detroit - Grosso (Orlando) 1:37

Toronto - McCreedy (Davidson, Kampman) .. 6:36

Detroit - Abel (Grosso) 12:30

Toronto - Schriner (Taylor) 12:59

Second Period

Detroit - Grosso 14:11

Third Period

No scoring

SECOND GAME (April 7, at Toronto)

Red Wings 4, Maple Leafs 2

First Period

Detroit - Grosso (Wares) 11:47

Detroit - Bruneteau (Liscombe) 14:17

Second Period

Toronto - Schriner (Taylor, Stanowski) 11:13

Third Period

Detroit - Grosso (Wares) 4:15

Detroit - J. Brown (Bush, Liscombe) 10:06

Toronto - Stanowski 14:39

THIRD GAME (April 9, at Detroit)

Red Wings 5, Maple Leafs 2

First Period

Toronto - Carr (Taylor, Kampman) 15:36

Toronto - Carr (Taylor) 16:06

Detroit - J. Brown (Bush, Stewart) 18:20

Detroit - Carveth (Bush, A. Brown) 18:58

Second Period

Detroit - McCreavy (Grosso, Bush) 13:12

Detroit - Howe (Grosso, Bush) 15:11

Third Period

Detroit - Bush (Liscombe) 7:11

FOURTH GAME (April 12, at Detroit)

Maple Leafs 4, Red Wings 3

First Period

No scoring

Second Period

Detroit - Bruneteau (Motter) 1:32

Detroit - Abel (Wares, Grosso) 9:08

Toronto - Davidson (Langelle, McCreedy) .. 13:54

Toronto - Carr (Taylor, Schriner) 15:20

Third Period

Detroit - Liscombe (Bruneteau, Howe) 4:18

Toronto - Apps (Stanowski, N. Metz) 6:15

Toronto - N. Metz (D. Metz, Apps) 12:45

FIFTH GAME (April 14, at Toronto)

Maple Leafs 9, Red Wings 3

First Period

Toronto - N. Metz (Apps, Stanowski) 9:24

Toronto - Stanowski 15:13

Second Period

Toronto - Goldham 1:59

Toronto - Schriner (Taylor) 4:11

Toronto - D. Metz (Apps, N. Metz) 14:11

Toronto - Apps (D. Metz, Goldham) 14:39

Toronto - D. Metz (N. Metz) 16:43

Third Period

Detroit - Howe (McCreavy, Liscombe) 3:12

Toronto - D. Metz (Apps, Stanowski) 5:31

Toronto - Apps (D. Metz) 9:20

Detroit - Motter (Howe) 13:57

Detroit - Liscombe (Howe) 15:39

SIXTH GAME (April 16, at Detroit)

Maple Leafs 3, Red Wings 0

First Period

No scoring

Second Period

Toronto - D. Metz 0:14

Third Period

Toronto - Goldham (Schriner) 13:32

Toronto - Taylor (Schriner) 14:04

SEVENTH GAME (April 18, at Toronto)

Maple Leafs 3, Red Wings 1

First Period

No scoring

Second Period

Detroit - Howe (Abel, Orlando) 1:44

Third Period

Toronto - Schriner (Carr, Taylor) 7:46

Toronto - Langelle (Goldham, McCreedy) 9:43

Toronto - Schriner (Taylor, Carr) 16:13

boarding houses were all] walking distance to the Olympia."

Quackenbush remembers the decade of the '40s fondly: "Mrs. Shaw's boarding house had four of us living there," he recalls. "[There were] only six teams in the NHL then. [We would] travel on trains [where there were] eternal card games. We knew all the other players–a camaraderie that would be missed today."

The 1940s were a successful decade for the Detroit Red Wings. They dominated all of the American clubs in the post-season, making it to the Stanley Cup finals on six occasions (1940-41, 1941-42, 1942-43, 1944-45, 1947-48 and 1948-49). Despite this, they were only able to capitalize on one of these opportunities, winning the Stanley Cup in 1942-43. In 1940-41, 1947-48, and 1948-49, they were eliminated in four straight games by their opponents.

The Red Wings' post-season battles with Toronto and Boston contain many colorful stories. Besides 1942-43, when they won the Stanley Cup, the most interesting of these post-season contests took place in 1941-42 and 1944-45. Statistics for every Stanley Cup final appearance made during the 1940s are provided. Actual stories of the 1942, 1943 and 1945 matches are also presented to accent the statistics.

The word frustration took on new meaning for the Detroit Red Wings that made it to the Stanley Cup finals in 1941-42. After winning the first three games of the series against Toronto, they were defeated in the remaining four games. Until they started losing, the Red Wings had everyone convinced that they would be champions. After the first three games, Toronto goaltender Turk Broda remarked that he felt the Wings were unstoppable. When things turned sour, it was a shock to both the players and fans who were thirsty for a Stanley Cup win.

THE FINAL GAME - APRIL 18, 1942

Maple Leaf Gardens was packed to the gills for the seventh game of the finals. Miles away, the city of Detroit expected the Red Wings to take home the Cup that night. The 16,218 Maple Leaf fans present at the game thought otherwise. Both teams had won three matches, and this was the contest that

determined the winner. Only one team would skate away with the prized, silver trophy.

The first period of the game was scoreless. Then, Detroit's Syd Howe scored the game's first goal in the second period, elevating the hopes of Detroit fans back home. Things looked good for the away team, and the excitement was starting to build. Victory was only a matter of minutes away! However, to the delight of the capacity crowd, Toronto scored three unanswered goals in the third period, and with an amazing comeback effort, won the game and the Stanley Cup.

In a 1942 *Detroit News* article, defenseman Jimmy Orlando discussed the defeat shortly after it happened. He said: "It still makes me slightly sick every time I think about what happened to us in the Stanley Cup final, but I don't think about it so often these days as I used to. We're getting over it a bit by now, I guess, but we'll never forget it."

Offering an explanation as to exactly what happened, Orlando added:

The main trouble was that they finally caught on to our style of play, and threw the same thing right back at us, only more so. Yes, we were playing knock-'em-down hockey, but the chief thing we did all through our 'hot spell' was to rush the other team all the time; keep the puck in their end. We were pretty successful with it all the way too, and against Toronto it worked, until they wised up. Then they did the same thing to us. But instead of rushing with four men as we had been doing, they rushed us with five. They gambled all out. They sent men into the corners to fight for the puck and ran every risk of being caught in order to get that puck. They didn't give a hang for breakaways. They played that all-out hockey, kept the puck in our end all the time, just the way we had been doing it to them, and they got away from it. Penalties hurt us bad, and our own fast pace caught up with us after two months, and the Leafs caught up with us, too. So they licked us.

Despite numerous chances, Detroit won the Stanley Cup only once during the 1940s, taking it in 1942-43. That season, the playoff format changed. The top four teams making it to the post-season played best-of-seven semifinal matches that determined who challenged for the Cup.

1942-43 STANLEY CUP VICTORY

FIRST GAME (April 1, at Detroit)
Red Wings 6, Bruins 2
First Period
Detroit - Stewart (Abel, Liscombe) 1:15
Boston - A. Jackson (Cain) 18:13
Second Period
Detroit - Bruneteau (Abel, H. Jackson) 1:12
Detroit - Abel 15:43
Detroit - Carveth (Douglas) 19:06
Third Period
Detroit - Bruneteau (Abel, Liscombe) 1:21
Detroit - Bruneteau (Stewart, Abel) 16:24
Boston - DeMarco (Guidolin, Gallinger) 17:53

SECOND GAME (April 4, at Detroit)
Red Wings 4, Bruins 3
First Period
No scoring
Second Period
Boston - Crawford (Chamberlain) 10:16
Boston - A. Jackson (Cowley, Cain) 11:04
Detroit - Douglas (Orlando) 17:08
Third Period
Detroit - Carveth (Orlando) 5:55

Detroit - Liscombe (Abel) 6:21
Detroit - Howe (Wares) 13:16
Boston - A. Jackson (Cowley, Hollett) 16:38

THIRD GAME (April 7, at Boston)
Red Wings 4, Bruins 0
First Period
Detroit - Grosso (Wares) 3:26
Detroit - Grosso (Liscombe) 10:16
Second Period
No scoring
Third Period
Detroit - Douglas 8:03
Detroit - Grosso (Wares) 18:41

FOURTH GAME (April 8, at Boston)
Red Wings 2, Bruins 0
First Period
Detroit - Carveth 12:09
Second Period
Detroit - Liscombe 2:45
Third Period
No scoring

In the 1942-43 semifinals, the first-place Red Wings beat the third-place Maple Leafs. With the exception of the New York Rangers, Detroit had scored fewer goals than any other NHL team that season. When the playoffs arrived, the line of Sid Abel, Don Grosso and Eddie Wares came alive, and the Red Wings played tough hockey, remembering the loss they had endured to Toronto the previous season.

In the second game of the series, on March 25, 1943, All-Star defenseman Black Jack Stewart mixed it up twice in the third period in front of 13,382 crazed Toronto fans. First, he had a battle with Reg Hamilton. "I pushed Hamilton into the boards and he gave me the butt end of the stick in the face," Stewart said in the March 26, 1943 issue of the *Detroit News*. "So I pushed him back. He dropped his stick and I figured he was looking for trouble so I dropped my stick and gloves." Stewart sent two solid blows to Hamilton's face and body. Hamilton managed to get only one punch in before officials separated the two. Stewart broke away from the officials, and Hamilton skated over to meet him again, where more blows were exchanged in almost

one full minute of uninterrupted fighting. Afterwards, the victorious Stewart skated off to have a gash above his eye stitched up.

The action didn't end there. Approximately 30 seconds after he returned to the ice, Stewart went to check Toronto forward Bob Davidson at the blue line. Davidson fell to the ice, clipping Jack on the head with his stick as he fell. Angered, Stewart slapped Davidson in the face with his stick, and the two dropped the gloves. After fighting for a short while, they lost their balance and fell to the ice, with Stewart on top of Davidson, pinning his shoulders to the ice. Stewart was given a 10-minute misconduct penalty since the infraction was his second of the contest, and missed the remainder of the game, which only had 2-1/2 minutes remaining.

During the series, the Maple Leafs won what, at the time, was the longest hockey game ever played on Olympia ice. Toronto's Jackie McLean scored at 1:12 a.m., after 70 minutes and 18 seconds of overtime to secure the victory. McLean wasn't officially credited for the goal until three-and-a-half days later, as it was disputed and required a decision from then-League president Red Dutton. "Actually, Poile made the shot but it hit McLean's stick on the way to the net, according to Referee Frank [King] Clancy," said Dutton in the March 28, 1943 issue of the *Detroit News*. "I talked to McLean; I talked to several Red Wings; I consulted Clancy three times; I studied the original of the *Detroit News'* photograph of the goal. I was sitting in the press box at the time. I didn't see who made the goal. I laid awake half of last night pondering the situation. I am taking my referee's word in the matter and am ruling that it is McLean's goal."

The Red Wings eliminated the Maple Leafs when Adam Brown, playing in only his second game for Detroit as a replacement for the injured Syd Howe, scored the game-winner. Before that, the two teams battled through 9 minutes, 21 seconds of sudden-death overtime. The 3-2 win was Detroit's fourth victory in six games, and put them into the Stanley Cup finals for the sixth time in 11 years. In the other semifinal series, the Bruins beat Montreal, who were missing an injured Rocket Richard. The nation of Canada was completely out of the race, and two American clubs faced off for the prized Stanley Cup.

STANLEY CUP FINALS

In the finals, things got off to a good start for Detroit when Mud Bruneteau scored a hat trick in game one of the series at the Olympia, helping his teammates win 6-2. The feat made him the very first Red Wing to score a hat trick in a Stanley Cup playoff game. "It was as easy as shooting sitting ducks," he said in the April 2, 1943 issue of the *Detroit News*. "Each time I had a perfect pass. That's playing real hockey. Don't forget I made all my goals on five passes from [Sid] Abel."

The second game, also played in Detroit, looked favorable for the Bruins, who took a 2-0 lead. However, the Wings came back and won 4-3. Detroit proved they were the better club in the following two matches. Boston's Arthur Jackson scored the last goal of the series for the Bruins in the third period of the second game, and the Red Wings held Boston off the scoreboard for the remainder of the series, taking the Cup in four straight games. Goaltender Johnny Mowers was unstoppable!

In the third game, the Wings won 4-0. However, the contest was not as boring as the score might seem

to indicate. The papers point out that the contest might have been closer had the Bruins not received some unlucky breaks. Detroit's Don "Count" Grosso was the game's hero. He had played with a secret cast on his stick hand during the regular season to protect a bone separation in his wrist. Once again, he was injured, an x-ray revealing a fracture. Despite the pain, he scored three of the four goals in that contest, and started the actual plays that led to two of them.

THE FINAL GAME - APRIL 8, 1943

The final game, which saw the Cup come to Detroit, was played in Boston on April 8, 1943. Prior to the game, Boston goalie Frankie Brimsek claimed his team didn't have the punch to come back and win as Toronto had done the previous season.

Brimsek was right, and Detroit shut out Boston 2-0 in front of 12,954 fans. The victory gave them their third Stanley Cup victory in 17 seasons. Joe Carveth and Carl Liscombe scored the game's only two goals. However, Detroit goalie Johnny Mowers was incredible between the pipes, and Carveth paid him due credit in the April 9, 1943 issue of the *Detroit News*, commenting: "There's no doubt who won that game—Mowers did."

An excerpt from the same *Detroit News* article described Mower's performance. It read: "Just how hard the Bruins fought is shown by the stops. Thirty times Mowers had to turn back Bruin shots. One he stopped with his head, in a third period which saw the Wings two men short at one point. Blood poured from a gash under his eye. Mowers refused to delay the game to be sewed up. He tended the goal the last five minutes with blood streaming down his face and it wasn't until the train was pulling out of Boston's South Station, with the last of the breathless Wings just piling aboard, that Dr., C.I. Tomsu took two stitches in it."

After the game, Dit Clapper, then Boston's playing coach, came over and congratulated Mowers, followed by Jack Adams, who hugged him and patted his cheek. Many of the players also joined in the congratulating. It was a rushed affair, however, as the team had only 20 minutes to catch the 11 p.m. train to Detroit. Mud Bruneteau and Alex Motter, both sitting out due to injuries, rushed to get the case holding the coveted Cup and shuttled it to the train station via taxi.

Once all of the players were safely aboard the train, Adams opened the black case in the smoking lounge of the train, and the celebration began. Carl Liscombe was the first to taste beer from the trophy, getting a little wet as the train suddenly jerked, signifying the start of their journey home.

James Norris was present, despite orders from his physician to remain resting in Florida, where he had been recovering from a bout of pneumonia. Despite some resistance, the players forced him to pose for pictures, and he left with a promise to greet them at the victory dinner, scheduled in Detroit the following week. The Red Wings were hockey champions!

1944-45 was the last wartime season NHL teams had to endure. Even though Detroit had won a third Stanley Cup by beating Boston in 1943, the bitter taste from the 1942 series against Toronto was still

in their mouths. The same two teams met once again in the 1944-45 Stanley Cup finals.

Oddly, this time it was the Maple Leafs who won the first three games. Their goalie, Frank "Ulcers" McCool, set a Stanley Cup record for successive shutouts, when he closed the door on the Wings 1-0, 2-0 and 1-0 in the first three contests. Detroit took the fourth game, played in Toronto, 5-3, and went on to win the next two contests as well.

It was almost the 1941-42 series in reverse. However, the Leafs took the seventh game, played on Olympia ice. They got on the scoreboard early with a goal from right wing John "Sudden Death" Hill, in what proved to be a low-scoring game. The middle period was scoreless. Detroit's Murray Armstrong managed to tie up the game 8:16 into the third period, but the Maple Leafs' Babe Pratt scored about four minutes later. Detroit couldn't manage to score again, and Toronto was victorious.

1944-45 STANLEY CUP PLAYOFFS

FIRST GAME (April 6, at Detroit)
Maple Leafs 1, Red Wings 0
First Period
    Toronto - Schriner 13:56
Second Period
    No scoring
Third Period
    No scoring

SECOND GAME (April 8, at Detroit)
Maple Leafs 2, Red Wings 0
First Period
    No scoring
Second Period
    No scoring
Third Period
    Toronto - Kennedy (Pratt) 6:05
    Toronto - Morris 12:03

THIRD GAME (April 12, at Toronto)
Maple Leafs 1, Red Wings 0
First Period
    No scoring
Second Period
    No scoring
Third Period
    Toronto - Bodnar (Stanowski) 3:02

FOURTH GAME (April 14, at Toronto)
Red Wings 5, Maple Leafs 3
First Period
    Detroit - Hollett (E. Bruneteau) 8:35
    Toronto - Kennedy (Hill) 9:19
    Toronto - Kennedy (Hill) 11:44
Second Period
    Detroit - Armstrong (M. Bruneteau) 9:20

    Toronto - Kennedy (Davidson) 10:20
Third Period
    Detroit - E. Bruneteau 1:11
    Detroit - Lindsay 3:20
    Detroit - Carveth (Hollett) 17:38

FIFTH GAME (April 19, at Detroit)
Red Wings 2, Maple Leafs 0
First Period
    No scoring
Second Period
    No scoring
Third Period
    Detroit - Hollett (Carveth) 8:21
    Detroit - Carveth (Quackenbush) 16:16

SIXTH GAME (April 21, at Toronto)
Red Wings 1, Maple Leafs 0
First Period
    No scoring
Second Period
    No scoring
Third Period
    No scoring
Fourth Period
    Detroit - E. Bruneteau 14:15

SEVENTH GAME (April 22, at Detroit)
Maple Leafs 2, Red Wings 1
First Period
    Toronto - Hill (Kennedy) 5:38
Second Period
    No scoring
Third Period
    Detroit - Armstrong (Hollett) 8:16
    Toronto - Pratt (Metz) 12:14

1947-48 STANLEY CUP FINALS

FIRST GAME (April 7, at Toronto)

Maple Leafs 5, Red Wings 3

First Period

Detroit - McFadden (Horeck) 7:20

Toronto - Watson (Apps) 8:21

Toronto - Klukay (Bentley, Costello) 9:03

Toronto - Apps (Mortson) 18:25

Second Period

Toronto - Mortson (Bentley) 14:31

Toronto - Meeker (Stanowski, Kennedy) 19:22

Third Period

Detroit - Conacher (Quackenbush, Lindsay) .. 4:28

Detroit - Lindsay 5:26

SECOND GAME (April 10, at Toronto)

Maple Leafs 4, Red Wings 2

First Period

Toronto - Bentley (Samis) 13:31

Second Period

Toronto - Ezinicki (Apps, Watson) 3:35

Toronto - Bentley (Costello, Klukay) 17:16

Detroit - Horeck (Abel) 18:18

Toronto - Watson 18:49

Third Period

Detroit - Gauthier (McFadden) 17:19

THIRD GAME (April 11, at Detroit)

Maple Leafs 2, Red Wings 0

First Period

No scoring

Second Period

Toronto - Watson (Ezinicki) 19:42

Third Period

Toronto - Lynn (Kennedy) 15:16

FOURTH GAME (April 14, at Detroit)

Maple Leafs 7, Red Wings 2

First Period

Toronto - Kennedy (Bentley) 2:51

Toronto - Boesch 5:03

Toronto - Watson 11:13

Second Period

Detroit - Reise (Pavelich, Horeck) 2:41

Toronto - Apps (Thomson) 4:26

Toronto - Kennedy (Lynn) 9:42

Toronto - Watson 11:38

Third Period

Toronto - Costello (Bentley) 14:37

Detroit - Horeck (Fogolin) 18:48

1948-49 STANLEY CUP FINALS

FIRST GAME (April 8, at Detroit)

Maple Leafs 3, Red Wings 2

First Period

Detroit - Gee (Lindsay, Howe) 4:15

Toronto - Bentley (Timgren, Klukay) 13:15

Second Period

Toronto - Thomson (Bentley) 16:02

Third Period

Detroit - Quackenbush (Lindsay, Gee) 15:56

Overtime

Toronto - Klukay (Thomson, Timgren) 17:31

SECOND GAME (April 10, at Detroit)

Maple Leafs 3, Red Wings 1

First Period

Toronto - Smith (Boesch) 8:50

Toronto - Smith (Barilko, Kennedy) 9:56

Second Period

Toronto - Smith (Kennedy, Mackell) 17:58

Third Period

Detroit - Horeck (Stewart, McFadden) 5:50

THIRD GAME (April 13, at Toronto)

Maple Leafs 3, Red Wings 1

First Period

Detroit - Stewart (Horeck) 4:57

Second Period

Toronto - Ezinicki (Gardner, Watson) 11:02

Toronto - Kennedy (Smith, Mackell) 12:40

Toronto - Mortson (Thomson, Klukay) 16:15

Third Period

No scoring

FOURTH GAME (April 16, at Toronto)

Maple Leafs 3, Red Wings 1

First Period

Detroit - Lindsay (Gee, Howe) 2:59

Second Period

Toronto - Timgren (Bentley) 10:10

Toronto - Gardner (Thomson, Ezinicki) 19:45

Third Period

Toronto - Bentley (Timgren) 15:10

Marty Pavelich, Harry Lumley, Jerry Coture, George Gee and Sid Abel during the late 1940s.

Humorously, in John DeVaney and Burt Goldblatt's book *The Stanley Cup*, Pratt recalled what he was doing just prior to this important seventh game. He said: "I was always kind of a bad boy in those days, you know. I did some drinking then, I don't any more, but anyway the coaches always had to keep an eye on me. I used to room with [Toronto] coach Hap Day. I remember the afternoon of the seventh game, we were in Detroit, and I was with Hap Day in his suite. I went to sleep. Poor Hap, he was pacing up and down the room for hours while I was snoring away. Finally, it was about six in the evening and I guess he couldn't take my snoring anymore, it finally got to his nerves. He grabbed the mattress of my bed, pulled it out, and kerplow! I landed on the floor. I woke up and I looked up at him and I said, 'Hap, Hap, what's the matter, what happened?' And he looked down at me and he said, 'You son of a bitch, it's two hours before the seventh game of the Stanley Cup, how the hell can you sleep?'"

THE MEN

HARRY (APPLE CHEEKS) LUMLEY

Born: November 11, 1926, Owen Sound, Ontario
Position: Goaltender
Junior: Barrie Colts
Minor Pro
 • Indianapolis Capitols (AHL): 1943-44, 1944-45
Detroit Red Wings: 1943-44 to 1949-50
Best NHL Season
 • 1953-54 (Toronto): 4,140 MIN; 1.86 GAA; 13 SO
Career Awards & Honors
 • First All-Star team: 1953-54, 1954-55
 • NHL All-Star Games: 1951, '54, '55
 • Hockey Hall of Fame, 1980
 • Vezina Trophy, 1953-54 (1.85 GAA in 69 games)
Milestones
 • While playing for Toronto, led the NHL in shutouts for two consecutive seasons.
Trades
 • Traded to Chicago in 1950 with Pete Babando, Al Dewsbury, Don Morrison and Jack Stewart for Bob Goldham, Sugar Jim Henry, Metro Prystai and Gaye Stewart.

BIOGRAPHY

Harry Lumley's NHL debut with Detroit came in 1943-44, at the age of 17. Embarrassingly, he allowed 13 goals to slip by him in two games. Such play on Lumley's part didn't continue long, however. In the more than six seasons in which he tended goal in Detroit, he led the Red Wings to the playoffs each season. In 1949-50, his last season in Detroit, he led the team all the way to the Stanley Cup.

As Terry Sawchuk was coming up, Lumley was moving westward—to the cellar-dwelling Chicago Blackhawks. "It's like you're with a first place team and then you go to a last place team," recalls Lumley. "It's quite a kick in the pants." After two seasons in Chicago, Lumley moved on to Toronto. He then spent three seasons with the Boston Bruins, and in 1962, ended his career in the minors with the Collingwood Shipbuilders.

After hockey, Lumley became a successful business man in his home-town of Owen Sound, Ontario, where he has been a partner in an auto dealership, Dominion Motors.

JOHN THOMAS (JOHNNY) MOWERS

Born: October 29, 1916, St. David's, Ontario
Position: Goaltender
Junior
- Niagara Falls Brights
- Niagara Falls Cataracts
- Pontiacs (M-O League)

Minor Pro
- Omaha Knights (AHA), 1939-40

Detroit Red Wings
- 1940-41 to 1942-43; 1946-47

Best NHL Season
- 1940-41: 3,040 MIN; 2.13 GAA; 4 SO

Career Awards & Honors
- Vezina Trophy, 1942-43
- First All-Star team: 1943
- Red Wings Hall of Fame: 1946

BIOGRAPHY

Along with brothers George and Gordon, Johnny Mowers moved to Niagara Falls, Ontario, in 1916, where his father, George, Sr., was a foreman for American Cyanamid Company. Mowers played all of his amateur (junior and senior) hockey in Niagara

Falls, also playing baseball for the City League, and football for Niagara Falls High School. However, hockey was his main game. "When I started to play as a kid I was the smallest in the gang so they made me play goal," he said in the November 10, 1940 issue of the *Detroit News*. "Later, in signing up for the Junior City League one year I thought I'd have some fun so I said I'd played defense. I didn't fool anybody. They made me go back to goal. It doesn't matter where you are, just so you're playing."

While playing for the then-mediocre Niagara Falls Brights, Mowers impressed Red Wings scout Carson Cooper by shutting out the Toronto Goodyears, a much better team, for 180 consecutive minutes. Soon after, Cooper brought him to Detroit from the Niagara Falls Cataracts. At training camp, Mowers made a lasting impression on Jack Adams.

Before earning a regular spot with the Red Wings, Mowers spent a half-season in the Michigan-Ontario League with the Pontiacs and served as a practice goalie for the Red Wings. The Pontiacs were a poor club and were defeated often. Despite this, Mowers' fine play eventually won him a professional spot with the Omaha Knights of the old American Hockey Association, where he helped them to a first-round playoff finish. He beat out goalies Jimmy Franks and Floyd Perras for a chance at the number one job with the big club the following season.

Remembering his earliest days with Detroit's system, in the same *Detroit News* article, he said: "Carson Cooper first scouted me, then Jack Adams saw me play one night in Toronto, and I came to play for Pontiac in the M-O League. I used to drive 90 miles to Toronto whenever I got a chance to see Tiny Thompson work in goal. When I was in the M-O League Tiny used to see me play. He's a peach of a fellow, that Tiny. He'd tell me what I did wrong and why it was wrong. After that, I got my chance with Omaha and now with the Wings."

Ironically, it was Mowers' idol, Thompson, who first told him he got the job with the big club. As Mowers was enjoying a milkshake in the Olympia's coffee shop one day, Thompson walked in and

Johnny Mowers was runner-up for the Calder Trophy his rookie season. Hockey Hall of Fame archives.

congratulated him on taking the goaltending job for Detroit away from him. Thompson pointed to the *Detroit Times'* sports page announcing the starting line-up for that night's game against the New York Americans. In an article by Joe Falls, which appeared in the May 14, 1982 issue of the *Detroit News*, Mowers remembered: "I was so scared that night I held onto every puck they shot at me, even from center ice. We must have set the record for the most faceoffs in one game."

During Mowers' rookie season, he was runner-up for the Calder Trophy. That season (1940-41), he nearly won the Vezina Trophy as well, with a 2.13 GAA, but lost out to Toronto's Turk Broda. When World War II beckoned in 1943, Mowers joined his brother and a few teammates (Jack Stewart, Harry Watson, Les Douglas and Sid Abel) and enlisted in the Royal Canadian Air Force. Before departing, a reporter asked him what he thought would become of the Red Wings because of the war. He was quoted in the July 22, 1942 issue of the *Detroit News* as saying: "Oh, don't worry about Jack [Adams], he'll have a lot of good kids on the ice and they'll play real hockey—

Opposite: Harry Lumley led Detroit to the playoffs many times. Imperial Oil-Turofsky/Hockey Hall of Fame.

everybody always does for Adams." While in the RCAF, Mowers played a considerable amount of hockey in England and Switzerland.

After the War, Mowers attempted to return to the Red Wings, but back problems prevented him from playing more than a handful of games in 1946-47. "I only saw him play a couple of games," recalled former teammate Harry Lumley. "He was in the service and then when he came back out of the service he played a couple of games and I guess they figured he didn't have it. You know when you're in the service you lose a lot."

In an excerpt from the March 9, 1943 *Detroit Red Wings Program*, the quiet Mowers was described as "a mixture of good humor and common sense, a sincere worker, and an uncomplaining member of the team. ... [He was] never one to blame an opposition score on the shortcomings of teammates, preferring to accept more than may be his just share of the responsibility."

Mowers turned to coaching in 1947-48, when he stepped behind the bench in Indianapolis. After coaching, he went into insurance sales and did very well. He kept a hand in the game, helping out many high school and amateur hockey teams over the years.

HUBERT GEORGE (BILL) QUACKENBUSH

Born: March 9, 1922, Toronto, Ontario
Position: Defense
Junior
- Brantford (OHA)

Minor Pro
- Indianapolis Capitols (AHL): 1942-43, 1943-44

Detroit Red Wings
- 1942-43 to 1948-49

Career Awards & Honors
- First All-Star Team: 1948, 1949, and 1951
- Second All-Star Team: 1947, 1953
- NHL All-Star Games: 1947-54

Trades
- Traded to the Boston Bruins in 1949 with Pete Horeck for Jimmy Peters, Pete Babando, Lloyd Durham, and Clare Martin.

BIOGRAPHY

Nicknamed "Bill" by an aunt who thought he was far too masculine to go by Hubert George, Bill Quackenbush played for the Red Wings for six seasons. Recalling some of his earliest hockey memories and the people who were most influential in his development as a player, Quackenbush says: "In Toronto, I remember skating on frozen roads to get to the outdoor rink. I would skate home for lunch. My influences were two: my father and Mr. Slade of Western Technical School. My father, John Quackenbush, a sergeant in the Toronto Police Force, regularly managed to get the group to early morning practice at Western Tech despite his working hours."

Before making it to the NHL, Quackenbush played junior hockey for Brantford of the OHA, where Tommy Ivan, whom he respected greatly, was his coach during his last season. In Brantford, he played with future Red Wing teammates Leo Reise and Doug McCaig. After being scouted by Carson Cooper, he went to the Red Wings in 1942-43, and played for their American League club in Indianapolis for development. That season, he played 10 games for the Stanley Cup-winning Red Wings, but broke his wrist, and ended up finishing the season with Indianapolis.

Quackenbush was perhaps the smoothest rushing defenseman the game has ever known, possessing good playmaking and passing ability and a special ability to stop a rush without sending his opponent crashing into the boards. A great poke-checker, he was adept at robbing the puck from opposing players. Seldom penalized, he could also check his opponent without tripping or holding him.

Over the course of his entire NHL career, Quackenbush racked up a mere 95 penalty minutes. In 1949, he became the first defenseman to win the Lady Byng Trophy (Detroit defenseman Red Kelly later won the award as well), racking up no penalties. At the time, the only other players to win the Lady Byng and not rack up any penalty minutes were forwards Max Bentley and Syl Apps. Reflecting upon the feat in the March 22, 1985 issue of the *Toronto Globe and Mail*, Quackenbush explained: "We played far more in the neutral zone. Now the whole game is played in the offensive and defensive zones. With all the forechecking in the game, you'll never see a defenseman go without a penalty today."

Describing his style of play, Quackenbush says: "My style of play did not include slashing, but did include conserving energy by anticipating, knowing the opponent's moves to allow maximum time on the ice—often half the game or more. ... [I was] a student of the game—analyzing all other players' moves and anticipating. I loved to play and be out on the ice."

Despite his penalty-free reputation, Quackenbush wasn't as innocent as his numbers make him appear. Describing him during his playing days in the same *Toronto Globe and Mail* article, former Boston Bruin Milt Schmidt said: "He grabbed a lot of people. Bill was very cagey at holding people in the corners. He was so strong, he could move you without being seen."

The one-and-only "fight" Quackenbush had as a player was, in reality, a shoving match with Chicago's Gaye Stewart. Neither man dropped the gloves, but both received majors for fighting! In the March 2, 1977 issue of the *Maple Leaf Gardens Program*, Quackenbush gave his feelings on fighting:

We had a powerhouse team. Black Jack Stewart was on it, very strong and a good fighter, too, and tough Leo Reise. I always seemed to play better when I got mad at something, but I tried to stay away from foolish penalties. I tried to play the game with composure, use my head and stay away from penalties — they could really hurt the team. They talk about rough hockey in those days — and there were some brutal games — but all the years I played amateur or pro I don't ever remember receiving a butt end, or giving one. That doesn't mean that there weren't some tough guys. Rocket Richard and I bumped against each other quite a lot, but in 14 years against Richard I never had any real problems. It was always good clean hitting.

After playing for Detroit, Quackenbush was traded to Boston in 1949, where he became a main component of their defense for seven years. According to Quackenbush, while there, he often played all but two or three minutes of entire games. The trade was tough for him to swallow, as the Red Wings won the Stanley Cup the year after he was traded. "I was mad as hell," he says today. In Boston, he played defense with his brother Max in 1951.

In the off-season, Quackenbush played softball, golf, and soccer to stay in shape, and went into business selling building materials. He graduated

from Toronto's Western Technical School in 1941, and attended Boston's Northeastern University, receiving an A.C.E. degree in 1962 from Lincoln Institute. After playing hockey, he was involved in different business endeavors and coached a variety of athletics at Princeton University, including men's hockey. He currently resides in Florida, and enjoys playing golf.

LEO CHARLES (RADAR) REISE, JR.

Born: June 7, 1922, Stoney Creek, Ontario
Position: Defenseman
Junior
- Junior B: Brandtford
Minor Pro
- Kansas City Pla-Mors (USHL), 1945-46, 1946-47
- Indianapolis Capitols (USHL), 1946-47
Detroit Red Wings
- 1946-47 to 1951-52
Best NHL Season
- 1950-51: 5 goals, 21 points
Career Awards & Honors
- NHL All-Star Games: 1950-53

BIOGRAPHY

Leo Reise spent 10 seasons playing in the National Hockey League, a little over five of them with Detroit. He started playing for a group called the Fruitland Farmer, who played for an F&S league in Hamilton, Ontario. After playing high school hockey, Reise played Junior B with Brantford, where his father was coach.

Reise's father, Leo, Sr., played defense in the National Hockey League for nine seasons with the Hamilton Tigers, New York Americans, and New York Rangers. When the younger Reise made it to the NHL, he was the only second-generation player to do so. As a child, Reise didn't receive most of his coaching from his father. "Actually most of that came not by personal coaching," he recalls. "I was lucky. When he was coaching, he used to let me dress with the teams and I would practice with them. Of course, they were amateur teams and they [were] always short somebody. So I used to fill in anywhere I could. So actually, when I got down as far as Chatham, when I was 15 or 16, I could keep up with most of the guys anyhow. I just normally fell into it, let's put it that way. Chatham, Ontario, won the Senior

B championship the year my dad coached."

Reise broke into the NHL with the Chicago Blackhawks in 1945-46. He came to the Red Wings during the 1946-47 season. "We had great hockey teams while I was there," says Reise, remembering his days in Detroit. "I came in '46. I got there about Christmas of 1946 from the Chicago Blackhawks. Before that I went to Red Wing training camps. Before the War, I went to the Detroit training camps probably when I was a kid, when I was still a junior. So when I finally got to Detroit, back from Chicago, I knew an awful lot of the players. It was like playing back home."

The change of teams really wasn't much of a switch for Leo. "From that standpoint, no difference," he says. "You know, a manager is a manager is a manager, and the difference was with the team itself. The Red Wings were a very friendly organization, there were no cliques or anything on the team. In Chicago, I was the real rookie and they had a lot of older guys there. So it was just a little bit different there, but I didn't have any problems anywhere. There wasn't much difference at all between one [team] or the other."

When asked to recall the most unforgettable games of his NHL career, Reise says:

Well, I guess maybe the one game we played in Montreal and I remember Tommy Ivan kept pushing me out on the ice and I kept skating and skating. In fact, I think we lost the game. But it got so they had to lift me off the ice. They had to pull me into the box and even the Montreal fans applauded when I came off the ice. It was probably one of those things I remember, one of the great things to remember. Another one I played in Chicago, when they finally decided they were going to send me down to Kansas City, where I played the first part of the year at their farm club. I played six games for Chicago. There were 18,000 people in the Chicago Stadium and I had made quite an impression with the fans and what not, and they started to chant, 'We want Reise.' The whole place said, 'We want Reise.' They weren't playing me in that game because the regulars were back, so I was sitting on the end of the bench and wasn't playing and then the fans started to chant. So finally Johnny Gottselig put me on the ice. It is one of the memorable things.

"I was one of the top defensemen in the league for six or seven years," says Reise. "That's where I rated myself, anyhow. I played in every All Star game then when I was in the league, so I was rated as a pretty good defenseman. ... I loved body checking. I used to hunt for them to hit. That's what I was as good at as anybody, and better off than most, frankly, body checking. When it got close to playoff time, I would push myself a little harder so that when the playoffs came, I would be flying. I don't know. I just applied myself. I made sure I didn't make the same mistake twice. I just worked hard and made an honest effort."

Since retiring from the game, Reise has also retired from a career in business, which had its roots in his playing days. During the off-season he worked as a salesman and accountant. One of his customers hired him when he quit playing hockey. Today Reise isn't as active as he once was, but still engages in many enjoyable activities. He skates two to three times a week, sails his boat and plays golf.

JOHN SHERRATT (BLACK JACK) STEWART

Born: May 6, 1917, Pilot Mound, Manitoba
Position: Defenseman
Died: May 25, 1983, Detroit, Michigan
Junior
- Pilot Mound
- Portage la Praire Terriers

Minor Pro
- Pittsburgh Hornets (IAL), 1937-39

Detroit Red Wings
- 1938-39 to 1942-43; 1945-46 to 1949-50

Career Awards & Honors
- First All-Star team: 1942-43, 1947-48, 1948-49
- Second All-Star team: 1945-46, 1946-47
- Hockey Hall of Fame, 1964
- Red Wings Hall of Fame, 1944
- NHL All-Star Games: 1947-50

Trades
- After playing in Detroit, Stewart moved on to the Chicago Blackhawks in a trade that included eight other players in July of 1950. The Red Wings traded Stewart, Harry Lumley, Al Dewsbury, Pete Babando, and Don Morrison to Chicago for Metro Prystai, Gaye Stewart, Bob Goldham and Sugar Jim Henry.

BIOGRAPHY

Black Jack Stewart was one of the toughest defenseman the game has ever known. The son of wheat farmer John Calvin Stewart, Stewart got his big break while playing junior hockey. Winnipeg businessman Gene Houghton, an associate of James Norris, Sr., recommended him to the Red Wings. Stewart signed with the team in 1938 and played for its Pittsburgh affiliate. In 1938-39, he was called up to help the Red Wings in their last 32 games.

In Detroit, Stewart was a key component in the team's defensive corps, along with Leo Reise, Red Kelly and Bill Quackenbush. He helped the Red Wings take home the Stanley Cup in 1943 and 1950. Although he was not a prolific scorer, Stewart had a special knack for scoring at the right time, such as in close games when his team needed a goal badly.

Stewart was a deceptive skater and had the reputation of being one of the hardest (but cleanest) hitters the game has ever known. It was his tough checking that earned him the nickname "Black Jack." In the May 26, 1983 issue of the *Detroit News*, he said: "I got the nickname when a player reportedly woke up in the dressing room and said, 'Who hit me with the blackjack?'" Even though he was a tough, punishing hitter, Stewart was not a dirty player. Once, Stewart led the NHL in penalties with a mere 73 minutes, one of the league's lowest totals ever.

Stewart is remembered for the scrums he had on a regular basis with Boston's Milt Schmidt. "They used to have a quite a donnybrook every time they played," recalled Stewart's former teammate Harry Lumley. "I don't know what it was. It was just like a dog and a cat attracted to each other. Every time they seemed to go on the ice, why they were at each other."

"Black Jack Stewart was a very good defenseman

and tough guy," remembered Wally Crossman, a long-time Detroit Red Wings employee. "He'd really hit a person coming down the ice. He was a hard checker and he was very well liked here because of that attitude he had. Then we had Jimmy Orlando, he played with him on defense. Jimmy was called into the American Army during the war, but he never reported. So he was deported to Canada. He couldn't play here again, so he never did come back, but Jack finished his hockey career here. They were [a pretty fearsome pair on the blue line]."

Sid Abel once said Stewart had an arm like a cement wall, and never backed down from anyone. "He was just unbelievable the way he played defense," said Abel in the May 26, 1983 *Detroit News*. "When I look back where Ted Lindsay, Gordie Howe and myself got a lot of credit for doing things and the club winning—I've got some of the old films and figure, my God, Jack Stewart was more instrumental in the team winning than the ones who got the credit."

"He was a fine man, and a fine gentleman," remembered former teammate Leo Reise. "Tough, rough, [a] real tough hockey player. Probably one of the toughest there was in the league. About *the* toughest. He and Milt Schmidt used to have battle royals. Not fighting, but just physical body checks. Jack was a real fine gentleman and a tough hockey player. I started playing with [him] in Detroit.

CASCIO

Black Jack Stewart, perhaps the toughest defenseman that ever lived.

He said: 'You look after your side, and I'll look after mine.'"

"I'll always remember Jack Stewart with respect," said former NHL defenseman Bob Goldham in the May 27, 1983 *Toronto Star*. "You quickly learned to respect him. Jack's share of the area behind the blueline was 'No-Man's Land' for invaders. When he stepped into you, you felt as if you'd walked on a land mine. ... Stewart could not only flatten you with a body check but he had the heaviest stick of any man I ever played against. I don't mean that he hit you with his stick, but when he laid that stick across your arms he was so terribly strong that, literally, you couldn't move."

Stewart was traded to Chicago in July 1950. In the Windy City, he proved to be a leader, and was team captain from 1950 to 1952. However, he was plagued by injuries, and while there, had an operation on his back to repair a slipped disc. He was released

by Chicago President Bill Tobin in February 1952.

Like his father, Stewart also served as a harness racing official with the Canadian Trotting Association. During the off-season he played softball and golf to stay in shape and was known as one of the best-dressed players in the NHL. After playing, Stewart turned to coaching, spending time behind the bench with many hockey teams. Among them were the Kitchener Juniors, the OHA's Chatham Maroons and Windsor Seniors, and Pittsburgh of the AHL. He retired from the game altogether in 1963.

JOSEPH GORDON CARVETH

Born: March 21, 1918, Regina, Saskatchewan
Position: Right wing, Center
Junior
- Regina Aces Juniors
- Pontiac Chiefs (M-O League)

Minor Pro
- Indianapolis Capitols (AHL): 1939-40, 1941-42, 1943-44

Detroit Red Wings
- 1940-41 to 1945-46; 1949-50 to 1950-51

Best NHL Season
- 1943-44: 21 goals, 56 points

Career Awards & Honors
- Red Wings Hall of Fame, 1978
- NHL All-Star Game: 1950

BIOGRAPHY

Although he played for Boston and Montreal, Joe Carveth spent most of his NHL career playing for the Detroit Red Wings. Before coming to play for the big club, Carveth skated for the Pontiac Chiefs. In 1938-39, he and linemates Les Douglas and Archie Wilder played on a line that broke all scoring records in the Michigan-Ontario League and won the M-O championship.

The following season, the three of them found themselves playing professionally for Indianapolis of the AHL. Carveth broke his leg and ended up missing the rest of the season. The following year, the three linemates were put back together, and strong pre-season performances enabled them to make the Red Wings. Carveth and Douglas were the only ones to stay with the Red Wings long-term. Unfortunately, once Carveth made the team, he broke his leg again when he collided with Hank Goldup of the Toronto Maple Leafs on Christmas Eve, 1940.

In 1941-42, Carveth started off in Indianapolis, but by mid-season, he was once again on Detroit's roster, where he remained until 1945-46. After stints with Boston and Montreal, Jack Adams decided to bring Carveth back to the Wings in 1949-50, where he finished his NHL career. "We decided we would rather have a veteran on the bench taking spot assignments than to keep a youngster there, who would do better playing regularly in the minors," said Adams in the November 13, 1949 issue of the *Detroit News*.

As an athlete, Carveth was not the fastest skater, but was a good stickhandler. He was not only utilized at right wing, but at center as well, where he proved to be very effective. Determination and deliberation were two characteristics that he embodied. Carveth played for the American Hockey League's Cleveland Barons after his NHL days were over.

SYDNEY HARRIS HOWE

Born: September 28, 1911, Ottawa, Ontario
Position: Center, Left wing
Died: May, 1976, Ottawa, Ontario
Junior
- Lansdowne Park Juveniles
- Gunner Juniors (JCHL)

Senior
- Rideau Seniors (OSCL)

Minor Pro
- Syracuse Stars (IHL), 1931-32

Detroit Red Wings
- 1934-35 to 1945-46

Best NHL Season
- 1943-44: 32 goals, 60 points

Career Awards & Honors
- Red Wings Hall of Fame, 1944
- Hockey Hall of Fame, 1965
- Second All-Star Team (left-wing): 1945
- NHL All-Star Game: 1939 (benefit game for Earl Seibert)

Milestones
- Howe formerly held an NHL record. One year during the playoffs against Toronto, he scored the first goal of the game in only 9 seconds. The record is now held by Don Kozak of the Los Angeles Kings.
- At one time, Howe came close to tying the record for most goals in one game, when he scored six against the New York Rangers on February 3, 1944. The record is currently held by Joe Malone, who scored seven goals against Toronto on January 31, 1920.

Trades
- In 1935, Detroit obtained Syd Howe and defenseman Ralph (Scotty) Bowman from the St. Louis Eagles for defenseman Teddy Grahm and the sum of $50,000.

BIOGRAPHY

Syd Howe was the main attraction for the Red Wings before the coming of another Howe by the name of Gordie, who is no relation. Like most players, Howe learned the game at an early age. As a child, he lived near Ottawa's First Avenue Public School. It was there, and on both Patterson's Creek and the Rideau Canal, that he learned to skate using a pair of double-runners. Two years later, he was skating with regular, single-blade skates and playing for the school's team. After completing his education there, he attended Glebe Collegiate High School, where he played in an intercollegiate league. In 1927, Howe was the first recipient of the Ronald J. Ames Memorial Trophy, given to "the outstanding male athlete combining sportsmanship, school spirit, deportment, [and] academic efficiency while maintaining an interest in other school activities."

While still playing for Glebe, Howe also played junior hockey for the Lansdowne Park Juveniles, who won the playground championship. After winning the championship, that team became the Gunner Juniors when it merged into the Junior City Hockey League. They went all the way to the 1927 Memorial Cup finals, only to be defeated by the Regina Monarchs. After junior hockey, Howe played for the Rideau Seniors in the Ottawa Senior City League.

Professional hockey was beckoning, and Howe turned professional with the Ottawa Senators in February 1929, at the age of 17. According to Howe, the Senators lent him out for his first two seasons there, first to the Philadelphia Quakers, and then to the Toronto Maple Leafs who utilized him with their farm team, the Syracuse Stars. After two full seasons playing exclusively in Ottawa, the Senators moved to St. Louis, becoming the Eagles in 1934-35.

In 1935, Detroit obtained Syd Howe and defenseman Ralph (Scotty) Bowman from the St. Louis Eagles for defenseman Teddy Grahm and the sum of $50,000, which at the time was an outrageous amount of money. James Norris, Sr., was not pleased with the way the team was going and decided that the move would be beneficial. In negotiations with T.F. Ahern, the Eagles' principal stock holder, Norris first attempted to get St. Louis' entire forward line of

Howe, Carl Voss and Glen Brydson, but the deal fell apart. In the end, he eventually acquired Howe, who Jack Adams had been after for three seasons. The move was right on the money. Howe was an exciting player to watch, and he brought large crowds into the Olympia.

Part of Howe's popularity came from his versatility, which allowed him to be utilized at center, on the wing, or at the blue line. Sid Abel once noted that Howe could also play goal, and considering his versatility, was not recognized for the great athlete he was. In the January 5, 1966 issue of the *Detroit News*, in an article by John Walter, Ebbie Goodfellow said: "Syd was the most versatile player the Red Wings ever had. Syd played center, left wing and defense— wherever he was needed." When injuries sidelined the team's regular netminders, Howe also filled in as a spare goalie on several occasions.

One memorable thing about Howe is that he played in the longest game in Stanley Cup history, along with Mud Bruneteau. Howe recalled that event, and in the March 22, 1975 issue of the *Ottawa Journal*, commented on the game following that ordeal: "We had many of the same players when we went into the quarter final against the Americans and it was such a tight-checking game and we were so tired that we were all hoping it wouldn't last long. I'll never forget the guys carrying me off the ice when I scored so early."

Besides going on to win the Stanley Cup in 1936-37 and 1942-43, Howe reached another career high point at the Olympia on February 3, 1944. In a 12-2 victory over the New York Rangers, he scored six goals in one game! He scored two goals in each period of that game. "They were going in the net tonight—another night they don't," he said in the

February 4, 1944 issue of the *Detroit News*. "I don't remember any goal in particular. The boys were feeding them to me nicely. No celebration for me [he said with a grin], I'm due at work at 7:10 a.m."

Amazingly, on January 24, 1944, several nights before his six-goal game, Howe scored a hat trick against the Rangers in front of 12,293 ecstatic fans. He did it during the third period of what turned out to be a 15-0 blowout at the Olympia! The hat trick made him the team's all-time leading scorer at the time, with 149 career goals.

Tommy Emmett, the very first publicist for the Detroit Red Wings, once said: "Syd Howe was a mechanical perfectionist, like the Detroit Tigers' Charley Gehringer. He wasn't a spectacular stickhandler or speedy, nor did he have a blinding shot. He was extremely powerful although he was only 5-feet-9-1/2 inches and weighed 165 pounds. And he was a tremendous competitor."

"He was [the main attraction in Detroit before Gordie Howe got there]," says former Red Wing Carl Liscombe. "At the time that I played hockey, I would have picked him as the best center man in hockey, all around, because he played about 40 minutes a game and he played all over the ice. He played center ice, he played left wing, he played right wing, he played on defense. Just wherever they needed him, that's where he played."

As a person, Howe was a very shy, modest man. He was known for his sincerity, workman-like qualities, and team spirit. He was not only good at hockey, but also at basketball, football, baseball and piano. Humorously, on Syd Howe Night, a piano was brought out to center ice and Howe played for the crowd! "[Off of the ice he was] very, very nice," says Liscombe. "He was like Gordie Howe, you never knew he was around. [He was a] real, real quiet guy."

In the off-season, Howe lived in Dearborn, Michigan, and worked for Ford Motor Company as a tool-maker. He died in Ottawa, Ontario, in May of 1976 at the age of 64 after a long illness.

Opposite: Syd Howe–Detroit's main attraction during the 1940s. Hockey Hall of Fame archives.

HARRY PERCIVAL (WHIPPER) WATSON

Born: May 6, 1923, Saskatoon, Saskatchewan
Position: Left wing
Junior
- Saskatoon Dodgers, 1939-40
- Saskatoon Junior Quakers, 1940-41
Detroit Red Wings
- 1942-43 to 1945-46
Best NHL Season
- 1948-49: 26 goals, 45 points
Career Awards & Honors
- Saskatchewan Sports Hall of Fame, 1987
- Hockey Hall of Fame, 1994
- NHL All-Star games: 1947-49, '51, '53, '55
Trades
- Acquired with Pat Egan and Murray Armstrong for $35,000 when the New York Americans folded. Traded from Detroit to Toronto in 1946 for Billy Taylor.

BIOGRAPHY

Harry Watson was a remarkable hockey player. He played left wing for 15 seasons in the NHL, two with Detroit. In 1942-43, he helped the Wings win their third Stanley Cup. Watson is remembered as a hard-working leader. Fast and strong, the bulky left-wing possessed great offensive and defensive ability.

Watson grew up in Saskatoon, Saskatchewan, where he played youth hockey. He attended Thornton Public School in 1936 and played in the annual city East vs. West All-Star game. He also played with the Saskatoon Wesleys, who thanks in part to his efforts, won provincial championships in Pee Wee (1935-36), Bantam (1936-37), and Juvenile (1938-39).

Commenting on some of the early influences on him, Watson remembered: "Well I always listened to Foster Hewitt on Saturday night and I really looked at Busher Jackson, Charlie Conacher, Joe Primeau back in those days. ... We had a good senior club in Saskatoon, the Saskatoon Quakers, so I always looked up to them and I hoped that some day I would be able to make the senior team there."

Watson made it to the NHL with the New York Americans in 1941-42. When the club folded at the season's end, he was claimed by the Red Wings. Remembering that first season in Detroit, Watson recalled: "The first year that I was there it was 1942-

43, and we won the Stanley Cup. It wasn't too big a thrill for me because I got benched in the last couple of games, and after we won it, we never even had a party after the game or anything. And the Stanley Cup ring is really something different. It was a flat, gold ring. It was printed backwards. You had to carry an ink pad around with you to stamp out Detroit, Stanley Cup Champions, 1942-1943 and crossed hockey sticks. So it is a rarity, I think, today. Anyway, it was something else. The ring got sent to me when I was out in Saskatoon, you know, so there was no presentations or anything. That was kind of disappointing."

After one season in Detroit, World War II beckoned, and Watson joined the Royal Canadian Air Force. During his stint in the RCAF, he was stationed in Saskatoon, Winnipeg, and Montreal. Besides playing for the Saskatoon Quakers while in the service, he also played for the military's hockey teams, and in 1944, helped the Saskatoon RCAF team win the Western Command Senior Hockey Championship.

After the War, Watson returned to the Red Wings but was traded to the Toronto Maple Leafs in 1946-47, where he spent the majority of his professional career. In Toronto, he realized his most successful years as a player, winning four Stanley Cups (1947, 1948, 1949 and 1951). While there, he played with Syl Apps and Bill Ezinicki and was often given orders to check opponents like Gordie Howe and Rocket Richard. Watson finished his career with the Chicago Blackhawks during the mid-'50s, when Detroit was enjoying their glory years.

In 1948-49, Harry Watson was runner-up for the Lady Byng Trophy, going the entire season without a penalty minute. Even though he was seldom penalized, at 6'-1", 203 pounds, Watson was no wimp, and is well-remembered for a fight in which he broke Murray Henderson's nose with one punch!

"I was just a guy that tried to look after my own position and run up and down the wing and try to do the best I could," says Watson. "I always got criticized because I wasn't rougher. Being a bigger guy, I never got into too many scraps or anything like that. Every club I ever played on, they gave me a bad time because I wasn't into the fights and everything."

After hanging up his NHL skates, Watson served as player-coach of the AHL Buffalo Bisons. When he finally retired from active play altogether, he was the last member of the New York Americans still playing. He later turned to coaching junior hockey, and in 1963 coached the Windsor Bulldogs to the Allan Cup.

Besides his direct involvement with the game, Watson has been associated with many charitable events and organizations such as the March of Dimes, Timmy Tyke, and the Markham Arthritis Society. He also served as both general manager and public relations director of Toronto's Tam O'Shanter Summer Hockey School, which at one time was the largest of its kind in North America. "We ran hockey schools for quite a few years and then I got into sales, which I am still doing," he says when asked about his current endeavors. "[I] have been into selling pricing machines with Pri-Mark ... [the] metal pricing guns that you see the kids in the grocery store punching out labels with."

WALLY CROSSMAN

Born in Montreal, Quebec, in 1910, Wally Crossman is a locker room attendant at Joe Louis Arena. He came to Mt. Clemens, Michigan, and eventually Detroit, with his family when they moved to the area. Although he never played for the Red Wings, Crossman is a fixture in the team's history. He has been associated with the club in one way or another since the Detroit Olympia was constructed. In the February 12, 1996 issue of *Michigan Hockey Magazine*, in an article by Dave Garr, he said: "There was this enormous hole in the ground where they were putting in the basement. I would nose around there almost every day to see how they were coming along. It was really exciting to watch."

Crossman hung around the Olympia after it was built, becoming a rink rat of sorts. "I hung around the Olympia. I didn't live far from there and I used to go down there and hang around while they practiced and everything. I just kind of eased myself in there. I hung around that old rink and they eventually asked me if I wanted to come in and be a [stick] boy. So I was the [stick] boy until the assistant trainer was called into service. They promised him a better job with the club after he got out of service, but when he came back he never got it. So he quit. [His name was] Ernie Burton. Then they asked me to stay on and help the club out."

Since that time, Crossman has been in the Red Wings' locker room for decades, seeing hundreds of Detroit's best hockey players pass through its door. From Jack Adams and Gordie Howe to Scotty Bowman and today's players, Crossman has seen it all. He is also the man who opens the door for players as they exit and enter the playing surface. In the same *Michigan Hockey Magazine* article, he said: "A guy really has to be alert behind the gate nowadays because those guys move so darn fast. Some of those guys are so darn anxious to get on the ice that they open the door themselves. If I'm not watching, they will swing the door open so fast that I can't catch it and I get a charley horse from it hitting me so hard."

Crossman attempted to retire his post recently. However, players, coaches and fellow employees convinced him to remain on duty. It is an honor to have Crossman on board at the Joe Louis Arena. He remains a true hockey fixture in Detroit Red Wings hockey!

A young Gordie Howe (top row, #13), poses for a team picture. JRK Photo.

CHAPTER SEVEN

GORDIE HOWE
THE MAN, THE MAGIC,
THE MILESTONES

GORDON (GORDIE) (MR. HOCKEY) (POWER) HOWE

Born on March 31, 1928, in Floral, Saskatchewan, Gordie Howe is, without a doubt, the most legendary hockey player to ever lace up the skates. He spent the majority of his amazing, 32-year professional hockey career playing for the Detroit Red Wings.

Several books, both authorized and unauthorized, and literally thousands of articles have been written about the famous Mr. Hockey. Both *Gordie–A Hockey Legend–An Unauthorized Biography* by Ray Macskimming, and *and...Howe!–An Authorized Autobiography* by Gordie and Colleen Howe with Tom DeLisle, are two current books that offer a wealth of details on the life of the man who wore the legendary number 9.

Between the covers of these books are many tales of the good and the bad things that have happened to Gordie Howe over the years. There are stories of struggles, hockey politics, pay inequities and private family life. These aspects of his life are not discussed here. This chapter outlines the great hockey career of Gordie Howe and provides a glimpse of the true greatness behind the name and the man who is Gordie Howe.

THE MAN

Gordie Howe was born in the wheat country of Western Canada. His mother gave birth to nine children. Howe's father, Ab, worked in the fields and for the city of Saskatoon to support his family.

In a *Sports Illustrated* article by E.M. Swift, Ab Howe, recalled that when Gordie was a boy, he viewed him as "clumsy and backward and bashful," and because of it, said he never thought Howe would amount to anything. In the same article, a piece of advice that the older Howe passed on to Gordie was revealed. Quite possibly, it may have been a guiding force throughout Howe's career. He said to Gordie: "Never take dirt from nobody, 'cause they'll keep throwing it at you." As the article points out, it was from his mother that he inherited his gentle side, and from Ab the mean side that came out on the ice when he was focused on his game.

As a child, Howe received his first pair of ice skates when a woman came to his family's door with a bag full of assorted items, which she was selling to buy milk for her children. Howe's mother bought the bag for $1, and when she emptied the sack, a pair of ice skates tumbled out onto the linoleum floor. Gordie took one and his sister Edna the other. One skate did not cut it for Gordie, however, and pretty soon he had them both on. It was on that cold day that he took his very first step toward hockey stardom.

Along the way, Gordie received a little motivation from a former NHL player. "Everything has a stroke of luck," he said in an article by Linda Solomon, which appeared in the *Detroit News*. "In my case, I saw a man driving in a great big convertible in the middle of the summer. It happened to be 'Sudden Death' Hill, a hockey player from Boston. I said, 'If that's what hockey can do for you, that's what I want.'"

As a youth, Howe practiced his hockey skills all year long. In the winter, he often skated on the regulation-sized rink in his neighbors' back yard, which belonged to Bert and Francis Hodges.

Howe played hockey in many pick-up games with other children, and for various different leagues and teams. Among them were different school teams, Kinsmen's peewee league teams, and a house league which was operated by the King George Athletic Club, which provided sporting activities for boys throughout the year. The King George School team on which Howe played won the league championship in 1941, 1942 and 1944. The latter season, Howe was the team's captain, and in 11 contests, they outscored their opponents 106-6. In 1942, a season in which he skated for both the school team and the Athletic Club, he made it to the provincial finals with the latter team.

After he developed into a recognizable player, many scouts were after Howe. He had already made one trip to the New York Rangers' training camp in Winnipeg before Detroit Scout Fred Pinkney, who at the time was also a timekeeper for the nearby Saskatoon Quakers, finally signed him. Pinkney had

In his only season with the Omaha Knights, Gordie Howe scored 22 goals and 44 points. JRK photo.

been watching Howe for some time. He gave Howe's father $100 to call him the evening before Gordie turned 16, when his rights could be officially secured.

Howe attended the Red Wings' training camp in Windsor, Ontario. He made the club, and Jack Adams signed him for $2,200, plus a $500 signing bonus. Howe went on to play for the Red Wings' number two farm team, the Omaha Knights of the U.S. Hockey League, which played its games at the Aksarben (Nebraska spelled backwards) arena. Along with Gordie Howe came Lefty Wilson and team captain Jimmy Skinner. In his first season there, Howe scored 22 goals and had 22 assists. Rather than being moved up to the organization's number one farm team, the Indianapolis Capitols, he made it to the big club the following season.

At first, Howe was a bit careless with his stick and didn't hesitate to mix it up with anyone. One memorable moment from his time at Omaha, recalled in an article by Milt Dunnell, had the players lined up for a scrimmage game. It was the Eastern vs. the

Western players. At the time, Tommy Ivan was the club's playing coach. A native of Ontario, he was an opponent of Howe's. Gordie ended up cutting him, requiring Ivan to receive six stitches.

In a *Sports Illustrated* article by E.M. Swift, Gordie's father recalled Howe's early days:

When he joined the Wings, I told the wife, 'I hope that boy never fights. He's got a blow that can kill a man.' He's both-handed, you know, like me. Worked on my crew two summers. Best man I ever had. Had him on the mixer with his brother Vern. He could pick up a cement bag in either hand—90 pounds. Weren't the weight so much as you couldn't get a grip on them, the sacks were packed so tight. He'd pick them right up by the middle. His brother played out in two days, but Gordon, he liked that mixer. He was strong, all right. Fella came with some counterweights for a dragline in the back of his truck, and Gordon says, 'Mr. Driscoll, you want these off?' Well, it weren't a one-man job, but Driscoll, he winks at me and says, 'Sure, Gord, right over here.' Lifted 'em out of there like it was nothin'. Driscoll like to fall over. Oh, he was strong.

When Howe made it to the Red Wings, he was still tough. In the same *Sports Illustrated* article by E.M. Swift, Howe's father said: "That first night he played for Detroit, I put my feet up by the radio and listened to the game, and pretty soon Gordon was in a fight, all right. And he got in another. The wife was terrible upset, worrying he might kill someone. He got in fights about the first ten games, and after a bit Mr. Adams calls him in and asks, 'Howe, you think you've got to beat up the entire league, player by player?' Gordon started to play hockey then. Mr. Adams, he treated Gordon like a son."

After moving up to the Red Wings, Howe's salary doubled to $5,000, but his contract included a clause that if he was sent to Indianapolis, his pay would be cut accordingly. This scared Howe, and for many years he was afraid of losing his job to another player. In the article by E.M. Swift, Ted Lindsay recalled: "He was always worried he couldn't make the team. Every year he was tough on left wingers in training camp because of it. He lived to play the game, and nobody was going to get the job away from him. Genuinely, sincerely, he felt he had to worry about his

position. He would say, 'Gee, I hope I make the team.' Or, 'That guy isn't going to get my job. He'll do it over my body.'"

In Detroit, Gordie was teamed up with Sid Abel and Ted Lindsay on the famed Production Line. Alex Delvecchio would later replace Abel. The line was an awesome offensive unit for the Red Wings during the 1950s. Howe became quite a goal scorer and was a key component of the Production Line. Howe's former coach Tommy Ivan once said that he didn't think Howe was fully aware of his puck wizardry and that he could have scored even more goals. Ivan said that because of Lindsay and Abel's incredible abilities, of which Howe was aware, Gordie often passed the puck to them.

During Howe's career, he developed an intense rivalry with Rocket Richard of the Montreal Canadiens, and it was often debated which of the two was the "greatest player." Former Red Wings trainer Lefty Wilson commented on the rivalry, explaining: "They were tough competitors. We never liked to lose to them and they never liked to lose to us, but that was what made big games, you know. [They were] great, great guys. But they were the big shots and they lived up to [it], no ifs, ands or buts. But they weren't overbearing or anything else like that. They just played the game and lived the life they wanted to live and that's the way it was."

Former Red Wing Harry Watson, who played against Howe in later years, checked many of the league's best players during his career. He compared Howe with the Rocket. "The other guy was the Rocket. You know, I checked him, or supposedly checked him, for about 10 or 12 years, and he was an exciting hockey player. From the blue line in, I guess, he was one of the best, and it was always an exciting spectacle when he scored a goal, where as Gordie Howe would go in and score a goal and he would be back at center ice before the referee was to drop the puck for the game to continue."

Despite all of the fame that Howe gained while with the Red Wings, he was not conceited, or stuck on the old adage that on the ice things were his way or no way. In an article by Shirley Fischler, which appeared in the *1986 NHL All-Star Game* program, Howe recalled an incident which exemplifies this statement. He said: "I've forgotten which All-Star game it was, or even, I have to admit, which centerman it was. But he was a kid and it was his first All-Star game. When I went up to him and asked, 'How do you want me to play?' I thought the kid was going to faint. He just sort of stood there goggling at me. But it was a perfectly logical question—lots of guys play different kinds of hockey at center ice and I had just spent about 18 years playing with Alex Delvecchio."

Howe remained with the Red Wings until 1970-71, after playing in three decades for them. At the time, in a September 9, 1971 *Toronto Telegram* article, he said: "I'm 43 and it's a young man's game ... [I'm having] some wrist trouble and my legs aren't what they used to be. One thing I've stuck to pretty much throughout my career, when it becomes more work than fun, I've had it. I've found practice extremely difficult and I just don't get up for a game anymore. And it was my mother's wish before she died that I get it (retirement) out of the way before I got seriously hurt."

In 1973-74, Howe returned to professional hockey when he signed a four-year deal with the New England Whalers for $1 million. He joined his sons Mark and Marty, and thus formed the very first same-team, father-son combination in professional hockey. Howe played in Houston until the team folded in 1976-77 and then played for the New England Whalers, who were assimilated into the NHL in 1979-80, Howe's last season of professional ice hockey.

THE MAGIC

To describe Gordie Howe accurately, it is necessary to hear the comments of the many players, coaches and friends that have been associated with him throughout the years.

"Howe is by far the greatest player I have ever seen, so it's hard to be surprised by anything he does. Yet, you never get the feeling you have seen it all. One of the things which never ceases to surprise me is his anticipation. It's like playing chess with a guy who is always two moves ahead of you. Gordie will put himself in a certain position and you won't know why. A couple of seconds later, you realize he's in the

proper place, now that the play has developed. ... You never hear him beef. He has a way of expressing himself, but he is not a complainer. As his center for the last 12 or 13 years, the best way I could sum up my feelings would be this: When you pass the puck to Gordie Howe, you know that the previous effort which went into the play is not going to be wasted. ... Gordie is not a dirty player. He is a rough player. Don't forget the number of people over the years, who tried to haul him back to their own level. [At the age of 43] there are still players willing to challenge him."
-Former Detroit Red Wing Alex Delvecchio, April 1, 1971 *Toronto Star*

"Gordie to this day doesn't have an enemy because of the way he treated people. He was wonderful around the rink. Hell, there was a guy called Jessie who used to lug beer cases around the Olympia. He's at Joe Louis [Arena] now. He and Gordie were the best of friends. I mean here's a guy that Gordie had no reason to even look at him, but Gordie was that type of guy. In fact, that shows what a family it was [at the Detroit Olympia]."
-Former Detroit Red Wings PR Director Elliott Trumbull

"Gordie was ambidextrous, he could shoot either left or right. He was a great team player,"
-Former Detroit Red Wing Harry Lumley

"Gordie Howe was the greatest hockey player, as far as I am concerned, that I ever played against. Everybody said what a dirty hockey player he was, but I never found him that way. He was an honest hockey player, and he worked hard. All of the guys that complained about him were the guys that took shots at him or speared him or gave him an elbow and he gave it back to you double. I never really had any problem with Gordie. Maybe it's because we are both from Saskatoon, I don't know."
-Former Detroit Red Wing Harry Watson

Opposite: With the Red Wings, Gordie Howe developed into the greatest player of all time.

"I wasn't with the club in the 1949-50 series when he got hit in the head there, but [from a physical standpoint] he never changed from day one until he quit, as far as I'm concerned. He was always nice, didn't get into any trouble. He would have a couple of beers, but nothing more, and just went along with the ride. He wasn't a big shot.

"Cripes, you couldn't put new equipment on him. Oh, cripes. My son broke his skates in, Sid Abel broke his gloves in, [Vic] Stasiuk wore his new personal shoes till he broke them in and then Howe would wear them. He never liked anything new. Delvecchio was the same way. Now you get these rookies coming in, 'I want a new this, new that, new this, new that,' because they are in the big league and they [think they are] big shots.

"He'd stay an hour-and-a-half after the game signing autographs. He was just a great kid. I'll tell you what he made the first year him and I signed. He made $2,300. I made $2,100. We thought we were millionaires! Can you imagine what he would be making today if he was a rookie? Oh, cripes. Yet the Rangers had him and they let him go. Well, they sent him back home. He was too young, probably, but they had him and then we picked him up from Saskatoon."
-Former Detroit Red Wings trainer Lefty Wilson

"I think Gordie was the best hockey player all around that I have ever seen. He could score goals, as he proved, and he was a good passer, he back-checked, he came back, every time you looked up he was back in your own end. He was rough and tough in the corners. To me he was a complete hockey player. Any facet of the game that you want to mention, he was right up there, 1, 2, 3. Some of the guys, your stars today, don't back-check too good and they are not too rough in the corners and stuff, but the Big Guy did everything well.

"I played against him for 15 years, so I got a taste of him in a lot of games. He was big and strong, too. He had everything that you want in a hockey player, everything. If you played it straight-up with Gordie, he played it straight-up with you, and that's part of the game. I think we respected each other and if he had his head down, I would get a piece of him and vice versa. In the corners, you know, you took him out rough and tough, no stick work or anything like that, and he accepted that. He'd do the same thing to you. But if you ever got the stick up, or cross checked him, or hooked him in the mouth, or whatever, you had better look out because he was going to get you back sometime. I have seen him wait game after game to get somebody that had done something to him. He had a good memory.

"[Off the ice, Gordie Howe was a] very humble individual. If you didn't know it was Gordie Howe, you wouldn't know him. He just was not a bragger or anything like that, just very easy going. But that changed when he got on the ice, especially if you elbowed him or gave him the stick or something. You had better watch out because he was going to get you back. He was a tremendous competitor, tremendous. Came to play every night. Even hurt he'd come to play good. Oh, I saw him play in so many good games, you know, especially when you are behind one or two goals, he seemed like he just wanted to take over and get the score even or go ahead. Like I said, he was a tremendous competitor."

-Former Detroit Red Wing Bill Gadsby

"[Gordie Howe was the] closest to being the perfect hockey player as I've ever seen. One night in Boston we lost and Gordie came out of the dressing room and said, 'Gee, Jimmy, I had a bad night. What am I doing wrong?' What can I say to him? This is my first year, too. I told him he wasn't doing anything wrong, that he just had a bad day. But that's the kind of person he was. He had a bad game and he was concerned about it. He wasn't too proud to ask for help. That's why he was so great."

-Former Detroit Red Wings coach Jimmy Skinner, November 26, 1976 *Detroit News*

"I knew Gordie and all of his kids. I sharpened their skates for them when they were little tots.

Gordie Howe in Detroit's home jersey.

Gordie is a very nice gentleman. He was equal with everybody, no matter who [they were]."

-Long-time Detroit Red Wings' locker room attendant Wally Crossman

I remember when I first started to play against him, he was like a [mysterious] guy. I had heard about him, but I had never seen him. A lot of guys used to say he used to have 15 feet around him, that's why he's so good. Give a guy 15 feet with that kind of ability and he can do anything with the puck. The way I played him and he played me, I guess we never had an encounter. I think once we almost brought our sticks up. I played hard against him, but I didn't play dirty. If you didn't play dirty against Gordie, everything was OK. Of course you always had to watch. He didn't forget.

He was the type of guy who could beat you, you know what I mean, like 'beat you,' meaning scoring a goal even though you tried your best. When a guy of 180

pounds tries his best and he's good, then a guy 200 pounds does his best and he's good, he's going to beat you once in a while. I saw him score some great goals on Glenn Hall, our goaltender [in Chicago].

I wasn't there, [but] I tell the story where Gordie and Lou Fontinato [had a fight]. Lou was a tough guy, and the game was on TV on a Saturday afternoon across the United States. Big Lou, Leapin' Louie they used to call him, was going after Gordie and Gordie figured, 'Well, I'd better take care of him.' Nobody would drop their gloves too often with Gordie. Word was round that he was a good fighter. But Louie dropped his gloves and

before they hit the ice, apparently that's the story I hear, Louie's nose was in his ear almost. You know, one-two punch. Also, I think Gordie had cut his ear with a stick. But any way, Lou got five minutes for fighting and so did Gordie, but Gordie got an extra five minutes for injuries to an Italian! That's just a joke about it, but apparently he really cleaned Lou Fontinato's clock. I've heard of how tough he was, but in all the games we played, I never saw him in a tussle. I saw him score some great goals. I saw him score a goal switching hands, he could shoot left or right.

-Former Chicago Blackhawks defenseman
Pierre Pilote

A young Gordie Howe & Ted Lindsay battle Teeder Kennedy and the Toronto Maple Leafs on January 1, 1947. Imperial Oil-Turofsky/Hockey Hall of Fame Photo.

THE MILESTONES

1946-1947

- Scores first NHL goal on October 6, 1946 in a 3-3 tie against the Toronto Maple Leafs. Opposing goaltender was Turk Broda, who had come up through Detroit's Farm System.

1947-1948

- Becomes a member of the famed Production Line, with teammates Ted Lindsay (left wing) and Sid Abel (center).

1948-1949

- Leads NHL in playoff goals (8) and playoff points (11).
- Named to the second All-Star team for the first time in his career.

1949-1950

- Plays on first Stanley Cup championship team with the Detroit Red Wings, who won the Cup on April 23, 1950.
- Is severely injured in playoff game against Toronto, and undergoes emergency brain operation at Detroit's Harper Hospital.
- Members of the "Production Line" of Lindsay, Abel and Howe finishes first, second, and third in NHL scoring, with 78, 69, and 68 points respectively.
- Named to the second All-Star team.

1950-1951

- Sets NHL record for most points in one season with 86.
- Leads NHL in both goals (43) & assists (43).
- Wins first Art Ross Trophy for most points in a season.
- Named to the first All-Star team for the first time.
- Scores his 100th NHL goal on February 17, 1951 (Rocket Richard Night) in a 2-1 win over the Montreal Canadiens. Goalie Gerry McNeil is in the nets for Montreal.

1951-1952

- Ties NHL season point record set previous season (86).
- Leads NHL in goals (46).
- Plays on second Stanley Cup championship team.
- Tied for lead with most playoff assists (5) and points (7).
- Wins second Art Ross Trophy.
- Wins first Hart Memorial Trophy as NHL MVP.
- Named to the first All-Star team for the second time.

1952-1953

- Sets new NHL season point record with 95.
- Leads NHL in goals (49).
- Leads NHL in assists (46).
- Wins third Art Ross Trophy.
- Wins second Hart Memorial Trophy as NHL MVP.
- Named to first All-Star team for the third time.
- Scores 200th career goal in Chicago against Al Rollins on February 13, 1953.

1953-1954

- Leads NHL in points (81).
- Leads NHL in assists (48).
- Plays on third Stanley Cup championship team.
- Wins fourth Art Ross Trophy.
- Scores the fastest goal ever scored from the start of a playoff game in 9 seconds.
- Named to the first All-Star team for the fourth time.

1954-1955

- Sets NHL playoff point record (20).
- Sets record for points in a final playoff series (12).
- Leads NHL in playoff goals (9).
- Plays on fourth (and last) Stanley Cup championship team. Scores the deciding goal in 3-1 win over the Montreal Canadiens on April 14, 1955.

1955-1956

- On February 7, 1956, becomes third man in NHL history to score 300 goals.
- Named to second All-Star team for the third time.

1956-1957

- Leads NHL in goals (44).
- Leads NHL in points (89).
- Wins third Hart Memorial Trophy.
- Wins fifth Art Ross Trophy.
- Named to first All-Star team for the fifth time.

1957-1958

- Sets NHL record for career assists (440).
- Wins fourth Hart Memorial Trophy.
- Named to first All-Star team for the sixth time.

THE MILESTONES

1958-1959

- Ties Maurice "Rocket" Richard's record for number of 30-goal seasons (9).
- Named to the second All-Star team for the fourth time.

1959-1960

- Sets NHL record for career points (977).
- Wins unprecedented fifth Hart Memorial Trophy.
- Named to first All-Star team for the seventh time.

1960-1961

- Sets record for career playoff assists (64).
- Ties for lead in playoff points (15).
- Named to the second All-Star team for the fifth time.
- Scores 1,000th NHL point in his 938th game, a 2-0 win over the Toronto Maple Leafs, on November 20, 1960.
- Becomes the NHL's leading scorer on December 1, 1960, by scoring his 1,092nd point.

1961-1962

- Plays in 1,000th NHL game on November 25, 1961.
- Sets record for number of NHL games played with 1,050.
- Sets the record for most 30-goal seasons (10).
- Named to the second All-Star team for the sixth time.
- Scores 500th career goal against Gump Worsley in a 3-2 loss to the New York Rangers on March 14, 1962.

1962-1963

- Leads NHL in goals (38).
- Leads NHL in points (86).
- Tied for lead in playoff points (16).
- Wins sixth Art Ross Trophy.
- Wins sixth Hart Memorial Trophy.
- Named to first All-Star team for the eighth time.
- Ties Maurice "Rocket" Richard for total All-Star team selections (14).

1963-1964

- Breaks Maurice "Rocket" Richard's record of 544 career goals (566).
- Breaks Maurice "Rocket" Richard's record of 126 playoff points (140).
- Leads NHL in playoff goals (9).
- Leads NHL in playoff points (19).
- Named to second All-Star team for the seventh time.
- Sets NHL record for All-Star team selections (15).

1964-1965

- Named to second All-Star team for the eighth time.
- Ties record for career assists in All-Star games (7).
- Ties record for points in an All-Star game (4).

1965-1966

- Ties record for consecutive NHL seasons (20).
- Named to the first All-Star team for the ninth time.

1966-1967

- Sets record for consecutive NHL seasons (21).
- Wins Lester Patrick Trophy for outstanding service to hockey in the United States.
- Named to the second All-Star team for the ninth time.

1967-1968

- Ties Doug Harvey's record by being named to the first All-Star team for the tenth time.
- Scores 700th NHL goal on December 4, 1968.

1968-1969

- Sets record for assists by a right winger (59).
- Sets record for points by a right winger (103).
- With his 11th nomination, sets record for number of times named to the first All-Star team.
- Scores 100th point of the 1968-69 season in the 76th game.
- Ends up scoring a career-high 103 points during the regular season.

1969-1970

- Sets record for 30-or-more goal seasons (14).
- Sets record for career playoff assists (91).
- Sets record for career playoff points (158).
- With his 12th nomination, breaks own record for being named to the first All-Star team.

1970-1971

- Extends record of consecutive 20-or-more goal seasons (22).
- Retires from NHL with career records for goals (786), assists (1,023), and points (1,809).
- Awarded the Order of Canada, that nation's highest honor, in recognition of his personal accomplishments as a citizen and sportsman.

THE MILESTONES

1971-1972

- Elected to the Hockey Hall of Fame on June 7, 1972.
- Number 9 is retired by the Detroit Red Wings. Owner Bruce Norris announces $1,500 annual scholarship in Howe's name. Vice President Spiro Agnew reads letter of congratulations to Howe from President Nixon.

1972-1973

- On June 19, 1973, signs four-year, $1 million contract with the Houston Aeros of the new World Hockey Association. Howe joins sons Mark and Marty, also with Houston, to make the first father-son combination to play on the same team in professional, major-league hockey.

1973-1974

- Leads WHA in assists.
- Named WHA's most valuable player for the first time.
- Named to the WHA first All-Star team for the first time.

1974-1975

- Named to WHA first All-Star team for the second time.

1976-1977

- Along with sons Mark and Marty, signs long-term contract to play for the New England Whalers of the WHA on May 23, 1977.

1977-1978

- Scores 1,000th career pro-hockey goal on December 7, 1977 in a game against the Birmingham (Alabama) Bulls. In goal for Birmingham was John Garrett.
- Becomes the first 50-year old to play professional hockey on March 29, 1978.

1979-1980

- After an eight-year absence from the league, returns to the NHL with the expansion Hartford Whalers on October 11, 1979.
- On January 3, 1980, becomes the first professional hockey player to play in five decades.
- Scores 800th regular-season NHL goal on February 29, 1980, in a game against St. Louis. In goal for St. Louis was Mike Liuf.
- Plays final NHL game on April 6, 1980 (1,767th) at Hartford against the Detroit Red Wings, scoring his 801st career goal against goalie Rogie Vachon.
- On June 4, 1980, retires at the age of 52 after 33 years as a professional hockey player. Becomes director of development for the Hartford Whalers.
- Retires with a combined (WHA & NHL) 975 goals, 1,383 assists, and 2,358 points.

OTHER HONORS

- In 1971, named "Hockey Player of the last Quarter Century" by Sport Magazine.
- In 1988, named "Hockey Player of the Decade" by The Hockey News.
- Member of the United States Hockey, Red Wings, and Omaha Halls of Fame.
- In 1974, became part of first father-son combination to play in international competition in the Canada-Russia series.

The famed "Production Line" of Gordie Howe, Sid Abel and Ted Lindsay.

CHAPTER EIGHT

THE IMMORTALS

TERRANCE GORDON (TERRY)(UKE) SAWCHUK

Born: December 28, 1929, Winnipeg, Manitoba
Position: Goaltender
Died: May 31, 1970, New York, NY
Junior
- Winnipeg Rangers: 1945-46
- Galt Red Wings (junior division): 1946-47

Minor Pro
- Omaha (USHL): 1947-48
- Indianapolis Capitols (AHL)

Detroit Red Wings
- 1949-50 to 1954-55; 1957-58 to 1963-64; 1968-69

Best NHL Season
- 1951-52: 4200 MIN; 1.90 GAA; 12 SO

Career Awards & Honors
- Hockey Hall of Fame: 1971
- Michigan Sports Hall of Fame
- Red Wings Hall of Fame: 1971
- First All-Star Team: 1951, '52, '53
- Second All-Star Team: 1954, '55, '59, '63
- NHL All Star Games: 1950-56, '59, '63, '64, '68
- Vezina Trophy: 1951-52, 1952-53, 1954-55, 1964-65 (Toronto: with Johnny Bower)
- Calder Trophy: 1950-51

Career Milestones
- Member of five championship teams.
- Member of four Stanley Cup teams (Detroit: 1950-51, 1952-53, 1954-55 and Toronto: 1966-67).
- Sawchuk played in more seasons and more games than any other NHL netminder.
- First on Detroit Red Wings' All-Time Goaltenders' List.
- Leads Detroit Red Wing goalies in:
  -Shutouts in one season (12 in 1951-52, 1953-54, 1954-55).
  -Wins in one season (44 in 1950-51, 1951-52), (40 in 1954-55).
  -Career shutouts: 85
  -Games by a goalie: 734
  -Most shutouts by a rookie goalie: 11 (1950-51).
  -Most minutes by a rookie goalie: 4200 (1950-51) (shares record with Glenn Hall).
  -Most consecutive shutouts by a goalie (three in 1954).

Trades
- Traded to Boston in 1955 with Marcel Bonin, Lorne Davis and Vic Stasiuk for Gilles Boisvert, Real Chevrefils, Norm Corcoran, Warren Godfrey and Ed Sanford.
- Traded to Detroit from Boston in 1957 for John Bucyk and cash.
- Traded to Detroit from Los Angeles in 1968 for Jimmy Peters, Jr.

BIOGRAPHY

As a youth, Terry Sawchuk was a center before he started playing goal. He was selected to play between the pipes because he had goalie pads at home. The pads had belonged to his brother, who died from a heart condition sometime before. In a Hockey Hall of Fame article, Sawchuk said: "The pads were there where I could always look at them . . . the day they put me in the net I had a good game. I've been there ever since."

Sawchuk played his first organized hockey in 1942-43. In three successive seasons, he played on the Bantam, Midget and Juvenile teams of the Winnipeg Red Wings. In 1947-48, before breaking into the NHL, Sawchuk played for Omaha of the U.S. League, winning the Outstanding Rookie Award, which came with an engraved gold puck and $250. In 1948-49, he played for Indianapolis of the American League, winning the Dudley "Red" Garrett Award as the Outstanding Rookie of the Year. Upon his emergence into the NHL, he once again received top rookie honors when he won the

Calder Trophy in 1950-51. He became the first player to ever win such honors in three professional hockey leagues.

Terry Sawchuk was a naturally gifted athlete. In Winnipeg, he had established a reputation for his baseball skills and was an excellent hitter. The St. Louis Cardinals baseball club made him an offer to play minor league baseball in their organization, but Sawchuk rejected it. He decided to pursue a career in hockey, where he felt his talents would be best realized.

According to an article by Arnold Irish, which appeared in the February, 1974 *St. Louis Blues Program*, while trying out in the summer of 1949, Chet Johnson, a former pitcher with the St. Louis Browns, told him: "Listen, kid, don't be scared of anything. I've had it pretty tough in my day, and I've been pushed around a lot. But let me tell you something, when I go out there on that mound, I tell myself I'm the best pitcher alive. You do the same and you'll be okay." Sawchuk never forgot those words the rest of his hockey career.

It appeared as if Sawchuk would never make it to

the Detroit Red Wings, who had a solid goalie in Harry Lumley. However, the opportunity to prove himself came when Lumley sustained an ankle injury. After allowing 16 goals in seven games and posting a shutout in a game against the New York Rangers, Sawchuk made a lasting impression. Later, when making a deal with Chicago, the Blackhawks insisted that Detroit throw in a goalie. Reportedly, the Red Wings offered Sawchuk, hoping that Chicago would instead demand Lumley.

Whatever the case, Lumley ended up in Chicago, and Sawchuk was in goal for Detroit, leading the NHL with 11 shutouts and a 1.98 GAA during his Calder-winning rookie season. Sawchuk not only made a lasting impression on the Red Wings, but on the game itself. In response to the screened shot coming into prominence, he brought the crouch-position of net-minding to the game for good.

Sawchuk is the only goalie in NHL history to record more than 100 shutouts (103). His first step towards this milestone occurred on January 18, 1964, when he blanked the Habs 2-0 in the Montreal Forum, surpassing the former record of 94 set by George Hainsworth, who played for Toronto and Montreal. On March 4, 1967, while playing for Toronto, Sawchuk shut out the Blackhawks 3-0 at Maple Leaf Gardens, recording his 100th shutout. Nearly three years later while playing goal for the New York Rangers, he recorded his final shutout in a 6-0 spanking of the Pittsburgh Penguins.

Sawchuk played on many successful teams during his career. However, out of the 106 Stanley Cup playoff games in which he played, the 1952 series is perhaps the most memorable. In that series, Sawchuk was outstanding, helping his Red Wing teammates win the Cup in eight games and posting a .62 goals-against-average. During the series, he posted a record-tying four shutouts.

In 1971, Sawchuk was the third goalie and 26th member inducted into the Red Wings Hall of Fame. His number one was retired by the team on March 6, 1994, and Sawchuk's family was able to hoist it up into the rafters at Joe Louis Arena, next to the

Opposite: Terry Sawchuk holds the New York Rangers at bay.

A young Terry Sawchuk, who went on to play in more games and more seasons than any other NHL netminder.

numbers of Gordie Howe, Sid Abel, Alex Delvecchio and Ted Lindsay.

Playing goal was stressful in itself, especially during a time when netminders did not wear masks. However, Sawchuk's life was filled with stress and adversity from a very young age. He lost his brother to a heart condition at age ten. Five years later, his father fell from a scaffold and became disabled. The accident placed the burden of supporting a family on Terry. Besides undergoing an emergency appendectomy, suffering a ruptured spleen and a bowel obstruction and contracting mononucleosis, Sawchuk was sidetracked by an almost-fatal car crash in which he suffered a collapsed lung.

One injury in particular plagued Sawchuk throughout his lifetime. At the age of 12, he injured his elbow in a football game and would later undergo operations to remove loose bone fragments. There were days that he could not raise a glass of water to his lips using his right hand. This helps

explain why Sawchuk's weakness was a shoulder-high shot on the right side.

Such were the setbacks he experienced away from the game. On the ice, the list continues. Sawchuk was decorated with over 400 stitches on his face before donning a mask in 1962. While playing in the minors for Omaha, his eyesight was saved after a sticking incident only because a very skillful eye surgeon happened to be in town. He broke bones and suffered concussions on more than a few occasions and had his left hand skated over, severing all of the tendons and making it impossible for him to ever make a fist. While playing for Boston, he suffered a nervous collapse. In 1966, he had surgery on his back to repair two ruptured vertebrae and a swayback condition that caused him various smaller problems such as headaches. He would also suffer with weight problems throughout his career. Early in his career, he had a hard time keeping it off, and later, a hard time keeping it on after Jack Adams initially ordered him to lose weight.

Sawchuk was a loner and, according to many people, often appeared unhappy. In later years, he struggled with a drinking problem that may have contributed to his untimely death. Considering all of the setbacks and hardships in his life, his unhappiness is understandable. However, he was a truly incredible individual to establish himself as the very best in the game.

In an article by Frank Orr, Gordie Howe described Sawchuk as "the best goalie I ever saw" and "everything that a goalie should be." "Terry simply hated to give up goals and it bothered him when he did," said Howe. "If many other goalies got bombed in the game, they went out after the game and got bombed themselves and forgot about it. Not the Uke. He would brood about a loss or a bad goal for days."

"I was his roommate on the road for many years and I never did quite figure the Uke out," said Marcel Pronovost in an article by Frank Orr. "When we woke up in the morning, I would say good morning to him in both French and English. If he answered, I knew we would talk at least a little that day. But if he didn't reply, which was most days, we didn't speak the entire day." In a July, 1970 article that appeared in *The Hockey News*, an anonymous Toronto Maple Leaf player said: "Ukey was in Toronto for three years and never made what you'd call a friend. The only one was Marcel Pronovost who'd been with him in the good days at Detroit."

The 1950s were a tremendously successful decade for the Detroit Red Wings. Sawchuk was largely responsible for that success, especially during the playoffs. Looking back on his contributions in John DeVaney and Burt Goldblatt's book *The Stanley Cup*, former Red Wings defenseman Bob Goldham said: "The key guy for us was Sawchuk. We called him Ukey—he was a Ukrainian boy. I played against all the great ones . . . Bill Durnan, Frankie Brimsek, Charlie Rayner . . . and Ukey was the greatest goaltender who ever lived. We could always count on him to come up with the big save. When I look back on those Stanley Cup series, what I remember is Ukey making one big save after another."

In the same book, Goldham commented more on Sawchuk as a person. "I roomed with him. He was a

Opposite: Gordie Howe considered Terry Sawchuk the best goalie he ever saw.

Terry Sawchuk was a member of five championship teams and four Stanley Cup teams during his NHL career.

tough guy to live with. Like all great athletes, his concentration on his job was so great that he ignored a lot of the other things. All he ever wanted to do was to be the greatest goaltender there ever was. He had a bad arm. They used to take bone chips out every year, and he used to put them in a bottle and save them."

Terry Sawchuk died in New York City on May 31, 1970, after sustaining internal injuries in an accident. The facts surrounding his death are still somewhat unclear and often debated. According to a published newspaper account in the June 9, 1970 *Toronto Globe and Mail*, on April 29, Sawchuk and roommate Ron Stewart of the New York Rangers were drinking at the E&J Pub, then a popular Rangers

hangout in Long Beach, New York. They were arguing over household responsibilities at the beachfront residence they shared at 58 Bay Street, as their lease was nearing expiration. A shoving match developed at the pub and, after the two were thrown out, it continued at their home in the presence of two witnesses: Rosemary Sasso, a friend of Stewart's who was a Canadian nurse, and Sawchuk's close friend Benjamin Weiner of Long Beach. Reportedly, Sawchuk pushed Stewart to the ground and Weiner attempted to restrain Sawchuk. However, the two of them fell onto Stewart when Weiner accidentally tripped on a barbecue grill. It was in this way that Sawchuk somehow sustained a pulmonary embolism.

Both this and an earlier report in the *Montreal Gazette* say that while the witnesses present at both the pub and beachfront home denied there ever being a punch thrown, the doctor who found Sawchuk pale, in pain and with low blood pressure had a different story. In the June 4, 1970 issue of the *Montreal Gazette*, Dr. Denis F. Nicholson of Long Beach said that Sawchuk told him he had both started and finished the fight. "Terry told me that Stewart had been bugging him all year, and he had gotten fed up," explained the doctor. He quoted Sawchuk as saying: "I punched him (Stewart) and knocked him down. They kicked us out of the bar and I hit him again. — I just kept knocking him down. At the house I tagged him again and knocked him down again. I jumped on him and fell on his knee."

In the same article, Stewart was baffled by Sawchuk's injury. In his first public statement, he said: "He fell on me, that's for sure. But all his lifetime Terry took much worse falls on the ice and he always bounced back ... and then he trips on top of me and suddenly his life is ended. It doesn't make sense. A fall like that, just like a thousand he's taken on that hard ice and nothing ever happened to him. And this thing happened, and Terry is gone. It's all like a bad dream when I look back now."

Regardless of the circumstances, a great goaltender had passed away before his time, leaving behind his former wife and seven children. In the same *Montreal Gazette* article, Stewart said: "You don't know how much Terry loved that woman. He was crazy about her. And his heart just melted over those kids of his."

SIDNEY GERALD (BOOT NOSE) ABEL

Born: February 22, 1918, Melville, Saskatchewan
Position: Center, Left wing

"I don't ever want to leave this game. I want to stay in hockey as long as I can." -Sid Abel, April 14, 1985 *Detroit News*

Junior Hockey
• Saskatoon Wesleys: 1936-37
Senior Hockey
• Flin Flon Bombers: 1937-38
Minor League Hockey
• Pittsburgh Hornets (AHL): 1938-39
• Indianapolis Capitols (AHL): 1939-40
Detroit Red Wings
• 1938-39 to 1942-43; 1945-46 to 1951-52
Best NHL Season
• 1949-50: 34 goals, 69 points
Career Awards & Honors
• Hart Memorial Trophy: 1948-49
• Michigan Sports Hall of Fame: 1967
• Red Wings Hall of Fame: 1944

• Hockey Hall of Fame: 1969
• First All-Star Team (Center): 1949, 1950
• Second All-Star Team (Center): 1951
• Second All-Star Team (Left Wing): 1942
• NHL All-Star Games: 1949-51
• Team Captain: 1945-46 to 1951-52
• Sid Abel Night: December 20, 1986, Joe Louis Arena
• Number 12 retired: Joe Louis Arena, 1994
Administrative:
"Coaching is tough on the nerves, but sitting up in the stands and watching the game is tougher." - Sid Abel (Red Wings News Release)

• Playing coach, Chicago Blackhawks: 1952-54
• Head coach, Detroit Red Wings: 1957-68; 1969-70
• General manager, Detroit Red Wings: 1962-71 (first 38 games)
• Head coach, St. Louis Blues: 1971-72
• General manager, St. Louis Blues: 1972-73
• General manager, Kansas City Scouts: 1973-75
• Head coach, Kansas City Scouts: 1975-76
• Coached NHL All-Stars: 1961, '63, '64, '67

BIOGRAPHY

A true hockey legend, Sid Abel was a smooth-skating play-maker for the Red Wings. With his fierce, competitive spirit, he established himself as a true leader in Detroit and was named team captain at the age of 24 in 1945-46. While in the Motor City, Abel centered two of hockey's most famous lines: the Liniment Line during the late 1940s with Don Grosso and Eddie Wares or Mud Bruneteau, and the legendary Production Line in the early 1950s with Gordie Howe and Ted Lindsay. His contributions on the ice resulted in Stanley Cups in 1942-43, 1949-50, and 1951-52. In each of those Stanley Cup-winning seasons and in both 1948-49 and 1950-51, he helped the Red Wings to first place finishes.

Mailman Goldie Smith, a part-time, Western Canada scout for the Red Wings, signed Abel to his first contract. However, before training camp (and before he mailed Abel's contract to Adams), Smith died. In an article by Bill Brennan, Abel recalled the incident, stating: "I didn't know about the missing contract and I was having a good camp when Jack Adams called me in and said 'Sid, we

don't have your contract.' By this time, I was hoping they wouldn't find the original because I figured I could sign again for more money. However, later when the executors were going through Goldie's papers they found my contract. That was it."

During the 1940s, Abel roomed with Alex Motter and Black Jack Stewart in a boarding house owned by Ma Shaw. In the April 14, 1985 issue of the *Detroit News*, he recalled those early days: "She didn't charge us much because she knew we didn't have much. We were rink rats. That's all we knew—hockey. Our whole lives were at the hockey rink. We'd get up early, eat breakfast and then go to the rink. We'd spend all day there. After the games they'd have free skating for the public, and we'd go back out on the ice and take part in that. Of course what we were doing was looking for girls."

During World War II, Abel continued to play hockey in Montreal with the RCAF (QSHL and MNDHL) and Montreal Car (MCHL). He also played in England for Jim Norris' Wembley

CASCIO

The "Production Line" of Gordie Howe, Sid Abel and Ted Lindsay.

Lions in 1945-46. Detroit was glad to have Abel back after the war, even if he did have to get back into NHL condition. Depicting Abel's value to the Red Wings, in the February 8, 1946 issue of the *Detroit News*, defenseman Jack Stewart said: "Just to have Sid in uniform and able to make a rush once in awhile is likely to be enough spark to get us through."

After playing, Abel took three seasons off and then turned to coaching when Jimmy Skinner became ill. As a coach, he had considerable success and his teams made it to the playoffs seven times in 11 years. A player's coach, he was behind the Red Wings' bench from January 2, 1957 until 1963, when he assumed the additional responsibilities of general manager, succeeding Jack Adams.

"I was lucky to start out playing in the NHL for a hell of a guy," says former Red Wing Gary Bergman. "Sid Abel is one of the finest gentlemen that ever came down the pike. He's a class act and you always knew where you stood with him and he'd do anything in the world to help you. He really was [a big influence on me]. He [was] definitely liked in the NHL. He was a first class guy. He was a first class guy because he was always straight with you. That was premier. Oh yes—good, bad or indifferent, you always knew and he was always fair and you can do

Opposite: Sid Abel once said that coaching was tough on the nerves, but that watching the game from the stands was tougher.

nothing but respect a guy like that."

In the April 28, 1966 issue of the *Windsor Star*, Abel revealed a bit of his coaching philosophy, explaining: "When you're forced to put on a uniform every day of the week it gets to be a chore. In my last few years, I practised only when I felt I needed it. I believe if you treat players right you get more out of them. I'd rather have a happy hockey player than one who hates my guts." While coach, he once made it his practice to utilize an advisory council composed of his most veteran players (Gordie Howe, Bill Gadsby, Marcel Pronovost and Alex Delvecchio) to discuss team problems and strategy.

Abel felt that coaching was much tougher than playing. In a *Detroit News* article, he once said: "As a player you can go out after a defeat and have a beer and a couple of guys will pat you on the back and tell you what a great fellow you are. As a coach you are more likely to find a couple of guys ready to knife you in the back. Coaching is a good way to lose friends."

As general manager, Abel earned the reputation of being a shrewd trader. Perhaps his brightest moment came when he acquired Frank Mahovlich, Pete Stemkowski and Carl Brewer late in the 1967-68 season in what many acclaim to be one of the greatest trades ever made. With the exception of the 1968-69 season when he was solely general manager, Abel fulfilled the dual role of general manager and coach until 1969-70 when Bruce Norris hired Ned Harkness.

Looking back on it all, in an article by Bill Brennan, Abel said: "Playing was the best ... it was the fun part of the career. Coaching was headaches, while being a general manager was not as bad ... being a player was the best."

Abel later ran a restaurant and pursued a career in sales for a heating firm. In addition to that, he stayed active with Red Wing hockey by doing commentary on both WJR radio and WXON television with Bruce Martyn. As a commentator, Abel had a reputation for his candid broadcasts, which on several occasions got him into hot water with team management. Abel went on the air long term in 1976-77. However, before that time, he gained experience working as a television analyst for five games with Budd Lynch in the early 1950s, before he departed for the Chicago Blackhawks.

Abel was named to the Hockey Hall of Fame in June of 1969, along with former team owner Bruce Norris. On April 29, 1995, his number 12 was retired to the rafters of Joe Louis arena. The gesture was an appropriate one to a man who has given so much to the sport of professional ice hockey in Detroit.

Today, Sid Abel is fighting a battle with cancer. He still follows the Red Wings' progress from his home in suburban Detroit. Abel's grandson, Brent, recently signed his first professional contract and will play goal for the St. Louis Blues.

ALEXANDER PETER (FATS) DELVECCHIO

Born: December 4, 1931, Fort William, Ontario
Position: Center, Left wing

"I've always wanted to make hockey my career. And I did. I wouldn't change a thing."
-Alex Delvecchio, November 24, 1974 *Detroit News*

Junior: Fort William Hurricanes
　　　　Oshawa Generals
Minor Pro: Indianapolis Capitols (AHL)
Detroit Red Wings: 1950-51 to 1973-74
Best NHL Season: 1968-69: 25 goals, 83 points
Career Awards & Honors
- Team Captain: 1962-74
- First All-Star Team: 1953 (center), 1959 (left wing)
- NHL All-Star Games: 1953-59, 1961-1966
- Hockey Hall of Fame: 1977
- Red Wings Hall of Fame: 1978
- Michigan Sports Hall of Fame
- Northwestern Ontario Sports Hall of Fame

- Alex Delvecchio Day: June, 1970
- Lady Byng Trophy: 1958-59, 1965-66, 1968-69
- Lester Patrick Trophy: 1973-74
Career Milestones
- Second only to Gordie Howe on Red Wings' Career Scoring Leader list.
- Number of All-Star Game appearances as a Red Wing (13) second only to Gordie Howe (22).
- Thirteen 20-or-more goal seasons.
- Played on six Prince of Wales Trophy-winning teams.
Administrative
- Head coach, Detroit Red Wings:
  -1973-74 (with Ted Garvin)
  -1974-75
  -1975-76 (with Doug Barkley)
  -1976-77 (with Larry Wilson)
- General manager, Detroit Red Wings:
  -1974-75 to 1975-76
  -1976-77 (with Ted Lindsay)

BIOGRAPHY

Alex Delvecchio spent 24 seasons playing center and left wing for the Detroit Red Wings. His distinguished career began in 1952 when, at the age of 20, he was called up from Indianapolis by Jack Adams. Delvecchio eventually replaced Sid Abel on the famed Production Line.

Former Detroit Red Wings coach Tommy Ivan commented on Delvecchio early in his career in an article by Marshall Dann, which appeared in the February 21, 1953 issue of *The Hockey News*. "Just watch how he keeps turning his head from side to side—swivel neck, we call him—while he's carrying the puck. He's always looking for a winger to pass off to. That may seem like a little thing, but how many players do you see that do that?" Because of his passing ability and the manner in which he kept his cool, Ivan dubbed Alex "our young old man" at the time.

Delvecchio went on to have an incredibly successful career with the Red Wings. A tough competitor, he was a terrific passer and skater and played a very clean brand of hockey. During his entire career, he amassed only 383 penalty minutes, never receiving more than 37 in any one season. A very durable athlete, his most serious injury occurred in 1956-57 when he hurt his ankle, causing him to miss 22 games. After that injury, he would miss only 21 more games during the remainder of his career. Altogether, he played in 1,549 regular season games and 121 playoff games.

Despite all of the honors awarded to him, Delvecchio was never one to seek the limelight. Many felt that he was often overlooked due to the high-caliber teammates with whom he played during his career, such as Gordie Howe. A Hockey Hall of Fame write up on Alex points out that he has "more goals than Ted Lindsay, more assists than Jean Beliveau [and] more points than Rocket

CASCIO

Richard. More of everything—except recognition."

"Delvecchio was one of the best passers I have ever seen in hockey," says former Red Wing Bill Gadsby. "He could just throw that puck to either wing and it was right on the tape all the time. Gordie Howe would tell you that. He would come to play every night. He was a real smoothy, Alex was. He didn't get in much trouble, but really got the job done. He played well with Howe and Lindsay—very, very well."

"Alex was just one of the smoothest players that I ever saw," says former Red Wing Gary Bergman. "He was one of the best centermen that ever played the game. He didn't have a great shot, he wasn't an exceptionally fast skater, but he was an exceptional passer. One thing you will notice that—certainly Gordie got his goals playing with him, but Gordie is going to create a lot of his own stuff—Alex's left wing always did well with him. Alex still had, even when he retired, he had that old stupid straight stick of his that was almost pointed like a right handed stick. And Alex was a left handed shot, so his back handed passes were always going to the left wing. ... Alex was just really a good passer and an exceptional reader of the play. I saw Alex toward the end of his career when the legs were kind of going. He could still check well because he was such a great anticipator and a good reader of the play. His record speaks for itself, but he's still one of the best."

Hall of Fame defenseman Pierre Pilote, who played against Delvecchio on many occasions, remembers him the following way:

He was smart. He was a smart hockey player. Very clever. He'd feather a pass, just on a guy's stick. I played against him in junior hockey. I remember. He was in

A tough competitor, Alex Delvecchio was a terrific passer and skater who played a very clean brand of hockey.

Oshawa at St. Catharines. He could skate good and he was big enough. He could shoot, he could pass, he could do everything. He was not an underrated player, he was an outstanding player. If he was on the ice, you had to watch him. He was smart. He caught me a few times. He knew that I would move up on a play and he'd try to get behind me and pull me around the board. They had a play worked out. He was a tough guy to defend against, especially when they had the puck in their own end. They played like a pool game off the boards there [in the Olympia]. You'd be somewhere and boom, right at that red line. You had to be very careful, or he'd get a break away on you. He was smart.

In the December 31, 1963 issue of the *Detroit News*, the late Terry Sawchuk said: "The tougher the game, the better he plays. When we get in trouble in our end, he can carry the puck out or pass it out.

He's an outstanding passer." Lefty Wilson added: "He surprises goalies with his shots from seemingly impossible angles. He snaps his wrists. He's like a fast ball pitcher. The puck is past you before you know it."

NHL Referee Paul Stewart holds Delvecchio in high esteem. He said: "I always liked Alex Delvecchio because somehow or another, he didn't look like a real athlete, but he just somehow or another seemed to get the job done. Yeah, he was slick. He didn't look hard boiled or mean like Lindsay looked. And Gordie Howe, of course I had played against, not when he was with Detroit, but I played against him in the WHA, and Gordie had just that power that you

Opposite: Alex Delvecchio was Sid Abel's eventual replacement on the "Production Line."

could feel coming out of him. But Delvecchio seemed to be slick with the puck."

In June of 1970, Delvecchio's home town of Thunder Bay, Ontario, paid tribute to his accomplishments by having an Alex Delvecchio Day, complete with a parade attended by nearly 30,000 people. On November 10, 1991, the Red Wings retired Delvecchio's number ten, hoisting it up to the rafters of Joe Louis Arena between former linemates Gordie Howe and Ted Lindsay. "I've been inducted into the Hall of Fame, and I've been on Stanley Cup winners, but this is something you always dream of," he commented in the *Times News* the next day. "Someday, my children and grandchildren can look at my jersey and know that's their dad."

On November 9, 1973, Delvecchio hung up his skates to become the coach of the Detroit Red Wings, becoming the second player in League history to spend over 20 seasons playing for one team, the other being his long-time teammate Gordie Howe. As a coach, Fats had the reputation of being an easy-going, low-key guy to play for. In an article by Earl McRae, he explained: "I'm reading this book. It's called the *Psychology of Coaching*. Coaching is not so much what you tell a guy but how you tell him. I respect my players and they respect me. It's not a lot of *teaching*. Hell, these guys know what to do, it's just, I don't know, it's just what you *are* that gets performance."

Delvecchio had an uncomplicated approach to the game. Revealing more of his coaching philosophy in the January, 1974 issue of *Hockey Pictorial*, he explained: "You can't play hockey by a lot of theories and systems. It's too fluid a game for that. You've got to make quick decisions on the ice and you can't be wondering if the decision fits into your system."

Toronto's Marcel Pronovost (3) and Tim Horton (7) try and prevent Gordie Howe and Alex Delvecchio from scoring on Terry Sawchuk. Graphic Artists/Hockey Hall of Fame.

ROBERT BLAKE THEODORE (TED) LINDSAY

Born: July 29, 1925, Renfrew, Ontario
Position: Left wing
Junior
- Windsor Spitfires
- Oshawa

Detroit Red Wings
- 1944-45 to 1956-57; 1964-65

Best NHL Season
- 1956-57: 30 goals, 85 points

Career Awards & Honors
- Art Ross Trophy: 1949-50
- Hockey Hall of Fame: 1966
- Red Wings Hall of Fame: 1962
- Team Captain (Detroit): 1952-1956

- First All-Star Team: 1948, '50-'54, '56, '57
- Second All-Star Team: 1949
- NHL All-Star Games: 1947-57

Trades
- Traded to the Chicago Blackhawks in 1957 with Glenn Hall for Hank Bassen, Forbes Kennedy, Bill Preston and Johnny Wilson.

Administrative
- General manager, Detroit Red Wings: 1976-77 (final 10 games) through 1979-80
- Head coach, Detroit Red Wings:
  -1979-80 (with Bobby Kromm)
  -1980-81 (with Wayne Maxner)

BIOGRAPHY

Undoubtedly one of the greatest left wingers of all time, Ted Lindsay is perhaps the most dynamic player who ever laced up the skates in Detroit. Born the youngest of nine children, Ted's father, Bert, was a well-known goaltender for the Renfrew Millionaires during the early 1900s. Bert Lindsay also minded the nets for the Montreal Wanderers and Toronto Arenas between 1915 and 1919.

Lindsay's family moved to Kirkland Lake, Ontario, in 1931. It was there that Ted became skilled at the game while playing minor and amateur hockey. He then went on to play Varsity hockey for Toronto's St. Michael's College in 1943, just like future teammate Red Kelly. In 1944, Lindsay started the season with St. Michael's. That season, they were defeated by Oshawa for the Memorial Cup. As it happened, Lindsay ended up on Oshawa's victory team when he was selected as a wartime replacement (teams were allowed to select up to four players from other clubs)

by Oshawa coach Charlie Conacher.

Detroit scout Carson Cooper spotted Lindsay playing in a St. Michael's game against St. Catharines. Cooper liked Lindsay right away, even though he was skating on a bad leg during that particular game. It wasn't long before Lindsay was on Detroit's roster after completing negotiations which included a promise that he would not be sent to one of Detroit's farm clubs.

Lindsay's career took off fast in Detroit. In 1950, he was awarded the Art Ross Trophy as the league's scoring leader (78 points, 69 games). As a member of the famed Production Line with Gordie Howe and Sid Abel, he was responsible for much of the team's success during the 1950s, when they won seven straight NHL titles and four Stanley Cups.

Lindsay was an excellent two-way player who didn't neglect the defensive component of the game. His enthusiasm and aggressive play in this area can be seen in the nearly 2,000 penalty minutes he amassed

CASCIO

"Terrible Ted" sticks it to an unfortunate Toronto Maple Leaf as Sid Abel looks on. Imperial Oil-Turofsky/Hockey Hall of Fame.

during his NHL career.

Away from the game, Lindsay was straightforward, courteous and articulate, and was a dedicated family man. However, he was famous for heckling spectators at games and was often personified as a rabble-rouser and rebel-at-heart. In addition to "Terrible Ted," he was also known as "The Blowtop of the Ice Lanes" and "Ol' Scarface" during his career. He often made statements unpopular with league officials. On one occasion, while playing in a game against the Toronto Maple Leafs, he drew both a misconduct and a game misconduct penalty with only 90 seconds remaining in the game. The penalties included $75.00 in fines, which Ted refused to pay. He also refused to write a letter of apology for remarks he made at the game, claiming that he would not sit in Mr. Campbell's "Kangaroo Court." Campbell ended up handing Lindsay a suspension,

which was later revoked when he signed a letter of apology dictated by Campbell.

In 1957, Lindsay served as president of the first NHL Player's Association. Members included Montreal's Doug Harvey, Boston's Fern Flaman, Chicago's Gus Mortson, Toronto's Jim Thompson and New York's Bill Gadsby. Their main concerns were the players' pension fund, a minimum salary for rookies, moving expenses for traded players and meal money.

For his involvement, Lindsay was traded to Chicago by Jack Adams. Glenn Hall accompanied Lindsay in the one-sided trade in which the only players of real value coming to Detroit were Forbes

Opposite: Ted Lindsay is one of the greatest left wings of all time.

In 1957, Ted Lindsay served as president of the first NHL Players' Association.

Kennedy and Johnny Wilson. Lindsay lost the support of those who had been backing the association, and it was basically dissolved for the time being.

"I played with him in Detroit and then we were traded together to Chicago," remembers Glenn Hall. "Ted was great. He really was. Again, I got in trouble in Detroit because I was told not to talk to Ted Lindsay. When I was playing junior in Windsor, Ted and Marty and these guys used to come over and encourage you over there. It was great when they came over to watch you."

Former Chicago Blackhawks defenseman Pierre Pilote, who defended against and played with Lindsay, says: "[Lindsay was a] pretty fiery guy, but he was the guy that I think could not do it by himself. He was the guy that needed to play with a good team to be good. I mean, he could set up [the] play and he could score, but he needed someone to set him up so he could score or he could set up somebody else. But for him to do the whole job himself, he was not a

single individual, he was like a team player. If he played on a good line, he was good, excellent. But if he played on a horse-shit line, he could not carry that line, where Gordie probably could."

After spending three seasons with Chicago and a brief period of time (1960-61 to 1963-64) in retirement, Lindsay returned to Detroit for one final season in 1964-65. Sid Abel, at the time Detroit's coach and general manager, offered him the opportunity. Many thought it was a crazy decision.

As stated in a write up of Lindsay by an unknown author, then-NHL president Clarence Campbell said: "This is the blackest day in Hockey History when a 39 year old man thinks he can make a comeback in the world's fastest sport." However, several months later, he had changed his tune, commenting: "This is one of the most amazing feats in professional sports. I didn't think it could be done. He has to be rated a truly amazing athlete!"

That season, "Terrible Ted" led the Red Wings to a Prince of Wales Trophy and a first-place division finish for the first time since he left the club. Former Red Wings' PR man Elliott Trumbull says that Ted Lindsay "made" the team that season. "Ted Lindsay came out of retirement and I give him a ton of credit," says Trumbull. "His mere presence kept those guys going. I mean, Teddy to this day, he's going to be 70, he still skates like he's determined as ever. You just can't take that out of him. He was out there at practice, working hard and well, he just brought the rest of that team with him. Because they all said, 'Jesus, if this guy can do it, we can do it.' One guy in particular, Bruce McGregor, they put him on the right wing with him. I can't remember who the center man was, but they had a hell of year. So Ted made that team really kick." After that season, Lindsay hung up the skates for good.

Lindsay's association with the Red Wings continued in another capacity when his playing days were over. On March 16, 1977, he signed a five-year deal to become the team's general manager, replacing Alex Delvecchio. He made numerous deals to

Opposite: The "Production Line" was an awesome offensive unit for Detroit during the 1950s. Hockey Hall of Fame archives.

improve the club while in that role, and Detroit went from one of the NHL's worst clubs to one that was able to finish second in their division. This success resulted in his being named Executive of the Year by both *The Hockey News* and *The Sporting News*. In 1980, three years after entering his five-year agreement with the Wings, Lindsay's duties were changed and Ted became head coach as well as director of player personnel.

Over the course of his NHL career Lindsay was named to the first All-Star team a record eight consecutive times, and once to the second. In 1966, he was inducted into the Hockey Hall of Fame. Because his family was not allowed to attend the ceremony, then reserved for only men, Lindsay refused to attend. He explained that his family had sacrificed a great deal during his career and that they

deserved to be there as much as he did. Instead of attending the ceremony, Lindsay was present at a graduation day at a hockey school he was operating in Port Huron, Michigan. During the 1991-92 season, Lindsay served as one of four Ambassadors of Hockey during the NHL's 75th Anniversary celebration.

Lindsay's number seven was retired by the Detroit Red Wings on November 10, 1991, during the same ceremony in which Alex Delvecchio's number was retired. Their numbers then joined Gordie Howe's legendary number nine, and the Production Line was "Immortalized."

Today, Lindsay works as an automotive manufacturer's representative in Rochester Hills, Michigan, where he plays in a winter hockey league and roller blades to stay in shape during the summertime.

CHAPTER NINE

WINGS OF FIRE
• THE 1950s •

Besides greats like Gordie Howe, Sid Abel, Terry Sawchuk, Alex Delvecchio and Ted Lindsay, Detroit had many fine athletes on its roster during the 1950s. It was these men who made the Detroit Red Wings the best team in the National Hockey League during the first half of that decade. With the exception of the 1955-56 season, when they finished in second place, the Red Wings were in first place from 1948-49 to 1956-57, taking home the Stanley Cup four times in six seasons. In 1955, the Red Wings set a standing record for the longest winning streak in NHL history, including the playoffs, when they won 15 straight games, six in the post season.

Commenting on the Red Wings during this glorious period of the team's history in an article by Howard Berger, which appeared in the February 12, 1988 issue of *The Hockey News*, Marcel Pronovost shed some light on what the team was like at the time, commenting: "There were so many highlights during the Detroit years that they seem to all run together. For my money, we were the closest-knit bunch in NHL history. There were no factions on those teams; everybody got along and we always looked forward to going to war together."

Bob Goldham, in John DeVaney and Burt Goldblatt's book *The Stanley Cup*, reflected deeply on this era. He said: "We had this tremendous pride in our organization in those days. All of us wanted to end up our careers as Wings. It counted for a lot. Tommy Ivan used to say that he could send our guys out on the road without a coach and never have to worry. The boys would show up at the games ready to play. Which is a compliment, when you think about it. It's something you have, I guess, the pride, and I guess the guys today have it. I don't know. But we sure as hell had it."

Former Detroit coach and general manager Jimmy Skinner was behind the bench when the Red Wings won the Stanley Cup in 1954-55. "There was a lot of loyalty in those days, compared to today," he says. "Players today, I think, are far better as far as their bodies and training and all that goes. But the big thing is loyalty, and I don't think there is very much loyalty in the National Hockey League today. It's, 'What are you going to give me next?' and stuff like that."

During this era, the game was much different from the way it is today, right down to the style of goaltending. Glenn Hall, who started out with the Red Wings, commented:

The goal keepers played a different style then than they do now. Now with the mask you can get hit. In those days, when you were down [you got hit]. A lot of them were down a lot. I butterflied, so I was standing more erect. When you did stack your pads, you stacked them away from your face, away from the shot. You got your feet into the pads or into the puck. So it was a little bit different game. The idea was still the same, they were trying to put the puck into a 4 x 6 spot, so that has never changed. Certainly the type of shots have changed. The

mask permitted the game to get faster and tougher and the helmets permitted it. I think it is too fast and too tough now. It's not so much with the masks, but with the helmets, because it's Kamikaze out there. I think you need to slow it down a little bit. What used to be called 'Charging and Boarding' in the corners is now considered a good check. You just run in and try to kill a guy. I don't think anybody when we were playing tried to hurt somebody. If the guy got hurt, they didn't mind, but they didn't go into the corner just to try and hurt somebody and I think that's happening regularly now.

The 1950s were part of hockey's fabled "golden age," the era that has come to be known as that of the "original six." With six teams and 120 men in the league, the rivalry and the competition were intense. Although rival teams would travel on the same train for home-and-home series', very few words were ever exchanged between them.

In the November 8, 1991 issue of the *Detroit*

News, in an article by Joe Falls, Red Wing legends Alex Delvecchio and Ted Lindsay expressed their feelings about the way things used to be. "You'd keep your head down when you walked past them [anyone from the other team]," said Delvecchio. "You might nod at one or two of them, maybe say hello to someone like Jean Beliveau. But that was it."

Lindsay's feeling were even stronger. He said: "I never spoke to any of them. I hated them, and they hated me. It was the way it was and the way it should be. It was wonderful."

THE MEN

GLENN HENRY (MR. GOALIE) HALL

Born: October 3, 1931, Humbolt, Saskatchewan
Position: Goaltender
Junior
- Humboldt Indians (SJHL): 1947-48, 1948-49
- Junior A: Windsor Spitfires (OHA)

Minor Pro
- Indianapolis Capitols (AHL), 1951-52
- Edmonton Flyers (WHL), 1952-53

Detroit Red Wings
- 1952-53, 1954-55 to 1956-57

Best NHL Season
- 1955-56: 4,200 MIN; 2.11 GAA; 12 SO

Career Awards & Honors
- Red Tillson Trophy (OHA MVP), second season with Spitfires
- First Team All-Star: 1957, '58, '60, '63, '64, '66, '69
- Second Team All-Star: 1956, '61, '62, '67
- NHL All Star Games: 1955-58, 1960-65, 1967-69
- Calder Trophy: 1956
- Conn Smythe Trophy: 1968
- Vezina Trophy: 1963, 1967 (with Denis Dejordy), 1969 (with Jacques Plante)
  -Hall's averages for his three Vezina seasons, in that order, were 2.55, 2.38 and 2.17, all very respectable.
- Hockey Hall of Fame: 1975
- Canadian Sports Hall of Fame: 1993
- The Hockey News/Itech King Clancy Memorial Award (continuing service to the sport of hockey): 1993

Opposite: During the 1950s, the Detroit Red Wings won four Stanley Cups and seven consecutive NHL championships.

BIOGRAPHY

Terry Sawchuk was not the only superb goaltender playing for the Red Wings during the 1950s. Detroit was also fortunate to have Glenn Hall. As a boy, Hall played forward on his public school's team. The goalie quit one day, and nobody would take his place. As captain of the team, Hall got between the pipes. That's how he began playing goal. He played pee-wee in 1944-45 and 1945-46 and juvenile the following season.

Hall played junior hockey in Detroit's system. He started out with the Humboldt Indians after being scouted by Detroit's Dave Pinkney and was eventually sent to their Junior A club in Windsor, Ontario. While playing for the Windsor Spitfires, Hall honed his skills to a fine edge, stopping a variety of shots from opposing teams that continuously penetrated his team's defense.

Commenting on his days in the Red Wings' farm system, Hall says: "[They were] great times. The organization was top notch. We had Lloyd Pollock who was general manager [and] Jimmy Skinner who was just a great coach, particularly for juniors. He taught you things that you really didn't know about, like the way you handled yourself and the intensity, how important intensity was. I thought he was a great coach. The trainer was absolutely great, like all trainers are. They've got a sense of humor that you can't believe. So I think that was important. They were great days for all of us, I think. I really did enjoy playing in Windsor."

Terry Sawchuk was Detroit's main goalie at the time, making Hall's chances for a jump to the big team seem dim at best. However, when Sawchuk suffered an injury that sidelined him for several weeks, Hall stepped up and did an outstanding job as a substitute. When, to the chagrin of many Detroit hockey fans, Sawchuk was traded to the Bruins in 1955, Hall got his crack at the big time and the team stuck with him. Jack Adams, in a February 4, 1956 *Toronto Daily Star* article by Jim Proudfoot, gave his reason for the trade, explaining: "We had to make a decision between Sawchuk and Hall. We decided to go with Hall and it was no snap decision. Glenn had played eight games with us in the past. He had shown us enough to prove he belongs in this league. He was more advanced at that time than Sawchuk was when he joined us."

Hall left no one disappointed and won the Calder Trophy (Rookie of the Year) with 12 shutouts and a 2.11 GAA in 70 games. The next season, he was named to the first All-Star team and posted a GAA of 2.24. Reflecting upon how he made it to the parent club, in a *Toronto Maple Leaf Program* article by Trent Frayne, Hall said: "Nobody said much to me. I knew if I ever wanted to make the big leagues I'd have to keep improving, so I used to go across the river to Detroit and watch the big guys in action. I used to like the way Turk Broda would cut down the angles when Toronto played the Wings, and I studied him, I guess. In fact, I guess I studied all of them, but just what I learned from them I dunno."

Today, Hall explains that at the time he played goal, the only way you learned was to watch other goalkeepers in action. As a rule, nobody handed out tips for improvement. Says Hall:

At training camp in those days there was nothing offered to you. You learned [by] stealing from the other guy, and that was simply by watching him. What's he doing in these conditions? No, there was nothing [in the way of tips]. You didn't expect any and you never gave any. Sawchuk and Lumley and these guys, they knew that I was probably after their job. I didn't think I was good enough to get it, but like again, just by being there I was after their job. So you weren't going to help a guy get your job. I think that's basically the way that the goalkeepers looked at things in those days. Sure, watch and pay attention. I'm sure they weren't worried about me taking their jobs because, as I say, I had lots of guys in Chicago that were there for the same purpose, to take my job. Like, I'd look at them and play. I'd say [if] the coach and general manager know anything, they will realize that he's not going to take my job.

Such a situation, and the fact that teams did not carry spare goalies years ago (the trainer would often fill in for an injured goalie), made it so that many goalies were loners. "You were the only guy," says Hall. "You were inclined to be a little bit of a loner and I liked it when people would say, 'Well, you're a loner.' For some reason, now it's looked at as a weakness if you're a loner. They'd say, 'How come you are a loner?' I'd say, 'Well, I used to like the company.' That's not too far from wrong. I could stand being by myself. A lot of people can't. I think I was just a run-of-the-mill goalkeeper in that type of thing."

Hall was with the Red Wings until 1956-57. He first came up to the big club as a substitute for an injured Terry Sawchuk in 1952-53. "I played a couple of times when Sawchuk was hurt," he says today, looking back. "I don't even know the years. It was 1955-1956 when I came up to stay, and prior to that there were two years where Sawchuk was hurt and I came up and played. One year I think I played two games [1954-55] and the other year I played five or six [six games in 1952-53]."

Commenting on his days with the Detroit Red Wings, he says: "The organization was great. I was there almost as long as I was in Chicago, really. I was 10 years in Chicago, but it was almost 10 years in Detroit because I played my junior hockey, and in those days it was an affiliation. Then I was four years in the minors and two years in Detroit. ... I played with Humboldt in junior, so I was really tied up with Detroit eight or nine years."

While playing for Detroit in a 1957 playoff game against Boston, Glenn Hall was hit in the mouth by a shot from Vic Stasiuk. After taking approximately 25 stitches in his mouth, he returned to the ice and finished the game. Looking back on the incident, Hall says:

It wouldn't happen today with the two goalkeeper system. I remember getting hit bad twice in the playoffs. Once with Detroit and once in 1967 in the spring, the last year before expansion. Obviously, today the goalkeeper is lying on the ice and crying when they got a little hang nail or something. I got up, not because I was tough or anything, but because Charlie Rayner and Turk Broda and Frankie Brimsek and all of those guys prior to me, that's what they did. The goalkeeper considered himself bein' tough. That was foremost in my mind; 'Don't let down the tradition.' Boy, you go in the closet

and cry. Don't cry on center ice. I think that you didn't get up for yourself, you got up for the old goalkeepers.

Although his injuries could have been prevented by wearing a mask, Hall wore one only in practice, believing that, in games, he was paid to take risks. He would often get violently nauseated before games but had no real problems once the game was under way. In a *Chicago Hockey Weekly* article, he said: "I just built myself up to an unbelievable peak. It was a combination of fright and desire. I was a little afraid of being hurt badly, but I was scared to death of playing poorly."

A streak of bad luck in the 1957 playoffs and an inability to get along with Jack Adams made for a trade to Chicago and Detroit's reacquisition of Sawchuk. Had he not been traded, Hall could have given Sawchuk a run for his money as the greatest Red Wings goalie of all time.

Former Red Wings trainer Lefty Wilson recalled how Hall got sent to Chicago. "[When] Glenn Hall got traded, it wasn't on his ability, it was personality. The old man [Jack Adams] followed him in the dressing room one day, right on his tail, and he said to Glenn, 'Glenn, I have done a lot for you.' Glenn said, 'Mr. Adams, I've done a lot for you.' He didn't have a real good playoff that year and they traded him. Personalities, I don't know what it is today, but in those days, it fit in like Jimmy Skinner and Jack Adams." In response to Lefty's story, Hall says: "I probably talked too much, but again, in those days you weren't permitted to express yourself."

Hall is best known in the world of hockey for his NHL record for consecutive games played by a goaltender, which to this day still remains unmatched. His consecutive streak of 502 games lasted from the beginning of the 1955-56 season and continued until the thirteenth game of the 1962-63 season, when he injured his back in a game against the Boston Bruins. Incredibly, the streak consisted of 30,120 successive minutes in front of the net! In addition to the 502 consecutive games he played in the NHL, Hall did not miss a game during the period (lasting nearly eight years—four in junior hockey and almost four in the minors) before he turned pro.

In all, Hall's career spanned 18 seasons of NHL hockey. "It wasn't that bad, really," he says, when asked about all of the time spent traveling from city to city. "I mean, you're back and forth. You're gone for a few days, but as far as that goes it wasn't extremely difficult. I suppose that it got long physically as well as mentally, but you were home with the family quite a bit. The biggest thing in those days was that you were away at Christmas time a lot, and that's what bothered me."

Hall was skilled in many ways, from his fast legs and hands to his ability to play the angles. Years ago, in *Sports Illustrated*, William Barry Furlong described Hall's unique style of net-minding: "Hall meets the shot with his feet wide, but his knees close together to form an inverted Y. Instead of throwing his whole body to the ice in crises, he'll go down momentarily to his knees, then bounce back to his feet, able to go in any direction." It was this style of play that allowed "the ghoulie" to record 84 shutouts in 906 games, leading the league in this department six times during his career.

Before retiring from the NHL, Hall spent some time with the St. Louis Blues. Because he got to live in the country while playing there and the team's style complemented his own, St. Louis was where he enjoyed playing the most. Hall recorded a 2.48 average in his first season with St. Louis, and a 2.17 average the next season (with Jacques Plante).

Today, Glenn resides near Edmonton, Alberta. Until recently, he was part-time scout and goaltending coach for the Calgary Flames. While working with the Calgary goalies, Hall didn't necessarily teach his old style of net-minding. While their coach, he once said: "I really let the guy figure it out. But I believe skating is the most important ingredient, [and] boy, oh boy, the mind runs very close to second. I think intensity. With no intensity you're not going to play well. I like a competitor. ... I'll talk on position; how high up you are, how and why the puck went in."

In *The Hockey News' Awards Special '93*, Calgary Flame's coach Dave King commented on Hall's abilities as a goaltending coach. Although he sometimes used video replays to show players where they made mistakes, most of the time he used his head: "It's amazing," said King. "He can tell you every minute move that led to a goal."

ROBERT (BOB) GOLDHAM

Born: May 12, 1922, Georgetown, Ontario
Position: Defense
Died: September 6, 1991, Toronto, Ontario
Junior
- Junior C: Georgetown, Ontario, 1936-37
- Junior B: Toronto Northern Vocational, 1937-38
- Junior A: Toronto Marlboros: 1938-39, 1939-40

Minor Pro
- Hershey Bears (AHL): 1940-41
- Washington Capitols (AHL): 1941-42
- Pittsburgh Hornets (AHL): 1947-48

Detroit Red Wings
- 1950-51 to 1955-56

Career Awards & Honors
- Second All-Star team: 1955
- NHL All-Star games: 1947, '49, '50, '54, '55

Trades
- Traded to the Detroit Red Wings in 1950 with Jim Henry, Metro Prystai and Gaye Stewart from the Chicago Blackhawks for Pete Babando, Al Dewsbury, Harry Lumley, Don Morrison and Jack Stewart.

BIOGRAPHY

Although he was not a flashy player, Bob Goldham was a true friend to the goaltenders he played with. Goldham turned pro with the Toronto Maple Leafs in 1941, when he was called up from their American League affiliate, the Hershey Bears. Once with the big club, he scored four goals and recorded seven assists in 19 games. In the playoffs that season, he showed great poise and maturity against Lynn Patrick and the New York Rangers, helping Toronto to win the Stanley Cup. He went on to win another Stanley Cup with Toronto in 1946-47. After only one season with the Leafs, Goldham spent three years with the Royal Canadian Navy.

When he returned to Toronto, teammates Hap Day and Bucko McDonald helped him develop an uncanny knack for blocking shots from the point or blue line, which became his "trademark." Goldham's primary focus became defending his goal, and he did it very well, often dropping to the ice to stop shots in the fashion of a second goalkeeper. Goldham was seldom fooled by fakes and had an excellent intuitive ability to move in front of opposing shooters at the right moment. Many held the view that his style of play was an excellent model for aspiring players to

pattern their play against.

On November 4, 1947, Bob Goldham was part of one of the most famous trades in league history when Toronto manager Conn Smythe included him in a five-player deal for Chicago's Max Bentley. Besides Goldham, Smythe also traded Gus Bodnar, Gaye Stewart, Bud Poile and Ernie Dickens.

Goldham spent three seasons with the Blackhawks. After arriving in the Windy City, he suffered a broken arm and was out for almost half the season. During his three seasons with Chicago, he gained a great deal of experience skating with future Detroit teammate Bill Gadsby.

Goldham finished his career with the Red Wings. In Detroit, he tasted champagne from Lord Stanley's chalice thrice more (1951-52, 1953-54 and 1954-55). While there, many held the opinion that nobody in the league could defend his goal as well as Goldham did, or with such tireless enthusiasm. Most of the time, he was paired with either Marcel Pronovost or Red Kelly at the blue line. His value to the team was not only as a hockey player, but as a person as well. "From the very first, Jack Adams recognized his qualities, not alone as a player, but as a team man and as a great morale builder for the club," said Jimmy Skinner, in the December 30, 1954 issue of the *Detroit News*. "He's comical on the road, [and] a great asset in keeping harmony on the club."

In an article by George Gross, Brian McFarlane once commented that "His teammates loved him not only in the NHL, but even later when he played for the old-timers. I remember playing with him in a game in which we were ahead of the opposition by six or seven goals. Someone asked him if it wouldn't be nice to let the opposition score a goal or two. Bob looked at the fellow and replied: 'I'll let them score–if they can go around me.' It wasn't that he wanted to rub it in, it only showed the tremendous pride he had in playing the game right."

Despite a style of play that increased his chances of losing teeth, Goldham made it through his professional hockey career without losing any. Former teammate Glenn Hall said: "I rode home with him after he finished his career, when he announced his retirement after a playoff game. He said to his wife, 'I got out of the game with all my teeth,' which was really something in those days.

That was a rarity, and the way he played, it was certainly unbelievable."

In the off-season, Goldham worked as a salesman for Caterpillar Tractor Company. He retired from hockey in April of 1956. After hanging up his skates from professional play, he coached Metro Junior B hockey at Woodbridge and Junior A at St. Michael's, where he coached future Toronto Maple Leaf Dave Keon. He later went on to become a very colorful and perceptive analyst for Hockey Night in Canada, teaming up with Bill Hewitt. He also continued playing in old-timer games, raising hundreds of thousands of dollars for noteworthy charities. On September 6, 1991, at the age of 69, Goldham passed away at Toronto General Hospital from a stroke.

LEONARD PATRICK (RED) KELLY

Born: July 9, 1927, Simcoe, Ontario
Position: Center, Defense
Junior
- Junior A: St. Michael's College Majors

Detroit Red Wings
- 1947-48 to 1959-60

Best NHL Season
- 1960-61 (Toronto): 20 goals, 70 points

Career Awards & Honors
- First All-Star Team: 1951-55, 1957
- Second All-Star Team: 1950, 1956
- NHL All-Star Games: 1950-58, '60, '62, '63
- Lady Byng Trophy: 1951, 1953, 1954, 1961
- Norris Trophy: 1954
- Team Captain: 1956-57, 1957-58
- Multiple recipient of Detroit Hockey Writer's MVP award
- James M. Citron Sportsmanship Cup (Local Detroit Trophy)

Milestones
- Played on nine Prince of Wales Trophy-winning clubs.
- Played on eight Stanley Cup winners.
- At one time, held the record for:
  - most years in the Stanley Cup playoffs (19)
  - most playoff games (164)
- Was runner-up to Gordie Howe for most regular-season games (1316).

BIOGRAPHY

Red Kelly was an amazing hockey player. After learning to skate at an early age, he played junior hockey at St. Michael's college, like future teammate Ted Lindsay. After that, Kelly went straight to

In 1951, Red Kelly became the second defenseman to win the Lady Byng Trophy. Altogether, he won the award four times during his career.

Detroit at the age of 19 and became a standout defenseman for over 12 seasons.

Tommy Ivan once described Kelly as the greatest all-around player in the game and said that he was nearly everything a coach could want in a player. In a March 15, 1950 *Toronto Globe and Mail* article, Ivan said: "We've used Kelly at every job except goalie and he's been outstanding wherever we put him. He may not get the all-star votes but I only wish I had ten like him."

Kelly was a different breed of blue-liner. Although a champion boxer while in college, he wasn't known for getting into scrums with the opposition. Kelly played a very fast, clean and fair style of hockey. He was well-known for his ability to check opponents in the corners without cross-checking or boarding them. He possessed a level head and was noted for his ability to keep his cool when things got hot. Kelly was also able to lead the rush well and was often utilized on both the power play and penalty killing units. This can be seen by the fact that he finished his career as a forward (left wing and center) for the Toronto Maple Leafs.

Kelly had a reputation for not swearing, drinking or smoking. Abstinence from the latter vice is noteworthy, since he worked on his father's tobacco farm during the off-season. He was a very religious man and reportedly attended church before almost every game. Kelly was a hard worker as well and, because of his exceptional physical condition, received a great deal of ice time.

In 1951, Kelly became only the second defenseman to win the Lady Byng Trophy. He won the trophy three more times during his career. He was also the first recipient of the James Norris Memorial Trophy, given to the league's best defenseman. The precedents do not stop there. On October 21, 1954, when Kelly scored a hat trick against the Boston Bruins, it was the only time in modern hockey history that a defenseman had scored three goals in one game.

Interestingly, Kelly was a Member of Parliament (York West) for three years (1962-1965). He was elected twice to the House of Commons (1962 and 1963). In the Autumn 1989 issue of *Canadian Parliamentary Review*, Kelly commented on his experience, explaining:

I suppose my first impression was one of awe. I was in awe of the atmosphere, of the rules and of the political personalities present. Eventually, I came to look at it more as a kind of sport, not unlike hockey. You had several teams, you had a Speaker who was referee. The Sergeant-at-Arms like the linesman was sometimes called upon to break up the fights (and I recall Gilles Gregoire and Re'al Caouette escorted out of the House by the Sergeant-at-Arms). You even had a Press Gallery to give us the thumbs up or thumbs down sign and in those days the "fans" in the public gallery occasionally broke into applause during some of the heated debates that characterized those years. There was no incident quite like the Rocket Richard riot at the Montreal Forum but

I did see at least one punch thrown outside the Chamber and I was in the House the day a bomb exploded in one of the bathrooms outside the Chamber.

After finishing his career with Toronto, Kelly went on to coach the expansion Los Angeles Kings in 1967, taking them to a second-place finish in the West Division. He remained with the Kings for two seasons and later went on to coach the Pittsburgh Penguins. Today, he lives in Toronto, Ontario.

RENE MARCEL PRONOVOST

Born: June 15, 1930, Lac la Tortue, Quebec
Position: Defense
Junior Hockey
- Windsor Spitfires (OHA), 1947-49

Minor League Hockey
- Omaha Knights (USHL), 1949-50
- Indianapolis Capitols (AHL), 1950-51

Detroit Red Wings
- 1949-50 to 1964-65

Career Awards & Honors
Junior & Minor-Pro
- USHL rookie-of-the-year: 1949-50
- Set USHL record for points by a defenseman (52 in 1949-50)
- Second All-Star Team, Indianapolis Capitols, 1950-51

NHL
- Red Wing Hall of Fame: 1978
- Hockey Hall of Fame: 1979
- First All-Star Team: 1960, 1961
- Second All-Star Team: 1958, 1959
- All Star Games: 1950, '54, '55, '57-'61, '63, '65, '68

Trades
- Traded to the Toronto Maple Leafs on May 20, 1965, with Autry Erickson, Larry Jeffrey, Ed Joyal and Lowell MacDonald for Andy Bathgate, Billy Harris and Gary Jarrett.

BIOGRAPHY

Marcel Pronovost played for 20 seasons in the NHL, 15 of which were with Detroit. The son of Claude Pronovost, a steam-fitter who worked on construction gangs, Marcel was one of 12 children. In an anonymously written article which appeared in *The Hockey News*, Pronovost was quoted as saying: "I was not born with a silver spoon in my mouth. We did not eat caviar, but we always ate. We lived in different houses. We slept two or three to a bed. The younger ones dressed in hand-me-downs from

the older ones. We made do. We had happiness. At Christmas time when the whole family got together with aunts and uncles and cousins we had a happy time."

Pronovost was scouted by Marcel Cote while playing juvenile hockey in Shawnigan Falls, Quebec. He turned professional in 1949-50 with Omaha of the U.S. Hockey League when he proved too skilled to play for the Spitfires. He won rookie-of-the-year and first-team All-Star honors and set a record for point scoring by a defenseman. An injury to Gordie Howe in the semi-finals caused the skilled two-way player to be called up from Omaha to fill the void created on defense when Red Kelly was shifted to forward to take Howe's place. His presence helped the Wings to defeat the Toronto Maple Leafs and then the New York Rangers in the finals. The following season found Pronovost starting out in Indianapolis of the American League, after he injured his cheekbone. In Indianapolis, he was named to the second All-Star team. He ended up finishing out the 1950-51 season in the Motor City, where he would remain for a long time.

Not a hard-hitting defenseman, Pronovost was a skilled stick-handler and puck carrier who possessed graceful skating ability. He was known for his fearless, electrifying rushes. He was also known for his tireless, steady, solid play and frequently played with injuries that side-lined most other players. Despite an endless series of injuries, Marcel Pronovost did not miss one game during a five-season stretch and in only five of his 20 NHL seasons did he play in fewer than 60 games.

Pronovost was also known for his leadership in the dressing room, in which he took great pride. In the December 1969 issue of *Hockey Pictorial*, Pat Quinn commented on the influence Pronovost had on him when he was a player with the Maple Leafs. "There are so many little things that become very important," he explained. "Marcel kept watching my every move in games last season [1968-69]. He mentally filed away my errors and then tried to show me how to correct them in practices. He will spend hours with any player who is receptive, willing to

listen and learn. I can appreciate how much he has done for me."

While skating for the Red Wings, Pronovost had the fortune of playing on four Stanley Cup winners and seven championship teams, sharing defensive responsibilities with men like Bill Gadsby, Red Kelly, Leo Reise, Warren Godfrey, Pete Goegan and Doug Barkley. Twice, he was chosen to both the first and second All-Star teams during a period of NHL history when great defenders were not in short supply, as the previous listing can attest to.

Besides the defenders, Marcel played alongside some of the greatest players in the game at that time, many of whom overshadowed the contributions he made to the team. Commenting on his days with Detroit in a November 27, 1965 *Globe and Mail* article, Pronovost explained: "In Detroit, I used to move instinctively. I knew where Howe and Delvecchio and Ullman would be and I knew what my defense partner was doing. I didn't have to look for them."

Several of Pronovost's brothers had stints in the NHL. Claud "Suitcase" Provonost played three games with Boston and Montreal in the late '50s; Joseph Jean Denis Pronovost played for Pittsburgh, Atlanta and Washington between 1968-69 and 1981-82; and Joseph Armand (Andre) Pronovost played for Montreal, Boston, Detroit and Minnesota between 1956-57 and 1967-68.

Pronovost ended his career as a playing-coach with Toronto's Central League affiliate, the Tulsa Oilers, in 1969-70. "I was not one of the better players, but I was one of the harder-working players," he said in an article that appeared in *The Hockey News*. "I wasn't afraid of anything and gave the game everything I had."

After retiring from professional play, Pronovost coached hockey with Tulsa and in the WHA with Chicago. He coached the Buffalo Sabres to a 105-point season in 1977-78 but was fired along with GM Punch Imlach the next season after a slow start. Besides serving as an assistant coach for the Red Wings during the 1980s, Pronovost has also coached the Hull juniors and OHL Windsor Spitfires and has worked for the NHL's Central Scouting Bureau and an investment company. He is currently a scout for the New Jersey Devils.

Opposite: Marcel Pronovost was known for his fearless, electrifying rushes and steady, solid play.

MARTIN NICHOLAS (MADMAN) PAVELICH

Born: November 6, 1927, Sault Ste. Marie, Ontario
Position: Forward (center and wing)
Junior Hockey
- Galt Red Wings

Minor League Hockey
- Indianapolis Capitols (AHL): 1947-48, 1949-50

Detroit Red Wings
- 1947-48 to 1956-57

Best NHL Season
- 1951-52: 17 goals, 36 points

Career Awards & Honors
- All-Star Games: 1950, '52, '54, '55

BIOGRAPHY

Marty Pavelich was once described by Tommy Ivan as the kind of player a team wants when things get dull on the ice. Although he was never the team's best player or an electrifying goal-scorer, Pavelich was very valuable to the Red Wings. It can be argued that his value is measured best by the goals he prevented opponents from scoring rather than those he scored. He had an uncanny knack for knocking the puck away from opponents and frequently broke up the opposition's plays.

Pavelich was known for his anticipation and determination and was among the best body-checkers in the game. As a hockey player, he was valued for his versatility. During his career, he played at center and both wing positions, and was one of hockey's greatest defensive forwards. Often on special teams, Pavelich gained the reputation as being one of the League's best penalty-killers.

Sportswriter Paul Chandler, in the February 15, 1948 issue of the *Detroit News*, provided an excellent description of Pavelich early in his career. He said: "Pavelich digs with the skates and likes nothing better than a broad jump, with a running start, into any given opponent. Pint-sized himself, his enthusiasm carries him into embroilments with big men. Sometimes they become angry, at which time teammates Jack Stewart or Gordon Howe come forth and offer protection for mighty Martin. ... Pavelich is a fierce back-checker and a good example of the 'Adams type of player,' which means a rough, hard-skating man, good at defense, who annoys

Marty Pavelich was known for his anticipation and determination and was among the best body-checkers in the game.

and heckles."

Pavelich spent his entire ten-season, NHL career playing for the Red Wings. His earliest hockey days were spent playing in the state of Michigan, across the border from his native Ontario. Once he broke into the junior ranks, he began to stand out as a player capable of making it to the NHL. Commenting on his transition from junior hockey to the pros, in a March 28, 1987 *Toronto Globe and Mail* article by Paul Patton, he said: "I had always been a high scorer in junior. But when I came up, they put me on a checking line and changed my whole style of play. We were always out against the other team's best scorers, doing whatever it took to win."

Ted Lindsay once said Pavelich had a great hockey mind, an insightful perspective, and could see more in a game and in a certain player than most pro scouts. Revealing some of his philosophy in the November 29, 1956 issue of the *Detroit News*, Pavelich said: "Hockey players are creatures of habit, just like everybody else. Seven out of ten times they'll

Metro Prystai was a junior hockey star before playing in the NHL.

METRO PRYSTAI

Born: November 7, 1927, Yorkton, Saskatchewan
Position: Center, right wing
Junior
- Moose Jaw Canucks (SJHL)

Detroit Red Wings
- 1950-51 to 1957-58

Best NHL Season
- 1949-50 (Chicago): 29 goals, 51 points

Career Awards & Honors
- 1950, '53, '54

BIOGRAPHY

Metro Prystai played all of his minor hockey in the Yorkton Minor Hockey system before moving to Moose Jaw in 1944, where he finished his high school education. Although he had a successful NHL career, Prystai was more of a star in junior hockey. During his final two seasons of junior, Prystai lead the SJHL in scoring.

In a *Times Herald* article, editor Mary Carty said: "I remember everyone in town, especially the kids, simply idolized him. Anyone who met him will certainly say that he was the most wonderful man. If anyone on another team had ever tried to rough Metro up, the crowd would probably have murdered him."

In Moose Jaw, Prystai played junior hockey for the Moose Jaw Canucks of the Saskatchewan Junior Hockey League. The Canucks won the Provincial Championship each of the three seasons in which Prystai played for them. During the first and last of those championship seasons (1945 and 1947), the Canucks went all the way to the Memorial Cup finals against Toronto St. Michael's. Prystai once commented that, despite the final two appearances, they had the best team in 1946, when Emile Francis was in goal. Despite having a strong team, the Canucks were eliminated by Edmonton that season.

Amos Wilson, a teammate of Prystai's on the Moose Jaw Canucks, said, that despite his popularity, Prystai never let it rush to his head. In the October 14, 1977 issue of the *Moose Jaw Times-Herald*, Wilson said: "I'll tell you one thing about Metro Prystai. He was a big, big star when he played in Moose Jaw. I still remember one year in the playoffs when Thatcher's hardware store had this huge picture of

make the same play in coming out of their own end, or under certain circumstances. By studying them you can anticipate what they're going to do."

During his career with the Red Wings, Pavelich played on all four Stanley Cup-winning teams during the 1950s and is one of the only four Red Wings to play on all seven consecutive, first-place championship teams (Gordie Howe, Ted Lindsay and Red Kelly are the others). Those seven consecutive finishes have never been surpassed by another team.

After hockey, Pavelich went into the plastics business with Ted Lindsay and Gordie Howe and later operated a company that had ties to the automotive industry. For a time, he also served as a minor league scout for the Red Wings. Pavelich's brother, Matt, was a long-time NHL linesman and was inducted into the Hockey Hall of Fame. Today, Marty Pavelich lives in the Western United States.

him in the window along with an advertisement to come see the Canucks play that night. But the great player that he was and the attention he received, he still remained one of the nicest guys you could ever hope to meet. He was as big a star as there ever has been in Moose Jaw, but it never affected his personality a bit."

With one year of junior eligibility remaining, Prystai made the jump to the big leagues to play for the Chicago Blackhawks. There, he joined the Bentley brothers, Doug and Max, who were also from Western Canada. In 1950-51, Prystai went to the Red Wings in a nine-player deal, joining Gordie Howe and Sid Abel, also from Western Canada. "I was disappointed because it looked like the Hawks were an up-and-coming organization but Detroit had so many good players that, after a while, I was happier than heck," he recalled in a *Toronto Globe and Mail* article by Paul Patton. "They used me as a swing man because I could play all three forward positions, though I spent most of the time on right wing. For a while I was with Ted Lindsay and Gordie Howe, then on a checking line with Marty Pavelich and Tony Leswick, then with Alex Delvecchio and Johnny Wilson."

After retiring from the Red Wings in 1957-58, Prystai moved back to his native Saskatchewan and went into the real estate and insurance business, and then into automobile sales.

EARL (DUTCH) REIBEL

Born: July 21, 1930, Kitchener, Ontario
Position: Center
Junior: Junior B: Kitchener Greenshirts
Windsor Spitfires (OHA)
Minor Pro: Omaha Knights (USHL): 1950-51
Indianapolis Capitols (AHL): 1951-52
Edmonton Flyers (WHL): 1952-53
Detroit Red Wings
• 1953-54 to 1957-58
Best NHL Season
• 1954-55: 25 goals, 66 points
Career Awards & Honors
• Rookie of the Year (AHL): 1951-52
• NHL All-Star Games: 1954, '55
• Harry Gormley Award: 1954-55
• James M. Citron Sportsmanship Cup: 1954-55
• Lady Byng Trophy: 1955-56
Trades
• Traded to Chicago in December of 1957 with Lorne Ferguson, Bill Dineen and Billy Dea for Nick Mickoski, Bob Bailey, Hec Lalande and Jack McIntyre.

BIOGRAPHY

Dutch Reibel spent the majority of his NHL career with the Red Wings. The youngest of six children, Reibel's father came to Canada from Germany and worked for a meat packing firm. When Reibel was a youth, Milt Schmidt of the Boston Bruins lived next door to his family. After receiving his first pair of skates for Christmas, Reibel started playing hockey when he was five years old. He first played for the Margaret Avenue School team and then for the Ward team (Bantam and Midget).

Recalling an early memory from his junior hockey days, in an September 15, 1955 issue of the *Detroit News*, Reibel said: "My father liked to see me play, came to the games, but my mother didn't." In the same article, he recalled an experience which made his mother swear his hockey days were over. As it happened, after playing a game for the Greenshirts in St. Catharines, he was returning home in a car containing five other children. The car stalled on the railroad tracks outside of Kitchener and a freight train smashed into the vehicle, breaking one boy's leg, another's pelvis and three of Dutch's ribs. Because his team was then short-handed, Reibel sneaked out of the house only a week later to play a game for the Greenshirts!

In 1948-49, Detroit scout Fred Cox spotted Reibel while he was playing for Kitchener, and it wasn't long before he was assimilated into the Red Wings' farm system and playing for the Windsor Spitfires. In Windsor, Reibel skated on a line with Glen Skov and Eddie Stankiewicz, and the team finished second to the Toronto Marlboros during the regular season. They went on to erase Toronto in the first round of the playoffs but lost to Guelph, who had a player by the name of Andy Bathgate on their roster.

Along with Marcel Pronovost, Johnny Wilson and Terry Sawchuk, Dutch turned professional with Omaha in 1950. It was there that misfortune struck when he broke his leg. "I wheeled behind the net, hit something, slid into the boards, [and] broke my left leg at the ankle. I was out until the last two weeks but we still won the league title and playoffs," he said in an article by John Walter, which appeared in the September 15, 1955 issue of the *Detroit News*.

The following season, the stocky centerman played for Indianapolis of the AHL, where he led his team in scoring (67 points) and finished fourth in the individual league point race. His performance won him rookie-of-the-year honors. However, after the season he rolled his car during the summer, resulting in damage to a nerve in his right eye. The injury caused him to be cross-eyed for a half-season. Rather than being promoted to the Red Wings, Reibel was forced to play one more season of minor league hockey for the Edmonton Flyers of the Western Hockey League. "I drove the goalies crazy in the Western League," he said in the same John Walter article. "They didn't know where I was going to shoot." The condition didn't hinder his performance, however. Playing on a line with Vic Stasiuk, he made the All-Star team and led the Western League in scoring.

Once Dutch made it to the big club, he found himself at center between Gordie Howe and Ted Lindsay, where Adams thought he would be the replacement for Sid Abel. He started out strong, but then fizzled out. Delvecchio eventually took his place as the regular center on the Production Line, and Reibel played between Bill Dineen and Marcel Bonin.

In the same John Walter article, Dutch compared what it was like centering each line, explaining: "Playing between Gordie and Ted was quite different than centering Bonin and Dineen. Ted and Gordie roam more, switch over, or sometimes they'll go up center, whereas Marcel and Bill patrolled up and down their wings. If Gordie goes up the middle, then I take his wing. When I go up the center on the way to the net, they'll adjust. After playing with them you begin to sense what's coming. However, with Gordie, you don't know what's going to happen. You just have to keep watching for a pass. Or he may shoot at the net. You have to keep on your toes."

Reibel won two Stanley Cups in Detroit. He almost won rookie-of-the-year honors during his first NHL season but finished second to Camille Henry of the New York Rangers. After a half season with Chicago, he finished his NHL career with the Boston Bruins in 1958-59.

JOHN EDWARD (IRON MAN, JOHNNY) WILSON

Born: June 14, 1929, Kincardine, Ontario
Position: Left wing
Junior
- Junior A: Windsor Spitfires (OHA)

Minor Pro
- Omaha (USHL): 1949-50
- Indianapolis (AHL): 1950-51, 1951-52
- Rochester (AHL): 1960-61

Detroit Red Wings
- 1949-50 to 1954-55, 1957-58 to 1958-59

Best NHL Season
- 1956-57: 18 goals, 48 points

Carer Awards & Honors
- NHL All-Star Games: 1954, '56

Career Milestones
- Played in 580 consecutive games (formerly an NHL record)

Trades
- Traded to Chicago from Detroit in June, 1955 with Tony Leswick, Glen Skov and Benny Woit for Dave Creighton, Bucky Hollingworth and Jerry Toppazzini.
- Traded to Detroit from Chicago in July, 1957 with Hank Bassen, Forbes Kennedy and Bill Preston for Glenn Hall and Ted Lindsay.
- Traded to Toronto from Detroit in June, 1959 for Barry Cullen.

BIOGRAPHY

During the 1950s, the Red Wings had a left wing on their roster who always came to play. Quite the iron man, Johnny Wilson played a streak of 580 consecutive games during his career. The streak, which included eight full 70-game seasons, ended on October 5, 1960, when the Toronto Maple Leafs assigned him to play for Rochester of the AHL. The feat was an NHL record until broken by Andy Hebenton.

Wilson was discovered while playing juvenile hockey in Shawnigan Falls, Quebec. He and his brother, Larry, impressed Red Wings scouts enough that the two were signed to play junior hockey for the Windsor Spitfires, then Detroit's Junior A affiliate. Wilson's family was behind them 100% and relocated to Windsor in 1947.

It wasn't long before Wilson turned professional. In 1949-50, he was assigned to play with the Omaha Knights of the United States Hockey League (USHL). That season, he was called up to play for the Red

Wings as a replacement player in one game. He was utilized again during the playoffs and had his name inscribed on the Stanley Cup during his first professional season. Wilson spent a year and a half with the Indianapolis Capitols before becoming a Red Wing long term.

Wilson was never a high scorer. However, he was a strong defensive player and possessed good speed and a hard, heavy shot. An excellent passer, he was considered one of the best wingmen in hockey during his career.

Wilson played for the Toronto Maple Leafs and New York Rangers after his days with Detroit were over. Shortly after retiring as a player, he turned to coaching. Wilson's career behind the bench began with the Ottawa Montagnards, a Canadian senior team. He led the Montagnards to a division championship and subsequently took them on a tour across Europe, representing Canada.

Wilson then coached hockey at Princeton University for two seasons. It was there that he learned a great deal about the art of coaching. "Association. Remember that word," he said in the February 1, 1972 issue of the *Toronto Globe and Mail*. "That's how anyone learns, by associating with others. I've found that associating with the football and basketball coaches, I learned a lot about coaching hockey. I can't explain it, but something is instilled in you. You learn how to react when things develop. You learn to get the maximum from an individual."

After Princeton, Wilson coached at the professional level with the Springfield Kings (AHL), leading them to the Calder Cup in 1970-71. He and his brother, who also played for the Red Wings and Blackhawks, had a friendly coaching rivalry going when the two coached in the American League. After a brief stint with the Los Angeles Kings in 1969-70, when he served as a replacement for Hal Laycoe, Wilson coached the Detroit Red Wings in 1971-72 (with Doug Barkley) and 1972-73.

The Red Wings let Wilson go when the team missed the playoffs in 1973. In the April 17, 1973

issue of the *Toronto Sun*, he commented on his release: "They [General Manager Ned Harkness and Vice President Jim Bishop] wanted a yes man as a coach. Mr. Bishop and Mr. Harkness wanted to coach the team. If I had stayed on in a situation like that ... I would have become a door opener. I'll match my track record at any time. We didn't make the playoffs, but we made some giant strides."

ROSS INGRAM (LEFTY) WILSON

Born in Toronto, Ontario, on October 15, 1919, Lefty Wilson, according to the record books, played goal in only three NHL games: for Detroit (1953-54), Toronto (1955-56) and Boston (1957-58). He is best known for being the long-time trainer for the Detroit Red Wings, a position he held with pride from 1950-1982. "I was in the organization for 38 years, six years in the minors and 32 with the big team," he says. "I've had a good life, I've enjoyed [it]."

Wilson was always in sports. He played some professional baseball with the Boston Red Sox before serving in the Canadian Navy during World War II. Recalling his early days and how he got involved with Detroit, Wilson says: "I was still in school, and we used to practice at the noon hour down at the Maple Leaf Gardens. I didn't do too well in junior and then I went back and actually played intermediate hockey in St. Catharines [Ontario]. Then, I went in the Navy. I was still a goaltender so I played for the Navy team. We played Detroit in Windsor for the Navy Fund. Jack Adams was there and Tommy Ivan and the gang, and they said, 'Left, when you get out of the service, give us a call.' That's what I did when I got out."

Adams soon pressed Wilson about his future, and Lefty chose hockey. He remained in the sport for 38 years. "[They wanted a] goaltender. Of course, when I went to camp I was the oldest goaltender there. I was 25 years old and I couldn't stop a balloon. So I said to Carson Cooper, the head scout, 'Carson, I'm going home.' He says, 'You go home and I'll cut your legs off.' So I stayed around. We were playing in Ann Arbor one night and Jack says, 'Left, we're going to send you to Omaha, Nebraska.' Omaha, Nebraska! I didn't even know where it was. So I went there with

Opposite: Johnny Wilson played in a streak of 580 consecutive games during his career. The feat is a former NHL record.

Besides serving as the team's long-time trainer, Lefty Wilson was also a spare goalie for the Red Wings.

Tommy Ivan, Jimmy Skinner, Gordie Howe and a bunch of the guys that played for the team. I knew nothing about either job. Omaha was a great little city. We won the championship."

Wilson never did play hockey in the NHL. However, he did fill in on three occasions, when injuries to Terry Sawchuk, Harry Lumley and Don Simmons necessitated his services. He also had the opportunity to serve as the trainer for Team Canada in 1976.

"That was another thrill of mine," says Wilson. "Why, when you've got the 35 hockey players, the best in the world we thought, or I thought, you work with them. They were a different breed. They were a bunch of guys [who] were the greatest, and you never had any trouble with them. You have the great stars like Howe and Delvecchio and Mahovlich and those guys, Lindsay and Abel, they were easy to get along with. They were a great bunch of guys, and I really enjoyed it immensely when I had them that year."

Today, Wilson is still active with the Detroit Red Wing Alumni Association and works at the Bay Pointe Golf Club during the summer months.

CHAPTER TEN

GLORY DAYS
• THE 1950s •
STANLEY CUP SUCCESS

During the 1950s, the Detroit Red Wings were able to secure four Stanley Cups in five seasons, bringing the franchise's total tally to seven. "Great team spirit and the will to win was the secret of the Wings' success," said Marty Pavelich in the March 10, 1956 issue of the *Detroit News*. "I don't think any group of hockey players in the NHL ever got to know each other better than the players who made up the Wings' seven championship teams. We ate, slept, and drank hockey. And in Jack Adams we've had a manager who took great personal interest in every one of his players. That's in rare contrast to some other clubs where players rarely see their general manager. Adams is at virtually every practice. He's there to talk to you, to praise or pep you up, to point out mistakes and to show you how to improve your play from his vast experience as a player, as well as 29 years of coaching and managing."

"We had good young players coming in from our farm club, so from there on they built up," says Wally Crossman, Detroit's long-time locker room attendant.

"Then Lindsay came to us in the 1940s. Howe came after Lindsay, then Red Kelly came, and from there they really built up a good team. Those were the nucleus of the Stanley Cup teams. We won three or four Cups in the 1950s, and then in 1956 or 1957, Adams broke [up] the team. He sent some of the players to Chicago and he got disgusted with Lindsay, because Lindsay was starting a union here amongst the players. He was traded to Chicago, too. Kelly was traded to Toronto."

Commenting on the Stanley Cup teams on which he played (1949-50 and 1951-52), Leo Reise remembered: "By the time we got to 1949-50, we had a pretty powerful team and it stayed powerful and got more powerful until we won the 1951-52 Stanley Cup. Some of those years we only lost 11 games or 13 games, so we had a real powerhouse. When you are flying like that, you know, management is very friendly. You don't have problems, very few people had problems that way. When you're winning, you're winning. Everybody is a nice guy."

1949-50 STANLEY CUP VICTORY

FIRST GAME: (April 11, at Detroit)
Red Wings 4, Rangers 1
First Period
New York - O'Connor (Gordon, Mickoski) . . 5:58
Second Period
Detroit - Carveth (Gee, Babando) 4:43
Detroit - Gee (J. Wilson) 9:33
Detroit - McFadden (Couture) 10:06
Detroit - Couture (Pronovost, McFadden) . . .13:56
Third Period
No scoring

SECOND GAME: April 13, at Toronto)
Rangers 3, Detroit 1
First Period
No scoring
Second Period
Detroit - Couture (Pavelich) 3:05
New York - Egan 10:39
Third Period
New York - Laprade (Stanley) 3:04
New York - Laprade .11:20

THIRD GAME: (April 15, at Toronto)
Red Wings 4, Rangers 0
First Period
Detroit - Couture (Kelly) 14:13
Detroit - Gee (Dewsbury) 19:08
Second Period
Detroit - Abel 19:16
Third Period
Detroit - Pavelich (Kelly) 16:55

FOURTH GAME: (April 18, at Detroit)
Rangers 4, Red Wings 3
First Period
Detroit - Lindsay (Stewart) 6:31
Detroit - Abel (Lindsay) 16:48
Second Period
New York - O'Connor (Kaleta, Mickoski) . . .19:59
Third Period
Detroit - Pavelich (Peters, Stewart) 3:32
New York - Laprade (Fisher, Leswick) 8:09
New York - Kyle (Kaleta) 16:26
Overtime
New York - Raleigh (Slowinski) 8:34

FIFTH GAME: (April 20, at Detroit)
Rangers 2, Red Wings 1
First Period
No scoring
Second Period
New York - Fisher (Leswick) 7:44
Third Period
Detroit - Lindsay (Carveth, Abel) 18:10
Overtime
New York - Raleigh (Lund, Slowinski) 1:38

SIXTH GAME: (April 22, at Detroit)
Red Wings 5, Rangers 4
First Period
New York - Stanley (Mickoski, Kaleta) 3:45
New York - Fisher (Laprade, Leswick) 7:35
Detroit - Lindsay (Stewart) 19:18
Second Period
New York - Lund (Egan, Slowinski) 3:18
Detroit - Abel (Lindsay, Carveth) 5:28
Detroit - Couture (Babando, Gee) 16:07
Third Period
New York - Leswick (Laprade, Fisher) 1:54
Detroit - Lindsay (Abel) 4:13
Detroit - Abel (Carveth, Dewsbury) 10:34

SEVENTH GAME: (April 23, at Detroit)
Red Wings 4, Rangers 3
First Period
New York - Stanley (Leswick) 11:14
New York - Leswick (Laprade, O'Connor) . .12:18
Second Period
Detroit - Babando (Kelly, Couture) 5:00
Detroit - Abel (Dewsbury) 5:30
New York - O'Connor (Mickoski) 11:42
Detroit - McFadden (Peters) 15:57
Third Period
No scoring
First Overtime
No Scoring
Second Overtime
Detroit - Babando (Gee) 8:31

With final series defeats to the Toronto Maple Leafs the previous two seasons, the Red Wings were hungry for victory in 1949-50. They met Toronto in the semifinals and beat their old foes. However, the victory did not come without sacrifice.

On March 28, 1950, in front of 13,659 Olympia fans, Toronto beat Detroit 5-0. It was the twelfth straight post-season beating they had given the Red Wings in four years. In that first game of the semifinal series, the team suffered much more than a lost game when Gordie Howe fractured his skull. Dirty hockey was being played that night. Altogether,

21 penalties were assessed, including four majors and a misconduct penalty. However, the tragic injury was not the result of foul play. Ted Kennedy of the Maple Leafs attempted to avoid a body check from Howe, who was speeding at him. The two players brushed one another, and Kennedy freed himself from the tangle and continued skating. Howe went hurtling headlong into the boards and crumpled onto the ice, face down. No penalty was given by referee George Gravel.

Howe was rushed to the hospital, semi-conscious and calling out for trainer Carl Mattson. Besides suffering a brain concussion and a cut eyeball, Howe's nose and cheek were badly fractured. Dr. Fred Schreiber, a brain specialist, was called in by the team's doctor to perform emergency, pressure-relieving surgery on Howe's brain, on which there was a pocket of fluid. The procedure took 90 minutes. Before he was removed from the ice, Howe apologized to Jack Adams for not being able to help out his team more!

After the surgery, Dr. Schreiber was quoted in the *Detroit News* as saying: "Howe came through satisfactorily. His condition is serious, but he has not been placed on the critical list. The fluid is draining and being absorbed by muscle tissue. He has been placed in an oxygen tent, but that is standard procedure after this kind of surgery."

Detroit won the next, fight-filled game in front of 14,297 fans. Two mass brawls erupted during the course of the game, each before the end of the second and third periods, respectively. The rough play caused then-NHL President Clarence Campbell to place two referees on the ice for the following third game in Toronto. The extra referee served as a referee subordinate and consultant to the chief referee. In the April 1, 1950 issue of the *Detroit News*, Campbell said: "It is clear from ... the first two games that the normal penalties provided are not sufficient deterrent to halt conduct which rapidly will bring the game of hockey into disrepute."

After the victory, in the March 31, 1950 issue of the *Detroit News*, Jack Adams said: "They played like champions. They were champions and they are champions. You don't make 88 points during the season playing canasta. They played the pants off Toronto and they did it with maybe the greatest

player in the world in the hospital."

At one point in the series, things looked grim for the Wings when Toronto led three games to two. However, Detroit goalie Harry Lumley came through in a big way during the last two games, and posted two consecutive shutouts. In the seventh and final game, Leo Reise scored at 8:30 of the first "sudden death" overtime period with a backhander he slid towards Toronto's Turk Broda. The goal allowed the Red Wings to make it to their third consecutive appearance in the Stanley Cup finals. Their opponents were the lowly New York Rangers, who had beaten Montreal in their five-game semifinal series. "We'd have won it in five games if Howe hadn't been hurt," said Jack Adams in the April 10, 1950 issue of the *Detroit News*. "He's one of the great hockey players, and no one knows how we missed him. It wrecked our best line and, for a time, our spirit."

The Red Wings were favorites to win the Stanley Cup. Adding to their favor, the Rangers were forced to sacrifice their home ice for a circus and played their "home" games at Maple Leaf Gardens, a building in which they had not won a game in three years. Despite the advantage, Detroit was still without Gordie Howe.

STANLEY CUP FINALS

In the finals, Detroit took the first game on home ice, played before 13,415 fans. Although the Rangers' O'Connor scored the series' first goal during the first period, Detroit scored four unanswered goals in the second, winning the contest. Not only were the Red Wings minus Gordie Howe, but Ted Lindsay and Jimmy Peters were also absent from the ice due to injuries.

The next two games were played in front of a Toronto crowd still bitter over Detroit's elimination of their team in the semi-finals. To the delight of fans at Maple Leaf Gardens, the Rangers took the first of those two matches. The Red Wings won the second, fightless match, blanking New York 4-0.

The Red Wings returned to Detroit for the next four games and lost the first two. New York coach Lynn Patrick was convinced that Detroit's players were wearing out from the lengthy semifinal match and the series at hand. Detroit lost the fifth game.

Harry Lumley and Pete Babando pose with the 1950 Stanley Cup, thanks to Babando's goal in double overtime. Hockey Hall of Fame archives.

Although they may have been tired, they did not let up, peppering New York goalie Chuck Rayner with 38 shots to the Rangers' 16.

The sixth game was a close 4-3 contest and was the most electrifying game of the post-season up to that point. Exactly 12,045 Olympia fans were on hand to watch their home town team beat the Rangers. In the match, Sid "Boot Nose" Abel came through in a big way for Detroit, breaking a 4-4 tie in the third period with an important goal on Chuck Rayner which won the game. The two clubs then faced off for what proved to be an action-packed, seventh game.

THE FINAL GAME - APRIL 23, 1950 (DETROIT)

Exactly 13,095 Detroit Red Wings fans were standing on their feet for the final game of the series, which after two periods of play was tied at three. New York started the game off strong by scoring the contest's first two goals midway through the first period. Stanley and Leswick each scored at 11:14 and 12:18, respectively. However, Detroit came back in the second period when Babando, Abel and McFadden all scored in the middle period. New York's O'Connor also scored, thus tying up the match.

No goals were scored in the third period, and the

game progressed into a first, then a second, overtime. Then, 8:31 seconds into the period, at 12:11 a.m., April 24, Pete Babando once again came through for Detroit, just as he had done in the second period. This time, however, he scored an historic, Stanley Cup-winning goal. Standing behind teammate George Gee, who was facing off against Buddy O'Connor, Babando received the puck from Gee and, without aiming, swung with all of his might. The puck sailed to the left of New York's goalie and into the net. The Red Wings were champions! It was the first time that the Stanley Cup was won in sudden-death overtime of a seventh game.

Equipment flew into the air as the weary Wings shouted in victory, hoisting coach Tommy Ivan to their shoulders. The Stanley Cup had not been in the possession of an American team since the Red Wings won it in 1943. NHL President Clarence Campbell presented the shining silver trophy to team captain Sid Abel, as team owners Jim Norris and Jack Adams walked to center ice. Chanting his name, the Olympia crowd roared for Gordie Howe to come to the ice as well. As the song "the moon shines tonight on pretty Red Wing ..." played from the organ, some of the players tossed their sticks into the crowd. In the dressing room, the champagne flowed, and some fans from the crowd came in to congratulate their home town players, who were true champions.

The Detroit team that graced Olympia ice in 1951-52 was perhaps the greatest of all time. That season, the Red Wings took the Stanley Cup home in eight straight post-season games. Terry Sawchuk allowed only five goals during the entire playoffs and shut out the opposition four times. Making this victory even more amazing is the fact that the Red Wings had to give up home-ice advantage to the Canadiens because of the circus, just as their opponents from New York had done in 1950. In a March 28, 1987 *Toronto Globe and Mail* article by Paul Patton, former Red Wing Marty Pavelich recalled: "In the final, we should have had home-ice advantage, but they had a circus in Detroit, so we opened in Montreal and beat them twice before coming home. It was just fantastic. We could have played all summer and never lost a game."

In a different Paul Patton article, Metro Prystai recalled Terry Sawchuk's performance in this series, commenting: "We never allowed a goal at home. We played four games and Terry Sawchuk had four shutouts. We won the final game 3-0 and I had two goals and one assist. Terry was 225 pounds and so big that you could hardly see the net, but quick as a cat. One year Jack Adams got mad as hell and said he was too big and told him to cut out drinking beer and lay off the potatoes, and he came back the next season thirty pounds lighter, but he was pretty sick from something."

1951-52 STANLEY CUP VICTORY

FIRST GAME: (April 10, at Montreal)
Red Wings 3, Canadiens 1
First Period
  No scoring
Second Period
  Detroit - Leswick (Pavelich) 3:27
Third Period
  Detroit - Leswick (Skov) 7:51
  Montreal - Johnson (Olmstead, Curry) 11:01
  Detroit - Lindsay (Abel) 18:44

SECOND GAME: (April 12, at Montreal)
Red Wings 2, Canadiens 1
First Period
  Detroit - Pavelich (Leswick, Skov) 16:09
  Montreal - Lach (Geoffrion) 18:37
Second Period
  Detroit - Lindsay 0:43
Third Period
  No Scoring

THIRD GAME: (April 13, at Detroit)
Red Wings 3, Canadiens 0
First Period
  Detroit - Howe (Stasiuk) 4:31
Second Period
  Detroit - Lindsay (Howe) 9:13
Third Period
  Detroit - Howe (Pavelich) 6:54

FOURTH GAME: (April 15, at Detroit)
Red Wings 3, Canadiens 0
First Period
  Detroit - Prystai (Delvecchio, Wilson) 6:50
Second Period
  Detroit - Skov (Prystai) 19:39
Third Period
  Detroit - Prystai 7:35

During the regular season, the Red Wings finished in first place for the fourth consecutive season, 22 points ahead of the second-place Montreal Canadiens. Both offensively and defensively, Detroit was a force to be reckoned with. The "Production Line" of Gordie Howe, Ted Lindsay and Sid Abel, combined with the line of Alex Delvecchio, Johnny Wilson and Metro Prystai, took care of the goals. Terry Sawchuk, winner of the Vezina Trophy, posted the NHL's lowest GAA. Four of the men on Detroit's roster (Gordie Howe, Ted Lindsay, Terry Sawchuk and Red Kelly) were All Stars.

In the semifinals, the heavily favored Red Wings eliminated Toronto in four straight matches. Toronto Manager Conn Smythe knew that it would be a tough fight between the two rivals. In the March 25, 1952 issue of the *Detroit News*, he said: "When the Red Wings beat us in the first round of the playoffs in 1950, they narrowly escaped losing the Stanley Cup to the New York Rangers in the final round. Their pride might have been stung, but they still won. Last spring, they didn't win. They were knocked off by the Canadiens. That's the blow that will send them roaring into the playoffs this year. They're not going to forget for a minute what happened to them last Spring."

In the following day's paper, after his team lost the first game in front of 14,316 Olympia fans, Smythe said: "We have 12 or 13 men who know they're defending champions. They'll stretch Detroit to the limit—the question is which team will break in the stretching."

As it happened, it was his beloved Maple Leafs who broke, and the Red Wings advanced to the Stanley Cup finals to face the Montreal Canadiens, who had eliminated the Boston Bruins in their semifinal series. In the April 2, 1952 issue of the *Detroit News*, Smythe admitted the truth after his team was washed away, saying: "[This is] Detroit's greatest team, much better than the Cup winners of two years ago, at least as good as that gang for which Bucko McDonald played."

STANLEY CUP FINALS

The first game of the Stanley Cup finals, played in Montreal on April 10, 1952, was marked with controversy. Detroit scored the game's first goal in the second period. Tony "Mighty Mouse" Leswick lifted the puck over Montreal goalie Gerry McNeil at a time when all of Montreal's defenders happened to be flat on the ice. Leswick netted another goal in the third period. Montreal's only goal of the game was also scored in the third.

The controversy came during the contest's last minutes. The game's timekeeper, a Mr. C.L. Lane from New York, was timing the game with a stopwatch. The Forum clock made the remaining time visible to the 14,533 fans present at the game. At the end of the third period, the announcer called out the customary "one minute remains in this game," and Montreal coach Dick Irvin pulled goaltender McNeil for an extra skater in an attempt to get a game-tying goal. On a pass from Sid Abel, it was Ted Lindsay who did the scoring—for the Red Wings.

After Lindsay's goal, the game continued—past the one minute mark—and went on for an extra minute of play before time was called. One story, given by a man who was near the Montreal bench that night, attempts to describe this occurrence. Supposedly a friend of coach Irvin's knew the Forum clock had a faulty buzzer and peeked over the timekeeper to get the "official" time for the announcer. The trouble was, he misread the watch and misinformed the announcer. Whatever the case, NHL President Clarence Campbell deemed the announcement correct and stated that the third period had actually been played for 21 minutes.

The Red Wings took the next two games, after which, in the April 14, 1952 issue of the *Detroit News*, Jack Adams said: "This is a fine team that has won everything else, and the guys intend to enter the record books as the first club to do the job in eight [games]." Joe Primeau, then coach of the Toronto Maple Leafs whom the Wings had eliminated, added: "They're a wonderfully balanced team. They just keep comin' and comin' at you, and if you do get through, down there at the other end of the rink is that Sawchuk." Destiny awaited an amazing Detroit Red Wings team in the final game.

THE FINAL GAME - APRIL 15, 1952 (DETROIT)

Before 14,545 screaming Detroit fans, the Red Wings eliminated the Habs in the fourth game of the series, 3-0. They proved to the world that, at the time, they were perhaps the greatest hockey team ever assembled. The men who made it all happen for Detroit during this game had not scored at all during any of the previous post-season games. They immediately proved their value.

In the first period, Metro Prystai got things going for Detroit when he scored at 6:50. Prystai's linemate, Glen Skov, with an assist from Prystai, scored the next goal at 19:39 of the middle period. Once again, it was Prystai who tallied for the Red Wings in the third and final period of the game with an unassisted goal at the 7:35 mark, ensuring Detroit's victory and the Stanley Cup.

After the victory, Montreal coach Dick Irvin shouted at the heckling Olympia fans and stormed off

the ice, locking the dressing room door to prevent Detroit reporters from entering. His players followed suit and forgot the traditional custom of congratulating their opponents on a job well done.

Altogether, the Wings outscored the Habs 11-2 in the final series. Sawchuk had sparkled between the pipes, allowing only two goals in the four final series games! During the entire eight-game post season, he had allowed only five goals and had shut out his opponents four straight times at the Olympia. In the April 16, 1952 issue of the *Detroit News*, he said that he was the most relaxed of all during the final game. He commented: "I don't think I had as many hard chances, either, and somehow I never had an idea that any would get through. Everybody up front was playing too well."

The 1951-52 Detroit Red Wings.

Back row (left to right): Assistant Trainer Lefty Wilson, Marty Pavelich, Glen Skov, Tony Leswick, Vic Stasiuk, Alex Delvecchio, Ben Woit, Gordon Howe, Marcel Pronovost, Enio Sclisizzi, Bob Goldham, Metro Prystai, Carl Mattson.

Front Row (left to right): Terry Sawchuk, Red Kelly, General Manager Jack Adams, Captain Sid Abel, Coach Tommy Ivan, Leo Reise, Ted Lindsay, Bill Tibbs.

1953-54 STANLEY CUP VICTORY

FIRST GAME: (April 4, at Detroit)
Red Wings 3, Canadiens 1
First Period
Detroit - Lindsay (Reibel, Delvecchio) 13:44
Second Period
Montreal - Geoffrion (Harvey, Masnick) 12:16
Third Period
Detroit - Reibel (Lindsay, Howe) 2:52
Detroit - Kelly (Pavelich, Leswick) 7:13

SECOND GAME: (April 6, at Detroit)
Canadiens 3, Red Wings 1
First Period
Montreal - Moore (Geoffrion, Beliveau) 15:03
Montreal - Richard (Moore) 15:30
Montreal - Richard (Moore) 15:59
Second Period
Detroit - Delvecchio 6:37
Third Period
No scoring

THIRD GAME: (April 8, at Montreal)
Red Wings 5, Canadiens 2
First Period
Detroit - Delvecchio (Howe) 0:42
Detroit - Lindsay (Kelly) 17:06
Second Period
Detroit - Wilson (Prystai) 4:57
Third Period
Montreal - Johnson 7:19
Detroit - Prystai (Delvecchio) 7:59
Detroit - Howe (Delvecchio, Woit) 11:32
Montreal - St. Laurent (MacKay) 15:02

FOURTH GAME: (April 10, at Montreal)
Red Wings 2, Canadiens 0
First Period
No scoring

Second Period
Detroit - Wilson (Prystai) 2:09
Third Period
Detroit - Kelly 19:53

FIFTH GAME: (April 11, at Detroit)
Canadiens 1, Red Wings 0
First Period
No scoring
Second Period
No scoring
Third Period
No scoring
Overtime
Montreal - Mosdell 5:45

SIXTH GAME: (April 13, at Montreal)
Canadiens 4, Red Wings 1
First Period
No scoring
Second Period
Montreal - Geoffrion (Beliveau) 12:07
Montreal - Curry (Olmstead, Masnick) 13:07
Montreal - Curry (Lach, Mazur) 14:25
Third Period
Detroit - Prystai 5:11
Montreal - Richard (Lach) 10:05

SEVENTH GAME: (April 16, at Detroit)
Red Wings 2, Canadiens 1
First Period
Montreal - Curry (Masnick) 9:17
Second Period
Detroit - Kelly (Delvecchio, Lindsay) 1:17
Third Period
No Scoring
Overtime
Detroit - Leswick (Skov) 4:29

In the regular season, Detroit recorded a sixth consecutive first-place finish, a feat that had never been accomplished by a major league sports team. After failing to win the Stanley Cup the previous season, the Red Wings were hungry. In the semi-finals, they met their old foes, the Toronto Maple Leafs, and beat them in five games.

In the fifth game of the semi-finals, Ted Lindsay scored a goal in second overtime that advanced the Red Wings into the finals. The game, tied at three, had progressed through a scoreless third period and one full period of overtime. Harry Lumley, then in

the nets for the Maple Leafs, recalled the goal in the April 2, 1954 issue of the *Detroit News*, saying: "The puck came out of a scramble on my left behind the net. Lindsay was all alone in front of me less than ten feet out when he fired in a backhander. It happened so quick I couldn't move."

At the Olympia 13,927 fans went wild with excitement when Lindsay put the biscuit in the basket at 12:08 a.m. Jack Adams, who was under orders to avoid the third periods of games, followed the doc's rules but returned for the *overtime* period! After the series-winning goal, King Clancy, then Toronto's coach, leaped over the boards and went over to congratulate Terry Sawchuk. Detroit, for the ninth time in the team's history, was going to the finals! In the same *Detroit News* article, a sarcastic Jack Adams gave his feeling on the upcoming series against the Habs. He said: "Dick Irvin said before the playoffs even began that Montreal had too much power for us. We probably won't win a game from them."

In their semifinal match, Montreal eliminated Boston. Goaltender Jacques Plante, who had replaced Gerry McNeil in goal, shut out the Bruins twice in that series, and a new center by the name of Jean Beliveau arrived from the amateur ranks for the largest sum ever paid to a rookie. Despite this, the Red Wings were still 2-1 favorites to win the Cup.

STANLEY CUP FINALS

In Detroit, the Red Wings' top defensive line of Marty Pavelich, Glen Skov and Tony Leswick was assigned to check Jean Beliveau, Dickie Moore and "Boom Boom" Geoffrion. They did a good job of it, and the Red Wings skated away with the first win of the series. However, they lost the next match at the Olympia 3-1. For 137 seconds, the Habs were on the power play. In 56 of those 137 seconds, they scored three times (at 15:03, 15:30 and 15:59). Two of the goals were scored in 29 seconds by Maurice "Rocket" Richard. During that first period, referee Red Storey infuriated the Olympia crowd when he failed to call Montreal for too many men on the ice and instead called Gordie Howe for high-sticking the Rocket. Detroit captain Red Kelly protested, but Storey insisted he had not see the infraction. In the last 36 minutes of the game, characterized by rough play, Storey called no penalties.

Jack Adams was infuriated, commenting in the April 7, 1954 issue of the *Detroit News*, "Do we throw away the rule book for the rest of the game? We advertised 60 minutes of hockey." Adams later commented that because he lived in Montreal, Storey should not have worked the games. He commented that other qualified officials from more neutral sites (such as Kitchener, Ontario) were available to officiate the games. After the contest, Storey had to be escorted out of the Olympia dressing room by six policeman, as a barrage of orange peels, newspapers and other assorted items flew at him.

The third game, played on April 8, 1954, in front of 14,481 Montreal fans, was a rough contest. Officiated by referee Bill Chadwick, the tables were turned in this match, as Chadwick called five players to the bench during the first 12 minutes. After that, there were no penalties for the next 38 minutes. Montreal ended up receiving twice as many penalties, with six to Detroit's three.

In the second period of the fourth game, Johnny Wilson got things going for Detroit by scoring first in a 2-0 win for his team. Shortly after Wilson's goal, Gordie Howe was assessed a five-minute penalty for slashing Doug Harvey. However, the Red Wings employed an excellent defensive effort and held off the Habs on their power play. Red Kelly ended up scoring the game's second and final goal late in the third period into an empty Montreal net. Detroit was now only one victory away from the Stanley Cup!

The Red Wings lost the next game in overtime after battling through three scoreless periods. They nearly missed winning the cherished trophy in front of 14,623 crazed Olympia fans when Glen Skov apparently scored during the second period. However, the goal was quickly disallowed by referee Bill Chadwick, who said Skov kicked the puck in. People in the press box noted that Skov was in the crease. In the April 12, 1954 issue of the *Detroit News*, Detroit coach Tommy Ivan said: "Glen told me the puck hit him in the chest, [and] dropped at his feet in a scramble in front of the net. The puck dribbled past Gerry McNeil and the red light flashed. I thought it was good, but referee Bill Chadwick explained that Skov kicked it in with his skate."

After disallowing the goal, the crowd, which was the second-largest of the season, went wild. Chadwick was nailed in the head with a bag of peanuts. Altogether, play had to stopped four times due to debris showering the rink. Besides the incident in which the goal was disallowed, other incidents excited the crowd. First was a roughing brawl. Then, Montreal's Tom Johnson cracked Alex Delvecchio over the head with his stick. Topping it all off, the fans thought that Chadwick failed to call a penalty on Rocket Richard.

The sixth game was even worse, as the Red Wings were able to squeeze off only one goal to Montreal's four. Both clubs were now tied at three victories. The

Red Wings were hungry for a win. Fueling their desire, they were asked to transport the Stanley Cup back to Detroit with their luggage.

THE FINAL GAME - APRIL 16, 1954 (DETROIT)

Before the final contest, in the April 12, 1954 issue of the *Detroit News*, Tommy Ivan said: "I'll grant the Canadiens outplayed us [in the sixth game], but we have some things working in our favor for Friday night. We'll be back at home. We'll have a couple days rest. We have fewer players and therefore the rest should mean more to us than to them."

Rest turned out to be a good thing for Detroit, as the seventh and deciding game went into overtime. Montreal scored the game's first goal at 9:17 of the opening period. Detroit's Red Kelly, assisted by Alex Delvecchio and Ted Lindsay, scored early in the middle period, and the game progressed into overtime after a scoreless third period.

A little over four minutes into overtime, Detroit's Tony Leswick came through in a big way and scored what has been dubbed a "fluke" goal to give the Red Wings their sixth Stanley Cup. It was the very first overtime goal Leswick had scored in an NHL game. As it happened, Detroit's Glen Skov battled a Montreal player to the right of the Habs' net. The puck made it to Leswick, who swung with all of his might. Montreal defenseman Doug Harvey saw Leswick's shot coming and attempted to block it with his hand. However, the shot ticked off of his finger, altering the flight pattern of the sailing rubber disc

and fooling Montreal goalie Gerry McNeil. The puck sailed past McNeil's right shoulder and hit the net up high, sending 15,791 Olympia fans to their feet in what has been called one of the loudest moments in the arena's history. McNeil was known for having a weakness for high shots. When asked if he had taken this into consideration, in the April 17, 1954 issue of the *Detroit News*, Leswick commented: "It's funny, but I didn't. I just shot as quickly as I could and it happened to go in high."

Goaltender McNeil said: "To lose on a goal like that. No, there was nothing screened about it. I saw it all the way. It was going to hit me on the chest. Doug Harvey put his hand out to try to stop it. He just ticked it with his glove and it deflected up into the corner, over my shoulder."

The Red Wings were presented with the Stanley Cup at center ice by NHL President Clarence Campbell, who was forced to cut his speech short due to the loud Olympia crowd that drowned out his voice. A group of fans in the crowd unveiled a large sign depicting the Red Wings as the new world champions. No officials from the Montreal Canadiens came to congratulate the Red Wings.

A celebration was held at the Sheraton-Cadillac Hotel. Montreal player Gaye Stewart, who had left Detroit in a trade for Tony Leswick, joined his former teammates at their celebration. Ted Lindsay made a toast to Goldham who had blocked many Montreal shots, calling him the greatest competitor in hockey. Once again, the Red Wings were hockey champions!

1954-55 STANLEY CUP VICTORY

FIRST GAME: (April 3, at Detroit)

Red Wings 4, Canadiens 2

First Period

No Scoring

Second Period

Montreal - Curry (MacKay, Mosdell) 5:09

Detroit - Delvecchio (Lindsay, Howe) 14:00

Third Period

Montreal - Curry (MacKay, Mosdell) 8:57

Detroit - Stasiuk (Howe, Lindsay) 13:05

Detroit - Pavelich 17:07

Detroit - Lindsay (Howe) 19:42

SECOND GAME: (April 5, at Detroit)

Red Wings 7, Canadiens 1

First Period

Detroit - Pronovost (Goldham) 2:15

Detroit - Lindsay (Howe, Reibel) 9:57

Detroit - Delvecchio (Stasiuk, Goldham) 16:00

Detroit - Howe (Reibel) 17:11

Second Period

Detroit - Lindsay (Howe, Reibel) 8:10

Detroit - Lindsay (Delvecchio) 15:48

Detroit - Lindsay (Reibel, Howe) 19:37

Third Period

Montreal - Mosdell (St. Laurent, Curry) 12:32

1954-55 STANLEY CUP VICTORY (CONTINUED)

THIRD GAME: (April 7, at Montreal)
Canadiens 4, Red Wings 2
First Period
Montreal - Geoffrion (Beliveau, Olmstead) .. 8:30
Montreal - Geoffrion 8:42
Detroit - Kelly (Stasiuk) 18:12
Second Period
Montreal - Geoffrion (Beliveau) 14:32
Detroit - Stasiuk (Pavelich, Delvecchio) 16:16
Third Period
Montreal - Leclair (Moore) 7:50

FOURTH GAME: (April 9, at Montreal)
Canadiens 5, Red Wings 3
First Period
Montreal - MacKay (Mosdell, Harvey) 0:40
Detroit - Reibel (Kelly) 12:38
Second Period
Montreal - Geoffrion 3:40
Montreal - Beliveau 8:25
Montreal - Johnson 9:07
Third Period
Montreal - Curry (MacKay) 2:33
Detroit - Reibel (Lindsay, Howe) 3:40
Detroit - Hay (Reibel) 12:00

FIFTH GAME: (April 10, at Detroit)
Red wings 5, Canadiens 1
First Period
Montreal - Beliveau(Harvey, Moore) 8:01
Detroit - Skov 12:59
Detroit - Howe 18:29

Second Period
Detroit - Howe (Delvecchio, Lindsay) 12:29
Detroit - Howe (Lindsay, Kelly) 16:20
Third Period
Detroit - Stasiuk (Delvecchio, Bonin) 2:09

SIXTH GAME: (April 12, at Montreal)
Canadiens 6, Red Wings 3
First Period
Montreal - Beliveau (Harvey) 7:30
Detroit - Delvecchio (Stasiuk) 13:36
Second Period
Montreal - Leclair (Geoffrion, Harvey) 3:45
Montreal - Geoffrion (Beliveau, Harvey) 5:21
Detroit - Delvecchio (Lindsay, Pronovost) 15:54
Montreal - Geoffrion (Beliveau, Bouchard) ..18:18
Third Period
Montreal - Curry (MacKay, Mosdell) 0:19
Detroit - Kelly (Leswick, Pavelich) 16:23
Montreal - MacKay (Olmstead) 18:55

SEVENTH GAME: (April 14, at Detroit)
Red Wings 3, Canadiens 1
First Period
No scoring
Second Period
Detroit - Delvecchio (Kelly) 7:12
Detroit - Howe (Pronovost) 19:49
Third Period
Detroit - Delvecchio 2:59
Montreal - Curry (Geoffrion, Beliveau) 14:35

In 1954-55, the Detroit Red Wings won the last Stanley Cup of the 1950s. The taste of victory would be sorely missed after this season, until Detroit reclaimed the cherished Cup again in 1996-97. The road to that victory proved to be perhaps the most colorful ever. Aside from the usual struggle for victory, it was marked by controversy, tear gas, riots and the assaulting of NHL President Clarence Campbell.

The road began during the regular season when, after sitting in third place, the Red Wings suddenly got hot. They started a record-setting, 15-game winning streak that eventually went two games into the Stanley Cup finals against Montreal. They had previously recorded a ten-game winning streak in 1952 but were on fire and broke what at the time was a record held by the Boston Bruins (14

consecutive victories in 1929-30). Late in the race for the regular season championship, Detroit's streak took them one point away from Montreal, then in first place. At that time, the Canadiens played a game against Boston, where a stick-swinging melee erupted. Maurice "Rocket" Richard punched NHL linesman Cliff Thompson, drawing a suspension from President Clarence Campbell for the rest of the season, including the playoffs.

The night after the Boston incident, Detroit met the Canadiens at the Forum, where fans threatened to kill Campbell if he showed up. First place hung in the balance. To the displeasure of the crowd, Campbell showed up. The Canadiens fell behind 4-1, and an array of garbage littered the ice. A tear gas bomb exploded. A fan assaulted Campbell, punching him in the face, and the police raced in to "put out the fire." Outside the Forum, looting, burning and mayhem erupted in the streets. Campbell forfeited the game to the Red Wings, who were then in first place. They won the following night's game and their seventh consecutive Prince of Wales Trophy as first place champions. After the incident, Rocket Richard, accompanied by his wife, left Canada for New York City to avoid the barrage of telephone calls and intrusions that became commonplace after the riotous game.

Quoted in the March 21, 1955 issue of the *Detroit News*, Montreal coach Dick Irvin didn't see the victory as favorable, exclaiming before he boarded the train: "Tear gas champions, that's what we'll have to call them. We won't win a game in the playoffs. Our boys feel they got the worst of it in that forfeit. I can't convince them otherwise. It was unfair to Lumley [Montreal's goalie], too. Sawchuk played 40 minutes less than Lumley, because only one period was played in Montreal. But Sawchuk gets the Vezina Trophy. How do you know how that game would have come out if they had finished it? Early in the season we led Detroit 3-0 with only two minutes left in the second period. Detroit won 4-3. In a later game, Detroit led us 2-0 after the first period. We won 4-2."

The Red Wings' streak continued after the regular season, enabling them to burn up the Maple Leafs in four consecutive games. "I'm not predicting we'll win the Stanley Cup, but it will take a superhuman effort to keep us from winning," exclaimed Jack Adams before their semifinal series in the March 22, 1955 issue of the *Detroit News*. Detroit, as Adams proclaimed, was unstoppable. The final goal in the fourth game was an empty-netter. Behind 2-0, the Leafs pulled goalie Harry Lumley for an extra skater. However, Tony Leswick, who had won the Cup for Detroit the previous season, slapped a 95-foot, backhanded shot into the Toronto goal after receiving a pass from Marty Pavelich. All of the Toronto players, with the exception of Ted Kennedy, came over to congratulate the Wings. Kennedy shook former teammate Bob Goldham's hand and skated off the ice.

Montreal coach Dick Irvin was discouraged by the loss of superstar Richard and commented that he did not see how his team could win without him.

However, in five games, the Canadiens eliminated Boston in their semifinal series. Between 200-300 police were present at Forum games after the previous violent eruption. In front of Clarence Campbell's box, a total of ten police stood facing him at one contest to protect him from any possible assaults. Rocket Richard, who had returned from his short New York visit, returned to the Montreal Forum as a spectator.

STANLEY CUP FINALS

Before Detroit and Montreal faced off for what turned out to be a seven-game final series, Jack Adams expressed his delight over the fact that it was Montreal, and not Boston, they were playing for the Cup. In the April 1, 1955 issue of the *Detroit News*, he said: "We're glad we're playing Montreal instead of Boston for the Stanley Cup. Not that Montreal will be an easier opponent. I'm not discounting them one bit, for they've gotten over the shock of losing Maurice Richard. But the Wings have 'come up' for their games with Montreal the latter part of the season, winning five of the last six, whereas, it was harder to get them keyed up for Boston."

The Habs, without Richard, were still formidable opponents. They had Bernie "Boom Boom" Geoffrion, who ended up as the NHL's regular-season scoring champion, one point ahead of The Rocket and Jean Beliveau, who was third in NHL scoring. In goal was the reliable Jacques Plante.

When the finals began, Jimmy Skinner, in his rookie season as Detroit's head coach, piloted his spirited team to two victories in the Olympia, extending their unbeaten streak to a record 15 games. The second of those two contests was a 7-1 spanking in front of 13,942 fans. In that game, Ted Lindsay scored four goals, three in the third period. Montreal's Dickie Moore skated over to Lindsay, wanting to drop the gloves, but Lindsay ignored him and coolly exited the playing surface. The referee ejected Moore from the game for that, and for his threats and violence towards a spectator, referee and linesman. After his productive game, Lindsay reminded everyone that, while they could win the Cup in two more games, they still had a challenging road ahead.

He was right, as the Canadiens won the next two contests in Montreal, breaking the Wings' winning streak on April 7, 1955 in front of 13,571 Montreal fans. The fifth and sixth games saw each team win a game apiece in their respective cities. After Detroit won the fifth game, 5-1 in front of the largest Olympia playoff crowd to that date, Montreal coach Dick Irvin predicted the Wings would eliminate his team at the Forum the following night! In the April 11, 1955 issue of the *Detroit News*, he said: "We've hit the bottom of the barrel here. We've gone as far as we can go. We're run down—we've played a game about every other night for the last month. We're infirm. This team is as bad off physically as any we've had in the playoffs in years." Despite his prediction, the Habs won the sixth game, 6-3. Once again, the series would be decided by a seventh match.

THE FINAL GAME - APRIL 14, 1955 (DETROIT)

In front of 15,541 fans, the largest Olympia crowd of the season, the Red Wings won their seventh Stanley Cup when they beat the Montreal Canadiens 3-1. After a scoreless first period, Alex Delvecchio and Gordie Howe each put a point on the scoreboard for Detroit. Delvecchio added another goal in the third period. Montreal right winger Floyd Curry scored for the Habs in the third period as well. However, it was futile for Montreal, as the Red Wings were victors when the final horn sounded.

They were presented with the Stanley Cup on the ice. Lindsay was quoted in the April 15, 1955 issue of the *Detroit News* as shouting to the crowd: "Earlier in the season they called us bums and I guess it took bums to win it." In the dressing room, beer flowed and the players shouted in victory. A celebration similar to the previous season's followed at the Sheraton-Cadillac. From the chair upon which he was standing, Ted Lindsay poured champagne from the Stanley Cup and made toasts to his teammates.

After the victory, in the April 15, 1955 issue of the *Detroit News*, Jack Adams said: "When some of these same boys were a little younger, we had teams that might have been better. But this bunch has 'em all beat on one score—it's the greatest clutch team I've ever had. They won every game that had to be won." In the same article, emphasizing the importance of team play, Bob Goldham added: "You can't win a National Hockey League championship and a Stanley Cup without 17 players."

Altogether, the Red Wings set four Stanley Cup Playoff records and tied another: Most points by an individual–Gordie Howe (nine goals for 20 points); most points by a line–Gordie Howe, Ted Lindsay and Dutch Reibel (51 points); highest-scoring NHL team in Stanley Cup history with 27 total post-season goals; highest scoring final series (47 goals); and most assists by an individual– (12, equaled by Ted Lindsay).

END OF AN ERA - BEGINNING OF A DYNASTY

After winning their seventh Stanley Cup, the Detroit Red Wings made it to the finals against the Montreal Canadiens in 1955-56 but were eliminated in five games. The Habs went on to win the Stanley Cup for the next five seasons, enjoying a "dynasty" of their own, until the Chicago Blackhawks won it in 1960-61. Toronto and Montreal continued winning the Stanley Cup after Chicago's temporary interruption, keeping the trophy out of the United States until 1969-70, when it was won by the Boston Bruins. However, the era of the 1950s will always have a special place in the memories of the many Detroit Red Wings fans who were fortunate to be alive at the time. It will stand out forever as the brightest hockey era the Motor City has ever known.

The 1964-65 Detroit Red Wings were the last team to make the Stanley Cup finals until 1994-95.

CHAPTER ELEVEN

THE END OF AN ERA
- THE 1960s -

Detroit started the 1960s off strong. They made it to the Stanley Cup finals four times and to the semifinals once between 1960-61 and 1965-66. However, the success that was so close soon faded away. The latter half of the decade marked the beginning of some very unsuccessful years for Detroit. From 1966-67 to 1982-83, the team would fail to make the playoffs every season except 1969-70 and 1977-78, when they reached the quarterfinals.

The close calls in the post-season were frustrating for Red Wings fans and players alike. Former Detroit defenseman Bill Gadsby explains: "We were in the finals and in the semifinals in the Stanley Cup playoffs quite a few times, but I guess it just wasn't in the cards to win it. We gave it a pretty good try a few years. The Red Wings had a pretty good hockey club, but just couldn't do the trick, so it was just one of those things. You know, we would have loved to win it, but if you can't and you give it a good try, it is kind of satisfying."

The 1960s also marked the end of the "original six" era, and the beginning of expansion, as the league doubled in size in 1967. However, before expansion, it was a still a time of intense rivalries between teams, and an era when defenseman began moving into the offense more than ever before. Elliott Trumbull, former public relations director for the Red Wings, described the era:

The rivalry. The Detroit-Montreal, Detroit-Toronto rivalry...I mean, there was hatred there. A cute little story, Jack Adams' wife, Helen Adams, used to sit behind the visiting bench. Jack's seat at the Olympia was behind the home bench, of course. But Mrs. Adams had the corresponding seat behind the visiting bench. And, of course, in those days the visiting team walked right through the lobby, through the corridor, right out onto the ice, right by the bench. They would have to pass by her. Well, it wasn't so bad if it was Chicago, Boston or New York, but when Montreal or Toronto came..... Mrs. Adams would be talking or something, and she would stop talking and look away. She would make sure she wouldn't be looking to her right, because that's the way they were, over her right shoulder, walking onto the ice. She'd look away, she wouldn't even look at them! This was the wife of the general manager. That's how much of a hatred there was.

You played the same team 14 times a year, seven times there, seven times at home. Everybody knew everybody on the team. They were sell-out crowds every night. It was fine, fine hockey. Two-to-one games, no ten-to-eight games or eight-to-six. This was when the teams played defense. Of course, the way the game is played now, I can't knock it, because that's the way it's played. Bobby Orr, he's the one that changed the whole game when he became an offensive defenseman. Yeah, they would rush the puck [in our era]. But still, their main objective was to get the hell back and protect the goal. But Orr, Christ, he'd be up in the forward line, in the

offensive zone more than back in the defensive zone. In fact, years ago, I jokingly said, 'Hey, they shouldn't call them defensemen any more, they should call them rear forwards.' I mean you've got five forwards on the ice. Like we have now with the Red Wings and these five Russians. I mean, the way they play, there's nobody in any position. They rove around like the Harlem Globetrotters. It is marvelous to see. The game has gotten so fluid. I suppose that if you looked back at the old days, you'd say, 'Geez, it's pretty static.'

STANLEY CUP FINAL APPEARANCES

During the 1960s, the Red Wings made it to the Stanley Cup finals on four occasions. Despite having a great deal of talent on their roster, they were not able to take home Lord Stanley's Chalice. These final appearances were the team's very last until 1994-95,

1960-61 STANLEY CUP FINALS

FIRST GAME: (April 6, at Chicago)
Black Hawks 3, Red Wings 2
First Period
Chicago - Hull (M. Balfour, Mikita) 9:39
Chicago - Wharram (McDonald, Mikita) . . .10:10
Chicago - Hull (Pilote, M. Balfour) 13:15
Second Period
Detroit - Lunde (Howe) 16:14
Third Period
Detroit - Johnson (Howe, Ullman) 19:18

SECOND GAME: (April 8, at Detroit)
Red Wings 3, Black Hawks 1
First Period
Detroit - Young (Stasiuk, Delvecchio) 8:10
Detroit - Delvecchio (Howe, Johnson) 17:39
Second Period
Chicago - Pilote 0:41
Third Period
Detroit - Delvecchio (Stasiuk, Howe) 19:22

THIRD GAME: (April 10, at Chicago)
Black Hawks 3, Red Wings 1
First Period
No scoring
Second Period
Chicago - Mikita (Pilote, Hull) 11:56
Chicago - Murphy (Pilote, Litzenberger) 14:19
Chicago - M. Balfour (Hull, Hay) 18:17
Third Period
Detroit - Howe (Delvecchio, Young) 9:28

FOURTH GAME: (April 12, at Detroit)
Red Wings 2, Black Hawks 1
First Period
No scoring

Second Period
Chicago - Hay (M. Balfour, Hull) 7:34
Detroit - Delvecchio (MacGregor, Howe) 8:48
Third Period
Detroit - MacGregor (Fonteyne, Godfrey) . .13:10

FIFTH GAME: (April 14, at Chicago)
Black Hawks 6, Red Wings 3
First Period
Detroit - Labine (Johnson, Ullman) 2:14
Chicago - M. Balfour (Hay, Hull) 9:36
Chicago - Murphy (Nesterenko, St. Laurent) 10:04
Detroit - Glover (MacGregor, Fonteyne) 18:49
Second Period
Chicago - M. Balfour (Pilote, Hay) 16:25
Detroit - Stasiuk (Howe, Pronovost) 15:35
Third Period
Chicago - Mikita (Vasko, Pilote) 2:51
Chicago - Pilote (Wharram, Mikita) 7:12
Chicago - Mikita (Murphy) 13:27

SIXTH GAME: (April 16, at Detroit)
Black Hawks 5, Red Wings 1
First Period
Detroit - MacDonald (Howe, Delvecchio) . . .15:26
Second Period
Chicago - Fleming 6:45
Chicago - McDonald (Mikita, Hull) 18:47
Third Period
Chicago - Nesterenko (Sloan, Pilote) 0:57
Chicago - Evans 6:27
Chicago - Wharram .18:00

when the Red Wings met the New Jersey Devils in the finals.

1960-61 STANLEY CUP FINALS

On April 16, 1961, before 14,328 Detroit fans, the Red Wings met the Chicago Blackhawks in the final game of the post-season. The Blackhawks took home their third Stanley Cup. It had been 23 years since the Windy City had been awarded the silver trophy.

"We weren't the best team in the league at that particular time," explains former Chicago great Stan Mikita. "As far as the regular season goes, I think we finished in third place. However, we had some great goal-tending from Glenn Hall and some good scoring from different people. That's what you need to win."

Detroit, who had finished the regular season in fourth place, beat the second-place Toronto Maple Leafs 4-1 in their semifinal series. The Blackhawks faced off with, and defeated, the Montreal Canadiens in their semifinal series, beating them 4-2

The first game of the series, held in Chicago on April 6, was won by the burly Blackhawks. The second game, played in Detroit, was a 3-1 victory in favor of Detroit. The third game was also a 3-1 game, but this time in favor of the Hawks. After traveling back to the Motor City, the fourth game was taken by the Red Wings. Detroit lost 6-3 in the fifth, action-packed game, held in Chicago.

THE FINAL GAME

The sixth game of the series was the key for Chicago. It was in this game that the team, described at the time by many experts to be the best that had ever represented Chicago in the NHL, worked its magic.

The game was dominated heavily by the Red Wings until early in the second period. At 15:24 of the first period, Parker MacDonald put Detroit ahead 1-0, scoring on the power play. Gordie Howe successfully executed a 40-foot drive which Glenn Hall stopped with his pads. However, MacDonald got the rebound and slipped it past Hall.

In the second period, Chicago gained momentum. Goals from Reg Fleming at 6:45 and Ab McDonald at 18:47 put the Hawks ahead 2-1. The Red Wings went on the power play after Wayne Hicks, who was filling in for Chicago's injured Murray Balfour, was penalized. While the Blackhawks were concentrating on defense to kill the penalty, Fleming made an unassisted rush towards the Detroit goal and scored on Hank Bassen after poke-checking the puck away from Red Wing defenseman Pete Goegan.

Many believed Fleming's goal to be the turning point of the game for Chicago. Although he agreed that particular goal was important, then-Chicago goalie Glenn Hall gave his impression of the game: "It's a combination of 20 guys or 18 guys, whatever you had in those days, and just getting a few good breaks. And believe me, you need the breaks."

McDonald's goal came after Stan Mikita made a pass to Bobby Hull. Bassen came out of the crease to meet Hull and was knocked over into left wing. McDonald, who was skating down left wing, leaped over Bassen and slapped the puck into the empty net.

Although Chicago was powerful during the second period, the Red Wings weren't exactly asleep. Glenn Hall made several saves that were critical to the Chicago victory. Still on the power play after Fleming had scored, Pete Goegan executed a hard, high shot from the blue line which Hall caught with his left, deep in the net. Three minutes later, Detroit went on the power play once again, and Gordie Howe ripped an almost identical shot at Hall, which bounced off his right arm and over his extended right hand. Hall made the save, once again deep in the net.

The third period was dominated heavily by Chicago, who scored three goals against the Wings, causing their confidence to slip. All of the goals were either the product of Detroit's defense giving up the chase, or breakaways. Eric Nesterenko, assisted by Pierre Pilote and Tod Sloan at 0:57, put another point on the scoreboard. Then, although he had scored only two goals during the season, and only one in the previous two seasons, Chicago defenseman Jack Evans scored an unassisted goal at 6:27. Finally, Kenny Wharram put in the final goal that ensured a Chicago victory at 18:00. The final score: Chicago 5, Detroit 1.

When the smoke finally cleared, Hall had made 21 saves, and Bassen had made 20. "Both clubs had the heart, the spirit, the desire," said Chicago Coach Rudy Pilous. "The flesh was a little weak at the end, but we just had a little more left."

1962-63 STANLEY CUP FINALS

FIRST GAME: (April 9, at Toronto)
Maple Leafs 4, Red Wings 2
First Period
   Toronto - Duff (Keon, Stanley) 0:49
   Toronto - Duff (Stanley, Horton) 1:08
   Toronto - Nevin 14:42
Second Period
   Detroit - Jeffrey (Ullman, Smith) 5:36
   Detroit - Jeffrey (Howe, Ullman) 8:05
Third Period
   Toronto - Nevin (Pulford, Shack) 5:08

SECOND GAME: (April 11, at Toronto)
Maple Leafs 4, Red Wings 2
First Period
   Toronto - Litzenberger (Pulford, Horton) 5:31
   Toronto - Stewart (Litzenberger, Kelly) 18:42
Second Period
   Toronto - Nevin (Stanley, Horton) 0:49
   Detroit - Howe (Delvecchio, M. Pronovost) . . . 1:32
   Toronto - Stewart (Litzenberger, Harris) 8:55
Third Period
   Detroit - Howe (Jeffrey, Ullman) 2:03

THIRD GAME: (April 14, at Detroit)
Red Wings 3, Maple Leafs 2
First Period
   Detroit - Stasiuk (Ullman, Smith) 0:33
   Toronto - Keon (Duff, Brewer) 14:56

Second Period
   Detroit - Faulkner (MacGregor, M. Pronovost) . . .8:13
   Toronto - Horton (Kelly) 13:06
   Detroit - Faulkner (A. Pronovost, M.Pronovost) ..13:39
Third Period
   No scoring

FOURTH GAME: (April 16, at Detroit)
Maple Leafs 4, Red Wings 2
First Period
   Detroit - Howe (Delvecchio, P. MacDonald) . 2:54
Second Period
   Toronto - Armstrong (Keon) 1:17
   Detroit - Joyal (Howe) 2:38
   Toronto - Kelly (Mahovlich, Baun) 17:41
Third Period
   Toronto - Keon 9:42
   Toronto - Kelly 17:45

FIFTH GAME: (April 18, at Toronto)
Maple Leafs 3, Red Wings 1
First Period
   Toronto - Keon (Armstrong) 17:44
Second Period
   Detroit - Delvecchio (Howe, M.Pronovost) . . . 0:49
Third Period
   Toronto - Shack (Douglas, Pulford) 13:28
   Toronto - Keon (Armstrong, Stanley) 19:55

In 1962, the Toronto Maple Leafs won the Stanley Cup with a roster full of older players that coach/general manager Punch Imlach acquired from other clubs. Critics called the victory a mishap. However, the Leafs proved them wrong by repeating in 1963. With big, strong hockey veterans like Johnny Bower, Ed Litzenberger, Allan Stanley, Red Kelly, Eddie Shack and Don Simmons, the Leafs had a great deal of depth and beat Montreal in the semifinals. They went on to beat the Red Wings, who in six games had eliminated Chicago in their semifinal series, winning the last four straight.

Despite the Red Wings having Gordie Howe, Alex Delvecchio and an aging-but-competent Terry Sawchuk in goal, the Leafs won the first two games of the series, both played in Toronto. Back home, they were able to win game three, but the first-place Maple Leafs won the remaining two games, taking the Cup in five.

In game three, Detroit fans tossed eggs at the Maple Leafs. Former Detroit defenseman Bill Gadsby remembers the game, commenting: "Oh, yeah. They were throwing a lot of things. That happened not only at the Olympia, but at a lot of the different places we played. But, it wasn't really right. Those eggs are kind of messy things. But the fans get riled up once in a while, and you know you can curtail them as good as you should. They get a little wild."

Besides eggs, Detroit fans tossed octopi. In John DeVaney and Burt Goldblatt's book *The Stanley Cup*, former Toronto Maple Leaf Frank Mahovlich remembered: "They threw everything at you in Detroit. What I remember best was seeing an octopus come down. There was a chap who had a [fish supply store], I guess, and every year at the Stanley Cup it was kind of a tradition. He'd throw this little octopus, and it would be alive until it landed flat on the ice and then it was a big blah. They just swept it away, the poor thing."

(Left to right): Gordie Howe, Norm Ullman and Alex Delvecchio.

1963-64 STANLEY CUP FINALS

FIRST GAME: (April 11, at Toronto)
Maple Leafs 3, Red Wings 2
First Period
    Detroit - MacGregor (Barkley) 4:31
    Toronto - Armstrong (Stanley, McKenney) ... 4:44
    Detroit - Howe (MacDonald, Delvecchio) ...10:25
Second Period
    No scoring
Third Period
    Toronto - Armstrong (Kelly, McKenney) 4:02
    Toronto - Pulford 19:58

SECOND GAME: (April 14, at Toronto)
Red Wings 4, Maple Leafs 3
First Period
    Toronto - Stanley (Kelly, Mahovlich) 11:57
    Detroit - Ullman (Gadsby, Jeffrey) 12:43
Second Period
    Detroit - Joyal (Barkley) 3:19
    Detroit - Smith (Howe) 16:15
Third Period
    Toronto - Kelly (Baun, Mahovlich) 11:57
    Toronto - Ehman (Bathgate, Stewart) 19:17
Overtime
    Detroit - Jeffrey (Ullman, Howe) 7:52

THIRD GAME: (April 16, at Detroit)
Red Wings 4, Maple Leafs 3
First Period
    Detroit - Smith 2:40
    Detroit - MacGregor (Barkley, Martin) 3:38
    Detroit - Smith (Ullman, Delvecchio) 14:47
Second Period
    Toronto - Bathgate (Mahovlich, Kelly) 4:16
Third Period
    Toronto - Keon (McKenney, Armstrong) 7:34
    Toronto - McKenney (Keon, Horton) 18:47
    Detroit - Delvecchio (Howe, A. Pronovost) ..19:43

FOURTH GAME: (April 18, at Detroit)
Maple Leafs 4, Red Wings 2
First Period
    Toronto - Keon (Horton, McKenney) 5:45

Second Period
    Detroit - MacGregor (Joyal) 5:57
    Detroit - Howe (Ullman, Jeffrey) 13:05
    Toronto Keon (McKenney, Armstrong) 16:09
Third Period
    Toronto - Bathgate (Mahovlich, Kelly) 10:55
    Toronto - Mahovlich (Pulford, Stewart) 18:09

FIFTH GAME: (April 21, at Toronto)
Red Wings 2, Maple Leafs 1
First Period
    Detroit - Howe (Delvecchio) 10:52
Second Period
    No scoring
Third Period
    Detroit - Joyal (A. Pronovost) 7:50
    Toronto - Armstrong (Mahovlich, Bathgate) .14:57

SIXTH GAME: (April 23, at Detroit)
Maple Leafs 4, Red Wings 3
First Period
    Toronto - Pulford (Stanley) 17:01
Second Period
    Detroit - Henderson (Martin) 4:20
    Detroit - Martin (MacMillan, Howe) 10:56
    Toronto - Pulford (Stewart, Brewer) 14:36
    Detroit - Howe (Delvecchio, Gadsby) 15:56
    Toronto - Harris (Armstrong, Baun) 17:48
Third Period
    No scoring
Overtime
    Toronto - Baun (Pulford) 3:07

SEVENTH GAME: (April 25, at Toronto)
Maple Leafs 4, Red Wings 0
First Period
    Toronto - Bathgate 3:04
Second Period
    No scoring
Third Period
    Toronto - Keon (Harris) 4:26
    Toronto - Kelly (Mahovlich, Stanley) 5:53
    Toronto - Armstrong (Mahovlich) 15:26

In 1964, the Detroit Red Wings finished the regular season in fourth place. In the finals, they met the third-place Toronto Maple Leafs, who had now won two consecutive Stanley Cups. Injuries plagued Detroit during the regular season, making its road to the playoffs difficult. However, they overcame adversity and eventually made it to the finals after eliminating Chicago in seven games.

The finals were filled with excitement. Toronto won the first contest when Bob Pulford scored with 10 seconds remaining in a 2-2 tie. Gordie Howe attempted to knock the puck away from Pulford, but did not get there in time. The second game progressed into overtime, until Detroit emerged victorious, tying the series. The winning goal came after Gordie Howe made a pass to Larry Jeffrey.

Frank Mahovlich, Alex Delvecchio, Gordie Howe and Roger Crozier were key players for Detroit during the 1960s.

Without Jeffrey ever moving his stick, the puck hopped off of it and past Toronto's goaltender, Johnny Bower.

When Alex Delvecchio scored with 20 seconds remaining in game three, the Red Wings were able to pull ahead in the series by one game. In that game, the Maple Leafs had been losing 3-0, but came back and tied up the match with only 73 seconds remaining.

Each team registered a win in the opposition's home rink before game six of the series. Detroit was only one win away from the Stanley Cup. In the sixth contest, a puck hit Toronto's Bobby Baun, breaking his ankle. After leaving the ice on a stretcher, he returned to play with it frozen, and did something that one Detroit defenseman will never forget.

"He got a lot of ink off of that broken ankle he was supposed to have," says Bill Gadsby. "I don't know how it could be broken and you play. He might have had a hairline fracture, but anyway, that's beside the point. Yeah, he came back. He probably

had a very, very sore ankle, but he came back on the ice and that [shot] went [off] my stick, [and] went over my shoulder. [It] was going to hit me in the face, really, and I put my stick up and hands to protect myself. It went off my stick, I looked over my shoulder and it was just going in like a lame duck in the top part of the net. Sawchuk never saw it. That was a big break on their part. It just happened to be that way, that's all. Maybe I should have let it hit me and there would have been no goal, but you never know about those things."

Whatever the case, the Maple Leafs won the game on Baun's overtime goal, on which he was assisted by Bob Pulford. Baun came back to play in the seventh and final game of the series, which Toronto won as well. Detroit never scored another goal in the series, as the Leafs blanked them 4-0 in the final contest.

A true sportsman, Gordie Howe went into the Maple Leaf's dressing room to have champagne with them after they won the Cup. He swapped sticks with Johnny Bower and remarked that he should have taken away Bower's stick a long time ago!

1965-66 STANLEY CUP FINALS

FIRST GAME: (April 24, at Montreal)
Red Wings 3, Canadiens 2
First Period
Detroit - Smith (Bathgate) 13:25
Second Period
Montreal - Backstrom (J. C. Tremblay) 4:23
Detroit - Gadsby (McDonald) 5:14
Third Period
Detroit - Henderson (Marshall) 2:14
Montreal - Harper (Rousseau) 2:36

SECOND GAME: (April 26, at Montreal)
Red Wings 5, Canadiens 2
First Period
Montreal - J. C. Tremblay (Beliveau, Cournoyer) . 6:55
Detroit - Bathgate (Prentice, Ullman) 18:39
Second Period
No scoring
Third Period
Detroit - MacGregor (Henderson, Ullman) ... 1:55
Detroit - McDonald (Gadsby, Smith) 2:45
Montreal - Cournoyer (Harper, Price) 12:00
Detroit - Smith (Bathgate) 12:28
Detroit - Prentice (Delvecchio) 16:25

THIRD GAME: (April 28, at Detroit)
Canadiens 4, Red Wings 2
First Period
Detroit - Ullman 4:20
Montreal - Balon (Harper, Richard) 15:40
Montreal - Beliveau 19:12
Second Period
No scoring
Third Period
Montreal - G. Tremblay (Beliveau) 1:45
Montreal - G. Tremblay (J. C. Tremblay, Rousseau) . 3:21
Detroit - Howe (Marshall, Delvecchio) 19:59

FOURTH GAME: (May 1, at Detroit)
Canadiens 2, Red Wings 1
First Period
No Scoring
Second Period
Detroit - Ullman (MacGregor, Henderson) ..11:24
Montreal - Beliveau (J. C. Tremblay, Duff) ...19:51
Third Period
Montreal - Backstrom (Duff, Roberts) 13:37

FIFTH GAME: (May 3, at Montreal)
Canadiens 5, Red Wings 1
First Period
Montreal - Provost (Backstrom, J. C. Tremblay) . 1:06
Montreal - Cournoyer (J. C. Tremblay, G. Tremblay). 19:21
Second Period
Montreal - Balon (Rochefort, Richard) 1:05
Montreal - Rousseau (Duff, Backstrom) 11:22
Detroit - Ullman (Henderson, Bathgate) 14:22
Third Period
Montreal - Duff (Richard) 5:31

SIXTH GAME: (May 5, at Detroit)
Canadiens 3, Red Wings 2
First Period
Montreal - Beliveau (Provost, G. Tremblay) .. 9:08
Second Period
Montreal - Rochefort (Richard, Balon) 10:11
Detroit - Ullman (Delvecchio, Howe) 11:55
Third Period
Detroit - Smith (McDonald, Bergman) 10:30
Overtime
Montreal - Richard (Balon, Roberts) 2:30

The 1965-66 season was a turning point for the Detroit Red Wings. After 1966, the team would be absent from the Stanley Cup finals until 1995. That season, the aging Red Wings faced off against first-place Montreal in the finals. In the semifinals, the Habs wasted the Maple Leafs in four straight contests, and Detroit eliminated Chicago in six.

With Roger Crozier in goal, Detroit took the first two contests, played on enemy ice. The next two matches were to be played at the Olympia. The Habs had only beaten Detroit on Olympia ice twice in as many years. However, they emerged as victors in both games, as well as the two after that. The latter game went into overtime, and ended with Montreal as Stanley Cup champions.

During game four, Roger Crozier twisted his knee, and was replaced in that contest by Hank Bassen. The Red Wings seemed to fall apart after that, and were outskated by Montreal. In John DeVaney and Burt Goldblatt's book *The Stanley Cup*, Montreal goalie Gump Worsley said: "Detroit has simply lost its speed. Howe is the greatest player I've ever faced. But Gordie doesn't have the steam he once did. Age has taken its toll."

In the last game, the temperature in Detroit was in the upper 80s, and the Olympia became steamy.

The two teams battled into overtime, and Crozier, who had returned to the lineup, sparkled between the pipes. It was a controversial goal by which the Canadiens took home the 13th Stanley Cup in their club's history. As it happened, Montreal's Doug Balon flicked the puck in front of the goal. It hit Henri Richard somewhere below the waist, and then bounced off of the ice and into the net. Some say that Richard, sliding along the ice, eased the puck over Detroit's goal line. Crozier tried to argue that Richard had carried the puck in with his hand, but the referee had already made up his mind. Detroit had lost.

THE MEN

ROGER ALLAN CROZIER

Born: March 16, 1942, Bracebridge, Ontario
Position: Goaltender
Died: 1995
Junior
- St. Catharines Tee Pees (Junior A) (OHA): 1959-61, 1961-62

Minor Pro
- Buffalo Bisons (AHL), 1960-63
- Sault Ste. Marie Thunderbirds (EPHL): 1961-62
- St. Louis Braves (EPHL), 1962-63
- Pittsburgh Hornets (AHL), 1963-64
- Fort Worth Wings (CPHL), 1967-68

Detroit Red Wings
- 1963-64 to 1969-70

Best NHL Season
- 1964-65: 4,167 MIN; 2.42 GAA; 6 SO

Carer Awards & Honors
- Calder Trophy (2.42 GAA - 6 shutouts), 1964-65
- Conn Smythe Trophy, 1965-66
- First All-Star Team: 1965
- Dudley "Red" Garrett Memorial Trophy (AHL Rookie of the Year), 1963-64
- Harry Holmes Memorial Trophy (Outstanding Goalie in the AHL), 1963-64

Career Milestones
- Led NHL in shutouts (3) during playoffs, 1968-69

Trades
- Traded from Chicago to Detroit with Ron Ingram for Howie Young in June, 1963.
- Traded to Buffalo by Detroit for Tom Webster in June, 1970.

BIOGRAPHY

Born the fourth of 14 children, Roger Crozier was among the smallest netminders in the NHL. An acrobatic, fall-down goalie, it was he who eventually replaced Terry Sawchuk in goal. However, Sawchuk later returned to the Red Wings and shared net-minding duties with Crozier. The development was one that benefitted Roger. In an article by Paul Rimstead, he explained: "He's just great with me. He's done it all. He tells me to forget a bad game. 'You've been a NHL goaltender for five years,' he says. 'You know you're not going to play bad forever.' Terry also told me that if I haven't got that good feeling and I know I'm on my way to a bad night to let him know, even if the game is only 10 minutes old, and he'll go in."

Crozier was quite the worrier when it came to his performance, and in 1967-68, lost confidence in his ability to tend goal, and temporarily retired for two-and-a-half months. He retired on November 6, 1967, and returned in January 1968. During his temporary retirement, he returned to the small, secluded town of Bracebridge, Ontario, and worked as a carpenter. In an article by Paul Rimstead, he elaborated on the incident, explaining: "It's the fear of playing bad [that worries a goalie most]. You can't afford to go out and feel shaky. There are 18 guys on your bench looking, 15,000 fans. The pressure is on you. Every team in this league needs great goaltending, so it's up to you—the guy in the net."

Pancreatitis and stomach problems plagued Crozier throughout his entire career. The 1965-66 season was no exception. After recovering from a bout with pancreatitis late in the season, he came back and helped Detroit make the Stanley Cup finals against Montreal. The Wings were victors in two of their first three games. Then, in the fourth, Crozier injured his knee. He came back to tend goal in the sixth game but the Red Wings were defeated by a controversial goal by Henri Richard.

After Detroit, Crozier made stops in Buffalo and Washington. Surprisingly, he enjoyed playing for the expansion Buffalo Sabres the most. In an article by Randy Schultz, which appeared in the October 31, 1986 issue of *The Hockey News*, he explained: "There were a lot of games I played with those early Sabre

Roger Crozier was one of Detroit's premier goaltenders during the 1960s.

teams that I could walk out of the locker room, win or lose, and feel satisfied that I had done the best I could. I really enjoyed my years in Buffalo."

In 1965-66, Crozier became the first goaltender from a losing team to win the Conn Smythe Trophy as playoff MVP. After retiring from the professional play, he served as both scout and general manager of the Washington Capitals. He was fired on August 27, 1982. Commenting on his release in the September 4, 1982 issue of the *Toronto Globe and Mail*: "They told me there was a conflict of personalities, philosophy and control. They wanted to run the organization by committee. ... I wasn't prepared to run upstairs every time a decision had to be made." After working for the Capitals, he later moved to Pennsylvania and served as president of the Maryland Bank in Wilmington, Delaware.

Doug Barkley nearly won the Calder Trophy his rookie season but lost by what at the time was the closest margin in NHL history. Hockey Hall of Fame / Detroit Red Wings.

DOUG BARKLEY

Born: January 6, 1937, Lethbridge, Alberta
Position: Defenseman
Junior
- Lethbridge Native Sons
- Medicine Hat

Minor Pro
- Calgary Stampeders (WHL), 1956-58
- Buffalo Bisons (AHL), 1958-62

Detroit Red Wings
- 1962-63 to 1965-66

Best NHL Season
- 1963-64: 11 goals, 32 points

Carer Awards & Honors
- Set a WHL record for most goals by a defenseman in 1961-62

BIOGRAPHY

Doug Barkley spent a total of six seasons playing defense in the NHL, until an eye injury prematurely ended his playing career. After spending his first two seasons with Chicago, the hard-checking defenseman finished his career with Detroit. Barkley nearly took home the Calder Trophy his rookie season, but lost by what, at the time, was the closest margin in NHL history to Toronto's Kent Douglas. In that race, Barkley finished with 99.2 points to Douglas' 99.4.

In 1965-66, Barkley made the second All-Star team with Roger Crozier. Teammates Norm Ullman and Gordie Howe were named to the first team. Detroit manager Sid Abel felt that Barkley's play was

such that it warranted a first-team selection. In the January 25, 1966 issue of the *Detroit News,* he said: "I'm genuinely surprised that Doug failed to get on the first team. I was certain Doug would beat out [Jacques] Laperriere [Montreal Canadiens defenseman]. Laperriere is a terrific hockey player, but in my opinion Barkley has done a better job. At the start of the season we were floundering around and our defense was the worst in the league. Barkley took over the load and helped stabilize us and now our defense has to be rated with the best and the major share of the credit has to go to Doug."

Barkley's career ended prematurely when, in a January 30, 1966 game against the Chicago Blackhawks, Doug Mohns accidentally hit him in the

Doug Barkley spent a total of six seasons playing defense in the NHL until an eye injury prematurely ended his career.

Looking back on his coaching experiences, Barkley expressed his opinion in an article by Paul Patton: "To be a success you have to be the choice of the general manager and have your own assistants," he said. "I was sort of pushed in by the management."

"It did take me quite awhile [to adjust]," he said in a January 12, 1971 *Detroit News* article. "When I was scouting those two years for Sid, I watched games and I would be kind of bitter. I'd think, 'I can play better than that guy.' Then, when Sid made me coach here last year I'd get out on the ice with those youngsters and hey, I find they are making them bigger and stronger and I was glad to get back on the other side of the fence."

In the same article, Barkley also commented on his scouting experiences, explaining: "[They helped me] a great deal. I can't say that I liked to scout. It was a lonely life. I covered all the leagues and the colleges. What bothered me most was eating alone. I kept thinking everybody was watching me. But I didn't mingle with players. Instead, I'd go and talk to the coaches and the managers and that's where you learn. Like a coach would say, 'I just can't get through to that guy,' and you'd discuss it. This is where you learn. It helped me when I became a coach."

Barkley once coached the London Lions, a team that was part of Bruce Norris' effort to start a European professional league. Today, he resides in Calgary, where he does color commentary for the Flames.

right eye with his stick, detaching his retina. Despite four operations to correct the injury, he was never able to regain his sight. As compensation, the league gave him $15,000 (Canadian) and the Red Wings $5,000. "The worst [injury] we had was when Barkley lost an eye," recalls former Detroit trainer Lefty Wilson. "That was the worst one. Yeah, Doug Barkley lost an eye and that was tragic. You don't know at the time, but as the days went on, it didn't look too good and of course he did lose it. It was a sad situation. I think it was the downfall of the Red Wings because they traded Pronovost to Toronto, then Gadsby quit and Barkley lost an eye."

After playing, Barkley turned to scouting and coaching for the Red Wings. After working in the front office as an administrative assistant to Sid Abel for three seasons, he coached Detroit's Central League development club in Fort Worth, Texas, posting a 15-16-4 record. He then had stints behind the Detroit bench in 1971-72 and again in 1975.

LEO JOSEPH BOIVIN

Born: August 2, 1932, Prescott, Ontario
Position: Defenseman
Junior
- Port Arthur West End Bruins (TBJHL), 1949-51

Minor Pro
- Pittsburgh Hornets (AHL), 1951-52

Detroit Red Wings
- 1965-66 to 1966-67

Career Awards & Honors
Junior
- Team Captain, Port Arthur West End Bruins (TBJHL), 1950-51

Professional
- NHL All-Star Games: 1961, 1962, 1964

Trades
- Traded from Boston to Detroit for Gary Doak, Bill Lesuk and an extra amateur draft choice (Steve Atkinson) on February 18, 1966.

BIOGRAPHY

Leo Boivin played for 19 seasons in the NHL (1951-52 to 1969-70), most of which were spent playing for the Boston Bruins, where he was a captain for four seasons. For almost two seasons, he played defense for the Detroit Red Wings (1965-66 and 1966-67), where he was a big contributing factor in their advancement to the Stanley Cup finals.

"I really had to work hard to keep my job," said Boivin in the August 23, 1985 issue of *The Hockey News*. "You have to remember that I played most of my career in the old six-team league. There were only 120 jobs available in those days and I consider myself fortunate to have played in the league as long as I did under those circumstances. I considered those players of that time 120 of the best in the world. I guess I had to be pretty good to be in such good company."

Due to his small stature (5'-7", 190), Boivin was nicknamed "Fireplug." Although he was small, he was determined to make the NHL from early on, and was as tough as they came. A hard-hitting, rugged, textbook body checker, Boivin was a defensive-defenseman. Tim Horton considered him to be the toughest defenseman to get past on the ice. He was famous for his hip-checks, which often sent opposing players into the air.

Former Detroit Red Wing Gary Bergman will always remember Boivin. When asked about him, Bergman replied (with a laugh):

Leo almost ended my career. When I came up in the early '60s, he was still playing for Boston. He was just here for a short time. I think he only came here for one year, or something like that. This was when we had lost bodies on defense, Doug Barkley lost his eye, Gadsby retired, and I think we needed a fill. I think Sid [Abel] was just groping at straws, because I think Leo was pretty

Leo Boivin was a rugged, hard-hitting, textbook body checker. Hockey Hall of Fame / Detroit Red Wings.

well over the hill when he got here, but he was a little fireplug. I think it was my first game against Boston, no it wasn't my first game, it was during the season, anyway. I threw one of those passes they talk about where, you know, you're looking over your shoulder admiring it, saying how pretty it is, and Leo came whipping across the ice with one of those hip checks of his. The next thing I knew I was looking up at the lights, literally. I was looking at the ceiling, flying through the air upside down. I tore up my knee a little. Then, in a couple of years, all of a sudden we are teammates. Leo was just...if I can say nothing else, he was just a tough, hard-working defenseman. I think he was only 5'-5" or 5'-6", but I mean, he had to weigh, I would guess that he was probably up in 180s to 190s. He was as solid as a 'brick crapper!'

Besides playing, Boivin has also worked as both a coach with the Ottawa '67s of the OHL, and the St. Louis Blues. However, he didn't see coaching as the right career choice for him, and turned to scouting with the Hartford Whalers.

WILLIAM ALEXANDER (BEAR) GADSBY

Born: August 8, 1927, Calgary, Alberta
Position: Defenseman
Junior
- Edmonton Canadiens

Minor
- Kansas City Pla-Mors (USHL)

Detroit Red Wings
- 1961-62 to 1965-66

Best NHL Season
- 1955-56 (New York): 9 goals, 51 points

Career Awards & Honors
- NHL First All-Star Team: 1956, '58, '59
- NHL Second All-Star Team: 1953, '54, '57, '65
- NHL All-Star Games: 1953, '54, '56-'60
- Hockey Hall of Fame, 1970
- Red Wings Hall of Fame, 1978
- Michigan Sports Hall of Fame, 1986
- Alberta Sports Hall of Fame, 1986
- Three-time runner-up, Norris Trophy

The Gadsby Damage Report
- 7 broken noses
- Left leg broken twice
- Over 600 facial stitches
- Both big toes and thumbs have suffered fractures
- Both shoulders separated
- 2 concussions

Trades
- Traded from Chicago to New York with Pete Conacher for Alan Stanley, Nick Mickoski, and Dick Mamourex in November of 1954.
- Traded from New York to Detroit in June of 1961 for Les Hunt and cash.

BIOGRAPHY

In 1939, at the outbreak of World War II, the steamship on which Bill Gadsby was traveling to Canada from England was torpedoed by a Nazi U-boat. After five hours in a lifeboat, the survivors were rescued by a British freighter. Several weeks later, the Gadsbys returned to Canada aboard the Mauretania. He and his mother had been visiting her family, who lived in Southgate, Lancashire, 20 miles outside of Liverpool, England.

In an article by Herb Ralby, which appeared in the December 1950 *Boston Bruins Program*, Gadsby recalled the horrifying experience, explaining: "We were knocked right out of our berths. I was too young to realize our real predicament. My mother rushed me up to our lifeboat station. She was as calm as could be though terribly frightened. I'll never forget the sights I saw. Men and women going crazy with panic. I saw horrible sights I'll never forget. ... I guess I was too young at the time to get the full significance of what happened. But when I did I shuddered and, brother, I still do when I think of it. What the heck are a few bumps and bruises in hockey after that."

Gadsby got his start in hockey at an early age, playing on the outdoor rinks of Calgary. Eventually, he went to Edmonton and played in a four-team junior league. He turned pro at the age of 18. "I went with Chicago and [played for] the Kansas City Pla-Mors," he says. "That was the number one farm team for the Chicago Blackhawks. I came up [to Chicago] 10 games later, in '46. I was lucky."

Chicago's scouts had their eyes on Bill all the way from bantam to junior. When the 6-foot Gadsby broke in with the Blackhawks, he was described as having a hard, accurate shot with passing abilities on a par with, if not better than, most men playing in the league. He was known for his "play for keeps" style of play, and his ability to block hard. Because he made a good number of his moves right out in open ice, he seldom was penalized.

In the fall of 1952, Gadsby came down with polio, but battled his way back and was runner-up for the Norris Trophy in 1956, 1958 and 1959. Nicknamed "Bear" because of his large size and hard-hitting style of play, Gadsby eventually found himself playing for the New York Rangers. With New York,

Bill Gadsby and Gordie Howe attempt to score on Glenn Hall as Chicago's Pierre Pilote looks on.

he realized his maximum potential as an offensive-defenseman, and spent time on the power play, playing the point with Andy Bathgate. Upon his arrival in Detroit, Gadsby changed his style to that of a defensive-defenseman, and earned himself a regular spot with the team. It has been said that with Detroit, he spent some games blocking almost as many shots as goalie Roger Crozier!

In the November 19, 1995 issue of the *Detroit News*, Gadsby recalled how he discovered Detroit was his new home. It was during a game against Detroit. Said Gadsby: "I took [Gordie Howe] into the boards and rubbed him up a little. He looked at me and said, 'Hey, dummy, don't do that — you're going to be on our team tomorrow.' I looked at him. 'Who says so?' Howe said, 'The deal's all set, so let up a little, will ya?' We beat the Wings 3-2 that night and the moment I stepped off the ice, our coach, Muzz Patrick, came up to me and said I'd been traded to Detroit. When I saw Gordie out in the hallway, he said, 'See, you dumb SOB—you played so well

tonight you might have cost us a place in the playoffs."

"I think playing here on such a good hockey club was a real lift," says Gadsby. "I was going to come here and play two years and then go back to Edmonton and coach the Juniors, but I got new life when I came here and made the All-Star team a couple of times. We had such good hockey clubs, it was a pleasure playing. When you are on any pro sport team and you are up there in the top all the time, boy you are a different person, believe me. We had a great group of guys here. The camaraderie was just excellent. We were winning most of the time. We finished in first place in '64. It was just a pleasure to go to work every day. I enjoyed practice, if you can believe that."

Gadsby later coached the Red Wings for a short time, posting a 33-31-12 record. He was named coach on June 3, 1968, by team president Bruce Norris, who in an Associated Press article the next day was quoted as saying: "I do not believe in contracts.

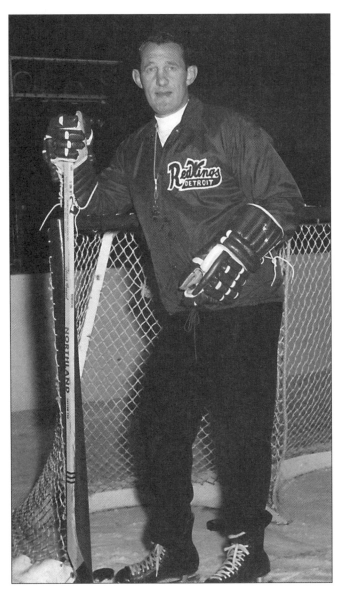

Bill Gadsby coached the Red Wings during the late 1960s.

press with a myriad of vague statements. According to an October 17, 1969 Associated Press article, Norris responded with comments like: "I think Bill is a fine man. I like Bill. ... I don't see how you can criticize the man. ... I just think coaching isn't what it used to be. ... We felt we weren't communicating as well as we should. We felt we needed a change for the club. ... Hockey is a sophisticated game and we felt we needed more sophistication."

Gordie Howe waved reporters off after hearing the announcement, saying that it made him sick. Once the crowd of 11,192 fans at the Olympia heard of the news, chants of "We want Gadsby!" echoed off the stadium walls.

Gadsby was a very popular coach with his players, and his dismissal was unsettling to them. Norris later named him as the club's director of professional scouting but fired him again on April 21, 1970, for reasons unknown.

Today, when asked about the incident, Gadsby says: "[Coaching is] always a tough job. That was real tough. We had pretty good clubs, but it was the biggest shock of my life when I got fired. We had beaten Chicago in Chicago, 4-2. The owner, Bruce Norris, had his arm around me that night. The next day, about 15 hours later, I got fired. It was a real shock. We were two straight, we were 8-1 in training camp, which didn't mean a lot, but it was a good start and we had a pretty good hockey club. It's a long story and I really don't like to get into it. Maybe that's in life, it was supposed to happen. It happened and like I said, it was in my craw for a quite a while, but I got on with the other part of life and got a good job and I moved on and enjoyed it. That was just one little instance in life, that's all."

Gadsby currently runs several adult hockey schools in the Detroit area. Incredibly, it wasn't long ago that Gadsby hung up his skates from playing in alumni games. Besides running his hockey schools, Bill is involved with the Detroit Red Wings Alumni Association, who play about 20 games a year for charity. Over the years, these alumni games have raised money for several worthy causes. "They get a bunch of guys together for another team and they'll play for the burn center or the Cancer Society, or any charity they want and the Red Wing Alumni are glad to do it," says Gadsby.

I'm happy and Bill is satisfied." It was unfortunate that the agreement for Gadsby to coach the team was not a formal one. On October 16, 1969, he received the biggest shock of his life when he was fired. To this day, he does not know why.

When the ax fell, Gadsby had started the team off 2-0. The night before, they had defeated Chicago. After the victory, Norris came down and gave Bill a congratulatory pat on the back. Then, an hour before the team's next game against Minnesota, Norris told Gadsby of his decision, which was made public moments after the game began at 8 p.m. Gadsby could not believe his ears, and Norris answered the

PAUL GARNET HENDERSON

Born: January 28, 1943, Kincardine, Ontario
Position: Left wing
Junior
- Hamilton Red Wings (Junior A) (OHA), 1960-63
- Goderich Sailers (Junior B)
- Hamilton Bees (Junior B)

Minor Pro
- Pittsburgh Hornets (AHL), 1963-64

Detroit Red Wings
- 1962-63 to 1967-68

Best NHL Season
- 1970-71 (Toronto): 30 goals, 60 points

Career Awards & Honors
Junior Hockey
- Max Kaminsky Memorial Award (OHA), 1962-63
Professional
- NHL All-Star Games: 1972, '73

Trades
- Traded from Detroit to Toronto with Norm Ullman, Floyd Smith and Doug Barrie for Frank Mahovlich, Peter Stemkowski, Gary Unger and the NHL rights to Carl Brewer in March of 1968.

BIOGRAPHY

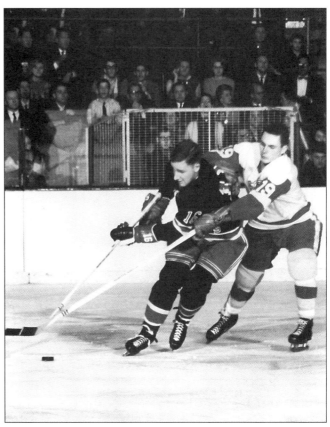

Paul Henderson checks Rod Sieling. Prazak Collection / Hockey Hall of Fame.

As a youth, Paul Henderson was raised in Lucknow, Ontario, where he played some of his earliest hockey. At a young age, scouts from Detroit, Toronto and Boston had their eyes on him.

After a successful tryout with Detroit in the fall of 1959, Henderson found himself playing for the Junior A Hamilton Red Wings of the OHA. However, in an effort to get more ice time, he later opted to play for the Goderich Sailers, then Detroit's Junior B team. In 1960-61, he played Junior B for the Hamilton Bees, and was occasionally called up to play for the Red Wings. The following season, playing once again for Hamilton, his team took home the Memorial Cup, given to the championship junior team in Canada. In 1962-63, Henderson had a very successful junior season and led the OHA in scoring with 49 goals in 48 games. For his gentlemanly play, he received the Max Kaminsky Memorial Award.

Henderson's professional debut came in 1963-64, when he played for both the Red Wings and the AHL Pittsburgh Hornets. During his NHL career, he was a very consistent and reliable player, recording seven seasons in which he scored at least 20 goals.

"I remember Paul, when he first played, skated

[and shot] like hell," says former Chicago defenseman Pierre Pilote. "He was a really good skater. Then he got traded to Toronto. But you had to be careful with him. He had the speed. Oh boy, you couldn't give him a step, or he was gone. But he didn't have the great scoring ability that, say for instance, Gordie [Howe] had. Otherwise, he would have got 100 goals. Boy could he skate. Great skater."

After playing for the Red Wings, Henderson was traded to Toronto, where he would continue playing successfully, After six seasons with Toronto, he jumped to the WHA Toronto Toros, later playing for the Birmingham Bulls. After the WHA merged with the NHL, Henderson played for both the Atlanta Flames and Birmingham Bulls, then part of the CHL.

In 1972 and 1974, Henderson played for Team Canada in the "Summit Series" against Russia. He became an international hero for his performance in the first series, referred to by some as "The Series of the Century." In 1972, he scored the game-winning goals in the series' final three games, scoring seven goals for a total of 10 points. Only Phil Esposito and

Pete (left) and Frank (right) Mahovlich made Red Wings hockey a family affair.

Alexander Yakushev scored more than Henderson.

Henderson's performance in the final game of that series, at approximately 3 p.m. on September 28, is remarkable. Doctors urged him not to play after he hit his head on the boards the night before. When the clock had arrived at the final minute of the game, and both teams were tied, Henderson skated out on the ice and took Peter Mahovlich's place. Playing on a line other than his own, he scored the game-winning goal with only 34 seconds left on the clock.

Recalling the goal, in a September 14, 1974 *Toronto Star* article by Jim Kernaghan, Henderson said: "I remember it vividly. There was no numbness or anything. Tretiak made a pad save on the first shot, and I drilled the rebound right back before he could recover. I knew it was going in. My first thought was, God, we've done it."

FRANCIS WILLIAM (FRANK) MAHOVLICH

Born: January 10, 1938, Timmins, Ontario
Position: Left wing
Junior
- Toronto St. Michael's [Junior A], (OHA): 1953-57

Detroit Red Wings
- 1967-68 to 1970-71

Best NHL Season
- 1971-72 (Montreal): 43 goals, 96 points

Carer Awards & Honors
Junior Hockey
- Red Tilson Memorial Trophy (MVP), 1956-57

Professional
- Hockey Hall of Fame, 1981
- Calder Memorial Trophy, 1957-58
- First All-Star team: 1960-61, 1962-63, 1972-73
- Second All-Star team: 1961-62, 1963-64, 1964-65, 1965-66, 1968-69, 1969-70
- NHL All-Star Games: 1959-65, '67-'74

Career Milestones
- In 1961-62, led the NHL in penalties during the playoffs
- In 1963-64, led the NHL in assists during the playoffs (11)
- In 1970-71, led the NHL in both post-season goals (14) and points (27)
- On March 21, 1973, scored 500th career goal against Vancouver
- In 1,181 games, scored 533 goals, for 1,103 points (not including the playoffs)

Trades
- Traded to Detroit in March of 1968 with Peter Stemkowski, Gary Unger, and the rights to Carl Brewer for Norm Ullman, Paul Henderson, Floyd Smith, and Doug Barrie.
- In January of 1971, traded to Montreal for Bill Collins, Guy Charron and Mickey Redmond.

BIOGRAPHY

Frank Mahovlich spent two full seasons, and parts of two others, playing left wing for the Detroit Red Wings during the 1960s. Although he spent the majority of his career playing for the Toronto Maple Leafs and Montreal Canadiens, the "Big M," as he was called, deserves recognition for the contributions he made in Detroit.

Mahovlich spent four seasons (1953-54 through 1956-57) playing Junior A hockey for Toronto St. Michael's. During his last season of junior, he scored 52 goals for 88 points in 49 games, winning the Red Tilson Memorial Trophy as the Ontario Hockey Association's MVP.

Mahovlich's professional career began with the Toronto Maple Leafs. An inability to get along with Toronto coach Punch Imlach saw him traded to Detroit after 12 seasons and four Stanley Cup wins. In Detroit, he played on a line with Gordie Howe and Alex Delvecchio, which was among the best in NHL. In 1968-69 and 1969-70, he scored 49 and 38 goals for 78 and 70 points, respectively.

During his career, some referred to Frank Mahovlich as the "Gentle Giant." Former Toronto Maple Leafs' owner Doug Ballard said that if he were only meaner, the Big M could have been an even more successful player. In the November 1970 issue of *Hockey World*, Ballard said: "A superstar has to have a mean streak in him. Gordie Howe sure does and so does Bobby Hull. But Frank doesn't and that's what he lacks." In the same article, Punch Imlach said of him: "He can do everything Hull can do and some things Hull can't. He is bigger and has longer strides and a longer reach. But Frank doesn't give his best effort all of the time. If he would push himself, he could score 60 goals, 80 goals, even 100 goals."

Despite the absence of a mean streak, Mahovlich was an incredible player, and during his career, played on six Stanley Cup-winning teams. A Hockey Hall of Fame write-up on Mahovlich says he was "a graceful, powerful skater with a shot that could smash Herculite, who put on goal-scoring displays of such brilliance there would be a hushed pause after the puck went in the net. Then, fans would nearly blow the roof off Maple Leaf Gardens with their cheers." Wherever he played, he could bring crowds to their feet with his exciting style of play.

Mahovlich continued to find success playing with the Montreal Canadiens, where he won two Stanley Cups. He later played for the Toronto Toros and Birmingham Bulls of the World Hockey Association, before hanging up the skates for good in 1977-78. Along with Mickey Redmond, Mahovlich attempted to make a comeback with the Red Wings in 1979-80 at the age of 41, but was unsuccessful. He had not played hockey for a year-and-a-half.

As a person, Mahovlich was very private, and preferred to keep his personal life personal. It was not unusual for him to visit an art gallery when the team was on the road, as he was interested in both art and music. At the time of his retirement, Mahovlich was operating a travel agency, which he continued to do for some time. Today, he is semi-retired, and travels a lot with groups for the agency.

NORMAN VICTOR ALEXANDER ULLMAN

Born: December 26, 1935, Provost, Alberta
Position: Center
Junior
- Edmonton Oil Kings (WJHL), 1952-54

Minor Pro
- Edmonton Flyers (WHL), 1953-55

Detroit Red Wings
- 1955-56 to 1967-68

Best NHL Season
- 1970-71 (Toronto): 34 goals, 85 points

Carer Awards & Honors
- First All-Star Team: 1965
- Second All-Star Team: 1967
- Hockey Hall of Fame, 1982
- NHL All-Star Games: 1955, '60-'65, '67-'69, '74

Career Milestones
- In 1964-65, Ullman led the NHL in goals with 42, and recorded 41 assists, second only to Stan Mikita's 87 points. That season, largely because of his play, the Red Wings finished in first place and Ullman was named to the first All-Star team. *The Hockey News* named him as their player of the year.
- Tallied 1,229 NHL points during his career, a total that grew slightly larger once he went to the WHA.

Trades
- Traded to Toronto in March of 1968, with Floyd Smith and Paul Henderson for Carl Brewer, Pete Stemkowski, Frank Mahovlich and Gary Unger.

BIOGRAPHY

Norm Ullman was discovered by Detroit scout Clarence Moher. While playing junior hockey for the Edmonton Oil Kings in 1953-54, his team made it to the Memorial Cup. At the time, the Oil Kings were the first junior team sponsored by the Red Wings to make it to such a pinnacle. A star-caliber junior player for Edmonton, Ullman nearly made it to the Red Wings after that season. However, an ankle injury sustained during a softball game delayed his debut.

After recovering from his ankle injury, Ullman joined the Edmonton Flyers of the Western Hockey League, late in the 1954-55 season. That season, he scored 25 goals and 34 assists for 59 points, helping his team win the WHL championship. His 21-season professional career soon began. Ullman proved himself a true iron man, playing in 1,410 games. During a 10-season stretch that began in 1957-58, he missed only 13 games.

During Ullman's first season in Detroit, he saw duty on different lines. The following season, he skated on a line with Gordie Howe and Ted Lindsay, scoring 16 goals and dishing out 32 assists. Stocky and curly-haired, the high-scoring Ullman was quite a hockey player. He was an excellent stickhandler and a very strong skater. Deceptively strong, Punch Imlach once said that Ullman was the best center that ever played for him.

Jack Adams nicknamed Ullman "Noisy" because he was such a quiet man. A Hockey Hall of Fame news release once pointed out that "he was one of the worst interviews in the game," and "consequently, he received scant attention from the media electronic or print." Thus, it has been said that Ullman was unappreciated by many who were not true students of the game. Ullman once admitted that he did not exactly relish being in the limelight. He was nearly as quiet on the ice as he was off of it and rarely displayed a great deal of emotion. When pushed by an opposing player, however, that man soon discovered that Ullman was not to be taken for granted. Perhaps

Opposite: Norm Ullman scored 42 goals for the Red Wings in 1964-65.

Ullman was not a man of words, but he didn't neglect to let his stick do the talking, and possessed plenty of team spirit.

Near the end of Ullman's days in Detroit he began to develop into more of a goal scorer, doubling the 21 he scored in 1963-64 to 42 the following season. In the October 30, 1966 issue of the *Detroit News*, Sid Abel gave a description of Ullman, who for a time skated on a line with Paul Henderson and Floyd Smith. Said Abel: "Normie is a finished hockey player. He's a puck carrier, a digger, a strong defensive player, has a good shot, has good speed and is a good playmaker. ... Personally, I think Normie would be a tough man to play with because of his style. But somehow or other the styles of Ullman and Smith mesh, especially when they are in deep. There are times when their styles don't mesh too well in the center ice area. Of course, they are close personal friends off the ice. ... Maybe this is a factor in their playing so well together."

While playing for Detroit, other teams often sent out their best lines to check Ullman. "The other coaches want to put their best lines on him," said Abel in the same article. "When we go against Chicago, he always draws the Scooters (Stan Mikita, Kenny Wharram and Doug Mohns). By the same token, I always want him on against the strong lines of the other teams."

Toe Blake, in the February 28, 1966 issue of *Sports Illustrated* said: "[Ullman] is not all that fast and sometimes I don't even know he is there. I sure don't expect him to be. And then the loudspeaker announces 'goal by Ullman' or 'assist by Ullman' and I know he *was* there all the time. I don't know how he does it. If I knew, I'd stop him. All I do know is he has been poison for us."

Unfortunately, Ullman played center during an era when Jean Beliveau, Henri Richard, Stan Mikita, Phil Esposito and Jean Ratelle were in the NHL spotlight. Because of this, he was overshadowed to some extent, as can be seen by his limited All-Star nominations.

Ullman was traded to the Toronto Maple Leafs in 1968. Prior to the trade, Ullman had held out during training camp until he came to terms on a contract. He was also serving as the president of the newly formed NHLPA, a position to which he was elected in January 1968. Some have suggested that these factors influenced his move to Toronto. However, years later, when asked to comment on the trade, Ullman offered another explanation. In the September 20, 1987 issue of the *Sunday Sun*, he said: "It was a huge trade. Toronto and ourselves (Detroit) were kind of struggling. They wanted to give each team a big shake-up."

When the Maple Leafs did not renew his contract, Ullman continued playing professionally for the Edmonton Oilers in the WHA, before finally retiring in 1977. During his 20-season career, Ullman was never fortunate enough to take home the Stanley Cup.

CHAPTER TWELVE
HARD TIMES
• THE 1970s •

The misfortune that began in the latter half of the 1960s continued throughout the 1970s. During this decade, the Red Wings were not the best team in the league. With the exception of the 1977-78 season, when they managed to make the quarter finals, Detroit missed the playoffs altogether. As an untitled Hockey Hall of Fame write-up reveals: "The Wings were a team in a state of upheaval, with coaches and players whirling through the revolving door. The on-ice product reflected that turmoil, playing sub-.500 hockey during [most of the decade]."

In an article by Allen Abel, which appeared in the December 5, 1980 issue of the *Toronto Globe and Mail*, then-goalie Jim Rutherford commented on the 1977 season, when local media refused to elect an MVP. "We would go good for a game or two, then fall apart," he said. "But I certainly wouldn't blame our record on the coaches. Marcel Pronovost and Ted Lindsay coached the team very well. You can't put the finger on one person when the whole organization

slides. One week, we would seem to have it turned around, then it would go the other way. When Wayne Maxner took over, everybody was playing on emotion for a while. But that doesn't mean everything is turned around." That season, Detroit experienced a 19-game winless streak and won only 16 of 80 games.

The reasons for the team's lack of success during this era are many and are not the result of any one isolated factor. Management, some bad trades, the loss of key players and a dwindling supply of talent all contributed to the frustration experienced by players and fans alike.

Former Red Wing Carl Liscombe feels the loss of marquee players contributed to the club's misfortune during the 1970s: "That's your Jack Adams," he says. "He depended on Gordie Howe. Gordie Howe kept Jack Adams in that rink for 25 years, because with Gordie Howe on that ice, you didn't need anybody else. Along with it, you have to remember that there was a guy named Alex Delvecchio. Alex played 22 years with the Red Wings, and he was a star every year. He was a number one center-ice man. With him and Gordie out there, they had a real hockey team. Along with that, Jack Stewart was in his prime there for about 10 years and they had some real good [players], they had Red Kelly and they had Quackenbush, all All Star hockey players. Detroit always had good players."

Liscombe further commented that the flow of talented hockey players into Detroit wasn't nearly as fast as it had been during the earlier years. "They had a couple of scouts, they had a scout named Carson Cooper. They had two of them, one in Western Canada and one in Eastern Canada, and those fellows knew hockey players. When they sent somebody down for a tryout, they were good hockey players. That's why half of the National Hockey League had Detroit Red Wing hockey players on them. All these years they had them on, because they [the Red Wings] couldn't have them all. They used to bring them down, train them, and trade them off. They had some real good ones."

Former Detroit trainer Lefty Wilson has similar feelings about the era. Says Wilson:

You still had Howe and you had Delvecchio. We didn't actually have the whole back-up, as far as the first line and the second line and the checking line and the fourth line. You never had good defensemen. I think the big downfall was when we lost those three guys in one season, the defensemen. Pronovost, Gadsby and Barkley. You lose three guys like that on your defense and you have nothing. We didn't have anything filling [the] system that we could bring up.

[The lean years were the result of] a little bit of everything, I believe. ... It just depends, I think, on your scouting system. If your scouting system is strong, which it was in the 1950s, we had better clubs in those days than they do in the league today, in the minor league. We only had 120 players in the big league. I remember Jack Adams when they won the Stanley Cup, and he sent 10 of our players to Chicago to support them. After that the league in Chicago still wasn't going good and they put a number of fellows on the block and Chicago could pick out two players. That's what kept Chicago going.

Wilson also feels that Red Wing pride suffered

during this era. He says:

Those guys [that they had] were good hockey players, but they weren't as good as the big teams that we had. They were run of the mill and they weren't...I put it all around to dedication. Dedication and the will to win and wearing the red uniform and everything else. They had pride and all this kind of stuff [during Detroit's glory years], but in those days [the 1970s] they didn't seem to have that. They lost something. [It was a] different attitude, different atmosphere, and they weren't gut hungry. [During the 1950s], we traveled on the trains and you'd never speak to the [opposing team]. They would be sitting across the table having breakfast and we would be on the other side having breakfast and you'd never say hello to them. The trainers talked because we had nothing to do with the playing, but we would talk, and very little. [Today] they are a lot different and of course the money is a lot different. That was the start, I guess, in the 1970s when the big money was starting to come in. [It was a] different attitude, [the players] didn't want to get hurt because they could last another two or three years. They never dug in and took chances like they did in the 1950s.

Bill Gadsby, who played for Detroit during 1960s, expressed many of the same feelings that other players gave, but also noted the effects of expansion, commenting:

A lot of guys retired and expansion came about. Expansion clubs had the first pick on a lot of players. When you get guys retiring four and five a year, and you can't replace them and you can't replace them with the good young guys, you're going to be in trouble for awhile. They made some bad trades here in the '70s, and things started going down hill. Once you get down, it's awful tough to get up again, really tough. It takes you four or five years. But they have done a real great job here in the last five or six years. They have really come around, and the Russian kids have really helped and the European guys. They have a very good nucleus of everybody, in all positions really, right from the goal keeper out.

I think Marcel Dionne was a good hockey player [during the 1970s], but he didn't have much to work with. They didn't have too many good hockey players for about five or six years. They were really struggling. They couldn't make any trades, nobody wanted some of the guys they had so they couldn't improve their team and their goal keeping was just mediocre. When you don't have good goal keeping and a good defense, you are in deep trouble. They made some bad trades and they had one or two good hockey players, like I said, but that's just not enough. You just can't cut it with that. [Attendance] dropped down naturally. They were losing all the time, and if you are not winning, it doesn't matter what city you are in, they are going to drop off. It doesn't matter where you are at.

As Gadsby said, the fans began to get fed up with the quality of hockey. Elliott Trumbull, a former Director of Public Relations for the Red Wings, recalled the thinning crowds and how the team's current management turned things around. Said Trumbull:

Yeah, it was getting really bad towards the end of the Norris regime. But this was like the fans always say, 'The only way to get the management's attention is stop going to the games.' When the gate receipts dry up, then they say, 'Oh Christ, we've got a problem here.' If the people still come out, they say, 'Hell, we don't have to make any changes, the product might not be winning, but the people are supporting it.' Well, back in the 1980s, just towards the end of the Norris regime, hell, they were getting half houses there. Let's see, they left Olympia in 1979 and they were getting half houses and even when they went to Joe Louis they weren't getting many people. The change came with the new management. It just gave the fans...whether the product was any appreciably better, I can't really say without looking at the records. But, at least it gave the fans a chance to realize they're trying, 'we've got new management here.' A new hope. Cause they were called the 'Dead Wings' and then in the Ned Harkness Era, there were some bad, bad eras there.

We didn't have the talent. They just didn't have the talent. ... The farm system just wasn't producing. We had the Pittsburgh Hornets ... and we had the Edmonton Oil Kings out there. Outside of guys like Normie Ullman, but of course he goes into the 1960s, we didn't bring up too many guys. I don't know.

Former Red Wing Marty Pavelich said: "I think what happened there is that after the [expansion]

draft, remember they started to expand, they lost players out of their farm system. I think ... it started before that. Adams kind of started it, and then after that they made some more trades and then the farm system was just pretty well depleted. There just wasn't anything left in the barrel and then there were more teams and less players to go around and I just think it was totally bad management there for some time."

Dennis Hextall was one of the Red Wings' better players during the decade of the 1970s. When asked what he thought was behind those unsuccessful years, he said: "Well, there was a lot of changes. People like Alex Delvecchio never got credit, but technically Delvecchio put that team together here that got into second place (in 1977-78). Ted Lindsay and Bobby Kromm took that team over and then they broke it up. And that sort of surprised me. That a guy that played the game the way Lindsay would, would allow those trades to take place. I never played against Ted, but anything you ever saw about him or read about him, he was a very fiery, competitive individual. I guess, based on the way he played, I was maybe a little disappointed in the way he put a team together. I thought he would have come in with a physical, hard working team, and yet the next thing I knew it was more European than it was North American."

Gary Bergman, a player noted for his leadership role in Detroit during the 1970s, said:

There were a multitude of reasons [the Red Wings fell apart in the 1970s], one of which bad trades were made. I think incompetent people were brought in to run the team. When they made the trades and we got a lot of the young guys, and when you don't have leadership, when you don't have a Sid Abel there....... Guidance and confidence are so important to young players, and when that doesn't happen. I don't care what company you work for, if you have bad management, and you have problems at the top, that stuff is going to filter down. You've heard that story a million times in your life and it's true. It just filters down through the system. Back then I had kids just...... I'm not going to mention his name, but I had a young defenseman that was playing that we brought up. I came out of the house one night and he was sitting on my front steps and had tears running down his cheeks. He said, 'What are we going to do? I'm trying to make my way in the NHL and

I don't know what to do. Nobody tells me. Where's this team going? What are we trying to accomplish?' There was a serious lack of guidance. I would blame it more on that [management] side than I would on the players. Certainly they made some bad trades, but in the sense that what they gave away was better than what they got. I still can't put all of the heat on the players that they traded for, because that would be an unfair statement.

THE MEN

JAMES EARL (JIM) RUTHERFORD

Born: February 17, 1949, Beeton, Ontario
Position: Goaltender
Junior
- Aurora (Junior C) (OHA): 1966-67
- Hamilton Red Wings (Junior A) (OHA): 1967-69

Minor Pro
- Fort Worth Wings (CHL): 1969-71
- Hershey Bears (AHL): 1971-72

Detroit Red Wings
- 1970-71; 1973-74 to 1980-81; 1982-83

Best NHL Season
- 1972-73 (Pittsburgh): 2,660 MIN; 2.91 GAA; 3 SO

Career Milestones
- Team Canada: 1977 and 1979 world championships
- In 1977-78, played goal for a Red Wings team that rose 37 points to finish second in their division.

Trades
- Traded to Detroit in January of 1974 by Pittsburgh with Jack Lynch for Ron Stackhouse.
- Traded to Toronto in 1980 for Mark Kirton.

BIOGRAPHY

Jim Rutherford played the majority of his NHL career with the Red Wings (three times), posting a career GAA of 3.65 over 457 games. He played junior hockey for the Hamilton Red Wings, where he was an All-Star (first team) goalie and recipient of the Hamilton team trophy as their most valuable and popular player. In 1969, he was Detroit's first draft choice (10th overall).

At a time when he wasn't pressured to play in almost every single game, the humble Rutherford once recorded three shutouts in a row. At the time, the feat tied a club record set by Glenn Hall in 1955 and also tied Rutherford's one-season high that he set while tending goal for Pittsburgh. The feat was even more notable when one considers the fact that, at the

time, the Red Wings were one of the weaker teams in the NHL. Rutherford gave much of the credit to his teammates. In the February 6, 1976 issue of *The Hockey News*, he said: "The key to those [shutouts] has been the team's play in front of me. ... The defense has been clearing the puck and moving players out from around the net and the forwards have been working hard."

Rutherford lists former teammate Ed Giacomin as being most influential on him. "I'd have to say he had more of an effect on me than anyone else in my professional career," he said. "We were roommates for two years and, although we didn't discuss goaltending that much, I learned a lot—watching him play and from the way he approached life."

Former Detroit Red Wing Gary Bergman remembered Rutherford, commenting: "The Little Roach. We called him Roachie because he was little. He was crawling around all the time. He was just a good goaltender. I think, unfortunately, he was too small. I saw goals go in on him some nights where he made the move right, he was there before the puck, but his arm wasn't long enough or leg wasn't long enough. Because he was a quick little guy. I think the biggest thing that was against Jimmy was his size. He was a quick little guy, and we were getting into the era when, more and more every year, at one time, just a few players on each team could really, really smoke the puck. We were slowly getting to the era where everybody was getting pretty good shots. So you had to be ready all the time and I think that's where the size really hurt him."

"Jimmy was a very good goaltender," says former Red Wing Nick Libett. "He was very quiet. I guess a typical goaltender, but very quiet. On game days, if he knew he was playing, he wouldn't say a word. Wouldn't say a word. Kind of like his personality. He's kind of a quiet person anyway but very good. He was small. Obviously, he was not a big goaltender, but I mean he could play. Obviously he could play, or he wouldn't have been in the league."

In 1982-83, Rutherford retired from the NHL. In a February 13, 1983 *Toronto Star* article, he said:

Opposite: Jim Rutherford's career spanned 13 NHL seasons.

"The time comes when you might as well stop kidding yourself. I've had a good career. I never won the Stanley Cup, but there have been lots of satisfying moments.... I think I got pushed around from time to time but I've never been one to complain. I often envied people who could pop off. Get rid of their beefs that way. I'd keep them inside. Not let them bother me, really. Just shrug them off and figure everything would turn out for the best. I guess I really do feel that way."

In the 13 NHL seasons that he tended goal, Rutherford played for 16 different coaches, including those with Team Canada. After playing, he served as director of hockey operations for Compuware in Detroit and was manager/coach of the Windsor Spitfires of the OHA.

GARY GUNNAR BERGMAN

Born: October 7, 1938, Kenora, Ontario
Position: Defense
Junior
- Winnipeg Braves (MJHL): 1958-59

Minor Pro
- Winnipeg Warriors (WHL): 1957-58, 1959-60
- Buffalo Bisons (AHL): 1960-61
- Cleveland Barons (AHL): 1961-63
- Springfield Indians (AHL): 1963-64
- Memphis Wings (CPHL): 1965-66

Detroit Red Wings
- 1964-65 to 1973-74, 1974-75

Best NHL Season
- 1967-68: 13 goals, 41 points

Career Awards & Honors
- NHL All-Star Game: 1973
- Team Captain: 1973-74
- Team Canada: 1972

Trades
- Traded from Detroit to Minnesota for Ted Harris in November of 1973.
- Traded with Bill McKenzie to Kansas City for Peter McDuffe and Glen Burdon in September of 1975.

BIOGRAPHY

Gary Bergman was a steady, dependable rushing defenseman who played for Detroit during the 1970s. He is one of the most popular players to ever play for the Red Wings and, at one point during his career, was rated among the top ten defensemen in the NHL.

Bergman was with the Red Wings when they were

a contender (1964-65), and his career carried over into an era in which the team was not very successful. "Bergie was a hell of a hockey player and he carried over from [the better days]," says former Red Wings' PR director Elliott Trumbull. "He had just started there when Lindsay and those teams were going out. So Bergie was a good carry-over into the 1970s. He was a damn good hockey player!"

While in the minors, Montreal owned the rights to Bergman. However, through a change in the rules, Sid Abel acquired him for Detroit. Recalling the day he made it to the pros, Bergman says: "Sid Abel got me for Detroit, so that was a rather exciting day. I was sitting up in Kenora fishing and somebody heard it on the radio and came running out on the lake to get me. I was getting rather despondent by then. I had been in the minors for four years and I really felt that I deserved a chance. ... There were only six teams then, and the hardest thing was making the team, getting in the league. Back then they didn't carry a lot of players and there were only 12 left defensemen jobs in the world and if you could get one, it was kind of a point of pride."

Recalling his first game with Detroit, Bergman says: "I have to tell you, I was really in awe the first time I sat down in the Detroit dressing room. I was thinking, 'What is a kid from the thistle-drinking Kenora doing here? Geez!' I felt the same way standing at the blue line for the National Anthem for my first game. I looked down the bench beside me and here's Marcel Pronovost and Bill Gadsby and Normie Ullman and Alex Delvecchio and Gordie Howe and Ted Lindsay, and I said, 'Holy geez, how lucky can a guy get? This is a pretty good little squad here.'"

Bergman's philosophy as an athlete was an admirable one. "The way I was taught [my philosophy was], to give it the best you've got every night that you go to the rink. Back then, you couldn't get into the league without your defensive skills. Because usually, everyone could carry the puck a little or diddle around with it, but if you spent any time in the minors it was to learn your defensive

Opposite: Gary Bergman was a steady, dependable rushing defenseman for Detroit during the 1970s.

skills. We thought nothing of blocking shots all night or body checking all night, but this running from behind stuff. When was the last time you saw a real good open ice check? That stuff happened every night. My philosophy was just go to the rink and try to be prepared, think properly, have your mind set right and shift by shift give it everything you've got."

Bergman once got into a tussle with Chicago's Bobby Hull. On February 9, 1966, Detroit goalie Roger Crozier hit Hull on the legs with his stick as he skated in front of the Detroit goal. Bergman stepped in between Crozier and Hull, who was charging after him. Bergman shoved Hull with his stick and received a whack on the head in return, thus starting a battle which saw Hull's hand swollen and sprained after the scrum. Bergman got away with a headache and a gash on his forehead which required four stitches to close!

Recalling the fight today, Bergman says:

I remember it well. We were in Chicago and I was skating up the ice and I heard some oohs and ahs. I don't know what happened back there. All I know is that Bobby and Roger got into it. I looked over my shoulder and I was the last man back and I thought, 'Oh geez, why me?' I turned around and I got to go bailing back in there. I jumped in between them and the first thing I got was a stick [from Hull], followed by his big fist, and [they] promptly split my forehead open. So we got into a little shuffling match. But that's the one thing I respect about the game then, and I really don't like about the game now. Every player that ever played the game back then had their pride bruised a little. It was all in how you picked yourself up. Now days, if you took the helmets off those guys they'd go from their 6'7" right back to their 5'8". We'll see what kind of men they are. That's just the way the game was played. Even though you whacked one another, there was still a certain amount of professional respect, and I think that's lacking in the game now.

Bergman played for Team Canada in 1972, the year they narrowly defeated the Russians. He played with fellow Detroit Red Wings Marcel Dionne, Mickey Redmond and Red Berenson. In the September 19, 1972 issue of the *Detroit News*, Bergman said: "Ironically, my greatest thrill in hockey came at the same time as my greatest humiliation. In that first game in Montreal against the Russians when I stood at the blue line for the opening face off, I was so proud I could bust. Then when we lost (7-3), it was my greatest humiliation. ... It is not a disgrace to lose, nobody wants to, but it's still no disgrace. But what we do, let's do it with dignity. With some class. There is one thing I want to be remembered for this, and that's that I gave my best...that I didn't dog it...that I worked as hard as I could."

Today, looking back, Bergman offered a more insightful look into his Team Canada experience, commenting:

First of all, I was so damn proud just to be chosen for the team. When I went to camp, as a matter of fact I'll never forget it, Harry [Sinden] called me Sunday morning. Janie and the kids and I were just going out the door to church, and I had to stop. Janie was saying: 'Would you get off the damn phone, we have to get to church.' It was Harry Sinden on the phone, asking me if I'd be part of the team. We went to Toronto for training camp, and he just happened to pair me with Brad Park and we just clicked. No conversation, no real big verbal communication, we just worked together. We were one of the few that played every game throughout the whole series and I think that's the reason. But that just showed that's always been my philosophy. To this day I can still look in the mirror every morning knowing that some nights it wasn't too great, but whatever I had in me the team got.

I think we knew in our hearts what we were up against. You know, we weren't properly prepared for it to begin with. They [the Russians] were prepared, they came out of the gate, just poof! We had been playing golf and drinking beer all summer until they brought us to training camp, and you don't go to training camp for a couple of weeks and take on a team like that, that's been training for months and months and months. But we felt really if we got in good enough shape to skate with them and start bumping them and moving with them, that we'd have a better-than-average chance. But the one thing that I think showed earlier in my career, I always felt I was a team player. I think that showed when I first came up, through the years that we had some pretty fair teams, and it showed in Team Canada. Because in my own mind, hockey is a very, very simple game, especially when you are surrounded by good hockey players because they simplify the game.

The emotions were so high. I mean, God Almighty, I think it was just short of a national holiday in Canada. They'd closed the schools for Pete's sake so everybody could watch the game. You talk about being under a microscope. When things were going bad for us, the best thing we ever did was get the four games over in Canada and get out of town, you know, 'Get out of Dodge' before they shot us. That was the best thing Harry did. He took us to Sweden for a week and we just got our stuff together. But I also felt ... proud of the sport deeply. Sure you were proud of representing Canada and the NHL, but I also felt deep in my heart that the reason I worked so hard was that I was also representing every other player in the NHL, and I'll be damned if I wanted to embarrass myself. I just felt very strongly about that. I wanted to come back and even if I skated out on the ice and they wanted to hit me, I wanted them down deep to feel that they respected me because I went and represented them well.

"Gary Bergman, he was a heck of a defenseman that I enjoyed watching because he played a real smooth game," says NHL referee Paul Stewart. "He was steady, didn't make too many mistakes with the puck and seemed to always find a knack or a way to get a piece of his body on the puck or tip it. He wasn't the type of defenseman that would take it end to end, but he always seemed to be the type of guy that could keep the puck in the zone or somehow break up a rush. Of course, he was bald and he was easy to notice. At the Canada Cup, he did a good job."

Today, Bergman lives near Detroit. He is the current president of the Detroit Red Wing Alumni Association.

REED DAVID LARSON

Born: July 30, 1956, Minneapolis, Minnesota
Position: Defense
College
- University of Minnesota Golden Gophers (WCHA): 1974-77
Detroit Red Wings
- 1976-77 to 1985-86
Best NHL Season
- 1982-83: 22 goals, 74 points
Career Awards & Honors
- All-Star Games: 1978, '80, '81
Trades
- Traded to Boston in March of 1986 for Mike O'Connell.

BIOGRAPHY

During the 1970s, the Red Wings were fortunate to have American-born defenseman Reed Larson on their roster. While playing for the University of Minnesota Golden Gophers, Larson was considered by many scouts to be the best college defenseman in the United States. At the age of 20, he decided to turn pro with the Red Wings. Larson played his first game with Detroit on February 12, 1977, in a game against the Minnesota North Stars. His first NHL goal came on October 26, 1977, in a 4-3 win over the Pittsburgh Penguins.

Larson possessed a quick shot and was very strong along the boards. He was also an excellent skater. "Reed could obviously shoot the puck," says former Red Wing Nick Libett. "He was strong as an ox, played hard and was very tough. Very tough. I don't think he knew how strong he really was."

While playing for the University of Minnesota, Reed Larson was considered the best college defenseman in the United States.

In June of 1987, something tragic happened to Larson. While driving, another car turned out of a side street and collided with his vehicle. The accident resulted in an injury. Larson explained his injuries in a November 12, 1987 *Toronto Globe and Mail* article by Frank Orr. Said Larson: "There was damage to the artery in my arm and the nerves didn't escape either. For a month and a half, I didn't have much movement or feeling in that hand and when I was able to wiggle my fingers, it was a big gain."

After microsurgery and extensive therapy, Larson was able to return and play again. However, it wasn't easy. "When I was coming back, I fooled myself a few times by thinking that some simple progress—being able to do something easy like picking up a coffee cup—meant that I was getting close to slapping the puck," he said in the same article. "When I would try something more difficult, it was a fight. The nerves are the spark plugs of your body and they ignite all the movements. For a long time, it was like my engine was running with bad plugs because my reflexes were slow."

On January 15, 1987, while playing for the Boston Bruins, Larson scored his 200th and 201st NHL goals in a win over the Hartford Whalers. At the time, very few defensemen had reached the mark. For a long time, Larson was the highest-scoring, U.S.-born player in the NHL.

MARCEL DIONNE

Detroit selected Marcel Dionne second overall in the 1971 Amateur Draft.

MARCEL ELPHEGE DIONNE

Born: August 3, 1951, Drummondville, Quebec
Position: Center
Junior
- Drummondville Rangers (QJHL): 1967-68
- St. Catharines Blackhawks [Junior A] (OHA): 1968-71

Detroit Red Wings
- 1971-72 to 1974-75

Best NHL Season
- 1979-80 (Los Angeles): 53 goals, 137 points

Career Awards & Honors
Junior Hockey
- Eddie Powers Memorial Trophy (OHA Leading Scorer): 1969-70, 1970-71

Professional
- Hockey Hall of Fame: 1992
- Lady Byng Trophy: 1974-75, 1976-77
- Art Ross Trophy: 1980 (LA)
- First All-Star Team: 1979-80 (LA)
- Second All-Star Team: 1980-81 (LA)
- NHL All-Star Games: 1975-78, '80, '81, '83, '85

Trades
- Traded to Los Angeles on June 23, 1975, with Bart Crashley for Dan Maloney, Terry Harper and a 1976 second-round NHL amateur draft choice.

BIOGRAPHY

Known as the "Little Beaver" because of his small size, Marcel Dionne's athletic abilities were evident from a very young age. He was known for his clean-cut, finesse style of play, which eventually won him two Lady Byng trophies. Once Dionne reached the junior ranks, he became a hockey star. In St. Catharines, he won back-to-back Eddie Power trophies (OHA top-scorer) with the Blackhawks and was named to the OHA All-Star team on two occasions (1970 and 1971). In three seasons of junior hockey, he accumulated 507 points.

Dionne broke into the NHL with Detroit, who selected him second overall in the 1971 NHL Amateur Draft. During his first season in the Motor

City, he led all rookies in scoring with 28 goals and 49 assists. The assist total was then a rookie record. In a *Hockey World* article by Norm MacLean, former Detroit general manager Ned Harkness said: "Dionne was the replacement for Gordie Howe in Detroit. Of course, no one replaces Howe, but in the minds of the fans he was to be the answer to our problems. Lafleur found replacing Jean Beliveau in Montreal a difficult task. Dionne did his job and captured the public imagination here in Detroit."

Interestingly, despite all of his career accomplishments, Dionne commented late in his career that he was not destined to be the main attraction. In a December 4, 1986 *Toronto Sun* article by Scott Morrison, he said: "When I went to the Red Wings' camp that year (1971), in Port Huron, I was lost. The veterans would look at me and say: 'What's this kid, all 5-foot-7 and 160 pounds of him, going to do for this team? ... I was born to be in the pack...to be second best ... Howe and Hull were guys I idolized, great players. Fans came to watch them. They filled buildings. I haven't. But I think I can play with anybody and I can live with it."

During his first four NHL seasons with Detroit, Dionne scored 366 points. The point total was more, in a four-year period, than Bobby Hull, Bobby Orr, Phil Esposito, Rocket Richard, Gordie Howe or any player in NHL history.

In the same article, Nick Libett commented on the then-rookie, saying: "Marcel can give you a nice lead pass. And he flies on those skates when he gets wound up. Wait until he gets a little experience." Unfortunately, when Dionne did get the experience that enabled him to attain a great deal of success, he was not wearing a Detroit sweater, but that of a Los Angeles King. He was traded to Los Angeles after frequent run-ins with both management and the Detroit media, refusing a $1,000,000 offer. His agent, Alan Eagleson, said that the decision was not one of money but of a personal nature.

Dionne spent the majority of his successful career in Los Angeles, where he gained fame playing center on the Triple Crown Line with Dave Taylor and Charlie Simmer. He spent the last three seasons of his career playing for the New York Rangers and retired at the end of the 1989 season.

DENNIS HAROLD HEXTALL

Born: April 17, 1943, Poplar Point, Manitoba
Position: Center
Junior
- Brandon, Manitoba (WHL)

Minor Pro
- Knoxville (EHL)

Detroit Red Wings
- 1975-76 to 1978-79

Best NHL Season
- 1972-73 (Minnesota): 30 goals, 82 points

Career Awards & Honors
- Shared team captaincy with Nick Libett and Paul Woods in 1978-79.
- NHL All-Star games: 1974, '75

Trades
- Traded to Detroit from Minnesota in 1976 for Bill Hogaboam and a second-round draft pick in 1976 Entry Draft.

BIOGRAPHY

Hockey has always been in Hextall's blood. His father, Bryan Aldwyn Hextall, was a right wing for the New York Rangers during the 1930s and 1940s and is a member of the Hockey Hall of Fame. His brother, Bryan Lee Hextall, was also a forward in the NHL and even had a brief stint with the Red Wings.

"[My dad played] when I was a small kid up in Canada," he says. "Of course we grew up in a small town, so we were skating all the time. He worked with us [on the ice], but we used to do so much [on our own], just the kids around those small farm towns where we were. You were always skating, you'd get whatever you could body wise and you'd have a scrimmage game. You might have three on a side or six on a side, whatever. But that's just the way we were as kids."

Hextall was an excellent junior hockey player in Canada. Recalling those early days, he says: "I played my junior in Brandon, Manitoba. I was in the Western League. Both years, we lost out in the Western Canada Finals to Edmonton. One year, they won the Memorial Cup. At that time, you only had two teams in the Memorial Cup—one from the West and one from the East. So technically, we were third one year in Canada and fourth the next year. ... The first year I was just there on the team, and the second year I lost the scoring championship by one point."

Instead of jumping up to the NHL, Hextall

Dennis Hextall was one of Detroit's better players during the 1970s.

decided to pursue his education at the University of North Dakota. He spent three years at the University of North Dakota and did not play his senior year. After college, he played for Knoxville of the Eastern League, and the New York Rangers offered him a pro contract. "Knoxville was New York's affiliate, and I played there one year," he says. "Then, the next year I went to camp and banged my knee up. That year, I ended up going from Omaha to Buffalo to New York [where] I played with the Rangers."

It was in the Eastern League that Hextall learned the survival skills necessary for NHL play, skills that one did not learn in college hockey.

That was a pretty tough league. You had to survive in that league. [You learned fast] or you didn't survive. It was a tough league. You got in that league, and there was a lot of fighting and everything else. [It was a surprise]

when you came out of college, because there was no fighting in college and, when I played junior hockey, I wasn't a fighter. But then I found out sort of quick that everybody's coming at you. It was just a matter of picking it up. So I went back a couple of summers and took boxing lessons from a guy in North Dakota. That sort of changed my attitude. If they wanted to come, I was going to be ready for them. Yeah, I was always a pretty good checker. You can look at junior hockey and minor pro and that...and you may be a goal scorer and stuff there, but every step you take up, it gets that much tougher to do stuff. When I hit the NHL, I scored goals, but I wasn't, per se, a goal scorer.

"I was a good, average player, or above average," says Hextall. "For six years, I led the team in scoring and in penalties, and I always had to play against the big centermen. When we played Chicago, I either had to check Bobby Hull's line or Stan Mikita's. We would go to Boston and I would get Esposito. Go to New York, I'd get Ratelle. I'd come to Detroit and chase Howe, Delvecchio and Mahovlich around all night. When I was in Minnesota and that, we always had to play against their big lines, and we were expected to score and keep their lines off the boards."

While playing for the Minnesota North Stars, Hextall got into a few memorable entanglements. In March of 1972, he and Wayne Cashman of the Boston Bruins had a stick-swinging melee near the end of the second period of a nationally televised game.

"We always had a tough go against Boston," he says.

That year, I had a knee operation and he had laced me across the leg twice coming down the ice. There were no penalties called and then at that point I just said, 'I'm going to even this up.' I turned around and speared him. I guess at the time you look at it and I was saying, 'Good, I got him.' But when you look at it now, you realize either one of us could have been seriously hurt. Had my stick been six inches higher, I might have gotten him right in the face. You know, he could have lost an eye. Then, after that, he took a swing at me. I was sort of backed. The referee and then, of course, Boston players were kind of mulling around. Cashman got up and took a run. He had a stick and he leaped over people and took a vicious swing. He could have clipped me pretty good, too. I think we have to look back and say, that's not the way the game should be played. We're very fortunate nobody got hurt, seriously. Like in the Maki incident. It could have been another one of those.

Looking back over his days with the Red Wings, Hextall recalled the most memorable moment. "We beat Atlanta [in 1977-78]," he says. "The one year they got in the playoffs, the whole team played well. We had to beat Montreal. We had a home-and-home [the team's played one another consecutively, with a game played in each of their respective home arenas] with them the last weekend and we had to win to get in second place. We went to Montreal, and I think the beat us by a goal. We came back the next night and we beat them on our ice. That put us in second place, so that weekend was good. But I would think the most satisfaction I had with Detroit was when we beat Atlanta the last night on our home ice. You know, the whole team played well both games. We weren't expected to win and we beat them on our home ice that night, I think 3-2."

Today, Hextall lives in the Detroit area. He is the past president of the Detroit Red Wings Alumni Association.

LYNN NICHOLAS (NICK) LIBETT

Born: December 9, 1945, Stratford, Ontario

Position: Left Wing

Junior Hockey
- Hamilton Red Wings [Junior A] (OHA): 1962-64, 1964-66

Minor League Hockey
- Cincinnati Wings (CPHL): 1963-64
- Memphis Wings (CPHL): 1965-67
- Fort Worth Wings (CPHL): 1967-68
- San Diego Gulls (WHL): 1967-68

Detroit Red Wings
- 1967-68 to 1978-79

Best NHL Season
- 1971-72: 31 goals, 53 points

Career Awards & Honors
- NHL All-Star Game: 1977
- Team Captain: 1973-74 and 1978-79
- Team Canada: 1979

BIOGRAPHY

Nick Libett was exposed to the game from an early age. His father played hockey in the old Michigan-Ontario League and was one of Canada's better softball pitchers.

As a youth, Libett played bantam hockey in a YMCA league. The league was suffering financially, and Detroit's Jack Adams put up sponsorship money so that it could continue. It wasn't without reason, however, as the Red Wings were interested in several of the league's players. Adams' sponsorship gave Detroit the rights to Libett. After he signed with them at age of 14, Libett eventually developed into an NHL regular for the Red Wings.

Libett did not possess a wealth of natural ability and had to work very hard for the results he was able to reap on the ice. He was an adept checker who wasn't afraid to scramble in the corners. Considered by many to have been among the best two-way forwards in the league, Libett played a strong positional game. In the March 31, 1972 issue of *The Hockey News*, in an article by Jack Berry, Libett's former coach Johnny Wilson said: "Nick is the best two-way left wing in the league and one of the best two-way left wings I've ever seen. He is the best forechecker, he comes right back, he kills penalties and he's strong. He's a great skater and he's got a wicked shot."

"I played with him for four years," says Dennis Hextall. "He was a big, strong winger, [who] went up and down, did his job [and] showed up every night. He played as well on the road as he did at home. I know from playing with Nick for four years, if something started out there, you never had to worry about him. You knew where he was, he was right behind you coming in. He was a great guy to play with."

During his career, Libett saw international competition. He played for Team Canada in 1979. "[Team Canada] was a highlight and a low [point]," he says. "The low [point] was that our team missed the playoffs. But the highlight was obviously playing as an older player and just having the opportunity to play. Even though most of the players on those teams were non-playoff teams that year, they still were very, very good hockey players. You had a chance to

Nick Libett played a streak of 389 consecutive games during his 14-season career.

article that appeared in *The Hockey News*, Libett commented on that fight in particular, and on fighting in general. "I'd say I won," he began. "I split him open and my hand is swollen from hitting him. The doctor says it's a bad bruise. I don't mind fighting but I don't go looking for them. It tires you out. We had a fight in Chicago but it didn't amount to anything—he just bounced around. I'd rather just grab the sweater and hit."

Today, Libett still remembers the fight. "I remember that because to this day, particularly in Detroit, people will come up to me and say—this is 20 some years, 24 years after the fact—they'll say, 'Nick I still remember...' and I will say to them without even—it was like a first goal—without even batting an eye, I'll say, 'Yes, you're going to mention the Magnuson fight.' I knew what they were going to ask. It was just a typical, and I know Keith now. Obviously, he's a gentleman and a smart, intelligent guy. He played hard and he always had a reputation of sticking his nose in it, and I don't think I'm the only guy that ever fought with him. I'd like to think that I won that one, but I just remember we just started [swinging]. It was just a good fight. He'd swing and miss, and I'd swing and hit. That's basically what happened. I think I did have a slight edge in that one."

Libett was quite an iron man. During his career, he once played in 389 consecutive games. The streak began in 1974 and ended when he injured his knee in February of 1979. Sadly, during the 14 NHL seasons in which he played, Libett made the playoffs only three times. In an article by Paul Patton, which appeared in the March 30, 1987 issue of the *Toronto Globe and Mail*, he said: "Before the second expansion, Detroit was asked to go into the Western Division, but Bruce Norris (the owner) didn't want to move. And Chicago went instead. They ended up making the playoffs all those years and we missed out. But I enjoyed playing in Detroit despite the losses. I liked the people and I just stuck it out. I never asked to be traded until late in my career when Ted Lindsay was running the team."

Libett finished his career with the Pittsburgh Penguins. After hockey, he went into business and owned his own company, Gibbons Libett Sales, which represented manufacturers from Japan, Taiwan and South Korea.

see what it would be like to play on a team that had that type of talent. You know, teams like Montreal had, years of teams like that. It was a thrill. It was enjoyable."

Libett also played in an exhibition game against the Russians on January 4, 1979. "That was good," he says. "We beat them, I believe, that game. That wasn't their national team, but they had some players that were on the national team. It was nice to see their style and how they attempted to move the puck and just a different strategy than we played. We beat them, I think, 5-4, and from what I remember we did outplay them. But again, you could see they had some talent."

In the spring of 1972 Nick Libett had a fight with Chicago's Keith Magnuson in front of a nationally televised audience. Besides all of the television viewers watching, then Vice-President Spiro T. Agnew and his wife were present at the game. In a March 31, 1972

MICHAEL EDWARD (MICKEY) REDMOND

Born: December 27, 1947, Kirkland Lake, Ontario
Position: Right wing
Junior
- Peterborough TPTs (Junior A) (OHA): 1963-67

Minor Pro
- Houston Apollos (CPHL): 1966-68

Detroit Red Wings
- 1970-71 to 1975-76

Best NHL Season
- 1972-73: 52 goals, 93 points

Career Awards & Honors
- First All-Star Team: 1973
- Second All-Star Team: 1974
- All-Star Games: 1974

Career Milestones
- Mickey Redmond was the first Detroit player to score 50 goals in one season. He scored 52 in 1972-73 and 51 the following season.

Trades
- Traded to Detroit from Montreal with Guy Charron and Bill Collins for Frank Mahovlich in 1971.

BIOGRAPHY

Mickey Redmond comes from a family rooted in hockey. His father, Ed, played defense for the Whitby Dunlops senior team during the 1950s. In 1958, the Dunlops beat the Russians in Oslo, Norway, for the world championship, and Ed hung up the skates. Mickey's brother, Dick, was a defenseman with Minnesota, California, Chicago, St. Louis, Atlanta and Boston.

Redmond spent a little over five of his nine NHL seasons with Detroit. He was a stand-out player from the very start. Redmond played junior hockey with the Peterborough Petes for four seasons, scoring a total of 136 goals. At age 15, he was named Rookie of the Year. In 1967, he scored 51 goals and won the Red Tillson Memorial Trophy for his gentlemanly play. While playing for Peterborough, Redmond earned All-Star honors twice.

Redmond broke into the NHL with the Montreal Canadiens in 1967-68, after playing 15 games with their Central League affiliate in Houston. One of his most unforgettable moments in Montreal occurred on April 13, 1969, during a Stanley Cup semifinal game against Boston. Serge Savard tied the game 3-3, with only 69 seconds remaining, and Redmond, who had spent the entire evening sitting on the bench, scored

Mickey Redmond had a reputation for his heavy, hard shot.

the game-winning goal during sudden-death overtime. The goal allowed the Canadiens to advance in the playoffs and win their second Stanley Cup championship in as many years. In Montreal, Redmond had the advantage of playing with, and learning from, veteran legends Henri Richard, Jean Beliveau, Claude Provost and J.C. Trembley.

Redmond was a gifted hockey player, possessing speed, size, and a hard shot. In an article by Jack Berry, which appeared in the April 12, 1973 issue of *The Hockey News*, former Detroit goalie Roy Edwards said: "I'd say that right now, Mickey has the hardest shot in the league. He's also got the second-best wrist shot I've ever seen. Gordie Howe had the best—not necessarily the hardest but the best—and when I saw Gordie, he was past his prime."

Redmond developed his hard, heavy shot by shooting metal pucks in the corridors of the Peterborough ice rink while playing junior and by spending hours in his parent's basement firing pucks when he couldn't find any ice. In an article written during his career, he remembered those developmental days, commenting:

"Dick and I used to shoot by the hour in the cellar—when we weren't on the ice somewhere. What I remember best was laying a cardboard box on its side and then putting a bottle right at the back of it. Dick and I would have a contest then to see who could break it first. It was quite a trick to drive the box hard enough and accurate enough to break the bottle. It's funny to look back on it now because to us it was just a fun, pleasant way to spend the time in the winter—and in the summer, too. But now it's paying off. Shooting is the thing I do best."

Sadly, in 1976, Redmond's career ended prematurely. He had been feeling pain in his back since October of 1974, but ignored it. When the pain became too much to bear, he sought medical help. Doctors discovered a ruptured disc. "The back pain became unbearable," said Redmond in the January, 1977 issue of *Sport*. "I couldn't even bend over to put on my skates, the trainer had to do it for me. In the morning, I'd go to the shower bent over, my chest ninety degrees to the rest of my body, and I had to let hot water pour over me for half an hour before I could straighten up. I couldn't sleep at night. Christ, it was terrible."

The injury caused permanent nerve damage to his leg. For a time, Redmond lost between 40 and 50 percent of the use of his right leg. Surgery was performed to correct the problem, but it was too late to repair the damage that had already been done. In the same Randy Schultz article, Redmond commented on the injury, explaining: "I'll have problems with my right leg for as long as I live. There are days when the leg is numb from the knee down. It gets tired very quickly if I walk on it too much. And I have many sleepless nights because it hurts so much."

Reflecting on his career, in the same article by Randy Schultz, Redmond said: "I was fortunate to play with two good centers while I was with the Red Wings—Alex Delvecchio and Bill Hogaboam. They fed me a lot of good scoring passes. But not making the playoffs while I was with the Red Wings was my biggest disappointment. We came close a couple of times, but we always seemed to fall short."

When his playing career was over, Redmond turned to broadcasting and became a member of both the Hockey Night in Canada and ESPN staff. He has worked for a steel company in Detroit as a sales representative and co-owned a restaurant in Boston with his brother, Dick. Currently, Redmond works for the Fox network and has been a member of the Detroit Red Wings broadcast team, along with partner Dave Strader.

CHAPTER THIRTEEN

A NEW BEGINNING
- THE 1980s -

The National Hockey League was an exciting place for some teams during the 1980s. Wayne Gretzky came alive with the Edmonton Oilers, and the World Hockey Association ceased to exist, with four of its teams joining the NHL. The decade began with the New York Islanders winning four consecutive Stanley Cups under head coach Al Arbor, and saw Edmonton flourish under coach Glen Sather.

For the Detroit Red Wings, things were not as bright. The struggling teams that characterized the 1970s continued into the 1980s. A number of coaches took their turn behind the Detroit bench. Among them were Ted Lindsay, Wayne Maxner, Billy Dea, Nick Polano, Harry Neale, Brad Park and Jacques Demers. A 1992 *Detroit News* article said that, for the most part, the 1980s "were terrible seasons, so long ago now. They were seasons when seats were empty and coaches were paraded through the hockey rink, to dream and to die. They were seasons when victories were scarce and there was little hope and the Stanley Cup was a foolish fantasy."

However, the 1980s marked a new beginning for the Red Wings. The Norris regime came to an end when, in 1982-83, current owner Mike Ilitch took control of the team, bringing new hope to a city that had not seen good playoff hockey since the mid-1960s. The club began to see post-season action once again, when in 1983-84, the Red Wings lost the division semifinal to St. Louis.

"I think the metamorphosis of Detroit started in the early 1980s, like 1982-1983," says NHL referee Paul Stewart. "I don't know when Ilitch bought the team, but you could see that the players that they were starting to get had better talent. The other thing was that they seemed to go back to a little bit more of their, I guess, tradition, where they were making an effort to bring Gordie Howe back into the family and all the other different things. Hanging up the flags and, of course, classing up the place. Then, when I started to have to do business with them in the mid-to-late-1980s, they were a team that wasn't quite there yet, but they had the core of a pretty good hockey team."

Above and left: Steve Yzerman, Glenn Hanlon, Gilbert Delorme and Joe Kocur celebrate the elimination of Toronto in the Norris Division finals. Rich Margittay Photos.

Commenting on the beginning of Detroit's improvement in the 1980s, former Red Wing defenseman Gary Bergman said: "Detroit was never short on the dollar. I don't know what it was like toward the end when Norris was there, because I wasn't there when he owned the team. But our payroll was always right there, close to leading the pack. I think when Ilitch took over, they were getting into the area where they had to spend some serious money, and he had it. Let's face it, [today], like Chicago, they're one of the most successful franchises in the league. They fill the barn every night and they put a good product on the ice. It would be getting into the last half of the '80s when they started heading in the right direction. They also made some real bad draft choices [before that time]. Forget about the trades, they made some serious big-time mistakes in the draft. I think they started heading in the right direction when they took players like Stevie Yzerman and those types of guys."

"We were in no way Stanley Cup contenders," said former Red Wing Dwight Foster, in the December 1995 issue of *Inside Line*, "but it was a great atmosphere. You knew Mike Ilitch was in the process of building the kind of team that is on the ice today. It was great to be a part of that building process at the very beginning."

Danny Gare, who came to Detroit after spending seven-and-a-half seasons with Buffalo, gave his feelings on the era in the April 1994 issue of *Hockey Digest*. Said Gare: "The rebuilding process in Detroit was a real challenge, but something I wanted to help [with] because of the new direction the team was headed—and I think I did. In Detroit, I again was on a 'checking line,' which I think may have hurt my chances as a potential Hall of Famer. But that's the situation we were in, and in order for our team to improve, I had to be in that role. It was a tough situation for me to do at times, but we did it."

Today, commenting further on the rebuilding process Detroit went through, he says: "Their organization, their drafting, and all of that was, I think, a little poor in the past. Until Mike Ilitch came along and put together a pretty good staff, along with Jim Devellano. They've got a strong team [now], and a lot of the credit has to go to the people that are around there. I know that Mike went out and spent some money to get people, and they've had some good leadership there. Scotty [Bowman] seems to be a good fit for them. They are very talented. Coffey has helped them a lot, and they have got good goaltending. With the talent they have, they will be up in the top three or four for some time."

During the 1980s, the Red Wings had a myriad of coaches behind the bench. At the close of the decade, they had Jacques Demers, an emotional, talkative coach who was quite popular with the fans. It was his term as head coach that marked the real metamorphosis of the Red Wings into the team that graces the ice of Joe Louis Arena today. Demers led the Red Wings to the conference championships twice (1986-87 and 1987-88). While he was behind Detroit's bench, the Red Wings finished second in the Norris division once (1986-87) and first the following two seasons.

Demers coached the Red Wings from 1986-87 to 1989-90. He was fired in 1990 when the Wings finished fifth, missing the playoffs. After coaching Detroit, the Montreal native, who as a boy was a rink rat at the Montreal Forum, coached the Canadiens to the Stanley Cup in 1992-93. "We had one bad year [in Detroit]," he said in the November 4, 1992 issue of the *Detroit News*, shortly before he took Montreal all the way. "I was shocked [when I was fired]. I respected the decision. I never said anything negative, and I think it's a reason I'm in hockey today. If I bad-mouthed anybody, I wouldn't be back in hockey."

THE MEN

GREGORY STEVEN STEFAN

Born: February 11, 1961, Brantford, Ontario
Position: Goaltender
Junior
- Oshawa Generals (OMJHL), 1978-80
- Oshawa Generals (OHL), 1980-81
Minor Pro
- Adirondack Red Wings (AHL), 1981-82
Detroit Red Wings
- 1981-82 to 1989-90
Best NHL Season
- 1987-88: 1,854 min, 3.11 GAA, 1 SO

BIOGRAPHY

Goaltender Greg Stefan spent his entire NHL career with Detroit. "He was a fearless goalie, like Grant Fuhr," said his former childhood friend Wayne Gretzky in the May 10, 1987 issue of the *Toronto Sun*. "I remember one game when Stef was 10 years old. He lost his stick and his gloves and dived across the crease to stop the puck with his face. My dad (Walter) was coaching the team. He said anybody with that much guts is going to be a professional player someday."

Gretzky and Stefan were good friends growing up in Brantford, Ontario. In the May 9, 1988 issue of the *Toronto Sun*, he recalled those days: "It was always something. We played hockey all winter long. We played all kinds of tournaments as kids, mostly because of Wayne. But if we weren't playing rep hockey, we were playing road hockey, or in the backyard. I guess that was about all we did. In the summer, it was baseball. It was always like that. We

Greg Stefan lifts his stick in victory as Detroit eliminates St. Louis in the 1988 Norris Division finals. Rich Margittay Photo.

were always together."

During his career, Stefan had the reputation of being a Jekyll and Hyde of sorts. On the ice, he was fiery and intense. Off it, he was quiet, reserved and easy going. His fieriness occasionally got him into trouble. Several times during his career, he got too creative with his stick. In March 1981, Stefan was handed a six-game suspension by the OHA for breaking his stick over the shoulder of Bart Wilson of the Toronto Marlboros. On April 13, 1985, he swung his stick at Chicago's Al Secord during the playoffs. The incident resulted in a suspension for the first eight games of the 1985-86 season.

Stefan continued his involvement with the sport after playing. Jim Rutherford hired him to be a goalie coach for the Detroit Whalers (formerly the Detroit Junior Red Wings) several years ago. Along with Peter DeBoer, Stefan served as an assistant coach to Coach / General Manager Paul DeBoer. In the December 21, 1995 issue of the *Detroit News*, DeBoer said: "Greg has been fantastic. Any time you can add a player with his background in the NHL, it commands immediate respect from the players. He's doing a super job." With the Whalers, Stefan's new team made it to the Memorial Cup finals and won the Ontario Hockey League title in 1994-95.

DWIGHT ALEXANDER FOSTER

Born: April 2, 1957, Toronto, Ontario
Position: Center
Junior
- Kitchener Rangers (OHA), 1973-78

Minor Pro
- Rochester Americans (AHL): 1977-78, 1978-79
- Binghamton Dusters (AHL), 1979-80
- Wichita Wind (CHL), 1982-83

Detroit Red Wings
- 1982-83 to 1985-86

Best NHL Season
- 1980-81: 24 goals, 52 points (Boston)

Career Awards & Honors
- Eddie Powers Memorial Trophy (OHA's leading scorer), 1976-77

BIOGRAPHY

Dwight Foster came to the Detroit Red Wings after several disappointing seasons with Boston, Colorado and New Jersey. The Bruins let him go to get the first pick in the 1982 entry draft, when they swapped first-round choices with the Colorado Rockies. After the Rockies moved to New Jersey, Foster discovered that he was not in their long-term plans. Rather than face a demotion to the minors, he asked for a trade, threatening to quit if the Devils failed to make a move within two weeks. He was soon sold to Detroit—for $1.

Foster was once one of the NHL's top prospects at the 1977 NHL entry draft. Jimmy Devellano, now Detroit's senior vice president, was then the Islanders' chief scout. He and his associates debated over whether the Islanders would select Foster or Mike Bossy. The Islanders took Bossy, the 15th pick overall. Foster was selected next by the Boston Bruins.

Nick Polano, Foster's former coach, commented on him in the February 7, 1982 issue of the *Detroit News*. He said: "Dwight's an aggressive type, a guy who's always hollering on the bench. He has the kind of enthusiasm that's contagious, and with his experience, he's definitely been an asset. He's what I call an 'up' guy."

Later, in the January 17, 1983 issue of the *Toronto Globe and Mail*, Polano added: "[Foster] just does so much for the team. He takes important faceoffs, kills penalties, works the power play and he has tremendous character."

A tough, grinding, aggressive, team player, Dwight Foster saw a great deal of time on the penalty-killing unit while playing for the Red Wings. In Detroit, he played on the "Troll Line" with Danny Gare and Bob Manno. In the December 1995 issue of *Inside Line*, current Red Wing Senior Vice President Jim Devellano said: "They were a group of crusty veterans who made up a solid checking line. They were certainly effective, but they weren't very pretty. So the fans dubbed them the Troll Line." Besides playing on a line with Gare and Manno, Foster also played on a line with Gare and Paul Woods.

Bad knees troubled Foster throughout his professional career and forced him to have several operations. In the same *Inside Line* article, he said: "My knee problems caused me to change my style somewhat. I had to earn a spot in their [Boston's] lineup three or four times, but I think that was good. Every time I went on the ice for Boston, it was with

the idea of showing them they didn't make a mistake when they drafted me. I wanted to show them I could contribute."

Today, Foster is vice president of Consolidated Benefit Plans, which is based in Southfield, Michigan. He is very active with the Detroit Red Wings Alumni Association and still skates with them in Alumni games.

GERARD GALLANT

Born: September 2, 1963, Summerside, P.E.I.
Position: Left wing
Junior
- Summerside (PEIHA): 1979-80
- Sherbrooke (QMJHL): 1980-82
- St-Jean (QMJHL): 1982-83
- Verdun (QMJHL): 1982-83

Minor Pro
- Adirondack (AHL): 1983-85

Detroit Red Wings
- 1984-85 to 1992-93

Best NHL Season
- 1988-89: 39 goals, 93 points

Career Awards & Honors
- Second All-Star Team: 1988-89

Career Milestones
- Two 70-plus-point seasons
- One 80-point season
- One 90-plus-point season
- In 1988-89, with linemates Steve Yzerman and Paul MacLean, Gallant was a member of the highest-scoring line in Red Wings history (140 goals, 319 points).

Gutsy and hard-nosed, Gerard Gallant was an effective two-way player for the Detroit Red Wings. Rich Margittay Photo.

BIOGRAPHY

Gerard Gallant learned to play hockey on the rinks of Summerside, Prince Edward Island. He was drafted by Detroit at the age of 17, in the 1981 entry draft, and spent the following two years playing junior hockey. Gallant didn't jump straight to the NHL from junior. Instead, he saw time with the Adirondack Wings, Detroit's AHL affiliate. He was not happy with the delay at first, but later said that the AHL stint was beneficial development-wise.

After starting out at left wing with the Red Wings, Gallant first played on a checking line with Danny Gare and Claude Loiselle. He was moved to

right wing in 1985-86 and was very successful until temporarily sidelined with a broken jaw sustained in a fight with Minnesota's Dirk Graham. Despite the injury, Gallant still finished the season with 20 goals and 39 points.

As a player, Gallant proved to be very versatile for Detroit. He could score, could play physically, and didn't neglect the defensive aspect of his game. He was gutsy, was hard-nosed and earned a reputation for being a player not easily intimidated. Columnist Jerry Green reflected upon Gallant at the time of his departure from the Red Wings in the July 22, 1993 issue of the *Detroit News*: "He was grit and smudges, an athlete of blood and muscle and heart and belief. He was seldom pretty when skating on the ice; there was nothing stylish about him. He was all of us who live and work here, in and around the city [of Detroit], in the nine seasons he played for the Red

---

Opposite: Dwight Foster was a tough, grinding, aggressive team player for the Red Wings. Rich Margittay Photo.

Wings. He was Every Detroiter. There was no other athlete in town who better symbolized the city in which he played."

"He's a real blue-collar type," said former Detroit Coach Jacques Demers in *Goal Magazine*. "I always admired Brian Sutter, and to me, when I came to Detroit, I said I had a second Brian Sutter in Gerard Gallant. His idea of playing is hard work, determination, consistency, game-in and game-out. That's the best compliment I could pay Gerard, because Brian was my captain in St. Louis and was a heck of an athlete. ... I had one of the greatest competitors in my 15 years of coaching in Brian Sutter. He was a competitor in the game, at practice and off the ice. Brian Sutter was totally committed to the St. Louis Blues. Win, win, win—do anything to win. Gerard Gallant is a carbon copy of Brian Sutter. Not gifted talent-wise, but gifted with great heart, great determination and great pride in wearing the uniform. He's a tremendously gifted person—gifted with character."

Besides playing on a line with Danny Gare, Gallant also played on a very successful line with Steve Yzerman and Paul MacLean. Many, especially their coach, considered Gallant and Yzerman to be Detroit's heart and soul for some time. In the October 6, 1988 issue of the *Detroit News*, former Red Wings' coach Jacques Demers said: "Steve Yzerman is the white-collar hockey player on this team. And Gerard, well, Gerard is the upper class of the blue collar. He is not as talented as Steve, but he's one of the hardest workers on the team. With Gerard, the only way for him to play is all-out. He doesn't know any other speed. Those two players are totally committed to being members of the Detroit Red Wings. They definitely are the heart and soul of this team."

Continuing to describe the pair, Demers became more psychological, explaining: "If the game goes wrong and there's a lot of pressure, players have their own way of dealing with it. Steve Yzerman will go to the net and score a pretty goal. Gerard will punch somebody in the nose."

Gallant's toughness occasionally got him into trouble. In January 1990, he drew a three-game suspension without appeal for striking linesman Jerry Pateman after a 6-4 loss to the North Stars in

Minnesota. Pateman pinned Gallant to the boards, and Gallant, apparently frustrated by the loss, struck Pateman on the chin.

After experiencing back problems and failing to see his contract with Detroit renewed, Gallant played for the Tampa Bay Lightning, signing on there as a free agent. He finished his career with the Detroit Vipers of the International Hockey League, who gave him a chance to play again. The Vipers valued Gallant for his leadership. In the October 25, 1995 issue of the *Detroit Free Press*, Vipers' coach Rick Dudley said: "He's still got a heavy shot and obviously takes care of himself. A coach can only make so many speeches in the locker room. And some players will just tune you out. But when you've got a leader like Gallant in the room, they're not going to forget things. Guys like him keep a team tight." Gallant retired for good in November 1995.

DANIEL MIRL GARE

Born: May 14, 1954, Nelson, British Columbia
Position: Center
Junior
- Calgary Centennials (WCHL), 1971-74

Detroit Red Wings
- 1981-82 to 1985-86

Best NHL Season
- 1979-80: 56 goals, 89 points

Career Awards & Honors
- Team Captain (Buffalo)
- Team Captain (Detroit): 1982-86
- Buffalo Sabres' Hall of Fame: 1993
- NHL All-Star Games: 1980, '81

Career Milestones
- In 1973-74, scored goals in 13 consecutive games, setting an WCHL record.

Trades
- Traded to Detroit from Buffalo in December of 1981, with Bob Sauve, Jim Schoenfeld and Derek Smith for Dale McCourt, Mike Foligno, Brent Peterson and future considerations.

BIOGRAPHY

Danny Gare comes from a family rich in athletic tradition. His father went to the same Toronto Maple Leafs' training camp as Tim Horton and played hockey in Lethbridge, Alberta. He also coached hockey at B.C. Notre Dame University, where he was instrumental in starting one of the first hockey scholarship programs in athletics. Recently, Gare remembered that tradition and the impact that his father had on his development:

[My father] died of Lou Gehrig's Disease just before I got traded [to Detroit in 1981], the same year. So it was a tough year for me when I got traded. ... He was a major influence. He was my mentor. He was the one that made me what I was. It's still a tough thing to talk about. He always took us out in the backyard, much like any Canadian father did, I think, at that time. He also ran the University Club there, and played Senior Hockey. So I was always at their practices, getting as much ice time as I possibly could, picking the pucks up, helping them.

Gare's brother, Ernie, is now a western scout now with Toronto, and his brother Morey coached at Northern Michigan when they won the NCAA title about five years ago. "We were a skating family," he says. "The girls were all figure skaters, and we were all hockey players."

Before breaking into the NHL with the Buffalo Sabres, Gare played junior hockey for the Calgary Centennials. Remembering those early days, he says: "I played with John Davidson, Bobby Nystrom, Mike Rogers, Jimmy Watson. We had a pretty good team, but we got beat out by Regina the year they won the Cup. ... Scotty Monroe was a big influence [on me]. I played on the line with Holland and Rogers, and we broke a lot of records out there. We had some good leaders. JD was a good leader, Nystrom was a great leader, Jimmy Watson was a great leader. Another guy, our captain, Brian Walker was a good guy. I was just 16 when I left home, played as a 17-year-old, and stayed there for three years. I was the captain my last two years there. I enjoyed that. Then I got drafted [by Buffalo]. That was the first year they went in the under-age."

Gare started his NHL career in Buffalo, where he enjoyed his most successful seasons. In his third season, he was named team captain. In the April 1994 issue of *Hockey Digest*, he said: "Buffalo was a great town for me to start my career in. It wasn't too big where you could get lost or caught up in things too quickly. They were people who really enjoyed the game. I think that really helped me, because of their enthusiasm. You couldn't get a ticket there; they were

Danny Gare was more of a checker than a scorer for the Red Wings.

sold out every night."

Current Detroit Red Wing Coach Scotty Bowman was behind Buffalo's bench while Gare played for the Sabres. It was Bowman who decided to ship him to Detroit, where he became part of their rebuilding process. Although he was never the goal scorer in Detroit that he had been in Buffalo, Gare was a solid contributor in the Motor City. He served as a tough checker for the Wings and was valued both on and off the ice for his leadership qualities. As in Buffalo, Gare was team captain in Detroit.

Recalling his days with the Red Wings, Gare says:

I was Mike Ilitch's first captain. ... I had Gallant on my right side, he was 17, I was 18, and Yzerman on my left side. I really enjoyed working with those youngsters. They were both rookies, and they became good leaders in their own right. They were real young kids at the time when I was there. We had some older guys too, like Walt McKechnie and Ivan Boldirev and Reed Larson. They weren't a very good team, but we came on and made the playoffs back-to-back, I think two years later, and it was the first time they'd done that in 20 years, so I felt good about that. Then there were some changes up in personnel. They brought in Harry Neal, and he didn't stay long. Then Brad Park came in. And then, they kind of cleaned house and brought in Jacques Demers. I was part of that house cleaning. I really enjoyed the Detroit area. I really liked the people there. The fans were unbelievable. We started to fill them [the seats] up towards the end of our reign there and it seemed that Mike Ilitch really marketed it well, and they got some better players. He went out and picked up a couple of free agents along the way, and then Yzerman came into his own, Gallant came into his own. I think a lot of it was that Brad Park was there. He was a good teacher. Darryl Sittler came for a while. Tiger Williams came, and towards the end of our reign, I think that one of the things that we really tried to impress on the younger players was what they had to do to prepare to play every night and to come to win.

Gare's most memorable moment in Detroit was when the Wings made it to the playoffs in 1983-84, marking the beginning of the team's resurrection from consistent playoff failure. Before that season, the team had made the playoffs only twice in the past 17 seasons, losing in the quarter-finals on both occasions.

Gare was more of a checker than a scorer in Detroit. He recently commented on the different role he was required to play with the Wings and how that role came about.

It was funny. I was hit by Scott Stevens in Washington my third year there. I'll never forget it. I still feel it in my chest area, my sternum. I bruised and crushed my sternum. I had to wear a flack jacket for that year and the next year because of the injury. I told Nick Polano, if we were going to go anywhere we had to put a checking line together. So I couldn't shoot the puck as well as I could, but I knew I was always pretty good defensively, and we put a line together with Dwight Foster and Bob Manno. We checked all of the top lines and we did a pretty good job of it at the time. The Troll

Patrol, that's was it was called. And it was well-liked by the people there. They seemed to enjoy it.

In the October 24, 1984 issue of the *Detroit News*, he offered his feelings on his different role at that time, saying: "My forte when I came into the league was scoring goals. But, obviously, there are other players on this team they [management] want to do that, and I understand that. When you're on a checking line, you don't take those extra chances. You don't break into the holes . . . you're looking over your shoulder to see your check doesn't get away. That's my job now, but I still feel I can contribute to the offense."

While playing for Detroit, Gare once received a death threat before a game against the Maple Leafs in Toronto, just as Ted Lindsay had many years earlier. An anonymous caller, who said he was calling from Las Vegas, Nevada, told Toronto's Global Television Network that if Gare played that night, it would be his last time on skates. Gare ignored the threat and scored two goals to help his team beat Toronto.

During his career, Gare had the honor of playing in the Canada Cup Tournament. Recalling the experience, he says: "[My most memorable moment] from the Canada Cup ... was probably in '76, when I played with [Marcel] Dionne and [Bobby] Hull on a line. Then, my back flared up and I didn't play many games after that. But I played real well in the '81 Canada Cup. We played with [Rick] Middleton and Lindsman. We were like the fourth line, but we did very well. We were very pesky, good forechecking guys. We seemed to catch a lot of teams off guard. But I really enjoyed that series also."

Gare finished his career in 1986-87 with the Edmonton Oilers, who won the Stanley Cup that year. Gare didn't play in the Stanley Cup finals, as he retired before the Oilers made it all the way. However, he did have the opportunity to play with the men who did.

After hanging up his skates from professional play, Gare served as the announcer for the Buffalo Sabres. He then became the color commentator for the Tampa Bay Lightning during the team's inaugural season. Coaching was in his blood and, along with former Boston Bruin Wayne Cashman, he eventually became an assistant coach to Terry Crisp in Tampa

Bay. He held that position for two years. Today, he is back in Buffalo doing radio for the Sabres and loving every minute of it.

JOHN ALEXANDER OGRODNICK

Born: June 20, 1959, Ottawa, Ontario
Position: Left wing
Junior
- Maple Ridge Bruins (BCJHL): 1976-77
- N. Westminster (WCHL-WHL): 1976-77-1978-79

Minor Pro
- Adirondack (AHL): 1979-80, 1992-93
- Denver (IHL): 1988-89

Detroit Red Wings
- 1979-80 to 1986-87; 1992-93

Best NHL Season
- 1984-85: 55 goals, 105 points

Career Awards & Honors
- NHL First All-Star Team: 1985
- NHL All-Star Games: 1981, '82, '84-'86
- Junior Hockey: Shared WHL Rookie-of-the-Year honors with Portland's Keith Brown in 1978.

Career Milestones
- Holds Detroit Red Wings' record for most goals in one season by a left wing: 1984-85 (55).
- Holds Detroit Red Wings' record for most points in one season by a left wing: 1984-85 (105).
- Shares the Detroit Red Wings' record for most points in one period: December 4, 1984 vs. Toronto (4).
- One of Detroit's all-time career scoring leaders.

Trades
- Traded from Detroit to Quebec on January 17, 1987, with Basil McRae and Doug Shedden for Brent Ashton, Gilbert Delorme and Mark Kumpel.

John Ogrodnick is one of Detroit's all-time scoring leaders. Photo courtesy of John Ogrodnick.

BIOGRAPHY

A 1992 *Detroit News* article says the years he played NHL hockey in Detroit "were the years when John Ogrodnick was the star player of the Detroit Red Wings, the single player with a knack for scoring goals." Ogrodnick was an important member of the Red Wings' team during the 1980s. He possessed a great shot and knew how to score goals.

Ogrodnick sparkled during his first training camp and, after spending some time seasoning with Adirondack (then Detroit's AHL affiliate), developed into one of the Red Wings' most exciting players during the 1980s. He played his first game in January of 1980 as an injury replacement. His junior hockey coach in New Westminster, Massachusetts, Ernie "Punch" McLean, always knew he would do well. In

the March 7, 1980 issue of *The Hockey News*, he said: "John should have been a first-round pick but people shied away from him. What happened in the draft is that everybody in the NHL grabbed the 18-year-olds that looked like potential superstars, the Ray Bourques, Keith Browns, Don McCarthys.... I knew the type of player he was. Once you're a goal scorer you can't take it away. When he came to us four years ago, he was a goal scorer and worked the other stuff in. The easiest way to explain it is, any kid who comes out of New West, if they last to be a junior there, 90 percent of them are NHL caliber. It's just a case of how long it takes some to get there. Some develop quicker because of their mental attitude. John Ogrodnick has the attitude."

In 1984-85, Ogrodnick became the third player in Detroit history to score 50 goals in a season (Danny Grant and Mickey Redmond were the

others). He went on to surpass Redmond's record of 52 goals that season, ending up with a total of 55 goals. It was an exciting moment for Ogrodnick, who accomplished the feat by scoring a hat trick during a game against Wayne Gretzky and the Edmonton Oilers, tallying his 48th, 49th and 50th goals of the season. The fact that Ogrodnick's parents and brother were among the sellout crowd at Northlands Coliseum made it even more memorable. Despite his efforts, the Oilers won, 7-6, with the Great One scoring five points. That season, Ogrodnick also became the first Detroit Red Wing to make the NHL First All-Star team in 12 seasons.

At the start of the following season, in the October 10, 1985 issue of the *Detroit News*, Ogrodnick commented on the feat: "Once the new seasons starts, you forget about what happened the year before," he explained. "That year [1984-85] is history. It goes down in the books and you forget it. I can't live on last years statistics. I've maintained a 40-goal average and, basically, that's my goal again."

The Red Wings were not the NHL's best team during the 1980s, but Ogrodnick was one of the NHL's better players. This posed somewhat of a problem. During his career, in an issue of the *Toronto Globe and Mail*, he commented:

A lot of people will tell you the grass is greener on the other side. But I like Detroit. My wife and I are happy, and we're satisfied. Sometimes, playing on this team is great, when we have won a few games, but, sometimes, it gets to you. When you allow so many goals to be scored against you consistently, it's depressing and that's where it shows up that we're not improving. I think when it gets to me most, personally, is when the season starts to wind down and you haven't made the playoffs and you're sitting in your living room halfway through April watching other guys play. That's when it really stings, the first week or two after the season. For four years now, I haven't had a sniff of the playoffs and that's a big thing to me. You can only play this game so long, and you've got to get as much out of it as you can.

Opposite: Bob Probert receives a blow from Minnesota's Shane Churla. Rich Margittay Photo.

Throughout his career, Ogrodnick was continuously plagued by rumors that he would be traded. The rumors became reality when he was traded to the Quebec Nordiques in 1987. Former Detroit coach Jacques Demers commented on the trade that sent Ogrodnick to Quebec in the January 20, 1987 issue of the *Detroit News*. He said: "John Ogrodnick was the second guy who had to carry this team after Steve Yzerman. Ogrodnick is a good player, a good guy. I like him. He did what I asked him to do. If Stevie didn't do it for us, the chance of winning was not there. Because of his personality, Johnny O. could not be that kind of player for us. In Quebec, he'll be just another very good player on a team with a lot of good players. John Ogrodnick will be a better player for Quebec, where he doesn't have to be the No. 1 or No. 2 guy, where he can just be himself." After five seasons with the New York Rangers, Ogrodnick came back to Detroit in 1992-93 and finished his career.

BOB PROBERT

Born: June 5, 1965, Windsor, Ontario
Position: Right wing, Left wing
Junior
- Brantford (OHL): 1982-84
- S.S. Marie (OHL): 1984-85
- Hamilton (OHL): 1984-85

Minor Pro
- Adirondack (AHL): 1985-86, 1986-87

Detroit Red Wings
- 1985-86 to 1993-94

Best NHL Season
- 1987-88: 29 goals, 62 points

Career Awards & Honors
- NHL All-Star Game: 1988

Career Milestones
- Career-high 398 penalty minutes, 1987-88
- Leads Red Wings in career penalty minutes with 2,090.

BIOGRAPHY

Bob Probert grew up in Windsor, Ontario, where his father worked as a policeman. As a youth, he went to watch the Red Wings play at the Olympia and, like many boys his age, idolized Boston's Bobby Orr. He was very active in sports, playing lacrosse, baseball, football and, of course, hockey. It was the latter sport that took him to the Ontario Hockey League, where he honed his skills playing junior hockey, and made it to the Memorial Cup finals in 1984-85. The following season, he broke into the NHL with the Detroit Red Wings and quickly established himself as one of the NHL's toughest, most feared players.

However, the road was not one without misfortune. Probert struggled with substance abuse problems while playing for Detroit. Sportswriter Mitch Albom, in the December 14, 1995 issue of the *Detroit Free Press,* commented on Probert's days with the team and his eventual departure to the Chicago Blackhawks. He said: "For a long, long time, Probert's life of booze, drugs, rehab and broken promises was daily conversation in this town. His waves made Detroit seasick. Every time he took on water, Detroit choked. But that kind of empathy can only go on so long. His hockey deteriorated. His fighting was less and less frequent. He couldn't even play when the team left the country—because of immigration limitations. What the Wings did was in spite of him,

not because of him. By the time he crashed his motorcycle in the summer of 1994, it was just another blot on one of the city's worst driving records. People were sick of his story. Maybe he sensed this. Certainly his agent did. He got a $6-million offer from the Blackhawks—a miracle in itself—and Bob Probert, fist-swinging hero of the working class, left town."

One could spend a great deal of time reciting the times that Bob Probert got into trouble with alcohol and drugs. The fact that he had a substance abuse problem is common knowledge. However, the fact that Bob Probert was a hockey player who contributed to the Detroit Red Wings during the decade of the 1980s, with both his fists and his stick, cannot be ignored.

In his book *Bad Boys—Legends of Hockey's Toughest, Meanest, Most-Feared Players!*, Stan Fischler commented on the fact that Probert is often praised for his fisticuffs and not his talent as a player. He said:

Steve Yzerman assumed the role of team captain at a very young age. Rich Margittay Photo.

"Probert's value far exceeded his powers of intimidation and his fistic ability. He has, over the years, demonstrated offensive prowess and the ability to put the puck in the net. But as long as journalists choose also to annually pick an NHL heavyweight champion, Probert will be as much discussed as a slugger as he is a scorer."

"Probert, he's a tough guy," says NHL referee Paul Stewart. "I stood in between him and [a guy] one night. ... at Detroit. I got between the two of them and it looked like an accordion. I had them stretched out. I'm pretty strong, and they are big fellows. They wrinkled me like an old tissue paper."

Probert's best season in Detroit was 1987-88, when he scored 29 goals for 62 points. That season, he played in the NHL All-Star game, assisting on a goal by Wayne Gretzky. He was also tied for seventh in NHL playoff scoring with 21 points and broke a Red Wings team record for single-season playoff scoring set by Gordie Howe (20 points) in 1955.

During his career, Probert has gained a reputation for mixing it up with opponents. His battles with Tony Twist and Tie Domi will be talked about for years to come. Former Red Wings trainer and goalie Lefty Wilson gave his feelings on Probert's career in Detroit and his role as a fighter. He said: "Probert? He was his worst enemy, himself. He had chance after chance after chance and he blew it. That's all you can say about him. But he's a good enough hockey player to forget about fighting. Even in the old days, we never tried to maim anybody. If a guy looked for a fight, they tangled. Cripe, we had to talk Howe into fights because he was getting mauled and pulled down. But we didn't try to maim anybody. But today, they hire these cement heads to injure the good players and try to knock them out of there."

So far, Bob Probert has done a commendable job of staying clean while playing for Chicago. In the October 11, 1995 issue of the *Chicago Sun Times*, he said: "Now my life is kind of even. Balanced. It used to be the highs were high and the lows were low. I just hang around the house and do things with the family. ... I don't know why I stopped this time. But if I continue this way [staying sober], I'll have the world by the balls. If I go back to the old lifestyle, I'll be dead in ten years. Five years."

STEVE YZERMAN

Born: May 9, 1965, Cranbrook, British Columbia
Position: Center
Junior
- Peterborough Petes (OHL): 1981-83

Detroit Red Wings
- 1983-84 to present

Best NHL Season
- 1988-89: 65 goals, 155 points

Career Awards & Honors
- All-Star Games: 1984, '88-'93, '97
- *The Sporting News'* NHL Rookie of the Year: 1983-84
- NHL All-Rookie Team: 1983-84
- Red Wings Team Captain
- Lester B. Pearson Award: 1988-89
- Team Canada: 1984
- World Championships: 1985, '89, '90

Career Milestones
- Second on Detroit's all-time list in goals, third in assists and points.
- Scored 1,000th point (assist) on February 24, 1993 vs. the Buffalo Sabres.
- Scored 500th career goal on January 17, 1996.
- In 1988-89, finished third in NHL scoring and set a Red Wings' team records with 65 goals, 90 assists and 155 points.

BIOGRAPHY

When Steve Yzerman came out of Tier II hockey to play junior for the Peterborough Petes, Yzerman's coach expressed doubts about his size. Those doubts were soon laid to rest when Yzerman proved he could handle himself.

It wouldn't be long before he was playing for the Detroit Red Wings, where he not only handled himself but was eventually named team captain at the age of 21, leaving a lasting impression on those around him. Commenting on his new role as a Red Wing, in the October 24, 1984 issue of the *Toronto Globe and Mail*, Yzerman said: "I felt when I first came up last year that the pace was going to be that much quicker than I was used to in junior. But then I found out that I could hold on to the puck. You get to know when you've got to move it and when you can keep it. You sort of get a feel for it. It takes time, but it comes along with your confidence."

Yzerman learned more than just how to hold on to the puck. In the January 17, 1988 issue of the *Toronto Sun*, former coach Jacques Demers said of him: "He's done it all for us. He's on the power play,

Steve Yzerman fires the puck. Rich Margittay Photo.

December 25, 1995 issue of the *Detroit Free Press*, he said: "When I was a kid playing hockey, everyone was a big scorer when they were a kid. When I went to juniors, I didn't get 50 goals. Even my first few years in Detroit, I was in the 30s. I was always considered more of a play-maker. I wouldn't say I'm really either. You think of Wayne Gretzky and Adam Oates as real play-makers. Brett Hull and Cam Neely as goal-scorers. I don't really fall into either one."

Former Chicago Blackhawk goalie Darren Pang commented on Yzerman's humble manner in the December 25, 1995 issue of the *Detroit Free Press*. He said: "Inside his expectations were loaded. Outside, there's no way he would ever talk about things like that [his strong points as a player]. He continues to keep a lot of things inside of him. I think you find that with a lot of guys, a lot of great guys, Hall of Famers. Inside, there's that driving desire to be among the best. I don't think that's ever changed for Steve. He's always had the drive, willingness, and stubbornness to succeed."

Yzerman's success began early, and his record speaks for itself. On January 31, 1984, at the age of 18, Steve Yzerman became the youngest person to ever play in an NHL All-Star game. Three seasons later, he became the youngest team captain in Detroit's history. In 1988-89, he scored 65 goals and 155 points. On six occasions, he has has 100-point seasons. On January 17, 1996, Yzerman scored his 500th career goal in Detroit. He is known for maturity, hard work and consistency on the ice.

In the December 25, 1995 issue of the *Detroit Free Press*, Red Wings' senior vice president Jim Devellano, said: "Certainly with the number of goals, number of points, number of games that he will have played with the franchise, there's no doubt that some years down the road, we'll be watching Yzerman's sweater raised to the rafters at Joe Louis Arena. And we'll have to make room for another bronze plaque in the dressing room because he'll go up there."

Former Detroit Red Wing Marty Pavelich thinks highly of Yzerman. He says: "I love Stevie Yzerman. He's a real fine young man. I think he's just completely dedicated to the game, totally. I mean, I saw him the time he hurt his knee, when he went down and injured his knee and looked like he might finish his career and boy, he came back. I heard that

he kills penalties, takes a regular shift, sometimes a defensive shift. He plays 32 to 35 minutes a game. He even fights now and then. Sometimes I just shake my head at the things he does."

Besides being one of the Detroit Red Wings' key players during the 1980s and today, Yzerman was, in many ways, a symbol of the team's re-birth. Says former Red Wing Nick Libett: "When Yzerman came, that's when the franchise started turning around and I think they even had some trouble the first year or two he was here as far as making the playoffs, but he hung in and obviously now they are probably the best team in the league."

Modesty has always been one of Yzerman's characteristics. Describing himself as a player, in the he worked real hard in the dressing room on weights and so forth, and came back stronger than ever. You never see Stevie Yzerman have a bad game. He might not have a game as good as some others, but he'll never have a bad game. [They made him team captain at a pretty young age], and he's handled it very well."

Former Detroit defenseman Gary Bergman also looks favorably upon Yzerman. "Unfortunately, Stevie had to spend a good part of his career, I would say, waste a good part of his career, trying to pick this franchise up by its boot straps," says Bergman. "[He got stuck into a leadership role at a young age and] wasn't prepared for it. He didn't want it. Steve is the nicest guy, all he wanted to do was go play hockey. He just wanted to play hockey. 'Leave me alone. I don't want this media crap.' You could just tell he didn't know how to handle the captaincy. He was just a young kid and he was just a good hockey player, but he was thrust into a situation that he didn't ask for. But I think under the conditions, he really handled it admirably, he really did. But as I said, he spun a lot of wheels and took a lot of miles off those legs trying to make a bad team look good."

Yzerman considered the job of team captain very carefully before accepting the job. "Other young guys had trouble handling the captain's job and that's why I had to think about it a little before agreeing to accept it. I wanted to be clear in my mind that I could handle it. I didn't want to take it, then give it up at Christmas because I couldn't do it. But it's a job you really can't be certain you can do until you've tried it." Tried it he has, and with a great deal of success.

Recently, when it was rumored that Yzerman was going to be traded, the crowd at Joe Louis Arena gave him a thundering cheer before the evening's game, in which the Wings beat the Oilers 9-0. When asked about the ovation and the trade rumor, Yzerman was very modest. In the October 14, 1995 issue of the *Detroit Free Press*, he said: "It [the cheer] was a thrill for sure. You get a real rush and it makes you feel good…. That was definitely the most exciting moment I've ever experienced at Joe Louis Arena…. It [the trade] may come into consideration sometime when as a hockey club you have to make a difficult decision. And if there's something they can do to improve the team, they have to do it." Luckily for the Detroit Red Wings, Yzerman is still on the roster, contributing in a big way as he always has.

The Detroit Red Wings hoist Lord Stanley's silver chalice high into the air. Rich Margittay Photo.

CHAPTER FOURTEEN
CHAMPIONS
• THE 1990s •

With the stroke of a broom, the 1997 Detroit Red Wings ended years of frustration and anguish when they put an end to the longest drought in Stanley Cup history. Not only was the victory well overdue, it came after two painfully close calls during what has become the brightest age of Detroit hockey in years.

During the 1990s, the Detroit Red Wings materialized into something all teams strive to be—champions. The wheels of success began turning while Jacques Demers was behind the bench during the late 1980s. There were gradual signs of improvement during the early part of the decade, and it wasn't long before Detroit's talent level improved to the point of Stanley Cup contention.

In 1994-95, the Detroit Red Wings won the President's Trophy for the league's best overall record. After flying straight through the first three rounds of the playoffs, during which they were undefeated on home ice, they made it to the finals, where they faced the New Jersey Devils. The accomplishment was a

treat for fans who hadn't seen their team in the finals for almost 30 years, and it was devastating when Detroit lost to the Devils in four consecutive games.

1994-95 STANLEY CUP FINALS

The first game of the finals, held in Detroit on June 17, 1995, saw the Red Wings fall to the New Jersey Devils, 2-1. The capacity crowd at Joe Louis Arena, at first loud with energy and excitement, grew more silent as the evening wore on. Detroit was stopped by a New Jersey team that employed the neutral zone trap, allowing the Red Wings to make a mere 17 shots on goal, their lowest total of the season. To make matters worse, halfway into the game Detroit center Keith Primeau left the game with an injured back.

Full of optimism, 19,875 fans packed into Joe Louis Arena for the second game three days later. Most of them were smiling when Sergei Fedorov scored in the third period, giving his team a 2-1 lead, which they held midway into that period. However,

1994-95 STANLEY CUP FINALS

NEW JERSEY DEVILS - DETROIT RED WINGS
FIRST GAME: (June 17, 1995 - Joe Louis Arena)
New Jersey 2 Detroit 1

New Jersey: Tommy Albelin, Martin Brodeur, Neal Broten, Sergei Brylin, Bobby Carpenter, Tony Chorske, Sean Chambers, Ken Daneyko, Bruce Driver, Bill Guerin, Bobby Holik, Claude Lemieux, Randy McKay, John MacLean, Scott Niedermayer, Mike Peluso, Stephane Richer, Scott Stevens, Chris Terreri, Valeri Zelepukin.

Detroit: Doug Brown, Shawn Burr, Dino Ciccarelli, Paul Coffey, Kris Draper, Bob Errey, Sergei Fedorov, Viacheslav Fetisov, Stu Grimson, Mark Howe, Vladimir Konstantinov, Nicklas Lidstrom, Darren McCarty, Chris Osgood, Keith Primeau, Bob Rouse, Ray Sheppard, Mike Vernon, Steve Yzerman, Vyacheslav Kozlov.

First Period
No Scoring
Penalties
Guerin (NJ) (Holding) 6:47
Konstantinov (Det) (holding the stick) 11:05
Second Period
1. New Jersey - Richer(Albelin, Broten) . .9:41 (PPG)
2. Detroit - Ciccarelli (Lidstrom, Coffey) .13:08 (PPG)
Penalties
Draper (Det) (Roughing) 9:35
Holik (NJ) (highsticking) 11:37
Lemieux (NJ) (hooking) 13:41
Daneyko (NJ) (roughing),
Ciccarelli (Det) (roughing) 15:54

Third Period
3. New Jersey - Lemieux (MacLean,
      Chorske) . . . . .3:17 (GWG)
Penalties
Brown (Det) (tripping) 4:48
Goalies
Brodeur (NJ), Vernon (Det)
Shots
NJ   9 - 10 - 9   28
Det   7 - 5 - 5   17
Referee: Bill McCreary
Linesmen: Brian Murphy, Kevin Collins

1994-95 STANLEY CUP FINALS

NEW JERSEY DEVILS - DETROIT RED WINGS
SECOND GAME: (June 20, 1995 - Joe Louis Arena)
New Jersey 4, Detroit 2

New Jersey: Tommy Albelin, Martin Brodeur, Neal Broten, Bobby Carpenter, Sean Chambers, Ken Daneyko, Jim Dowd, Bruce Driver, Bill Guerin, Bobby Holik, Claude Lemieux, Randy McKay, John MacLean, Scott Niedermayer, Mike Peluso, Stephane Richer, Brian Rolston, Scott Stevens, Chris Terreri, Valeri Zelepukin.

Detroit: Doug Brown, Shawn Burr, Dino Ciccarelli, Paul Coffey, Kris Draper, Bob Errey, Sergei Fedorov, Viacheslav Fetisov, Mark Howe, Vladimir Konstantinov, Vyacheslav Kozlov, Mike Krushelnyski, Nicklas Lidstrom, Darren McCarty, Chris Osgood, Bob Rouse, Ray Sheppard, Tim Taylor, Mike Vernon, Steve Yzerman.

First Period
No Scoring
Penalties
Stevens (NJ) (roughing) .0:37
Ciccarelli (Det) (Slashing) 5:57
McCarty (Det) (Roughing) 8:49
Broten (NJ) (highsticking) 9:27
Second Period
1. Detroit - Kozlov (Ciccarelli, Fedorov) . . .7:17 (PPG)
2. New Jersey - MacLean (Niedermayer, Broten) 9:40
Penalties
Brodeur (NJ) (delay of game) 6:56
Guerin (NJ) (slashing), McCarty (Det) (slashing) 8:58
Errey (Det) (charging) 16:01
Dowd (NJ) (interference) 18:30

Third Period
3. Detroit - Fedorov (Brown, Fetisov) 1:36
4. New Jersey - Niedermayer (Dowd) 9:47
5. New Jersey - Dowd (Chambers,
      Albelin) . . . . .18:36 (GWG)
6. New Jersey - Richer (Niedermayer) .19:36 (ENG)
Penalties
Holik (NJ) (boarding) 4:58
Goalies
Brodeur (NJ), Vernon (Det).
Shots
NJ   3 - 9 - 11   23
Det   7 - 6 - 5   18
Referee: Terry Gregson
Linesmen: Ray Scapinello, Wayne Bonney

1994-95 STANLEY CUP FINALS

NEW JERSEY DEVILS - DETROIT RED WINGS
THIRD GAME: (June 22, 1995 - Meadowlands Arena)
New Jersey 5, Detroit 2

Detroit: Doug Brown, Dino Ciccarelli, Paul Coffey, Kris Draper, Bob Errey, Sergei Fedorov, Viacheslav Fetisov, Vladimir Konstantinov, Vyacheslav Kozlov, Martin Lapointe, Nicklas Lidstrom, Darren McCarty, Chris Osgood, Keith Primeau, Mike Ramsey, Bob Rouse, Ray Sheppard, Tim Taylor, Mike Vernon, Steve Yzerman.

New Jersey: Tommy Albelin, Martin Brodeur, Neal Broten, Sergei Brylin, Bobby Carpenter, Sean Chambers, Tony Chorske, Ken Daneyko, Bruce Driver, Bill Guerin, Bobby Holik, Claude Lemieux, Randy McKay, John MacLean, Scott Niedermayer, Mike Peluso, Stephane Richer, Scott Stevens, Chris Terreri, Valeri Zelepukin.

First Period
No Scoring

First Period
1. New Jersey - Driver (Broten, MacLean) ....10:30 (PPG)
2. New Jersey - Lemieux (Carpenter, Stevens) 16:52

Penalties
Primeau (Det) (slashing),
Lemieux (NJ) (roughing) 1:09
Konstantinov (Det) (holding the stick) 8:56
Holik (NJ) (tripping) 10:58
Lapointe (Det) (unsportsmanlike conduct),
Guerin (NJ) (unsportsmanlike conduct) ...16:58

Second Period
3. New Jersey - Broten (Stevens, MacLean) ....6:59 (GWG)
4. New Jersey - McKay(Holik, Driver) 8:20

Penalties
Broten (NJ) (holding the stick) 11:01
Primeau (Det) (tripping) 16:03
Carpenter (NJ) (cross-checking) 19.47

Third Period
5. New Jersey - Holik (Guerin, Richer) ...8:14 (PPG)
6. Detroit - Fedorov (Fetisov, Brown) ...16:57 (PPG)
7. Detroit - Yzerman (Sheppard, Lidstrom) ....18:27 (PPG)

Penalties
Albelin (NJ) (highsticking) 2:30
Konstantinov (Det) (highsticking) 4:25
Draper (Det) (highsticking) 5:17
Primeau (Det) (cross-checking) 6:31
Holik (Det) (interference) 8:44
Richer (NJ) (hooking) 12:28
Ciccarelli (Det) (roughing), Taylor (Det) (roughing), .
Lapointe (Det) (double roughing minor),
Zelepukin (NJ) (double roughing minor),
Guerin (NJ) (boarding, roughing),
Brylin (NJ) (highsticking, roughing) 15:37

Goalies
Vernon, Osgood (Det), Brodeur (NJ)

Shots

Det	7 - 5 - 12	24	
NJ	15 - 8 - 8	31	

Referee: Kerry Fraser
Linesmen: Kevin Collins, Brian Murphy

in the final 10 minutes New Jersey scored three unanswered goals, securing another victory. The Stanley Cup was slipping away. To win the prize, Detroit needed to play smarter and harder. In the June 21, 1996 issue of the *New York Times*, Paul Coffey said: "Now is not the time to separate. Now is the time to stick together. It's always good, when you're losing games, to get on the road. You stay together as a team for three or four days. We'll lean on each other."

As the series moved east to New Jersey, Detroit's luck did not change as Coffey had hoped. The Red Wings lost the third game on June 22, 5-2. In New Jersey, 19,040 fans were present at Byrne Meadowlands Arena to see the Devils record

their third consecutive win. By the time Detroit was able to get on the scoreboard in the third period, the Devils had already established a 5-0 lead. Sergei Fedorov and Steve Yzerman scored two goals in that final period. However, it was too late. New Jersey had won again. In order to win the championship, the Red Wings had to do what only one other team in NHL history—the 1942 Toronto Maple Leafs—had done to them 53 years earlier. They had to win the next four straight games.

After the third loss, coach Scotty Bowman came down hard on his team. In the June 23, 1995 issue of the *New York Times*, he said: "We never were humiliated and embarrassed like we were tonight for two periods. A lot of players in the league would give

1994-95 STANLEY CUP FINALS

NEW JERSEY DEVILS - DETROIT RED WINGS
FOURTH GAME: (June 24, 1995 - Meadowlands Arena)
New Jersey 5, Detroit 2

Detroit: Doug Brown, Dino Ciccarelli, Paul Coffey, Kris Draper, Bob Errey, Sergei Fedorov, Viacheslav Fetisov, Stu Grimson, Vladimir Konstantinov, Vyacheslav Kozlov, Mike Krushelnyski, Martin Lapointe, Nicklas Lidstrom, Darren McCarty, Chris Osgood, Keith Primeau, Mike Ramsey, Bob Rouse, Mike Vernon, Steve Yzerman.

New Jersey: Tommy Albelin, Martin Brodeur, Neal Broten, Sergei Brylin, Bobby Carpenter, Sean Chambers, Tony Chorske, Ken Daneyko, Bruce Driver, Bill Guerin, Bobby Holik, Claude Lemieux, Randy McKay, John MacLean, Scott Niedermayer, Mike Peluso, Stephane Richer, Brian Rolston, Scott Stevens, Chris Terreri.

First Period
1. New Jersey - Broten(Richer, Chorske) 1:08
2. Detroit - Fedorov (Lapointe, Fetisov) 2:03
3. Detroit - Coffey (Brown, Fedorov) . . .13:01 (SHG)
4. New Jersey - Chambers (Driver, MacLean) . . .17:45

Penalties
Errey (Det) (hooking) 11:03
Daneyko (NJ) (roughing) 13:36
Primeau (Det) (goaltender interference) 15:35

Second Period
5. New Jersey - Broten (Niedermayer,
Guerin) . . . . .7:56 (GWG)

Penalties
Daneyko (NJ) (slashing) 0:30
Lapointe (Det) (roughing),
Stevens (NJ) (roughing) 10:09
Guerin (NJ) (interference) 12:43
Konstantinov (Det) (hooking) 19:12

Third Period
6. New Jersey - Brylin (Rolston, Guerin) 7:46
7. New Jersey - Chambers (Brylin, Guerin) . . .12:32

Penalties
Grimson (Det) (roughing) 10:24

Goalies
Vernon (Det), Brodeur (NJ)

Shots
Det   8 - 7 - 1   16
NJ   8 - 8 - 10   26

Referee: Bill McCreary
Linesmen: Wayne Bonney, Ray Scapinello

their eyeteeth to even get one shift in the finals. It's totally unacceptable as a player, as a coach. The entire group has to take the full responsibility. It was an embarrassment to the National Hockey League. This is a showcase series, the finals. You get this far to be down like we were, the score ended up a good publicity score. For us, that's about the only thing I can say about it."

THE FINAL GAME - JUNE 24, 1995

Game four was a carbon copy of the previous game, with the Devils again beating the Red Wings 5-2 in front of 19,040 fans. The victory gave them the first Stanley Cup in their team's history. Sixty-eight seconds into the first period, Neil Broten scored the Devils' first goal. Fifty-five seconds later, Sergei Fedorov answered for the Red Wings. A rare defensive flop by the Devils allowed Paul Coffey to score again for Detroit. With 6:59 remaining, Coffey scored on one of four shots Detroit made on Devils'

goalie Martin Brodeur. With 2:35 seconds to go in the opening period, the Devils tied the game with a goal by Shawn Chambers.

The beginning of the middle period was strong for Detroit, and things looked good when the Devils' Ken Daneyko took a penalty 30 seconds into the action. Despite the power play, Brodeur held the Wings at bay with five saves in the period's first four minutes. New Jersey then came back and secured the lead when Neil Broten scored at 12:44. When Bill Guerin was penalized, giving Detroit another power play opportunity, the Devils did not even allow a shot on goal. The stinginess continued into the final period. The Devils allowed Detroit only one shot on goal, while scoring two of their own, winning the Cup.

Undaunted by their playoff misfortune the previous season, the Red Wings remained positive. They had the talent to win, and remained focused. In

The Red Wings change lines during the 1994-95 Stanley Cup playoffs. Rich Margittay Photo.

1995-96, they were big favorites to reclaim Lord Stanley's silver chalice for the Motor City. Few could deny their power when the team skyrocketed through the regular season with tremendous skill, losing only 12 games between October and April.

Detroit's stellar regular season performance enabled them to break the NHL record for most wins in a season, set by Scotty Bowman's Montreal Canadiens in 1976-77. They also came close to the record for most points in a season set by that Montreal team (132), scoring 131 points. Besides that, the Red Wings also tied the NHL record for home wins (36), set by the Philadelphia Flyers in 1975-76, and scored a league-high 144 more goals than they allowed.

Unfortunately, the sweet taste of Stanley Cup victory eluded the Red Wings once again, and they lost the Western Conference finals to Colorado. Besides losing the series, Detroit also lost some blood

in game six when Colorado's Claude Lemieux hit Detroit's Kris Draper from behind, resulting in serious injury. Draper spent the summer recovering, and a bad seed between the two teams had been planted.

One of the components Detroit lacked was size. Bigger, more physical players would help open things up and increase scoring chances. Scotty Bowman realized this and beefed up the roster in 1996-97. The acquisition of Brendan Shanahan from Hartford and Tomas Sandstrom from Pittsburgh, as well as bigger roles for Darren McCarty and Martin Lapointe gave Detroit the muscle mix it needed.

Regular season success is great, but is far from the sweetness of Stanley Cup victory. Knowing this, the Red Wings were driven by images of the silver trophy in 1996-97. They refused to accept anything but the attainment of their number one goal. When the playoffs arrived, little red and white Detroit Red

Wings flags began to appear in increasing numbers on car windows across the state. The energy was in the air, and die-hard fans were just as hungry for victory as the men on the ice.

Detroit started the playoffs off strong, putting St. Louis and Anaheim on ice. Then, they faced off against their archenemies from Colorado in the battle for Western Conference supremacy. Far from an ordinary playoff series, both teams possessed a deep hatred for each other, stemming from the Claude Lemieux incident the previous season. When the two teams met on March 26, 1997, the strong feelings surfaced and resulted in a brawl that saw Darren McCarty clobber Lemieux, and opposing goaltenders Patrick Roy and Mike Vernon engage in center-ice fisticuffs.

Before the two teams met in the playoffs, Brian Burke, NHL senior vice president and director of hockey operations, met with their respective general managers and issued a warning that foul play would be dealt with severely. In the May 15, 1997 issue of the *Detroit News*, Detroit's Martin Lapointe said: "They don't like us and we don't like them, and that's fine. That's the way it should be." Colorado's Brent Severyn, new to the team in 1996-97, said: "The world's watching. In the heat of battle, you never know what's going to happen. I've never seen two organizations hate each other as much as these two."

The bitter feelings were reminiscent of those harbored by opposing players during hockey's golden age. "I never spoke to any of them," Ted Lindsay once said of his opponents, in the November 8, 1991 issue of the *Detroit News*. "I hated them, and they hated me. It was the way it was and the way it should be. It was wonderful."

The six-game series was hard-fought and eventful, especially towards the end. In the end, Detroit emerged as the victor. Although they played hard and limited Colorado to a mere 19 shots, Detroit lost the opening game, 2-1. However, they won the second contest, 4-2, equalizing the match. Vyacheslav Kozlov came through for Detroit in game three, scoring two goals, including the game-winner—his second of the playoffs—in a 2-1 win. During that game, Detroit's Mike Vernon also gave an outstanding performance, keeping the Red Wings alive. During

the game, he made a total of 27 saves, thwarting nine shots on three Colorado power plays during the first period.

Things got hot—and rough—in game four, as the Red Wings smoked the Avalanche, 6-0. The heat came not only from the score, but also from emotions that were running high, and from the colorful dialogue between the Avalanche and on-ice officials. During the first period, referee Paul Devorski called five consecutive minor penalties on Colorado. Near the end of the game, several fights erupted, including one in which Detroit's Brendan Shanahan beat Colorado's Rene Corbet to a pulp. Colorado Coach Marc Crawford screamed insults at Detroit Coach Scotty Bowman and attempted to get to the Red Wings' bench. His actions resulted in a $10,000 fine by the NHL.

In game five, Colorado was without the services of Peter Forsberg, who was nursing an injured right thigh. Forsberg's replacement, Yves Sarault, made his presence known by putting a big hit on Detroit's Larry Murphy against the back of Detroit's net. Murphy shook it off, and returned for more action. Then, Vladimir Konstantinov drew a foolish delay-of-game penalty at 6:22 of the second period, giving Colorado a five-on-three advantage. Facing playoff elimination, Colorado managed to skate away with a 6-0 win, avenging the loss suffered in game four.

In the end, Colorado's attempt to stay alive was futile and the Red Wings eliminated them, 3-1, in game six at Joe Louis Arena.

Sergei Fedorov played a big part in the game. After injuring himself during the first period while trying to check Colorado defenseman Aaron Miller, he later returned to the ice and scored the game-winning goal that sent the Avalanche packing. "Sergei is an unbelievable talent," said Kris Draper in the May 27, 1997 issue of the *Detroit News*. "When a player like him gets hurt, you want him back as soon as possible. When he came back, he sat next to me and asked how I felt. I told him I felt great. He said, 'Me too.' When one of your best players says that, that's all you want to hear. Then he comes out and gets the game-winning goal. It was a perfect script for him."

It wasn't until Brendan Shanahan scored an empty-net goal with 30 seconds left in the game that fans and player alike could breathe a sigh of relief and be certain that the finals were just around the corner.

"If you're going to beat a champion, you can't outpoint them," said Scotty Bowman in the May 27, 1997 issue of the *Detroit News*. "You have to knock them out. We didn't want to go back to Colorado. When you can knock out a Stanley Cup winner with one game, you should do it. You don't want to, when you're my age, be looking back and say you didn't show up for the game. You'd never forgive yourself."

After the series, Colorado Coach Marc Crawford admitted Detroit was the better team. In the June 16, 1997 issue of *Michigan Hockey Magazine*, he said:

"I thought that the Red Wings were by far the better team in the series. They played with a lot of intensity, a lot of desire, they played together."

By beating the Avalanche, the Red Wings established themselves as Western Conference champions, but they knew the ultimate prize fight was still ahead. In the May 27, 1997 issue of the *Detroit News*, Steve Yzerman said: "I didn't want to make a big deal out of it [winning the Clarence Campbell trophy as Western Conference champions]. The majority of our team played in the Stanley Cup finals a couple of years ago, and they realize that finishing second means absolutely nothing."

1996-97 STANLEY CUP FINALS

PHILADELPHIA FLYERS - DETROIT RED WINGS
FIRST GAME: (May 31, 1997)
Red Wings 4, Flyers 2

First Period
1. Detroit - Maltby 4 (Draper) ....6:38 (SH)
2. Philadelphia - Brind'Amour 11
   (Lindros, Niinimaa) ....7:37 (PP)
3. Detroit - Kocur 1 ....15:56

Second Period
4. Detroit - Fedorov 6 (Murphy, McCarty) 11:41
5. Philadelphia - LeClair 8 (Renberg, Lindros) ..17:11

Third Period
6. Detroit - Yzerman 5 (Murphy) 0:56

Shots on goal
Detroit	8 - 12 - 10	30	
Philadelphia	10 - 9 - 9	28	

Power-play Opportunities
Detroit   0 of 5
Philadelphia   1 of 5

Goalies
Detroit: Vernon 13-4 (28 shots, 26 saves)
Philadelphia: Hextall 4-1 (30 shots, 26 saves)
A: 20,291 (19,511)

1996-97 STANLEY CUP FINALS

PHILADELPHIA FLYERS - DETROIT RED WINGS
SECOND GAME: (June 3, 1997)
Red Wings 4, Flyers 2

First Period
1. Detroit - Shanahan 7 ....1:37
2. Detroit - Yzerman 6 (Murphy, Fetisov) ....9:22 (PP)
3. Philadelphia - Brind'Amour 12
   (Niinimaa) ....17:42 (PP)
4. Philadelphia - Brind'Amour 13
   (Niinimaa, LeClair) ....18:51 (PP)

Penalties
Coffey, (Phi) (holding) 4:29
Coffey, (Phi) (holding) 7:24
Lapointe (Det) (charging) 10:21
Fetisov (Det) (highsticking) 17:09
Larionov (Det) (holding) 18.37

Second Period
5. Detroit - Maltby 5 (Kocur) 2:39

Penalties
Maltby (Det) (roughing) 6:54
Coffey (Phi) (roughing) 6:54
(Det) bench served by Brown (too many men) ..9:03

LeClair, (Phi) (elbowing) 12:13

Third Period
6. Detroit - Shanahan 8 (Lapointe, Fedorov) ...9:56

Penalties
Lapointe (Det) (roughing) 10:27
Dykhuis (Phi) (roughing) 10:27

Shots on goal
Detroit	14 - 9 - 5	28	
Philadelphia	14 - 9 - 8	31	

Power-play Opportunities
Detroit   1 of 3
Philadelphia   2 of 4

Goalies
Detroit: Vernon 14-4 (31 shots, 29 saves)
Philadelphia: Snow 8-4 (28 shots, 24 saves)
A: 20,159 (19,511)
Referee: Terry Gregson
Linesmen: Wayne Bonney, Gord Broseker

1996-97 STANLEY CUP FINALS

PHILADELPHIA FLYERS - DETROIT RED WINGS
THIRD GAME: (June 5, 1997)
Red Wings 6, Flyers 1

First Period
1. Philadelphia - LeClair 9 (Desjardins, Brind'Amour) ....7:03 (PP)
2. Detroit - Yzerman 7 (Kozlov) ....9:03 (PP)
3. Detroit - Fedorov 7 ....11:05
4. Detroit - Lapointe 3 (Brown, Fedorov) 19:00

Second Period
5. Detroit - Fedorov 8 (Kozlov, Shanahan) ..3:12 (PP)
6. Detroit - Shanahan 9 (McCarty) 19:12

Third Period
7. Detroit - Lapointe 4 (Fedorov, Vernon) ..1:08 (PP)

Shots on goal
Philadelphia   8 - 7 - 7   22
Detroit   10 - 12 - 7   29

Power-play Opportunities
Philadelphia   1 of 7
Detroit   3 of 5

Goalies
Philadelphia: Hextall 4-2 (29 shots, 23 saves)
Detroit: Vernon 15-4 (22 shots, 21 saves)
A: 19,983 (19,983)

1996-97 STANLEY CUP FINALS

PHILADELPHIA FLYERS - DETROIT RED WINGS
FOURTH GAME: (June 7, 1997)
Red Wings 2, Flyers 1

First Period
1. Detroit - Lidstrom 2 (Maltby) 19:27

Penalties
LeClair (Phi) (holding) 3:23
Larionov (Det) (interference) 4:31
Lindros (Phi) (interference) 9:22
Falloon, (Phi) (holding stick) 13:21

Second Period
2. Detroit - McCarty 3 (Sandstrom, Yzerman) ..3:02

Penalties
Konstantinov (Det) (interference) 9:27

Third Period
3. Philadelphia - Lindros 12 (Desjardins) 19:45

Penalties
Samuelsson (Phi) (slashing) 1:32

Podein (Phi) (highsticking) 11:54
Draper (Det) (slashing) 14:39

Shots on goal
Philadelphia   8 - 12 - 8   28
Detroit   9 - 10 - 8   27

Power-play Opportunities
Philadelphia   0 of 3
Detroit   0 of 5

Goalies
Philadelphia: Hextall 4-3 (27 shots, 25 saves)
Detroit: Vernon 16-4 (28 shots, 27 saves)
A: 19,983 (19,983)
Referee: Bill McCreary
Linesmen: Wayne Bonney, Gord Broseker

In the fight for Lord Stanley's ultimate prize, the Red Wings faced off against the Philadelphia Flyers, who had eliminated the New York Rangers in their semifinals series. The big, physical Flyers were favorites to win. They hadn't been to the finals for 10 years.

The action began in Philadelphia, the City of Brotherly Love, but the feelings between the two teams were far from affectionate—this was war. The first battle was held on May 31, 1997, in front of a capacity crowd at Philadelphia's CoreStates Center. The Red Wings gained momentum early when left wing Kirk Maltby scored the contest's first goal. Joe

Kocur also scored to give Detroit a 2-1 lead after one period. Then, the Flyers began to collapse. During the second period, Sergei Fedorov scored the game winner on Ron Hextall with a 35-foot wrist shot. Steve Yzerman fired in an insurance goal during the final period with a 59-foot slapshot from inside the blueline. Playing smart, defensive hockey, Detroit won 4-2.

During the game, Vernon came through with big saves, just as he had done against Colorado. Two that were particularly spectacular happened during the second and third periods, against John Druce and Trent Klatt respectively.

Steve Yzerman and Philadelphia's Eric Lindros face off during the 1997 Stanley Cup finals. Rich Margittay Photo.

With a victory under their belt's, the Red Wings prepared for game two, taking advantage of a two-day recess. In Philadelphia's camp, Coach Terry Murray opted to bench Hextall and go with Garth Snow in game 2. Although Murray had hopes of shaking things up, the move did little to improve the quality of Philadelphia's goaltending. Murray stood behind his move. In the June 27, 1997 issue of *The Hockey News*, he said: "Things were working so well with us with both goaltenders. Snow was playing outstanding...you can't forget that. You can't say, 'You played great, now I'm going to forget you.' If we had played well in game one—and even if we lost—I probably don't make the change from Hextall."

Detroit skated away with another 4-2 victory in the second contest, also held in Philadelphia. As the Flyers' net-minding continued to suffer, Detroit's excelled. Vernon continued to come through with big saves, and the Red Wings kept playing smart hockey. By 9:22 of the opening period, Detroit had taken a 2-0 lead. Philadelphia's Rod Brind'Amour netted two

power play goals late in that period to tie the game. Then, Kirk Maltby came through for Detroit with the game-winning goal in the second period. Brendan Shanahan tapped in the contest's final goal, his second of the game, during the third period.

Shanahan, acquired by Detroit in October 1996 from Hartford, had performed superbly under pressure. "It's better than not facing any pressure," he said in the June 5, 1997 *Chicago Tribune*. "If you're the kind of person that wants to be a professional athlete, you enjoy pressure. We all share the load. I think, to a man, we all know that everybody is responsible for the success."

The series moved to Detroit for games 3 and 4. Two games stood between the Red Wings and the Stanley Cup. A capacity crowd packed the friendly confines of Joe Louis Arena to cheer for the Red Wings. The Flyers scored the first goal of the game on the power play when Detroit's Darren McCarty was sent off for interference. Two minutes later, Yzerman scored a power play goal for Detroit—his seventh of the playoffs—on a centering pass from Kozlov. Philadelphia failed to capitalize on a two-man advantage that lasted for 80 seconds, and from that point on, the game belonged to Detroit. In all, they scored six unanswered goals, with Fedorov and Shanahan each netting two. During the third period, the crowd at Joe Louis Arena began chanting: "Sweep, Sweep, Sweep." When the smoke cleared, Detroit had won, 6-1.

"We have got to find a way to stop the bleeding," said Flyers' coach Terry Murray after the loss. "No doubt that game tonight, it was an embarrassment. Detroit came out and really took it to us. We got the first goal of the game, which we really wanted to do. It has been something that we thought was a problem in the first two games. And they came right back and gained the lead, almost at will. We have got to find a way, a complete total effort from everybody. We've just got to find a way to get the job done here for one game."

The Red Wings were now only one win away from ultimate victory. The odds were in their favor. Only one team in NHL history—the 1942 Toronto Maple Leafs—had fought back from a 3-0 deficit to win the Cup. Excitement and jubilation filled Detroit's locker room after the win. "Tonight, we really played well in all areas," said Detroit's Larry Murphy. "The problem is, do we get caught up in all that. We've got to try and repeat how we played tonight—and that's in all areas of the game."

Scotty Bowman also let it be known that the battle was not over. "We are three-fourths of the way, that is the way to look at it," he said. "There is no other way you can look at it really. People are going to write and say things. The people that are going to decide the game are in the two [locker] rooms and I told the team about getting the right focus. You don't win a series with three games, there's not a three-out-of-five series. Obviously, we are going to try to show up [Saturday] like we did tonight."

THE FINAL GAME - JUNE 7, 1997

When the playoffs began, the Red Wings set their sights on the stuff of dreams, the stuff every young hockey player fantasizes about—winning the Stanley Cup. The city of Detroit had also set their sights on

Detroit and Philadelphia face off during the 1997 Stanley Cup finals. Rich Margittay Photo.

Lord Stanley's silver prize.

Prior to the big game, the city of Detroit and the state of Michigan were alive with excitement. The craziest, most loyal hockey fans on the planet were ready for a sweep. Garbed in red and white, some with their faces painted, some carrying brooms as a symbol of their desires, were everywhere. On Michigan roadways, virtually every vehicle sported a Detroit Red Wings window flag. Store windows and signs all had messages of support for Hockeytown's boys. Even neighborhood Burger King restaurants were patronized by hoards of hockey fans seeking souvenir pucks that featured their favorite players.

Space at Joe Louis Arena was a scarce resource. Scalpers were selling front row tickets for $2,500, and standing room-only seats sold for $600! According to an article in the June 8, 1997 issue of the *Detroit News*, two brothers who had purchased upper-level seats at face value were offered $800 apiece for the tickets. "It was tempting," said Eugene Gunnery. "Eight-hundred bucks buys a lot of beers." Sean Gunnery wouldn't hear of selling his ticket. "Seeing Stevie Y raising the Cup over his head is worth its weight in gold," he said. "There shouldn't be a dry eye in the house. You can't put a price on that."

Bruce Martyn, who had served as the team's broadcaster for 31 years, returned to the call the special game when his successor, Ken Kal, extended the invitation. The final moment of truth, that the team had worked towards, hoped for and dreamed about for many years had finally arrived. The Red Wings stood on the verge of victory. The game began, and a city watched in anticipation.

With less than one minute remaining in the opening period, Detroit got on the scoreboard first when Nicklas Lidstrom netted a goal on a 55-foot slap shot from the point. During the playoffs, Lidstrom had struggled, scoring only twice on 78 shots. The goal had the sweet taste of champagne for Lidstrom, and he established a lead that the Red Wings never lost. When asked about the goal in the June 8, 1997 issue of the *Detroit News*, Lidstrom said: "After all those shots—finally, I got a goal. If Sergei or Stevie or Brendan scores, that's OK. If we're playing like this and the team is winning, then that's what counts."

Darren McCarty scored the game/Stanley Cup-winning goal early in the middle period. As it happened, Detroit's Tomas Sandstrom took a hit along the boards, but was able to make a pass to McCarty, who carried the puck out of his zone, and into Philadelphia's. Moving quickly, McCarty faked Philadelphia defenseman Janne Niinimaa by weaving to the left. McCarty then proceeded to fake Philadelphia goaltender Ron Hextall by drawing him to the left and then quickly moving right for the score into an exposed net.

"Mac has been doing it for us all year long," said Kris Draper of the goal in the June 8, 1997 *Ann Arbor News*. "He scored huge goals for us in the playoffs and now obviously [this] is the icing on the cake. It is good to see a guy like that get a big goal in a big game."

Eric Lindros managed to put the Flyers on the scoreboard late in the third period when Terry Murray pulled Hextall for an extra attacker, but it was no use—the Red Wings were champions, and the city of Detroit had already begun to celebrate a long-awaited Stanley Cup victory! By losing game 4, the Flyers became the third straight team in recent years to be swept in the finals, joining Detroit (1995) and Florida (1996).

The 19,983 Red Wing fans went crazy after the win. Energized, their cheers shook the arena. NHL commissioner Gary Bettman presented captain Steve Yzerman with the Cup. Yzerman, who had toiled for 14 years without tasting champagne from the silver chalice, hoisted it high and skated around the rink to the absolute pleasure of the fans.

Scotty Bowman, the winningest coach in hockey, won his seventh Stanley Cup with an NHL record third team. After the win, he put on skates and toured around the rink with the Cup in his hands—something he had never done before. "I always wanted to be an NHL player and skate with the Cup, and you never know how many chances you'll get," he said in the June 8, 1997 issue of the *Detroit News*. "So I figured I'd go for it. It was pretty heavy, but light too."

In the same article, Nicklas Lidstrom looked back over his career with Detroit and said: "We've had a lot of ups and downs over those years. We had some good teams in the past, but always it was something.

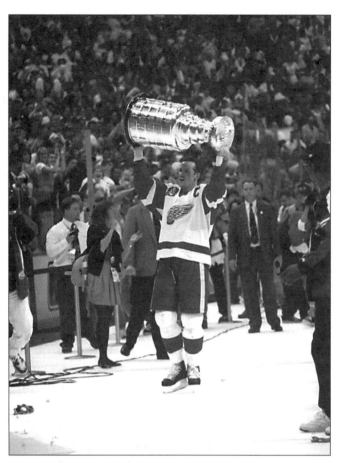

The team chemistry is as good [this year] as it's ever been. Even though everyone didn't get as much time as others, they all contributed. We got some big goals from a few guys who didn't play as much as the others. Winning the Stanley Cup is so great. We were really due for one, eh? It's a relief, too."

Today, unruly celebrations have become commonplace after championship sports victories. Red Wings fans showed the world they had class. Although the streets were alive with excitement and cheer after the big win, things remained under control—no cars were overturned, no buildings were looted. On Tuesday, June 10, the orderly celebration that began after Saturday night's game continued in downtown Detroit. Lining up hours in advance, approximately 750,000 fans eventually filled the streets to watch a victory parade from the Fox Theater to Hart Plaza.

Left: Steve Yzerman holds a long-awaited Stanley Cup above his head for all to see at Joe Louis Arena. Below: Elated fans, players and officials share their excitement after Detroit's 1997 Stanley Cup win.
Rich Margittay Photos.

Captain Steve Yzerman (left) and Brendan Shanahan (right) talk to fans and media after winning the 1997 Stanley Cup. Rich Margittay Photos.

The 40-piece parade included "Stanley," the giant Octopus, and "Paws," the Detroit Tigers' mascot, appropriately dressed in a Red Wings jersey. The champions traveled in red Ford Mustang convertibles. Hoisting the Stanley Cup at the rear of the caravan was captain Steve Yzerman, accompanied by his family and team owner Mike Ilitch. Mike Vernon, also accompanied by his family, rode along with the Conn Smythe Trophy. Even the State House of Representatives canceled its session in Lansing, Michigan, to partake in the day's celebrations. The streets of downtown became a virtual sea of red and white, a visual representation of the love and support Detroit fans have for their hockey team.

After the victory, sportswriter George Cantor wrote a heartfelt article that appeared in the June 10, 1997 issue of the *Detroit News*. In it, several fans gave their feelings on the victory. However, the most passionate statement was made through deeds, not words. The article talks about seven-year-old Max Schwartz, who along with several friends, stood on a street corner near his house the day after the big win. He displayed a poster asking cars to honk if they were a Red Wings fan.

"They kept a running tally on the back of the poster and by the time we finally dragged him away he had 600 marks on it," said his mother, Leslie. "All I know is we had the noisiest neighborhood in town. He can't stop drawing the Red Wings' insignia on every piece of paper he can get his hands on. And he went to school on Monday in a Wings T-shirt that comes down to his ankles. But he refused to leave the house wearing anything else." Max's actions are symbolic of the way an entire city feels now that the Stanley Cup is back in the Motor City.

Steve Yzerman holds a long-awaited Stanley Cup above his head for all to see at the public celebration. Rich Margittay Photo.

Steve Yzerman addresses the Motor City at the 1997 Stanley Cup victory celebration. Rich Margittay Photo.

THE MEN

Today's brand of Detroit Red Wing hockey is characterized by bigger, faster players than fans have known in past decades. Today, the game of hockey has evolved into its most progressive form ever. Unlike the days of the "Original Six," today's NHL includes 26 teams. Increasing television coverage and expansion into cities not traditionally known for being hockey hotbeds, such as San Jose, California, and Tampa Bay, Florida, have marked the beginning of a new era for both the league and the sport itself.

How would the legendary Red Wings of yesteryear stack up against today's boys? The question is an interesting one. Former Detroit Red Wing Marty Pavelich has one possible answer. "Howe would be outstanding today," he says. "Lindsay would be. Most of the guys I played with would be great hockey players because we were better coached as kids in those days [and] because our junior clubs were better. These kids today come out of junior hockey [and] don't go down to the minors. Some of our guys had to go to the minors for awhile, learn some more. It is so fast for these kids today. They come out of college, they come out of junior hockey and they come right into the NHL."

Many of today's players could have skated with the greats of yesteryear. In 1996, Bill Gadsby commented: "There are a lot of players on this team that could [have played] back in the team's glory days. There is a lot of talent on this hockey club right now, a lot of talent."

WILLIAM SCOTT (SCOTTY) BOWMAN

Born: September 18, 1933, Montreal, Quebec

Career Awards & Honors
- Hockey Hall of Fame (Builder): 1991
- Jack Adams Trophy: 1977, 1996
- *The Hockey News'* NHL Executive of the Year: 1983-84, 1996-97
- *The Hockey News'* NHL Coach of the Year: 1967-68 (St. Louis), 1976-77 (Montreal), 1996-97 (Detroit)

Career Milestones
- Holds record for most NHL games coached
- Seven Stanley Cup titles as a coach
- Only coach in NHL history to coach three teams to the Stanley Cup.
- Six Prince of Wales Trophies
- 25 seasons as an NHL coach
- Coached Detroit to the President,s Trophy in 1994-95 and 1995-96.
- Only NHL coach to win over 1,000 games (1,013 regular season games).
- Has reached the Stanley Cup finals 11 times in 24 seasons.
- Ranks first on the all-time playoff coaching ledger in victories, games, playoff series and series won.
- Only Toe Blake has won more Stanley Cups as a coach (eight).
- First individual to be named *The Hockey News'* NHL Coach and Executive of the year in one season.

BIOGRAPHY

The Detroit Red Wings have been fortunate to have the winningest coach in NHL history behind their bench in recent years. To describe Scotty Bowman—a task former Detroit Red Wing Shawn Burr once compared to explaining an abstract painting—is not easy.

In his highly acclaimed book, *The Game*, former Montreal Canadiens' goaltender Ken Dryden said the following of Detroit's coach: "Scotty Bowman is not someone who is easy to like. He has no coach's con about him. He does not slap backs, punch arms or grab elbows. He doesn't search eyes, spew out ingratiating blarney or disarm with faint, enervating praise. He is shy and not very friendly ... Abrupt, straightforward, without flair or charm, he seems cold or abrasive, sometimes obnoxious, controversial, but never colorful.... He is complex, confusing, misunderstood, unclear in every way but one: He is a brilliant coach, the best of his time. He starts each season with a goal—the Stanley Cup—and he has no

other.... A good season is the Stanley Cup; anything else is not."

"Without a doubt, Scotty Bowman is the most intelligent coach I've had," said former Red Wing Mark Howe in the June 16, 1995 issue of *USA Today*. "I learn from him every day. He's an enigma at times. Sometimes you don't know if he's half crazy or where he's coming from. But he knows what he's doing. His knowledge of the game is second to none."

One of the most successful coaches of all time, Bowman's involvement with the game started as a player. However, his playing career was ended prematurely at the amateur level by a head injury in 1952. The injury that Bowman sustained marked the beginning of his administrative career. Under the tutelage of former Montreal Canadiens' coach Sam Pollock, Bowman successfully coached junior hockey within the team's system. He coached the Montreal Junior Canadiens and the team's minor league affiliate in Omaha.

Today, Bowman has retained the ability to successfully "shape" young, up-and-coming hockey players. A recent article in the June 3, 1993 issue of the *Detroit Free Press* said: "Bowman thinks he has the most impact on marginal players: young players still developing their styles and older players past their primes. Bowman benches them, ignores them for long periods of time, making them worry and wonder why. Then, in the midst of a slump or rash of injuries, he returns them to the lineup. And frequently, they will give the kind of inspired performance that contributes to a timely victory."

When the NHL's first expansion occurred in 1967-68, Bowman became the first coach and general manager of the St. Louis Blues when Lynn Patrick offered him the job. During the four seasons in which he coached the Blues, his team made it to the Stanley Cup finals three times and won two division titles.

After St. Louis, Bowman returned to Montreal and coached the Canadiens from 1971-79, winning five Stanley Cups and six division titles in eight seasons. In 1979, Bowman began a new role as general manager, coach and director of hockey operations for the Buffalo Sabres, where he remained until 1987.

"Coaching is a lonely life," he said in the February 13, 1976 issue of *The Hockey News* "You do so much soul-searching. You can't get too close to the players. You have to have someone you can confide in. You miss your family 40 games on the road.... I expect to win, but I always expect to win. I have lived long enough to know you never know what life holds for you, and you have to make the best of what is dealt you."

After coaching Buffalo, Bowman joined CBC-TV's "Hockey Night in Canada" staff as a television analyst. He couldn't stay away from coaching for very long and was soon behind the bench again, this time in Pittsburgh. After joining the Penguins' front office as director of player development and recruitment in 1990-91, he replaced "Badger" Bob Johnson the following season when Johnson became ill. That season (1991-92), the Penguins won their second Stanley Cup in as many years.

At the age of 62, Bowman joined the Detroit Red Wings on June 15, 1993, becoming Detroit's 22nd head coach. The following year, he assumed the additional title of director of player personnel. Bowman piloted the Red Wings to the Stanley Cup finals in 1994-95, but the team lost to the New Jersey Devils. Two seasons later, he took Detroit all the way to Lord Stanley's Cup, ending the city's 42-season drought and becoming the only coach to win the trophy with three different teams. His surprise decision to use veteran goaltender Mike Vernon and the acquisition of Brendan Shanahan were key elements in the victory. On December 29, 1995, he broke the record for most NHL games coached (formerly held by Al Arbour) when he coached his 1,607th game in Dallas.

Besides being a successful NHL coach, Bowman has also achieved success at the international level. He coached Team Canada to a Canada Cup victory in 1976, also coaching them in 1981. In 1979, Bowman coached the NHL All-Stars in a three-game series against the Soviet Union.

At of the close of the 1996-97 season, Bowman's future with the team was unclear. His coaching contract had expired, but two years remained in his agreement for him to serve in a consulting or scouting role with the Red Wings. In the end, he decided to stay behind the team's bench, signing a new agreement for two seasons. Bowman relinquished his responsibilities as general manager to Ken Holland.

TIMOTHY CHEVELDAE

Born: February 15, 1968, Melville, Saskatchewan
Position: Goaltender
Junior
- Saskatoon Blades (WHL): 1985-88
Minor Pro
- Adirondack Red Wings (AHL): 1988-90, 1989-'90, 1993-'94
Detroit Red Wings
- 1988-89 to 1993-94
Best NHL Season
- 1991-92: 4,236 MIN, 3.20GAA, 2 SO
Career Awards & Honors
Junior Hockey
- WHL East All-Star Team: 1988
Professional
- NHL All-Star Game: 1992
Career Milestones
- Most minutes played (in a season) by a Red Wings goalie (4,236, 1991-92).
- Most games (in a season) by a Red Wings goalie (72, 1991-92).
Trades
- Traded to the Winnipeg Jets with Dallas Drake for Bob Essensa and Sergei Bautin on March 8, 1994.

BIOGRAPHY

Donning a pair of white goalie pads someone gave him for free while playing in the minor leagues, Tim Cheveldae played his first NHL game at the age of 20 against the Calgary Flames. Although the game ended up with the Red Wings on the losing side of a 3-2 overtime decision, Cheveldae did a more than adequate job. He played for six seasons in Detroit, half of which were spent partly with the team's AHL affiliate in Adirondack.

Late in the 1989-90 season, injuries to a number of players had affected the team. Cheveldae was called up from the minors to help. He responded by giving a stellar performance, losing only twice in a stretch of 17 games. Glen Hanlon, then the team's back up goalie, praised the younger netminder in the March 23, 1990 issue of the *Toronto Globe and Mail*. He said: "We knew all along he was a good goalie. He's had two years in the minors to learn how to play the game. He's so much farther advanced than most goalies at 21 or 22. He has a good head about himself and he's well liked by his teammates."

In a *Detroit News* article, Cheveldae commented on how he approached post-season hockey. He said:

"I just have to play my game. It's just a game. I learned that in the playoffs, there's lots of hoopla, but that doesn't affect what goes on the ice. It's just like the game that you play in September and the one you played when you were 12 or 13. It's like the Super Bowl. There's two weeks of hoopla, but then the game is played on the field, just like it was during the regular season. I knew I just had to go out there and play my style. At first I was thinking, 'Gee, I have to play this way or play that way.' I was doing little things different—standing too much upright, not challenging, standing too far back in the net. They're just little things."

In the end, it was mainly playoff hockey that got Cheveldae into trouble. He received a considerable amount of heckling from Detroit fans when the team was eliminated in the first round of the 1992-93 playoffs, and his play deteriorated. To make matters worse, his mother passed away the summer after that loss. In the September 14, 1993 issue of the *Detroit News*, he defended his play, explaining: "I'm sure some people do blame me for what happened in the playoffs. I don't think I played that bad. Everyone has their own opinion—I have mine, you have yours, the fans have theirs. An opinion is just an opinion. It isn't right, it isn't wrong."

After the poor performance, coach Scotty Bowman voiced his confidence in Cheveldae at the beginning of the following season (1993-94), saying that he had put the past behind him. However, Cheveldae played in only 30 regular season games that season and was eventually traded to Winnipeg in March of 1994.

CHRIS OSGOOD - BIOGRAPHY

The son of John and Joy Osgood, Chris started playing hockey at the age of five. He played organized hockey right up to the junior ranks in Medicine Hat, Alberta, not having to leave home as so many junior hockey players do. He has come a long way since then. In 1991 he was Detroit's third-round pick in the NHL Entry Draft and has since emerged into the top goalie for the Red Wings.

Osgood's NHL debut came in 1993-94, and, as a rookie, he found himself defending Detroit's goal in the first round of post-season play against the Sharks.

CHRIS OSGOOD

Born: November 26, 1972, Peace River, Alberta
Position: Goaltender
Junior
- Medicine Hat (WHL): 1989-91
- Medicine Hat, Brandon, Seattle (WHL): 1991-92

Minor-Pro
- Adirondack (AHL): 1992-93, 1993-'94, 1994-'95

Detroit Red Wings: 1993-94 to present
Best NHL Season
- 1995-96: 2,993 MIN, 2.17 GAA, 5 SO

Career Awards & Honors
- Junior Hockey: WHL East Second All-Star Team, 1990-91
- NHL Rookie of the Month: February, 1994
- NHL All-Star Games: 1996, '97
- NHL First All-Star Team, 1995-96
- William M. Jennings Trophy, 1995-96 (with Mike Vernon)
- MasterCard NHL Play of the Year, 1995-96

Career Milestones
- First NHL shutout (3-0) on February 24, 1994 vs. Hartford Whalers.
- Recorded shutout in playoff debut on April 20, 1994.
- In 1995-96, broke Terry Sawchuk's team record with a 13-game winning streak.
- In 1995-96, tied for first in NHL for best GAA (2.17).
- In 1995-96, set Red Wings record for longest unbeaten streak by a goalie (21 games).

Detroit was favored to win the series. However, in the third period of the seventh game, Osgood did not clear a pass from Detroit's end, and it resulted in a series-winning San Jose goal. After shedding a few tears in the locker room, Osgood learned from the experience and moved on.

Former Detroit Red Wing Gary Bergman commented on the incident. He said: "I felt so terrible about that for him because that same play happens 20 times a game and I've looked at that tape 20 times. There are certain things that players do when they see the goalie going to play the puck. None of the players around there did it. There were two guys that could have reached out and checked the

---

Opposite: Tim Cheveldae set a team record for most games played in a season by a goalie (72) in 1991-92. Rich Margittay Photo.

guy that got the puck and they just looked at him and that's part of the game of hockey. As you know, you see mistakes happening you have to cover up. That's why it's a team sport. The kid took a lot of undue heat; the media was tough on him."

Quiet and modest off the ice, Osgood has a fiery and competitive demeanor while between the pipes for the Red Wings and has developed a reputation for his competitive spirit. As a goalie, he is a very positional player. He does not have to make difficult acrobatic saves very often, as many of the opposition's shots seem to hit him directly. Since arriving in the Motor City, Osgood has refined his game a great deal, becoming more and more proficient. "He's maturing as a great goaltender in this league," said Mike Vernon in the February, 1996 issue of *Inside Line*. "He's just patient. And patience is what you have to have to be a great goaltender. You can't be too anxious to stop the puck. Let the shooter make the first move and react from there."

"Chris reminds me a lot of Grant Fuhr," said Paul Coffey in the May 28, 1996 issue of the *Detroit News*. "He's so cool. Nothing bothers him. He's 23, and he doesn't act or react like a 23-year-old would."

Former Red Wing defenseman Gary Bergman elaborated further on Osgood, commenting:

I love Osgood, I really do. I think the one thing that really helps him is his attitude. I think the other thing that's helped him is he's playing with Mike Vernon. I've been around when they are together, and they get along well. Certainly, no matter what sport you are in, [when] there's two players in a position, I think its unhealthy if there's not a little competition between them. You have to want to play, otherwise you shouldn't be there. But I think they respect one another for that and yet they are intelligent enough to handle it. That there's no bickering or in-fighting. But I think Ozzie is fortunate that he's had the team in front of him. You know he's had to put up some pretty good numbers.

The kid is just a hell of a goaltender. He came up with some big saves for them, but he's still on the learning curve. You can tell that by some of the goals he lets in. But if it's going to be your future, you've got to learn. There's only one way to learn, you don't learn from drawings and pictures and description, you learn by jumping in the barrel and getting your brains beaten in

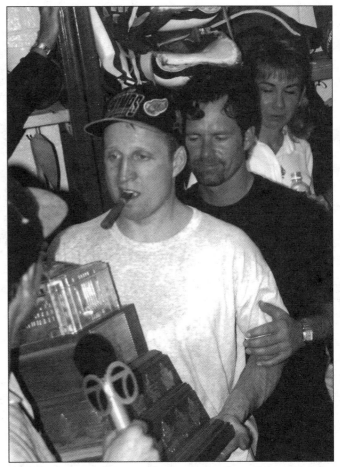

Mike Vernon meets the press after winning the Conn Smythe trophy as 1997 playoff MVP. Rich Margittay Photo.

a few times. There's no teacher like experience, especially in that position.

"Osgood's got great potential in the games that I have watched him," says Bill Gadsby. "He has played fantastic. For a young kid, he's got lots of poise, he's quick. He looks like he's going to be money in the bank, as we say."

On March 6, 1996, in a game against the Hartford Whalers, Osgood became the third goalie in NHL history to be credited for a goal. He was the second goalie in league history to actually shoot the puck into the other team's net. That season, during the playoffs, Osgood made an incredible save on Colorado's Joe Sakic in Game One of the Western Conference finals. As it happened, Osgood first stopped a shot on the right side of the net. Sakic picked up the rebound and attempted to score with a low shot on Osgood's exposed left side. However, Osgood dove to meet him and was able to make an unbelievable glove save. The Red Wings ended up losing that game 3-2 in overtime. Despite the outcome, Osgood's goal is something to remember. It was judged the MasterCard NHL Play of the Year by Fox, CBS and ESPN broadcasters.

In 1996-97, Osgood had a successful regular season that included unbeaten streaks of six, seven and eight games but was used a backup to goaltender Mike Vernon during the playoffs. Only time will tell his fate in Detroit. But if the past is any indicator of the future, Osgood may very well be the first Detroit Red Wing to win the Vezina Trophy since the legendary Terry Sawchuk. "He's always challenging himself to be the best; always checking for goals-against and save percentage," said Associate Coach Barry Smith in the Playoffs 1996 issue of *Inside Line*. "He's not just happy to be in this league. He wants to be No. 1 or No. 2."

BIOGRAPHY

Before coming to Detroit, veteran goaltender Mike Vernon played NHL hockey in his home town of Calgary. Despite the additional pressure and criticism, he proved to be a very consistent netminder for the Flames, and both he and the team enjoyed a considerable amount of success together. Vernon's peak in Calgary came when they won the Stanley Cup in 1988-89.

In 1996-97, Detroit coach Scotty Bowman surprised everyone and opted to rely upon Vernon's experience during the playoffs. Bowman once commented on Vernon in the January 20, 1995 issue of the *Detroit News*: "He gives us something that will make the other teams stop and think. He is a veteran goaltender, and a good one, and that can give us a big psychological edge. Our opponents will just have to look at us in a different way. It's a lot like when I had Ken Dryden in Montreal. What he did for us,

MIKE VERNON

Born: February 24, 1963, Calgary, Alberta
Position: Goaltender
Junior
- Calgary (WHL): 1980-83
Minor-Pro
- Oklahoma City (CHL): 1981-82
- Colorado (CHL): 1983-84
- Moncton (AHL): 1984-85, 1985-86
- Salt Lake City (IHL): 1985-86
Detroit Red Wings
- 1995-96 to present
Best NHL Season
- 1995-96: 1,855 MIN, 2.26 GAA, 3 SO
Career Awards & Honors
Junior Hockey
- WHL First All-Star Team: 1982, 1983
- WHL Most Valuable Player: 1982, 1983
- Named WHL Top Goaltender: 1982, 1983
Minor-Pro
- CHL Second All-Star Team: 1983-84
NHL
- William M. Jennings Trophy: 1995-96 (with Chris Osgood)
- Conn Smythe Trophy: 1996-97
- Second All-Star Team: 1988-89 (Calgary)
- NHL All-Star Games: 1988-91, 93
- NHL Player of the Month: January, 1989
- Team Canada: (Silver Medal, '91 World Championships)
- *The Hockey News'* NHL Playoff MVP: 1996-97
Trades
- Traded to Detroit by Calgary for Steve Chiasson on June 29, 1994.

Mike Vernon with the Conn Smythe trophy. Rich Margittay Photo.

Mike Vernon won the William M. Jennings Trophy (with Chris Osgood) in 1995-96. Rich Margittay Photo.

besides playing great goal, was give us a psychological edge. He was a thinking man's goalie, and he made the other teams think when they played us."

"Tim Cheveldae and Bob Essensa did not have the respect around the league Mike Vernon does," said Detroit's Assistant General Manager and Goaltending Consultant Ken Holland in the June 17, 1995 issue of the *Detroit Free Press*. "He gives you credibility, he's cocky and confident and it rubs off on the players."

Along with fellow netminder Chris Osgood, Vernon won the William M. Jennings Trophy for playing on the team with the fewest goals-against in 1995-96. The following season, at 34 years of age, he was Scotty Bowman's surprise choice during the post-season. He excelled during the playoffs, starting in all

20 of Detroit's post-season games and finishing all except two.

Vernon's key saves were instrumental in the Red Wings' winning the Stanley Cup. Accordingly, he won the Conn Smythe Trophy as playoff MVP, finishing the post-season with a 16-4 record and a 1.76 GAA. Steve Yzerman almost won the award but lost by the closest margin since the trophy was introduced in 1965. "I really wasn't too concerned about [winning the Conn Smythe]," said Vernon in the June 27, 1997 issue of *The Hockey News*. "I just wanted to win the Cup. That was the bottom line. We are all consummate winners in my mind and the team in front of me just played a great round of hockey. Just winning was the important thing."

PAUL DOUGLAS COFFEY

Born: June 1, 1961, Weston, Ontario
Position: Defense
Junior
- S.S. Marie Greyhounds (OHA): 1978-79
- S.S. Marie & Kitchener (OHA): 1979-80

Detroit Red Wings
- 1992-93 to 1995-96

Best NHL Season
- 1985-86 (EDM): 48 goals, 138 points

Career Awards & Honors
Junior Hockey
- OHA 3rd Team All-Star: 1978-79
- OHA 2nd Team All-Star: 1979-80

NHL
- First NHL All-Star Team: 1984-85, 1985-86, 1988-89, 1994-95
- Second NHL All-Star Team: 1981-82, 1982-83, 1983-84, 1989-90, 1995-96
- NHL All-Star Games: 1982-86, 1988-'94, 1996
- Norris Trophy: 1984-85, 1985-86, 1994-95

Career Milestones
- Has played on four Stanley Cup-winning teams: 1984, '85, '87 (Edmonton), '91 (Pittsburgh).
- First NHL defenseman to register 1,000 assists .
- Has played in over 1,000 games.
- NHL record holder for most goals, assists and points by a defenseman.
- Seven-time scoring leader among defensemen.
- NHL record for goals in one season by a defenseman (48 in 1985-86).
- Five 100-plus point seasons.

Trades
- Traded to Detroit with Jim Hiller and Sylvain Couturier for Jim Carson, Gary Shuchuk and Mark Potvin on January 29, 1993.
- Traded by Detroit to Hartford with Keith Primeau for Brendan Shanahan and Brian Glynn on October 9, 1996.

BIOGRAPHY

Paul Coffey learned to play the game in his native town of Weston, Ontario, where his father, Jack, taught him the fundamentals. After two seasons of junior hockey, Coffey was drafted in the first round of the 1980 draft and stepped up to the NHL. He scored his first NHL goal on October 22, 1980, on Calgary Flames' goalie Dan Bouchard and has since developed into one of the game's most incredible players. Known for his powerful skating ability, he has had the additional fortune of playing with teammates like Wayne Gretzky, Mark Messier, Mario Lemieux, Sergei Fedorov and Steve Yzerman, resulting

in four Stanley Cup rings.

Coffey has proven himself valuable time after time during the post-season. He knows what it takes to win, including playing with pain. One example is the 1984-85 post-season. Coffey carried his team through the early stages of the playoffs and sparkled all the way through the final round, helping the Oilers won the Stanley Cup. He did this despite an injured foot and a sore hip that required an injection to kill the pain before each game. Although Wayne Gretzky took the playoff MVP award, coach Glen Sather thought Coffey should have shared it.

Ten seasons later, during the 1994-95 Stanley Cup finals, Coffey was still showing his value to his team. Former NHL veteran Mark Howe claimed Coffey was perhaps the Red Wings' biggest asset. In the October, 1995 issue of *Inside Line*, he said: "[He] was by far our best player. When we needed a big goal, he was involved. I can't think of another guy who did as much as he did."

"He just loves playing and loves to win," continued Howe in the same article. "He has the God-given ability, the way he can skate. And he works hard at it. ... Part of it is his skating, but he can get the puck and not telegraph a play, snap the puck to somebody and catch the opposition off guard."

"I've seen Paul make some unbelievable plays," said Dino Ciccarelli in the March 24, 1995 issue of the *Detroit News*. "Paul is the best defenseman to ever play this game. ... I played against him for 12 or 13 years, so I've seen what he can do to you. Now I've played with him for two-plus seasons and I've seen what he can do for our team. I haven't seen anyone who skates like Paul does, shoots like Paul does or passes the way Paul does. He's the best there is."

NHL referee Paul Stewart recently gave an excellent description of Coffey. He said: "They talk about how Fedorov is a great skater, and there is no doubt about the fact that Fedorov is a great skater, but I've always said that Paul Coffey can go faster East-to-West than most guys do North-to-South. He does this just by scooting. Somehow or another, he seems to glide sidewards. He's moving forward, but he's going sidewards at the same time. He just has that unique, it's almost like watching a space craft in space. You don't see the power, but all of a sudden the thing moves. Coffey's got great temperament.

He's got this whole thing in perspective and he's a good guy out on the ice to deal with as a referee, and I enjoy watching him play."

Coffey has reached many milestones during his career. He has played in over 1,000 NHL games and recently became the first NHL defenseman to register over 1,000 career assists. At the age of 33, he took home his third Norris Trophy, nine years after winning his second. Coffey ranks it as the sweetest of the three trophy wins, given his age and all of the effort and competition involved. Today, Paul Coffey plays for the Philadelphia Flyers.

Right: Nicklas Lidstrom was runner-up to Pavel Bure for the Calder Trophy in 1992.

Below: Paul Coffey and Vladimir Konstantinov watch as octopi are removed from the ice during the 1994-95 Stanley Cup finals. Rich Margittay Photos.

NICKLAS LIDSTROM

Born: April 28, 1970, Avesta, Sweden
Position: Defense
International
- Vasteras (Swedish Elite League): 1988-91

Detroit Red Wings
- 1991-92 to present

Best NHL Season
- 1995-96: 17 goals, 67 points

Career Awards & Honors
- Upper Deck All-Rookie Team: 1991-92
- Canada Cup: Sweden, 1991
- World Championships (Sweden): 1991, 1994
- NHL All-Star Games: 1996

Career Milestones
- Gold medal: 1991 World Championships
- Runner-up to Pavel Bure for Calder Trophy: 1992.
- Named one of Sweden's top three players: 1990 World Junior Championships.
- In 1991-92, tied Red Wings club record for assists by a rookie defenseman, tying Marcel Dionne's overall team freshman assist mark (49) and Reed Larson's rookie defenseman point mark (60).

BIOGRAPHY

Before being selected in the 1989 NHL Entry Draft, Swedish-born Nicklas Lidstrom won two championships with his junior hockey team in Sweden, excelling with Vasteras of the Swedish Elite League. He played his first hockey for Detroit in 1991-92. During that first NHL season, Detroit coach Bryan Murray commented on Lidstrom in a December 20, 1991 *Associated Press* article: "He's played tremendous for a young guy," said Murray. "Nicklas has been one of our key people all season. He moves the puck and gets us out of trouble a lot. He's been an important player on the point for us. He also kills penalties ... he plays all of the time."

Besides adjusting to life in a new country, Lidstrom has had to adjust to the NHL's smaller ice surfaces and intense schedules, where back-to-back games are the norm. "I think over here [the United States], with such a long season and so many games, you have to be ready to play every game," he says. "Sometimes, if you are little bit injured, you have to play through it, unless it is real serious. I think the biggest thing is just to get ready to play every night."

In the November, 1995 issue of *Inside Line*, Lidstrom commented on his style of play and how he

adjusted it to fit the NHL: "I had to simplify my game," he said. "I had to play safe, minimize mistakes and get rid of the puck a lot quicker. That's why I always try to be in the right position, because I'm not going to go out and put the big hit on someone. That's just not my game. ... People are always looking for the big hits, but that's not what I'm all about. I'm not the biggest guy out there, so most of the time if I did try to crush somebody I would probably lose. I still take my guy out, but I do it a little different way."

"Lidstrom's a smooth player," says Gary Bergman. "I look at Lidstrom a lot in the same way [as Vladimir Konstantinov]. He's a smoother skater, he's got the big shot, [and] I think he plays his position very well. I just think once in a while he has a mental lapse, that's all. He just kind of goes to sleep defensively."

Lidstrom was a key component in Detroit's 1997 Stanley Cup win. Despite the fact that he had difficulty converting on many scoring attempts, his defensive play was invaluable. He came through for the Red Wings with the first goal in the team's 2-1 win over Philadelphia in Game Four of the Stanley Cup finals.

DINO CICCARELLI

Born: February 8, 1960, Sarnia, Ontario
Position: Right wing
Junior: London (OHL): 1977-80
Minor-Pro: Oklahoma City (CHL): 1980-81
Detroit Red wings: 1992-93 to 1995-96
Best NHL Season: 1981-82: 55 goals, 106 points
Career Awards & Honors
Junior Hockey
- OHA Second All-Star Team: 1977-78

NHL
- NHL All-Star Games: 1982, '83, '89, '97

Career Milestones
- On March 28, 1995, became the 101st NHL player to appear in 1,000 regular-season games in a contest against the Mighty Ducks.
- Scored 500th goal on January 8, 1994 vs. LA.
- Scored 1000th point with a goal against the Calgary Flames on March 9, 1994.
- Twice has exceeded 50 goals, 100 points in one season.
- Holds NHL record for most goals by a rookie in one playoff year (14 in 1981).

Trades
- Traded to Detroit from Washington for Kevin Miller on June 20, 1992.
- Traded to the Tampa Bay Lightning in 1996 for a conditional Draft pick.

BIOGRAPHY

At five-foot-ten, 185 pounds, Dino Ciccarelli is far from being one of the league's biggest physical players. However, he is known for his heart and fiery, physical style of play. Lou Nanne, former Minnesota North Stars' president, recalled Ciccarelli's feistiness the first time he set eyes on him. In the April 15, 1990 issue of the *Toronto Sun*, he said: "I first saw him in 1978 when I went to London to scout Bobby Smith. I sat right behind the London bench. He was a tiny guy who was bouncing off everyone, but he electrified the crowd every time he took [to] the ice."

While playing junior hockey for the OHL's London Knights in 1978-79, Dino had a close call that could have ended his career as a hockey player. During practice, he broke his right femur while sliding into the boards. The injury resulted in a 16-inch rod being placed in his leg. Doctors told him he would never play competitively again. After dealing with an infection which caused a portion of his leg to be removed, Dino battled his way back and, in

September of 1979, signed with the Minnesota North Stars, who remembered his bounciness. The following year, he spent a portion of the season playing for Oklahoma City but was eventually called up to the big club. During his first full NHL season (1981-82), he scored a career-best 55 goals for 106 points in 76 games.

Ciccarelli played for the North Stars until March 7, 1989, when he was traded to the Washington Capitals with Bob Rouse for Mike Gartner and Larry Murphy. Humorously, in a recent edition of *Inside Line*, Dino recalled one of the more embarrassing moments of his career that happened while playing for Washington. He said: "My first game after being traded to Washington was in Montreal. The second shift of the game I caught an elbow and got knocked out cold. When I started to come out of it, I couldn't figure out why I had a Washington jersey on. I thought I was still a North Star."

When contract negotiations with the Capitals got sticky, Dino came to the Red Wings in a trade for Kevin Miller in June of 1992. In Detroit, Ciccarelli

was a solid contributor, and his style of play was an asset to the team. In a 1992 *Detroit News* article, Ciccarelli said: "I can't play on the fringes. I don't have the talent to play that way. I mean, I'm a quick skater but I'm not fast. About 10-12 feet in front of the net, those are my boundaries."

In the same article, defenseman Brad McCrimmon said: "He can go to the net better than anyone I've played with or against. You're always wrestling with him in front of the net. He's pesky. And as fast as he goes down, he comes back up. He's sure scored a lot of goals from that 10-foot area."

Speaking of goals, Ciccarelli scored his 500th on January 8, 1994, in a 6-3 win over the Los Angeles Kings. Other players in the 500 goal club include Gordie Howe, Bobby Hull, Phil Esposito, Guy Lafleur, Marcel Dionne and Wayne Gretzky.

Former Red Wing defenseman Bill Gadsby recently commented on Ciccarelli, while Dino was still playing for Detroit "He's a good man to have around," said Gadsby. "He can stir up things and he can get you a lot of big goals. He's a feisty little guy and he comes to play every night. He's got a great 110 percent effort, they need guys like that. He stands in front of the net and he's not very big, takes a beating, but it pays off for him."

NHL referee Paul Stewart also offered an opinion of Ciccarelli. He said: "Well, I always kid him because I always tell him the green light's on, man. Do whatever you want. Like any relationship, it takes time to build it, and I think Dino and I have a relationship now where he pushes right to the edge, he gets right to that limit and then he knows when to back off. And I think that's a real sign of his being a veteran hockey player. I think the other thing is that, with the coach, they've all sort of found their way as far as what they are expected to do and what he expects them to do."

In 1996, Ciccarelli was traded to Tampa Bay in exchange for a conditional Draft pick. His first season with the Lightning was a successful one. Ciccarelli scored 35 goals for 60 points and was a starter in the 1997 NHL All-Star game in San Jose.

Opposite: Dino Ciccarelli has played in over 1,000 NHL games. Rich Margittay Photo.

MARK STEVEN HOWE

Born: May 28, 1955, Detroit, Michigan
Position: Defense
Junior
- Toronto Marlboros (OHA - Jr. A)
- Detroit Junior Red Wings (SOJHL)
- US Olympic Team (International)

Detroit Red Wings
- 1992-93 to 1995

Best NHL Season
- 1985-86 (Philadelphia): 24 goals, 82 points

Career Awards & Honors
Junior hockey
- Most Valuable Player (SOJHL): 1970-71
- Outstanding Forward (SOJHL): 1970-71

Other
- SOJHL First All-Star Team: 1970-71
- US Olympic Team: 1972
- WHA Rookie of the Year: 1973-74
- WHA First All-Star Team: 1978-79
- WHA Second All-Star Team: 1973-74, 1976-77
- *The Sporting News* All-Star First Team: 1982-83, 1985-86, 1986-87
- *The Sporting News* All-Star Second Team: 1979-80
- NHL First All-Star Team: 1982-83, 1985-86, 1986-87
- NHL All-Star Games: 1981, '83, '86, '88
- Emery Edge Award: 1985-86

Career Milestones
- Retired as the second-highest scoring defenseman in pro-hockey history (behind Paul Coffey).
- NHL plus-minus leader: 1986 (Philadelphia).

BIOGRAPHY

Mark Howe recently hung up the skates from a 22-year career in professional hockey. It all began in the Red Wings' amateur hockey program, where he played peewee, bantam, squirt and junior B. As a child, he had an advantage over most kids, getting to skate on the ice of the Detroit Olympia. In the April 20, 1987 issue of the *Detroit News*, Gordie said of his son: "[As a child], he was an entrepreneur. He used to sell my pictures at school. After games at Olympia, he'd tell me, 'I'm going to help clean the building out.' Then he had five hours of free ice time."

After playing junior hockey in Toronto, Howe played for Houston of the World Hockey Association with his father and brother Marty. After playing for New England of the WHA and Hartford of the NHL, he spent ten seasons with the Philadelphia Flyers, earning a reputation as one of the NHL's best defenseman.

Mark Howe played professional hockey for 22 years. Rich Margittay Photo.

Revealing some of his philosophy in the September 15, 1992 issue of the *Detroit News*, Howe said: "I've always been serious. I'm not into the showman part of the game. I'm not flashy. I play my game. There are things I try to avoid. I know what Dad did. I know what I can do. I'm extremely proud to be Colleen and Gordie Howe's son. But I am my own person."

Howe was signed by the Red Wings as a free agent without compensation on July 8, 1992. Being Gordie Howe's son, it would have been difficult for Mark Howe to play in Detroit earlier in his career, given the expectations fans might have had. However, Mark said that finishing his career in Detroit was a business decision and a chance to play for one of the NHL's strongest teams.

Howe learned early on that pain was part of the

game. At the age of 15, he underwent knee surgery and a spinal tap. During Howe's career, he experienced many injuries. In the March/April 1996 issue of *Inside Line*, in an article by Dave Barkholz, it was revealed that "Howe suffered major injuries to both knees, separations of both shoulders, broken teeth, a seriously jammed neck, and life threatening internal injuries when he was nearly impaled on a pipe goal mount. That injury, which occurred when Howe was playing with Philadelphia, prompted the NHL to switch to magnets to hold nets in place."

NHL referee Paul Stewart admired Howe's athletic qualities a great deal. He says: "I was sorry that Mark Howe finished up—it happens to all of us—and that he didn't get a shot at the Cup. He did [get a shot], but he didn't get his name on the Cup. He was always a tremendous competitor. A guy I remember playing against. Tremendous wrist shot. A great shooter. He was a real good shooter and a real tough kid. He came to play and played hard."

Howe hung up the skates after the 1994-95 season and is currently a scout for the Red Wings. He spends time looking for talent in the International Hockey League and works with defensemen who play for the Adirondack Wings, Detroit's American Hockey League affiliate. He also makes special publicity appearances for the Red Wings.

KEITH PRIMEAU

Born: November 24, 1971, Toronto, Ontario
Position: Center and Left wing
Junior
- Hamilton (OHL): 1987-88
- Niagara Falls Flyers (OHA): 1988-90

Minor-Pro
- Adirondack (AHL): 1990-91, 1991-92

Detroit Red Wings
- 1990-91 to 1995-96

Best NHL Season
- 1993-94: 31 goals, 73 points

Career Awards & Honors
Junior Hockey
- OHL Second-team All-Star: 1989-90

Career Milestones
Junior Hockey
- Led OHL in points (127) and goals (57) and was third in assists (70) in 1989-90.

Trades
- Traded by Detroit to Hartford with Paul Coffey for Brendan Shanahan and Brian Glynn on October 9, 1996.

BIOGRAPHY

Before making it to the NHL, Keith Primeau was a junior hockey star. He helped his Adirondack teammates win the AHL's Calder Cup in 1992. Once in the NHL, Primeau got off to a slow start. During his second season with the Red Wings, he publicly requested a trade, claiming that he was having difficulties moving forward and getting opportunities. He commented on the fact in the June 3, 1995 issue of the *Toronto Star*, saying: "There was a lot of pressure. Everyone expected all of [1990's top picks] to step in and contribute right away to teams that were struggling in the standings. That a couple did only added more pressure."

Primeau wasn't traded as he requested and slowly developed into a talented power forward for Detroit. As he matured, his skating skill and large size meshed and he became a more coordinated hockey player. In the October, 1995 issue of *Inside Line*, coach Scotty Bowman described Primeau: "Some players are judged just on the numbers. [Keith] gives you more than just production. The rest of the game is harder to judge. He's aggressive, he's good defensively, he's conscientious. He's a complete player. A complete player is harder to measure. You can't just look at the book for numbers. He takes faceoffs, he's intimidating to play against, he likes challenges. He's a premier player. And players like that are hard to find."

Primeau was eventually traded to the Hartford Whalers with Paul Coffey. In Hartford, he continues to post respectable numbers and in 1996-97 scored 26 goals and 51 points.

THE RUSSIAN CONNECTION

During the 1990s, an unprecedented number of Russian hockey players have played for the Red Wings. Vyacheslav Kozlov, Igor Larionov, Sergei Fedorov, Vladimir Konstantinov and Viacheslav Fetisov have brought an international flavor to NHL hockey in the Motor City.

Coach Scotty Bowman commented on their effectiveness in the April 12, 1996 issue of *The Hockey News*. He said: "They move the puck around, they don't take low percentage shots. When you have the puck in your possession and the other team doesn't get any quick transition turnover plays, it helps your defense." Bowman made history when he became the very first coach in NHL history to play an all-Russian unit.

Bill Gadsby thinks highly of Detroit's Russian players. He recently commented:

They are fantastic. It's worth the admission price of the ticket to see these guys play because they play tic-tac-toe with that puck. It looks like they have it on a string, and they work hard. Guys like Fedorov could probably be the best player in the world. That's quite a statement to make, but if he's going, he's unbelievable. The guy can do everything. He likes the rough going and he checks hard and he is probably the best skater in the league and he's smart. He's got tremendous hockey sense and the guys that are playing with him are right there with him, Larionov and Kozlov and Konstantinov. When they put the five on the ice, I tell you they are something to watch. And the fans here love it. A lot of times, he [Scotty Bowman] puts the five of them on the ice [at the same time] and they really do a job, believe me.

Former Detroit Red Wing Carl Liscombe, who played during the 1930s, said the following of the Russians: "I like Fedorov. He's got an awful lot of talent. He can skate, he can do everything. A couple of their defensemen, those Russian defensemen, they are good hockey players. But they are getting old, too. They are [a lot of fun to watch]. And Detroit passes the puck. As of right now, they are the best passing team in hockey today, there's no doubt about it. Sometimes it's unbelievable the way they pass that puck around."

Critics have raised the question over the Russians' passion to win the Stanley Cup. In the April 12, 1996 issue of *The Hockey News*, Detroit Red Wing Igor Larionov addressed the criticism and explained why it is unfair. He said: "Russians have played in this league for seven years. Some of the guys have become Americans, got passports, so I don't think we can divide North American guys and Russians. This whole team, we're working together."

VIACHESLAV FETISOV

Born: April 20, 1958, Moscow, Russia
Position: Defense
International
- CSKR (USSR), 1974-89

Detroit Red Wings
- 1995-96 to present

Best NHL Season
- 1989-90 (New Jersey): 8 goals, 42 points

Career Awards & Honors
- Soviet National League All-Star Team: 1979, 1980, 1982-'88
- NHL All-Star Game: 1997
- Leningradskaya-Pravda Trophy (top-scoring defenseman): 1984, 1986-'88
- Soviet Player of the Year: 1982, '86, '88
- Captain, Central Red Army Team
- "Honored Masters of Sport"
- Gold Stick Award (Europe's Top Player): 1984, '86, '90
- Olympics (silver medal: 1980; gold medal: 1984, '88)
- World Championships: 11 appearances

Trades
- Traded to Detroit from New Jersey on April 3, 1995 for 3rd round pick in 1995 Entry Draft.

BIOGRAPHY

Defenseman Viacheslav Fetisov played most of his professional hockey in Russia, and most of his NHL experience has been with the New Jersey Devils. It was only recently that he came to Detroit.

Fetisov is remembered for his participation as a key player in the 1980 Olympics, the United States' "Miracle on Ice." In a strange twist of fate, Mike Ramsey, who played for the United States, and Fetisov became teammates in Detroit years after the intense international competition that once stood between them. In 1979, the Soviets beat the NHL All-Star team in two of three games, one of which they won 6-0. So, it was a surprise when the United States beat the Soviets for the gold medal in what is considered one of the biggest upsets in sports history.

Commenting on the moment that the United States won, in the January 7, 1996 issue of the *Detroit News*, Fetisov said: "I hadn't seen many teams dancing in front of me. I think it was the greatest team in Soviet hockey history. Huge disappointment ... for players, for fans, for government. For me it was big loss, biggest loss in my life, but not as big as for older

teammates. I felt sorry for [goaltending legend Vladislav] Tretiak."

Retirement will most likely be in Fetisov's plans in the near future, given his age. But for now, he remains one of Detroit's five Russian players, valued for his contributions to the team. NHL referee Paul Stewart is a big Fetisov fan. He says: "I like Fetisov. He and I played against one another. I've always thought he was a gritty guy and he was a classy guy. In '87, at the Canada Cup, it's a custom for the captain of the team to come up and shake hands after the game with the referee. Gretzky was a captain and Fetisov was a captain. Gretzky came up and then Fetisov came over [to shake hands], even though they lost a tough game. I thought he was a classy guy. He has big hands and he's pretty mobile for 35 or 36 years old. He does pretty well."

Tragically, Fetisov was involved in an accident with teammate Vladimir Konstantinov and a team masseur on June 13, shortly after the team victorious Stanley Cup win. He sustained a bruised chest and lung, as well as a knee injury, but was released after five days in the hospital.

VLADIMIR KONSTANTINOV

Born: March 19, 1967, Murmansk, Russia
Position: Defense
International
- Central Red Army (Soviet Elite League), 1984-91

Detroit Red Wings
- 1991-92 to present

Best NHL Season
- 1996-97: 5 goals, 38 points

Career Awards & Honors
- NHL Second All-Star Team: 1995-96
- *The Hockey News'* Second All-Star Team: 1996-97
- Upper Deck All-Rookie Team: 1991-92
- Team Captain (Red Army and Soviet National Team)
- World Championships: four appearances

Career Milestones
- In 1989-90, was second in scoring for defensemen in Soviet Elite League.
- Led the NHL with a plus-60 rating in 1995-96.

BIOGRAPHY

Vladimir Konstantinov's hockey education began at the age of 17 in the Soviet Elite League. A former Red Army teammate of Sergei Fedorov, he was discovered by Detroit's past director of scouting Neil

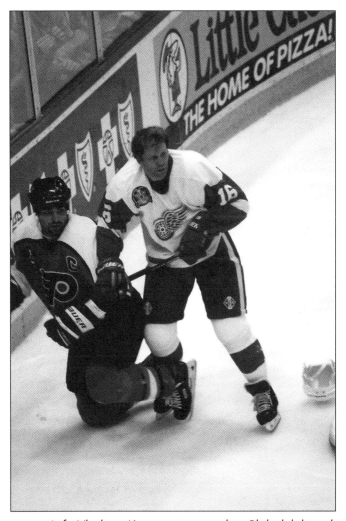

Left: Vladimir Konstantinov sends a Philadelphia player to his knees during the 1997 Stanley Cup playoffs.
Right: Vladimir Konstantinov shows his excitement during the 1997 Stanley Cup victory parade. Rich Margittay Photos.

Smith and European scout Christer Rockstrom at the 1989 World Junior Championship. A brawl developed between Canadian and Russian players and, according to Rockstrom, Konstantinov was the Russian who best held his own.

Like many of his foreign colleagues, Konstantinov has since had to adapt to the smaller ice rinks of the NHL. In Konstantinov's case, however, it has been to his advantage, as he has been able to make open-ice hits more efficiently. Although he is not a big goal-scorer, Konstantinov is hard-working, defensively solid and very mobile. In Russia, he was the captain of his hockey team and brings those leadership skills to the Red Wings.

As an athlete, Konstantinov is valued highly for his versatility. In the May 17, 1996 issue of *The Hockey News*, Detroit's vice-president, Jimmy

Devellano, said: "I think what makes Vladimir Konstantinov so special is that he gives you gives you the whole package. I'm not sure that I've seen a lot of defensemen over the years give you the whole package. Some will give you offense, some will give you defense, some will give you toughness. Vladimir, this year for the first time, has given us everything."

In the same article, Devellano expressed disappointment over the fact that Konstantinov was not a finalist for the Norris Trophy, commenting: "People sometimes get selected on reputation or because they've been selected so many times in the past. It would appear to me a little bit of that happened. Anybody who has followed the Detroit hockey club knows that Vladimir Konstantinov has been as good a defenseman as there has been in the NHL. I can tell you this much, I wouldn't trade him

Detroit fans sign a shrine erected for Red Wings players injured in a tragic limousine accident. Rich Margittay Photo.

variety of answers emerged, both affirmative and negative, most agreed that he pushes the rules to their limit on the ice. Teammate Ray Sheppard said: "Yes, He's always jabbing at you, hands in your face. But he's smart about it. He knows when to hit and when to take his whacks. That's why he's disliked by most players in the league."

In the same article, Martin Lapointe said: "No. He's just aggressive, real aggressive, not dirty. Russians sometimes are just fancy; they won't hit. He's the opposite. He hits and he gets hit. Look at the scars on his face and his nose has been broken a couple of times."

Steve Chiasson added: "I wouldn't want to take the abuse he takes. He just gets creamed out there. I don't know how he can take it sometimes. He's like Gumby out there; he just keeps bouncing back."

Konstantinov and defensive partner Nicklas Lidstrom were key elements in Detroit's 1997 Stanley Cup win. Tragically, Konstantinov's future remains uncertain. He was involved in a serious automobile accident along with teammate Slava Fetisov and team masseur Sergei Mnatsakanov on Friday, June 13, shortly after the team victorious Stanley Cup win.

for any defenseman in the NHL."

Many feel that Konstantinov is a dirty player. Some compare him to the likes of Chicago's Chris Chelios. Former Detroit Red Wing Gary Bergman said the following of Konstantinov in a recent interview: "I think he's a good player. I never thought I'd end up liking a Russian, after 1972. But I also have to take my hat off to Vlad.... [People in] Chicago probably feel over there like we feel about [Chris] Chelios here. [We] hate his guts, but [we] would like to have him on our team. The one reason I respect him, and especially Vlad, is because ... he takes it and doesn't bitch, and he dishes it out and doesn't bitch. You have to admit that as mean as he is with that stick and all the crap he does, he takes a pretty good pounding himself and he's not a big person. But gee, you never hear him whine. He just goes about his job and tries to do it the best he can."

In the February 4, 1994 issue of the *Detroit News*, a few of Konstantinov's teammates gave their opinions on whether or not he is a "dirty" player. While a

SERGEI FEDOROV

Born: December 13, 1969, Pskov, Russia
Position: Center
International
- CSKA (USSR): 1986-90

Detroit Red Wings
- 1990-91 to present

Best NHL Season
- 1993-94: 56 goals, 120 points

Career Awards & Honors
- Hart Trophy: 1993-94
- Selke Trophy: 1993-94, 1995-96
- Lester B. Pearson: 1993-94
- 1993-94 Player of the Year: *The Hockey News, The Sporting News, Hockey Digest*
- NHL All-Star Rookie Team: 1990-91
- NHL First All-Star Team: 1993-94
- NHL Second All-Star Team: 1995-96
- NHL All-Star Games: 1992: '94, '96
- Canada Cup: 1991
- World Championships (Gold-Medal-Winning Soviet National Team): 1989, '90

Career Milestones
- Shares Detroit's club record for game-winning goals with Carson Cooper (1928-29).
- Four-goal game (first three goals successively for a "natural hat trick"): February 12, 1996 vs. LA.

Sergei Fedorov won the Hart Trophy in 1993-94. Rich Margittay Photo.

BIOGRAPHY

One of the greatest European hockey players on skates today, Sergei Fedorov was born in Russia, where he learned the game in his native city of Pskov. At the age of nine, his family moved to northern Russia. Like many children his age, he devoted winters to hockey and summers to soccer.

Eventually, Fedorov went to play hockey in Minsk, where he was discovered by the Soviet Red Army. They invited him to their training camp in 1986, and he spent four seasons playing in the Soviet Elite League. In the November 1, 1990 issue of the *Toronto Globe and Mail*, Russian hockey legend Igor Larionov said that, as he and teammates Sergei Makarov and Vladimir Krutov once were, Fedorov was a big piece in Russia's international hockey picture. "Definitely, they were to follow us," he said. "Fedorov, Alex Mogilny and Pavel Bure were the three counted on by (Coach Victor) Tikhonov for future success of the national team ... and for Tikhonov's success."

Fedorov came to America in 1990. His team was in Seattle participating in the Goodwill Games, and he made the choice to walk away and secure a work permit in the United States. Even though he technically did not defect, the move upset the Soviet Hockey Federation. Although the situation was eventually smoothed out, the Federation threatened to put a halt on their agreement with the NHL that allowed Soviet players to play in North America. In November 1994, Fedorov returned home for the first time when the Russian Foreign Ministry issued him and Alexander Mogilny new passports so that they could play on a Russian all-star team in a series of exhibition games.

Fedorov's point production steadily improved after he came to the NHL, culminating in a 120-point season in 1993-94. That season, he was named to the NHL first All-Star team, won the Hart and Selke trophie, and the Lester B. Pearson Award. He continues to stand out as one of the NHL's premier players, and in 1995-96, led the Detroit Red Wings in goals, assists and points. He is known for his enthusiasm and positive attitude, not to mention his ability to skate like lightning—he won the NHL SuperSkills skating competition held at the 1992 and 1994 All-Star games.

Coming to a new country was not easy for Fedorov. The move required a lot of difficult adjustments. It is during such a time that one needs supportive teammates. In the December 17, 1993 issue of the *Detroit News*, Fedorov commented on the players he looks up to. When asked if there were any, he said: "Yes, especially when I came to Detroit — Stevie [Yzerman] for one. Every player was a little example for me of what I should do and what I should not do. I try to see how everything works. I don't just look at stars. I look at role players, everybody, and try to learn. Of course you look up to players like Mark Howe, Ciccarelli, [Steve] Chiasson, [Ray] Sheppard, Stevie. All of those players play a long, long time. They can share that."

In the same *Detroit News* article, Fedorov's teammate Martin Lapointe said: "He can control the game from one end to the other. I'm always telling other players how great he is. But he doesn't act like a star. He'll always talk about his teammates instead of himself. He's the best guy I've ever known as a person and as a hockey player. I watch him all the time. It's great to have a role model like Sergei."

Former Detroit Red Wings Associate Coach Doug Maclean expressed his feelings concerning Fedorov in the April 3, 1992 issue of the *Toronto Sun*. He said: "I don't know if everyone realizes what this guy is. He's a big scorer who still checks the other team's best line. When we play Chicago, he plays against (Jeremy) Roenick. When we play Toronto, he plays against (Doug) Gilmour. He's a great player offensively and a great player defensively. And he's quick. He has the quickest first three strides in the league, and laterally there isn't a better skater."

"I love watching Fedorov," says former Red Wing Marty Pavelich. "When he puts the afterburners on, oh my God, that's just something to see. Last night he did it. I watch him and it's just a joy. I mean, he's worth the price of admission just to see him play!"

NHL referee Paul Stewart is also fond of Fedorov. "[Sergei Fedorov is a] good kid," he says. "He's got a good smile. He looks at you out of the corner of his eye and he smiles a little bit. He knows he's not fooling you. When he wants to go at the puck, there aren't too many guys that can take him off it."

VYACHESLAV KOZLOV

Born: May 3, 1972, Voskresensk, Russia
Position: Left wing
International
- Khimik (Soviet Elite League), 1987-92

Minor-Pro
- Adirondack (AHL): 1992-93, 1993-94

Detroit Red Wings
- 1991-92 to present

Best NHL Season
- 1995-96: 36 goals, 73 points

Career Awards & Honors
- Rookie of the Year (Soviet Elite League), 1989-90
- World Junior Championships: 1989, '90
- World Championships: 1991, '94
- Canada Cup, 1991
- Goodwill Games (Soviets Won Gold Medal): 1990

BIOGRAPHY

Vyacheslav Kozlov came to the Detroit Red Wings after being discovered by Jimmy Devellano in 1987 at a U.S.-Soviet tournament in Lake Placid, N.Y. At the time, Kozlov was only 15 years old. Detroit scouts Bill Dineen and Neil Smith were also present. Devellano said to Dineen that he had followed Wayne Gretzky since the age of 12 and that Kozlov was by far the most talented 15-year-old hockey player he had ever set eyes on. In the December 4, 1993 issue of the *Toronto Sun*, Devellano recalled the find, commenting: "We saw a little buzz bomb — No. 13 — scooting all over the darn ice. He was playing so well and he was just a wee little guy. But we realized size didn't mean much because this was a real special player."

Before the Red Wings got him to the United States, Kozlov was involved in a serious car crash. On the way to training camp, a bus turned in front of the car they were driving, killing his Red Army teammate, Taras Kirilov. The injuries to Kozlov were very severe. Making matters worse, the Red Army stopped payment of his salary after he was injured, prompting him to move to the United States. Since that time, the talented skater has developed into a powerful weapon in Detroit's five-man Russian arsenal.

During his first NHL game, on March 12, 1992, Kozlov got two assists, the first of which came on a goal by Sergei Fedorov on Kozlov's first shift. The next season, he scored his first NHL goal in Los Angeles on October 8, 1992. However, most of that season was spent developing with the club's AHL affiliate in Adirondack. In 1993-94, Kozlov stepped up with the big club and established himself as a regular contributor with his superb one-on-one skills. In 1994-95, he tied a Red Wings club record with four game-winning goals, including the Western Conference clincher in double overtime against Chicago.

IGOR LARIONOV

Born: December 3, 1960, Voskresensk, Russia
Position: Center
International
- Khimik (USSR): 1977-81
- CSKA (USSR): 1981-89

Detroit Red Wings
- 1995-96 to present

Best NHL Season
- 1995-96 22 goals, 73 points

Career Awards & Honors
International
- Soviet National League All-Star: 1983, 1986-88
- Soviet Player of the Year, 1988

BIOGRAPHY

Igor Larionov is one of the greatest Russian hockey players of all time. He broke into the NHL with the Vancouver Canucks in 1989-90, and was later claimed by the San Jose Sharks in the NHL waiver draft on October 4, 1992. Today, he compliments four other Russian players on the Detroit Red Wings' roster.

Larionov is known for being outspoken when it comes to his beliefs, a characteristic which got him into some trouble in his native Russia. After arriving in Vancouver, he penned a book about the "tyranny of the Soviet hockey regimen," according to an article in the January 1996 issue of *Inside Line*. In that article, he said: "[In Russia], I had fun on the ice because I played with great hockey players. Off the ice was kind of hell; 11 months a year in training camp."

Upon arriving in Detroit, the 35-year-old Larionov had a big impact on younger Russian players Sergei Fedorov and Vyacheslav Kozlov. Teammate Chris Osgood commented on the fact in the April 12, 1996 issue of *The Hockey News*, saying: "He [Larionov] was their idol growing up in Russia. That was a big thing for them to play with him. He gives it to them sometimes if they do the wrong thing or if they get lazy. They're going to listen to a guy like that. It's like us and Paul Coffey, but those guys don't know Paul Coffey as well as they know Igor Larionov."

In the January, 1996 issue of *Inside Line*, Sergei Fedorov confirmed Osgood's statement, explaining: "[Larionov is] one of those experienced players who knows everything about hockey—and about life. He's a very intelligent and quiet guy off the ice. Any help you need, you can always ask him. No matter what the question is, ask him

anything. I mean *anything*."

Larionov also has had an impact on the team in general. In the same issue of *The Hockey News*, it was noted that coach Scotty Bowman identified him as the biggest difference between the Red Wings of 1994-95 and the following season's team. He is known for his creativity on the ice and his ability to out think the opposition. Bowman boasted that, after Larionov joined the team, his creativity improved Detroit's offense by 20 percent. Hopefully, Larionov will remain with the Detroit Red Wings and continue to be an integral part of the team's Russian unit.

EPILOGUE

Dear Detroit Red Wings fan,

It is my hope that you have enjoyed reading about the history of the Detroit Red Wings; one of America's most storied National Hockey League teams.

Of the three teams that I played for, I think I was treated the best here in Detroit, all around. Highlights from my career include winning first place in 1964 and going to the playoffs more years in a row than I did with any other team. Making the All-Star team in Detroit was a feather in my cap, too.

When I came to Detroit, I joined Gordie Howe, the greatest guy who ever laced 'em on. I banged heads with him for 15 years as an opponent and then finished up my career with him for the last five. A big highlight of my professional career was playing our twentieth year together; we both turned pro in '46. I quit in '66, so that was 20 years for both of us, and we were the second guys to do it.

The pages of this book brought back a lot of great hockey memories.

Best regards,

Bill Gadsby
Bill Gadsby, #4
Hockey Hall of Fame, 1970